THE NEW RISE IN REAL ESTATE

Published by CelebrityPress™, Orlando, FL
A division of The Celebrity Branding Agency®

Celebrity Branding® is a registered trademark
Printed in the United States of America.

ISBN: 9780983947066
LCCN: 2012932554

This publication is designed to provide accurate and authoritative information with regard to the subject matter covered. It is sold with the understanding that the publisher is not engaged in rendering legal, accounting, or other professional advice. If legal advice or other expert assistance is required, the services of a competent professional should be sought. The opinions expressed by the authors in this book are not endorsed by CelebrityPress™ and are the sole responsibility of the author rendering the opinion.

Most CelebrityPress™ titles are available at special quantity discounts for bulk purchases for sales promotions, premiums, fundraising, and educational use. Special versions or book excerpts can also be created to fit specific needs.

For more information, please write:

CelebrityPress™,
520 N. Orlando Ave, #2
Winter Park, FL 32789

or call 1.877.261.4930

Visit us online at www.CelebrityPressPublishing.com

THE NEW RISE in REAL ESTATE

Contents

CHAPTER 1

Are Real Estate Agents to Blame?
How to Avoid Being Ripped Off When You Buy or Sell Your Next Home

By Jay Kinder

"The Strategy of Pre-eminence is the foundation on which you build your ideology. To be the most trusted expert advisor in your field, you cannot allow your clients to make decisions that are not in their best interest, even if that means referring them to your competition. You have to learn to connect with your clients and identify their non-verbalized fears, concerns, goals and desires solely for the purpose of giving them superior guidance above all else." ~Jay Abraham

Make no mistake about it: The real estate industry is broken, and it could cost you thousands upon thousands of dollars when you buy or sell your home. Let me draw a comparison for you. I'm from Oklahoma, and the required amount of hours to receive your "provisional" real estate license is a whopping 90 hours. In contrast, you're required to have 1,500 hours to become a licensed beautician.

Shocked yet? You will be.

You would think that all real estate agents have been skillfully trained in managing the variables involved in the home buying and home selling process. You would think that their brokerage, franchise or otherwise, would have systems in place to consistently monitor and measure the success of their agents and the advice they give their clients. They don't.

This year, across the country, the success rate of agents listing a home—and it actually selling—is less than 50 percent. That means you could list your home for months and months, and your odds of selling are no different than pulling a nickel out of your pocket and calling heads or tails. The downside to this coin flip could be devastating. What if you have to move to another area? What if you contracted to build a new home already? What if you couldn't afford to pay for two places to live? What if this process unexpectedly drained your savings and put your family's financial situation at risk?

In most cases, you'll negotiate away your home's equity due to the timing and financial crunch an untimely home sale might cause. In many cases, this is encouraged by your real estate agent. According to National Association of Realtors (NAR), the original list-price-to-sales-price ratio is a whopping 11 percent difference. On a $200,000 home that would be a total loss of $22,000 to you as a homeowner!

So why is it that some homes sell in 90 days or less while others lag on the market for months and months, often never selling at all? This is where the expertise of your real estate advisor makes all the difference. Many agents today aren't accurately trained to determine the value of your home, much less managing the process. You've probably heard the term "CMA." It stands for comparative market analysis. It takes into consideration the agent's choices for comparable homes that have sold recently and making adjustments to see what your home's value *should be*.

This is an archaic method that many agents still use today. The problem is that the average agent shouldn't be "choosing" the comparables first of all, and secondly it leaves out many variables that ultimately could cost you thousands of dollars.

For example, CMAs don't tell you if the home was overpriced for months before a large price drop; they don't tell you if the home was professionally staged; if the home was painted blue, yellow, red and purple; or if the carpet wreaked of cat urine.

What about those highly motivated sellers who lost a job or are getting a divorce? Do these factors determine the value of your home? Absolutely not! More important, they don't play an active role in how you should *position* your home in today's market to attract the highest offer.

Another amazing statistic is how much the average agent invests in the marketing and sale of your home. Recently, NAR reported that the average agent invested less than $300 per month in the online marketing for all of their clients combined. Where does all that commission go?

It's simple. The average agent only sells seven homes per year, and there are nearly 1 million of them, so instead of investing those dollars into their business (if you want to call it that), they need that money to live on. You understand, right? Heck no! This is your largest investment!

Prognosis without diagnosis is malpractice. You would probably run from any physician who prescribed a cure without first doing a thorough examination, wouldn't you? Then the same should be considered when hiring a real estate agent to advise you through the sale of the largest purchase you'll make in your lifetime.

If the average real estate agent sells around seven homes per year, that's hardly enough experience to even know what questions to ask, much less give you the proper advice and guidance. Maybe I'm being hard on these agents. After all, we all know someone who's a real estate agent. You probably even have a friend who's an agent. I'd be willing to bet that he's a very nice person, too. This friend is honest, goes to church on Sunday, and even brings you a big turkey on Thanksgiving. These are all great qualities in a person. Surely, he can be trusted with the sale of your home, right?

Here's the bottom line: In the last 15 years, I've consulted with no less than 4,100 homeowners who either wanted or needed desperately to sell their home. There's a proven, repeatable system that can be followed to sell your home for up to 18 percent more money than the methods of average real estate agents.

When it comes to selling the largest asset you own, you owe it to yourself to do your due diligence. You owe it to yourself to hire an expert advisor. The only training in the real estate industry that can deliver you an expert advisor is the training provided by the National Association of Expert Advisors. The Certified Home Selling Advisor is a designation only the top agents in the country hold. It's the sign of the new real estate agent.

The days of the average, part-time, real estate agent are long gone. When you hire an agent, hire a Certified Home Selling Advisor. You can research your area online at www.naea.com.

About Jay

Recognized throughout the real estate industry, Jay Kinder is a business phenom, going from small-town kid to master business-growth strategist. Nobody in the tiny town of Walters Oklahoma, population 2,142, would have voted this notably ornery and average student most likely to be a millionaire, but that didn't stop him from building an impressive real estate brand positioning him as one of the top 10 Coldwell Banker Agents Worldwide, Small Business Administration Young Entrepreneur of the Year, *Realtor* magazine's 30 under 30, *Wall Street Journal's* top 25 agents worldwide, and a laundry list of high achievement awards all by the age of 30. By the time Jay was 25 years old, he had become a local celebrity and brilliant strategist. By the time he was 28, his passion for real estate expanded as he and his business partner Michael Reese, a top agent who got into real estate after seeing Jay's incredible business success, decided to open the doors to their successful businesses and began recreating their own success by helping agents like them master massive growth and celebrity stardom in their own real estate markets. This new business, Kinder Reese Real Estate Partners has been credited with helping thousands of real estate agents strategically grow their businesses with their proven and market tested idea. Jay and Mike now share a passion for growth-minded individuals who have a burning desire to add value to people's lives while enjoying a higher quality of life.

CHAPTER 2

Anyone Can Be a Real Estate Agent

Up Your Odds by Hiring an Expert Advisor!

By Michael Reese

There's a "new rise in real estate," and this time homeowners are finally the winners. For decades the American dream of homeownership has been one of the most stressful processes a person could go through during their lifetime. With buying and selling a home successfully being ranked as one of the best ways Americans can accumulate wealth over the last hundred years, real estate agents have been able to fly under the radar with no real value proposition, except for a rising real estate market for homeowners.

Real estate agents can no longer survive on hope. With more than half of all licensed real estate agents not even writing an offer last year, the traditional agent is just not getting the job done. If the real estate agent population were a chart, it would look like a waterslide at your local water park. Agents have been forced with some very hard decisions to either pay their annual dues or hang it up and get a real job.

This isn't the reality for all agents; a few are prospering from the "new rise in real estate," being forced to build large teams of talented individuals just to handle the abundance of new clients and closings. With economies of scale taking place the consumer wins by benefiting from the resources these agents have while giving them a clear competitive advantage over those consumers who are looking for results.

27

Consumers *should* demand results: I've never met a home buyer who wanted to pay more for a home or a seller who didn't want the highest offer. Both buyers' and sellers' wants and needs are either fulfilled or ignored based on the decisions resulting from the business principal "who before the what." Many top companies in America train top managers and executives to understand this very important fact about any business. So what does "who before the what" mean? It means that before you do anything in business, no matter *what* it is, the most important first step that affects all the other variables down to success or failure is *who* you choose on your team to do it with.

So *who* should you look for, no matter *what* your real estate goals? The answer is what industry insiders refer to as expert advisors. What I'm about to share with you is the honest but true confessions of a top producer. Over my 10-year career selling real estate, I've sold more in most years than a traditional agent would sell in a 30-year career. This has given me a very unique opportunity to understand what works and what doesn't. My objective in writing this chapter is to help all consumers understand and to help define the gap between a traditional agent and an expert advisor.

I've personally identified three very specific traits of an expert advisor for both home buyers and sellers. Understanding these will help you avoid the biggest mistake made in the home buying and selling process: hiring the wrong *who*. The first trait is easy to spot and really just echoes the same "who" principle. Who exactly are you hiring? When you hire an agent you have a choice no different than if you hired someone to build you a brand-new home. Imagine you where interviewing home builders and one specific builder came out with no real formal training, or let's say he was self-taught at electrical and plumbing. This particular builder's past clients where only happy 50 percent of the time and the other 50 percent, if surveyed, said they were dissatisfied. Would you hire that builder to build your brand-new, expensive home? No!

Let's continue for the few who might have said yes. What if he had no clear plan he could show you to explain exactly what he was going to do. When you asked him for a blueprint, he responded, "I don't like to use those; I don't really see the use, since I'm going to be doing everything all by myself, from the foundation, drywall and electrical to even the plumbing." Now most of you clearly wouldn't want to hire a jack of all trades to help build your dream home.

This is the exact same process I see home buyers and sellers go through when they hire an agent. They typically end up hiring a self-taught, solo practitioner, with no real proven plan to either sell the home or find the home buyer the best possible deal the market has to offer.

The good news is this is easily preventable. By asking a few good questions on the front end, you could save a lot of time on the back end of this process. I do warn those of you who might think about skipping this step because you already have a friend, family member, or neighbor *who* has a real estate license. If you don't have the time to do what it takes to find the right "who," then you'll be forced to make the time to do it over when your home fails to sell or you end up wasting precious time looking at homes that don't match your criteria. Maybe worse, you end up buying a home to find out months or years later that your family or friends got a smokin' deal on the home of your dreams.

So how do you prevent all these painful scenarios? The first thing you can do to protect yourself is to find a team of agents to help you. Running a real estate business is more than one job, so you want a team of specialists working for you. Just like a good dentist, a good agent should have a lot of clients. With a lot of clients both buying and selling, you want to hire a team with both Certified Home Buying Advisors (CHBA) and Certified Home Selling Advisors (CHSA).

It's a fact that the good deals don't last long. It's been my experience that the really good deals might not last a week. You can prevent these hidden opportunities from slipping through your fingers by working with a team CHBA. They're typically showing hundreds of homes weekly, sometimes even daily, and communicating between each other about their clients' needs and wants. The team working together increases the odds your agent will know about the home that's right for you. Many times the team might have internal inventory coming soon that no other buyers even know about. The fact that the cost to you is the same whether you have a team or a solo practitioner helping you makes hiring a team a no brainer. If you're selling or buying, the fact remains that buyers benefit from teams with market share, and sellers benefit from teams with lots of clients looking to buy. Once the contract is executed, that teamwork really helps expedite the behind-the-scenes process, which significantly enhances the client experience.

All real estate agents manage their business differently, but the expert advisor understands the benefits of having a closing team. In my business, we have a closing coordinator, who manages the contract, deadlines and deliverables from the time the home goes under contract until the time it closes. Most agents overlook a lot of important issues like deadlines that don't really hurt anyone unless something goes wrong. Agents have to meet a variety of deadlines, from turning in earnest money that prevents sellers from selling to someone else to option fees that protect the buyer's home inspections. Many times these fees aren't turned in on time, based on specific performance deadlines in the contract.

How does this happen? Easy. An agent forgets because he's too busy taking pictures of his new listing or showing a new client around. He might even be returning that five-day-old voice mail. The fact is the traditional agent who's working as a solo practitioner doesn't have the luxury of having someone whose specific role and responsibility is to make sure the deadlines are covered.

If you're selling your home, do you think an agent's ability to sell your home is increased by the amount of home buyers he's working with who are qualified and looking for a home that matches your home's criteria? Of course!

That happens with a marketing team, which leads me to the second thing you need to ask your agent when interviewing them. What's your plan? A true expert advisor has a plan for both buying and selling a home. The plan should make sense to a home seller. It should consider any outside threats that might prevent the home from selling. There should be a plan for getting the home exposure—how is the agent going to allocate their marketing budget to create a demand for your home? Is he going to stage your home? Is he going to offer bonuses; if not why? Do he have a buyer-profiling system? Most agents don't even have a system or plan for answering the phone calls after normal business hours or on a weekend. If your agent doesn't have a plan that makes sense that he can articulate—even make visible—then he plans to fail.

There are three types of buyers: in town, out of town, and buyers working with another agent. Your agent must have a way to target these buyers to increase the showings from other agents and keeping it top of mind. You need to demand maximum exposure of your property to increase showings, which, in effect, increases the odds of you receiving an offer.

The third question you should ask your agent is what training or certifications does he hold. In some states, as many as 1 in 17 adults hold a real estate license, and more than half of those didn't even write an offer last year. The market changes, and it costs you nothing to have an agent who is staying on top of the market. If you're buying, you owe it to yourself to work with a certified home buying advisor who's certified by the National Association of Expert Advisors. As a seller, I would only work with a CHSA because they can show you a proven, repeatable plan to sell your home that makes homeowners more money than traditional methods.

If your agent has a team, a plan, and is committed to his career by investing in additional training above and beyond the basic real estate license, then you significantly increase the odds of a positive experience and overall outcome being achieved. In many states, it's harder to become a truck driver, even a licensed beautician, than it is to become a licensed real estate agent. It's a fact that all agents aren't created equal. If you're looking to hire an agent, you should demand results by finding an expert advisor. There's no fixed price for a home, and ultimately, the price you sell or pay for a home can be greatly influence by getting good advice, which starts with hiring a CHBA or CHSA.

If you're looking for an agent who holds one of these prestigious designations, visit the association website by going to www.NAEA.com; or those looking for an expert advisor in North Texas, visit www.MichaelReese.Me, or call our office at (972) 625-7355.

About Michael

Michael Reese, a Lawton, Oklahoma, native, started his real estate career approximately seven years ago, but he's been groomed for sales and excellence his entire life. The son of a Command Sergeant Major said that in his house, his mother had only one way to do things—"exactly and completely; there was no gray area." As a result of this adherence to following through, Mike has excelled in every sales job he's had. In fact, as a teenager, he was asked by his school to not sell the candy his mother bought for him in bulk at the store because he was outselling the school itself and cutting into their profits.

In 2002, after a visit with his friend Jay Kinder, Michael decided that real estate was the career for him. In his first two years in the business, he sold more than 100 homes. In his third year alone, he exceeded that two-year total by more than 24 homes. By the end of his fifth year, at only the age of 27, he achieved what most real agents dream of, earning more than $1 million GCI in a 12-month period. By the end of his sixth year, he had sold more than 500 homes in his short real estate career, and he's on pace to sell almost 250 homes this year.

In 2006, he and his team at Keller Williams were voted the "Best of Business" for Frisco, Texas. He was also voted a member of the prestigious "30 under 30" group for realtors across the United States. In 2007, Michael ranked within the top 5 for Keller Williams in the southwest region and currently holds the ranking of No. 19 worldwide.

Understanding that you get more when you give, Michael regularly speaks to new agents entering the ranks at the Champions Real Estate School in the Dallas area. He values what he learned there and wants everyone to be successful in his or her real estate career. He has also created systems and programs within his real estate business that allow his agents to be successful and still have balance in their lives. These same programs have created a great real estate enterprise that delivers amazing results to his clients.

His philosophy is very simple: He believes that you don't have to be the best realtor, just the best marketer. The one with the most clients makes the most money. The more people you can get in front of, the better chance you have to sell more homes and the more people you can help.

Michael currently does coaching with Jay for real estate agents from around the country, and he's in talks to do some training for a variety of organizations nationwide that serve the real estate industry. His goal is to serve others to help them meet and exceed their wildest dreams and expectations.

CHAPTER 3

The Art of the Deal:
Negotiations

By JW Dicks, Esq

Real estate mogul Donald Trump called negotiating "the art of the deal" and used that phrase as the title of his first book. Country music legend Kenny Rogers sang, "You've got to know when to hold 'em, and know when to fold 'em." They were both right. Negotiating is an art that has to be learned. And one of the key elements is knowing when to hold onto your position and when to wait for a better deal. Between those two extremes a lot of money is made and lost. It's true that to a certain extent negotiators are born, not made. To some degree at least, the ability to hammer out a good deal is a God-given talent that some people are blessed with and some aren't—just as a few of us are blessed with a 95-mile-an-hour fastball, and most of us aren't. But that doesn't mean you can't improve on what you have and get better than you are, no matter what your level is at this moment. Even the greatest pitchers have a pitching coach, and Donald Trump learned about real estate deals at his father's knee. So education and training can help you get better at whatever you do, including negotiation.

This chapter focuses on skills taught to me by my mentors. We're also going to discuss some lessons taught to me in the School of Hard Knocks, when someone more skilled than I was "ate my lunch" at the table. Hey, it happens to the best of us. Sometimes, if the other side is very good at what it does, you don't even know it has happened. And sometimes, you're happy that you learned something new, even if it was at your own expense.

NEGOTIATION STRATEGY #1:
UNDERSTAND THAT "NO" DOESN'T ALWAYS MEAN "NO"

If you want a great lesson in negotiating, spend a day with a 5 year old. They're the best. First, they're fearless, because they're too young to have been burned very often. Second, they're very much into themselves, because neither their parents nor their teachers have been able to break them of the habit of being what they want to be or getting what they want to get.

If a 5 year old wants a piece of candy, he isn't going to ask you just one time and take your first "no" as the final answer. No, indeed! He'll ask you until you say "yes," or at least make a counteroffer that sounds acceptable.

This is the first rule of negotiating. "No" is just the beginning. "No" is the first step in finding out exactly what the other side means and how that position can be viewed in a positive light. You might as well face it from the beginning: Negotiating is the process of getting rejected. In fact, it's the very process of rejection, bad as it sometimes feels, that gives you the opportunity to find out what the other side really means. If you hate rejection, get over it or find someone else who handles it better and can be the negotiator in your stead.

This isn't necessarily an admission of failure. Many times, I used third parties to handle negotiations because they can often say and do things that you can't do for yourself.

Additionally, if you use another person as a middleman negotiator, that person can always bow out if things don't go well, and you can ride in on your white horse and save the day for both sides. The point is that you need to understand the process, recognize your skills or lack thereof, and create an environment of negotiating that works for you—no matter who's actually running the process.

NEGOTIATION STRATEGY #2:
CONTROL THE PLAYING FIELD

In football, as in most sports, there's something called the "home field advantage." In fact, much of the football season is played with one eye on getting into a position where your team will have the home field advantage in the playoffs.

The playing field in real estate is equally important. You want to control the context, and the process, as much as you can. One of the most skilled negotiators we know is an attorney whom we've dealt with on many occasions. Sometimes he's on our side of the transaction, and (unfortunately) sometimes he's on the other side, representing himself or one of his companies. When he negotiates, he always tries to control the playing field by being the first to introduce the contract to be used in the transaction. He isn't overly aggressive about it. On the contrary, he's pointedly helpful, always offering to manage the process of creating the contract document.

Very few people turn down his offer. Why? Because it's expensive for them to hire an attorney, because drafting contracts is time-consuming, and because in some of the complicated transactions he's involved in, it's very difficult to structure contracts both creatively and in a legally enforceable way. So most people readily relinquish that responsibility. When they do, they give up a lot. While the contract isn't the only element of control in a real estate transaction, it's an important one. Frequently, it defines the terms of the deal, and if you're the one who originally defines what things mean, then you start with a big advantage.

The first thing you need to find out is what type of contract you're dealing with. If it's a so-called "standard contract," you immediately need ask, What kind of "standard"? Is it a standard buyer's contract, a standard seller's contract, or something else entirely? The distinction is important because there's a big difference. Here's one example from a contract that favors the seller: The buyer shall be given 15 days to inspect the property. But suppose the inspection clause reads as follows: The buyer shall be given 60 days to conduct a property inspection by an inspector of his choice. In the event the buyer determines that the property fails the inspection, at his sole discretion, then buyer and seller shall have 90 days to correct any deficiency.

Well, it still looks reasonably fair. After all, 60 days doesn't seem like too much time to arrange for an inspection, especially in a busy market. But the buyer actually has 150 days (i.e., 60 + 90) just for the inspection process. The drafter of the contract has in effect created a five-month option on the property for the buyer, where he can control what happens to the property without having any money at risk. In today's real estate environment, five months is an eternity. You can control the property and, ultimately, keep it, flip it or walk away. This flexibility is gained just by setting the table to your advantage.

Some of you may be thinking, "I would never sign a contract like that!" And maybe you wouldn't. But the reality is it happens all the time. First, in most cases, the "60 + 90" issue (or the equivalent) never even gets red-flagged in discussions.

Most people, even lawyers, read contracts very quickly, and a simple, boring clause like this tends to get lost in a multipage legal document. Second, the inspection clause doesn't sound particularly one-sided because the language says, "The buyer and the seller are given this time?" Hey, that's fair, isn't it? Not really, but it sounds fair enough.

Even if the party objects to "60 days"; they'll probably demand only that it be reduced from 60 to 30 days. If my attorney friend was in the deal and the issue was raised, he'd quickly volunteer to change it to 30 days, adding something like, "No problem at all; it's just the inspection we're talking about here?" In the process, he'd make you (the seller) feel slightly foolish for even raising the issue. And henceforth, you'd feel that much more uncomfortable about raising other issues in the contract, including far more important ones.

Here are several other ways to control the playing field in a real estate transaction:

1. ***Meet your counterpart in your office.*** In your office, you control the environment and the administrative staff. But as with all rules, you'll find there are times to make exceptions.

   Sometimes you may want to meet in the other party's office so he's more comfortable. It depends on the situation. It's part of the art of negotiating.

2. ***Control the production of any documents in your transactions.*** This includes contracts and leases. As I've already said, controlling the workflow controls what the document says at the outset. Of course, it's likely to get changed as the negotiations go back and forth, but at least the contract and other documents start out the way you want them to. Following this rule will cost you out-of-pocket money, because in most cases it means your attorney will be doing the drafting, and you'll be paying the bill.

But concentrating on these relatively small amounts of money is a huge mistake, especially if it means giving up control of the contract process.

3. ***Control the closing.*** All other things being equal, you want to hire the closing agent and name the place of closing. This isn't to imply that either you or the closing agent will do anything underhanded. What you're trying to do is control the environment, making it easy to move a transaction along. If people are stressed because of their environment, they're more likely to be argumentative, even on small points.

A closing by its very nature is adversarial. By custom, the parties meet in the same room, each hears the financial picture from the other side, and anything one party dislikes necessitates a shift of money from one side of the table to the other. I don't like these types of closings. I often try to arrange separate times for the buyer and seller to sign documents—or, at a minimum, arrange separate rooms. Yes, this sometimes results in delays, when the other party has a problem that needs my input. To counter this, I tell the closing agent how to get in touch with me if needed.

4. ***Control who inspects the property.*** If you hire the inspector, you know she's going to be looking after your interests. When possible, I always try to be present when any inspections are done so I can hear the informal comments about the inspection. Sometimes the inspector will know the property, or at least the area, and by talking about it will give you extremely valuable information.

5. ***Control who conducts the property survey.*** The survey shows you encroachments on the property. If you're writing the check and talking to the surveyor directly, you'll find out more than if you don't speak to him. Encroachments, even small ones, can be a thorny problem, because they most often involve your direct neighbor. Commonsense tells you that you don't want to start off on a bad footing with your neighbors if you don't have to. If there's an encroachment, have the seller clean it up before closing, because she'll be moving. Let her be the bad guy.

6. Control who writes the title policy, particularly the exceptions in the policy. I've already addressed this challenge. Title exceptions are what the title company says it isn't covering. If you don't read these exceptions and get the company to delete them from the policy, you aren't buying much coverage. Title companies have been at this a long time, and their data centers know what to exclude. Don't let them do it.

7. Control which lender is used and which financing terms are acceptable. The buyer chooses the lender, of course, but the seller can affect the terms by eliminating language favorable to the buyer in the contract. For example, if the contract says, "subject to the buyer getting financing at the prevailing rate," you as the buyer are much more locked into the deal than if the contract says, "subject to the buyer getting financing on terms acceptable to him at his sole discretion."

8. Control the type of deed to be issued. A "general warranty" deed conveys the most rights, so as a buyer that's what you always want the seller to give you. A "quit claim" deed conveys the fewest rights; for example, it doesn't even warrant that the seller owns the property. Make sure you're getting the type of deed you want and need.

NEGOTIATION STRATEGY #3: USE A PARTNER TO HEAD OFF PRESSURE RESPONSES

Let's imagine you're sitting at the table facing the other party in a real estate transaction, and a serious problem pops up. What next? If you're the decision maker on your side, you may feel compelled to make a decision right there on the spot. If you're an old hand in the industry and are experienced at negotiations, you may do fine under this kind of pressure. But the less experienced you are, the more it can cost you, because you aren't conversant with all the moving parts of a transaction. If you're up against a skilled player, she'll know exactly how to put you into a position of making a decision at exactly the most inopportune time for you.

Successful real estate players like Donald Trump conduct their negotiations themselves. Why? Because they've been in business so long that they know where they can go with a particular transaction, and they can think on the spot. (They also recognize that their presence alone may have a positive influence on the negotiation.) If you don't have this kind of experience and stature, your best course of action may be to say, "Let me check with my partner."

It doesn't matter what kind of partner you're referring to.

Maybe it's a business partner, or your spouse, or just an associate whose advice you value. The point is, you need to buy a little extra time to think about what was just offered or rejected, and maybe get that partner's advice.

You can also use this strategy to turn the tables in your favor. For example, you could say, "Well, that seems reasonable enough, but I really need to discuss it with my partner. So let's go ahead and put it in writing, and I'll take it to him to discuss."

See how you've changed the playing field? You've required the other side to put its position in writing, and you've bought yourself a period of time to think about this new position—without the other side being able to change its mind easily. If you're a buyer, this move is almost always to your advantage because you can effectively take the property off the market for at least that period of time.

NEGOTIATION STRATEGY #4:
USE THE POWER OF SILENCE

"You can hear a lot by listening," as the legendary Yogi Berra is supposed to have said.

This quote reminds us that listening is one of the most important aspects of negotiating. Normally, the more you talk, the more you lose, because you give the other side more and more information about your true bargaining stance, and that rarely helps you get the best deal.

There are some very bright people on my staff whom I never take to a negotiation, because there's no telling what they'll say. Their disclosures are innocent and well intentioned, but they tend to hurt our negotiating position. Think about it.

Assume you're buying a property. What signal does your team send when one of its members says, "Oh, we have the perfect furniture for this room!"? It tells the other side, loud and clear, that you've already mentally bought the property and moved in. As soon as this has been said, you can forget about negotiating, because the seller knows you'll back down.

Sellers also often give away the store by giving little hints about what's happening in their lives—if you can get them talking. I was once negotiating to buy a house. In talking to the wife of the couple who owned the property, she happened to mention that she was going away that weekend. When I asked where, she said she was flying up to see her husband, who had already moved on to his new job. Then and there, I knew that the sellers were likely to be very flexible in their negotiations because I knew the couple was now living apart. The point is, always be cautious about what you're saying and mindful about the information you may be giving to the other side.

When in negotiations, try thinking of yourself as a counselor. Your job is to be open and to ask questions in a warm and friendly matter. Act as if you're going to try to help the other side with its problem, because, in fact, you are. Listen to the other side's comments, and ask friendly follow-up questions. The more you can learn, the more likely it is that you can formulate an offer that will work both for you and for them. Approaching negotiations in this vein is more fun, often more successful, and personally more rewarding. And if you meet this same party in another transaction, that deal may prove even more successful.

NEGOTIATION STRATEGY #5:
EMPLOY TAKE-AWAY OPTIONS

The most successful strategy I use, in almost all types of negotiations, is the "take-away." Frankly, I debated about whether to include it in this book because it works so well, and there's a chance that some of our opponents will read these pages. Ultimately, I decided that I couldn't leave out such a powerful strategy.

The take-away is used when a negotiation has reached a stalemate, or the other side is being unreasonable. When the other side says something like, "I wouldn't even consider that offer," your first response should be, "I understand exactly how you must feel." (This is a softening statement that sets up what's to follow.) You should then continue by saying something like, "We appreciate your time, and we hope we can work together sometime in the future," or some other appropriate sort of comment.

At that point, you can wait for the other side to respond, or you can just begin to pack up to leave. Whatever you do, keep quiet—because the next person who speaks…loses!

What you normally hear, after the silence, is a retraction of some or all of what the person just said. If you don't hear such a retraction, you'll know that the speaker was serious about his (unacceptable) position, and you might as well move on. Either way, you have the information you need: either to resume negotiations or to go to the next deal. You can't win them all, and time is money. The sooner you find out whether or not you're in the game, the better.

NEGOTIATION STRATEGY #6:
USE THE "COLUMBO CLOSE"

You may recall the television series "Columbo," in which Peter Falk played the role of a detective who appeared to be a bumbler. In fact, the bumbling was a tactic. When interviewing a suspect, he'd ask lots of questions, then, when he was finished, he'd get up to leave. But when he was almost out the door, he'd turn and say, "Ah, just one more question." That question would always turn out to be the zinger. The suspect, thinking the grilling was over, would be caught off guard. The tables were turned. In negotiations, the "Columbo close" can be used in a similar fashion. Imagine you're in the final phase of your negotiation. Everything seems to be done. Then, in your best Peter Falk voice, you casually ask, "You know, I was just wondering if . . ."

You'll have to fill in the rest of the sentence. Maybe it's, "You know, I was just thinking, if you don't mind, could we make the inspection period 90 days, instead of 30? I really would be more comfortable, if that's OK with you."

Or maybe, "You know, if we increased the price I pay you for the property, but you agreed to pay all the closing costs, it would save me having to pay cash out of my pocket, and you'd get the same net cash from the sale. That works for you, doesn't it? And you'll be amazed at how often it will work for them.

NEGOTIATION STRATEGY #7:
USE A CONVERSATIONAL APPROACH

Everyone ultimately develops his or her own style of negotiating. Some people are reserved, some are loud, and others fall somewhere between the two extremes. It really doesn't matter which style you use; you just have to determine what works best for you. One style that works for many people is a conversational approach, centered on questions that are used to determine the seller's objectives in relation to price, terms and timing—the three factors that will determine the deal. I've found that questions starting with "would you" or "could you" work best because they convey consideration and thoughtfulness.

For example, if the seller says he wants 20 percent down, and that amount doesn't work for you, your response could be, "Well, would you consider breaking that up for me, with 10 percent down and a note for the balance in two years at 8 percent? Or "Could you break that up for me, and take 10 percent now and the balance in a note at 8 percent?" If you ask the question in a nonthreatening manner, it's likely to be received that way by the other party. He may still say "no," but if he does, he'll often say why, and that answer will give you more information as to what he's trying to accomplish.

The more you can find out about what the other side needs, the better you can structure the deal to meet those objectives, instead of simply getting into an unproductive cycle of offer and counteroffer. You may ultimately find that there's no good deal available for you. Well, again, the faster you find that out, the faster you can move on to something else.

NEGOTIATION STRATEGY #8:
USE YOUR STAR NEGOTIATOR

There's a common assumption among many authors of real estate books that you should handle your own negotiations. I don't agree. The person who should negotiate your deal is the one who's most likely to bring about a success. Sometimes that's you, and sometimes it isn't.

Earlier, I pointed out that great negotiators (like great athletes) have a gift. You want the best person on your team—your star negotiator—making your arguments for you. If that's you, great. If it isn't, then find the best person in your network of professionals to do it for you.

After years of experience in many different circumstances, I consider myself to be a very good negotiator. But I'm well aware that there are many situations where there are better people for the job. Sometimes I use people who have a relationship with the other side of the transaction. Sometimes a development deal I'm doing requires a credible expert—on, say, environmental problems—to explain my stance on that issue to the other side. The point is, if for any reason you feel that someone else can negotiate better than you, be humble and wise enough to admit it and bring that person in. Your goal is to bring about a successful deal, and that may mean that you do nothing but find the deals and turn them over to someone with the skills to represent you in the rest of the transaction. Don't lose focus on your deal-making objective.

NEGOTIATION STRATEGY #9:
NEVER NEGOTIATE AGAINST YOURSELF

One serious mistake in negotiation is to make decisions on behalf of the other party. For example, suppose you're preparing to make an offer that you think is realistic. But then you think, "Uh oh, the seller isn't going to accept that!" Then you raise your offer even before the seller hears it. Before you say that you would never do something that foolish, let us assert that everybody does it, and often for an honorable reason: We tend to put ourselves in the other person's shoes. Well, try not to do that if it leads you to negotiate against yourself. Structure your offer based on what works for you, and let the seller make up her own mind. You may be pleasantly surprised.

Another time this comes up is when you make an offer, and the seller doesn't do anything in response, so you make another offer. Don't bid against yourself! Get the other party to counter, even if it's for full price. At least if you get a full-price counter, you can bind the contract with just your signature. Remember, time is money. If the other party doesn't counter and you make yet another offer, you're wasting a lot of time.

NEGOTIATION STRATEGY #10:
DON'T FALL IN LOVE WITH THE DEAL

If you fall in love with the deal, it's going to cost you. The motto for negotiations is, and always will be, he who cares less, wins.

There are many reasons to fall in love with a deal. Sometimes we fall in love with the property. (I've warned you about that!) Sometimes we get wrapped up in a deal because we've told people we were doing it. Sometimes we fall in love with a deal because we've already spent the profits, at least in our mind's eye.

Don't fall victim to these kinds of mistakes. The best deals you make are the ones that you have carefully analyzed and structured to meet your needs. If you depart from the script because you "want to do the deal," you're almost sure to make mistakes. I've done this ourselves, and it has been expensive.

Negotiating is an art. It requires a solid knowledge of your product and your goals, and the ability to think on your feet. Some of you will be very good at this. All of you can get better; it just takes practice. And it helps a great deal if you can learn to enjoy the process as you go.

THE NEGOTIATIONS CHECKLIST

- **Don't take rejection personally**. Learn to deal with the word no. It's nothing personal. The word "no" is often followed by the word "because," and the words that follow "because" often tell you what you need to know in order to succeed.

- **Do what you can to control the playing field**. The home-field advantage is real. You want to control both the context and the process, if possible. One way to do this is to take on (or have your lawyer take on) tasks that are either burdensome or complex. The person who controls the text of the evolving agreement, for example, holds a lot of power.

- **Don't get stampeded**. If you start feeling pressured—say, in response to a new offer that has just been put on the table—resist that pressure. Say that you'd like that last offer in writing so your partner can review it. It doesn't much matter who your partner is, or even if you have one. You need to buy time and (most likely) get some outside advice about this new offer.

- **Listen more than you talk**. People love to talk about themselves. Use that fact to your advantage—and meanwhile, refrain from talking too much yourself.

- *Use take-aways, the Colombo close, and would-you's.* Every negotiation is different. Each has its own rhythm and takes its own twists and turns. Get familiar with a range of negotiating tactics, and use them when they're helpful. The goal with all such tactics should be to either: 1) close the deal, or 2) find out that there's no deal to be had.

- *Never negotiate against yourself.* It sounds too obvious to dwell on, but everybody does it. Put your best offer together, and give the other side a chance to respond. Don't second-guess yourself before the other party has even had a chance to respond. (Again, you'll be wasting your valuable time.)

- *Never, never fall in love with the deal.* It's the same idea as "never falling in love with a building." Don't let a deal get its own momentum. It doesn't matter if you've got an ego stake in making it work. If it can't work, let it go. The deals you fall in love with tend to get very expensive.

About JW

JW Dicks, Esq. is an attorney, best-selling author, entrepreneur and business advisor to top Celebrity Experts. He has spent his entire 35-year career building successful businesses for himself and clients by creating business development and marketing campaigns that have produced sales of over a billion dollars in products and services. His professional versatility gives him a unique insight into his clients' businesses to see untapped opportunities to capitalize on, allowing him to use his knowledge of how to structure and position their business to take advantage of them.

He is the Senior Partner of Dicks & Nanton P.A., a unique membership-based, legal and business consulting firm representing clients who want to expand their business. JW helps his clients position their business and personal brand to take advantage of new vertical income streams they haven't tapped into, and shows them how to use associations, franchises, area-exclusive licensing, coaching programs, info-marketing, joint ventures, and multi-channel marketing to take advantage of them.

In addition to consulting and mentoring clients, JW is also a successful entrepreneur and America's leading expert on personal branding for business development. He is co-founder of the Celebrity Branding Agency, representing clients who want to get major media coverage, marketing and PR, and position themselves as the leading expert in their field. His Best-Selling book, *Celebrity Branding You!,* is in its third edition and new editions are currently being published for specific industries. He also writes a monthly column for Fast Company Magazine's Expert Blogg on personal branding, and has written hundreds of articles, blogs and special reports on the subject.

JW has led national conferences and conventions and has spoken to over 160,000 business leaders on branding, business joint ventures, capital formation, investing, and legal and business growth strategies. He is the Best Selling author of 22 business and legal books – including *How to Start a Corporation and Operate in Any State (a 50 Volume set), Celebrity Branding You!, Power Principles for Success, Moonlight Investing, The Florida Investor, Mutual Fund Investing Strategies, The Small Business Legal Kit, The 100 Best Investments For Your Retirement, Financial CPR, Operation Financial Freedom, Game Changers, How to Buy and Sell Real Estate, Ignite Your Business Transform Your World,* and more.

JW is the editor and publisher of The Celebrity Experts® Insider, delivered to clients in over 15 countries, and serves as the guide for entrepreneurs and professionals who are leading experts in their field. He has been called the "Expert to the Experts" and has appeared in *USA Today,* the *Wall Street Journal, Newsweek, The New York Times, Entrepreneur* magazine, and on ABC, NBC, CBS, and FOX television affiliates. Recently, JW was honored with an Emmy nomination as Executive Producer for the film, *Jacob's Turn.*

JW's business address is Orlando, Florida and his play address is at his beach house where he spends as much time as he can with Linda, his wife of 39 years, their family, and two Yorkies. His major hobby is fishing, although the fish are rumored to be safe.

CHAPTER 4

How to Sell for Top Dollar in 30 Days or Less

By Jeff Smith

You're feeling lucky—you finally landed that new dream job. Reality soon sets in as you realize the process of selling your home might become your biggest nightmare. How do you possibly sell your home before the job starts? Do you split up the family? How long can you cover the expense of your family living in two cities? Can you sell your home for the amount you need to make the move? How will this ever come together?

Fortunately, there's a proven way to maximize your price, determine how quickly your home might sell, and positively manage the outcome. No matter where you live, where you're going, or why you're moving, angst almost always accompanies the unknowns in a home sale. I have yet to meet a home seller who wants to get less money and take longer to do it. It just doesn't happen. All home sellers want to sell for the highest amount of money and as quickly as possible.

Although you can't control interest rates, the supply of homes, or other economic issues affecting your market, many key variables in the home-selling and -marketing process are within your control. These variables directly impact the selling price and the time it takes to sell. Through proper planning and preparation, you can position your property in the market to be so compelling compared to the competition that you can, with a large degree of certainty, predict mathematically the chance of your home selling in your specified period of time. Managed properly, these key variables can influence the perceived value of your home, eliminate 80 percent of the negotiating at the time of the offer, and guarantee a sale in less time and for the highest price the market will bear.

Up market, down market, big city, little city, homes are selling up and homes are selling down. No, it's not a Dr. Seuss book; it's the real word of real estate and the key principle of "price elasticity." Price elasticity simply means in any given market, a variable or elastic price range exists in which a home might sell, given its unique set of characteristics. We've found that this range can be up to 18 percent. It's commonplace to see homes with the same characteristics on paper in the same area sell for, say, $300,000 and $354,000, respectively. All homeowners can maximize their equity and sell at the upper end of their elastic range while minimizing their time on the market by intelligently managing each key variable that we'll discuss.

Before you look at the key variables to maximize your sales price and minimize your time on the market, determine what selling times are possible. You can do this by determining the absorption rate (sales rate) for your property, which is simply a measurement to predict your chance of selling in a given time period. Divide the number of like-kind properties selling on a monthly basis by the number of like-kind active properties in your area. For example, if 59 homes are for sale, plus yours, then 60 similar homes are available. If 12 of those are selling on average per month, then you can predict, with some degree of accuracy, that you have a 20 percent chance of selling within 30 days, a 40 percent chance of selling within 60 days, and a 60 percent chance of selling within 90 days. The question then becomes, "How can you position your home to be one of the 12 homes chosen in the next 30 days?"

At this point, you'll analyze, compare and rank each competing house to your house, based on a certain set of criteria—location, condition, lot size, features, amenities and, of course, price. If the calculation reveals that 12 of the available homes will sell in the next 30 days, then you must get your home to the head of the line. You need to execute several controllable key variables that will affect the outcome by creating a home that has the highest perceived value in the market—a home that's so compelling that you might anticipate multiple offers for it.

Assuming you don't want to compete on price alone, let's review a few strategies that will increase the value or the perceived value of your home to buyers:

- **Condition:** Conduct a room-by-room audit of any repairs and improvement items that, if done, would elevate your home to the top of the pack. Do the carpets need to be cleaned or do they need to be replaced? If so, with what could you replace them? In each room, ask yourself what you should do and what you could do. Keep in mind that all repairs and improvements must have a positive return on investment before you place them on the short list. You'll know the extent of your repairs and improvements by referencing the competing homes on the market. Remember, you're vying for a position in the top 12 homes in your market-place. If you can't meet or beat your competition on condition, then you might have to compete on price.

- **Lifestyle upgrades:** What could dramatically make your home stand out from the competition? Can you add some flair for a few bucks? If no competing homes have granite countertops, then imagine how yours will stand out with shiny, new counter-tops. Although such an upgrade might be inappropriate for your price range, maybe new light fixtures and fancy kitchen-cabinet hardware is all you need. Try to add something that doesn't exist in your price range or at least not in your competitors' homes.

- **Staging:** Staging is showing off your home with furnishings and decor that typically are found in homes at a higher price range than yours. By staging, you're subtly telling a story and selling a desirable lifestyle to home buyers, who will perceive a greater value in the home, even though they're buying your house mi-nus the decorations. Staging can be as simple as rearranging fur-nishings or as dramatic as hiring a certified professional staging company to furnish and decorate your home completely. The idea is to create and sell a desired lifestyle.

- **Presentation:** Look at your home from a buyer's eyes. Start at the curb and walk through the home as if you were a buyer. Are all of your senses being tantalized, from sight to smell to touch? Try to stir up their emotions, create a story, and pull their heartstrings. Few real estate offers are made until an emotional attachment has occurred.

- **Pre-inspection:** Always negotiate from a position of knowledge. A pre-inspection by a certified home inspector can provide you with that. Share the inspection report with your potential buyers so they feel comfortable with the true condition of the home. They can put their best offer forward, having no need to hold back to compensate for unknown deficiencies. You can identify repairs that will add value to your home or repairs that might need to be reflected in the price. The inspection, upfront, will identify any potential threats to the transaction. You'll sleep better knowing that you've minimized the chance of restarting the process after losing a buyer at inspection time. Finally, you eliminate a buyer's secret weapon they often use to beat you up at the inspection, because it ends up costing you $2 to $4 for every $1 the repair would have cost you.

- **Home warranty:** Offering a home warranty will give your buyers peace of mind that they're buying a home that's guaranteed to be in a good condition for 12 months or more. New homeowners nearly always spend money in repairs during the first year—repairs that would have or could have been avoided with a home warranty policy covering the home. The appeal to your potential buyers is that you're ensuring they will have no anticipated out-of-pocket expenses if they purchase your home.

- **Pre-appraisal:** Hire a licensed appraiser to give a full written appraisal on your home. Price the home at or, better yet, below this written appraisal. Be sure to display the appraisal so the buyers are fully aware of the appraised price and the incredible value you're offering. Most likely, your buyers will pay your price when a licensed third-party professional substantiates it.

- **A real estate expert:** Don't hire just any real estate sales person; hire a real estate expert advisor who has a proven and repeatable system to manage all the variables in the home-selling process. Doing so will ensure that you achieve the highest possible price in the shortest period of time. Your expert advisor will expose the property properly to targeted buyers and increase demand by using unique and innovative marketing approaches. The expert advisor has the experience, tools, tactics, and team to negotiate for top dollar; that is, if you have to negotiate at all after doing the proper preparation.

Although many more variables can affect the price and time on market, executing just these few key variables will ensure that your family can move together without taking on multiple housing expenses. Be assured that you're not a victim of the market and that you're being accountable and responsible by doing everything in your control to maximize the net dollars to you and your family. Done correctly, you will position your home at the highest end of the elastic range, and you'll understand how long your home might be on the market based on how you stack up to the competition.

The perceived value of your home will increase and will attract buyers who appreciate your product and approach and are willing to pay you top dollar. Who knows, you could even have multiple offers. Remember, 12 homes were selling per month, and any or all of the 12 buyers could think your home is No. 1.

To learn more about the seven principles of real estate, the more than 150 different variables in the home-selling process, and the system that guarantees you the most amount of money in the least amount of time, visit www.TheHomeSmithsTeam.com.

About Jeff

Immediately after graduating from college with a business degree in real estate and finance, and unwilling to follow his classmates into the corporate world, Jeff chose to control his own destiny and make a true difference in other people's lives. Fast-forward several years later, and Jeff has indeed made a difference. He has been instrumental in moving more than 1,000 families and counting. Jeff is the team leader and rainmaker for his successful real estate company, The HomeSmiths Team, a part of Keller Williams Realty in Denver.

Jeff's priorities in life are, in order, God, family, and business. Jeff's top-three core values are integrity in everything, growth in all things, and contribution through servant leadership to all.

Always the consummate learner, Jeff has been trained by the best in the business in the United States and Canada. He believes in doing only the right thing at the right time for the right reason. And the reason is you.

Over the years, Jeff has created a proven, repeatable system to help homeowners sell their homes fast and for top dollar, and a system to help his buyers find the best properties at the best price.

Jeff holds the CRS, GRI, and CNE accreditations, and is a Certified Home Selling Advisor with the National Association of Expert Advisors.

To contact Jeff and The HomeSmiths Team about his seven-step system and how to control all the variables in the home-buying or -selling process, call (303) 480-1399, email jeff@homesmiths.com, or visit www.TheHomeSmithsTeam.com.

CHAPTER 5

The End of Traditional Real Estate

By Chad Goldwasser and Greg Cooper

Just like a local hardware store and travel agents in strip centers, the traditional real estate agent will be extinct within the next 10 to 20 years. The traditional realtor—defined as an independent contractor with inconsistent tools and training, while still trying to do everything themselves—will be replaced with a new breed of professional; one that is highly trained and equipped with the tools, resources, and systems that will allow them to provide clients with truly incredible customer service. They'll have proven, repeatable processes that will allow them to get the highest price possible for their clients' homes in the shortest amount of time possible. They'll also be better able to help buyers analyze properties to purchase with a more long-term outlook of the investment potential of the homes they're purchasing. Given that a home is generally most people's largest asset, this is a critical need for consumers.

You may wonder why this is going to happen. Well, currently in the real estate industry there are no set ways of doing business. Even within the large national brands, there are few to no standards for the agents involved. The large, national real estate brands have lost control of their agents due to the way the companies are structured. The large brands often sell off vast geographic areas to area developers, then those developers sell off individual offices to local brokers. The local brokers then hire independent contractors. These agents are then basically left to fend for themselves with little to no brokerage support. Real estate is one of the only businesses left in which the agent is expected to be a master marketer, salesperson, graphic designer, accountant, negotiator, and the list goes on. Also, to get started in the business, all you have to do is take three to five short classes and a 45 minute licensing test. Practitioners are then free to go out and take on the sale of people's biggest asset—their homes. There's no other industry where a person is given such huge financial responsibility for another person's asset purchase with so little preparation or practice.

WHAT WILL THE NEW MODEL LOOK LIKE?

The most successful brokerages in the coming decade will be focused on consumer-centric practices. The new realtors will go through multi-step training programs that will allow them to be the most professional agents in the world. Just as a financial planner has to take numerous state and national certifications to allow them to work with consumer financial accounts, so will the new real estate agents. These new agents will be expected to meet high standards, and they'll have to be certified in many facets of the real estate business; this will allow them to deliver the greatest client experience possible.

New agents will have to go through mentor or apprentice programs before they're allowed to work with clients. They'll be guided through their first few transactions by more senior agents. By working under senior agents, they'll learn the proper way to do the business, instead of the current method of learning on the job and making mistakes as you go.

HOW WILL IT COME TO PASS?

This transformation will start at the brokerage level. The most highly successful brokerages will take a higher percentage of the agent's commission, but with that additional revenue, the agents will be provided with services above and beyond that of which a traditional brokerage would be able to provide. The brokerage will be able to take on the responsibilities that are normally left to the traditional agent who's a jack of all trades and a master of none. The brokerage will provide services, including transaction management and consistent marketing of listed properties. They will also have high-level training programs with certification courses and mentorship programs in place before agents can work with clients.

A company leading this charge into the future is Goldwasser Real Estate, based out of Austin, Texas, and managed by Chad Goldwasser and Greg Cooper. Goldwasser Real Estate started their business in 1998 and became one of the top sales teams in the country by training their agents at a different level than all other brokerages. With a concentration on serving people at the highest level, they were able to build a team that quickly vaulted to the top of their industry. Goldwasser Real Estate was Keller Williams' No. 1 team (out of approximately 80,000 agents) before they decided to use their unique way of doing real estate to create a new style of brokerage.

THE FUTURE OF REAL ESTATE

So what is Goldwasser Real Estate doing differently? At Goldwasser, they believe that the real estate industry is on the verge of a major shift away from primarily independent agents who are left on their own to manage all aspects of real estate transactions. They have the training, coaching, platforms, systems, technology, and processes in place to help their agents succeed at a very high level. Independent real estate agents already know the challenges of working on their own and juggling the hundreds of varied tasks associated with each real estate transaction. As stated earlier, these solo agents typically work for a broker who provides little support. That's why Goldwasser Real Estate employs a full-time staff of administrative professionals to assist their agents and manage the hundreds of details involved in each listing of a property and home purchase. Goldwasser Real Estate's model allows agents to do what they do best—sell homes.

A REVOLUTIONARY MODEL

Goldwasser Real Estate provides the tools and support to ensure success. How do clients get the most money for their home? By creating demand! In order to sell a home for the most amount of money in the shortest amount of time, a client and his or her agent must create demand by properly preparing the home and exposing it to the highest number of qualified buyers. It's that simple. At Goldwasser Real Estate, they specialize in full-service, premier marketing and sales tactics and strategies designed to create demand, including their extensive online marketing strategies. Compare the services offered by Goldwasser Real Estate agents to those offered by a typical traditional agent.

Goldwasser Real Estate uses proven systems and strategies specifically designed to help clients get the best price for their home. Their consumer-focused and professional approach helps sellers feel safe, secure and confident with one of the biggest decisions of their lives. Exactly what does that mean for their clients? Agents work with clients to plan their sale by collecting information and developing a home-sale strategy, prepare their home to sell by applying high-impact marketing tactics, and perform by executing the plan to deliver the best price for the home.

PHASE 1: PLAN AND COLLECT INFORMATION AND DEVELOP HOME-SALE STRATEGY

Careful planning is the foundation of a successful home sale. Much of the planning stage involves gathering information about the client and his or her home so there's a clear picture of everything involved. Based on this information, they work together to set realistic expectations about the home selling process.

The planning phase includes learning about the client's needs, conducting a best-price analysis, conducting a home staging consultation, pre-inspection and a competitive review. At the end of this stage, the agent and his or her support staff have enough information to prepare a home for sale.

Assess Home Seller's Needs

Agents are best able to serve their customers when they get to know them and understand their unique needs. Therefore, it's important to be sure the client and their agent understand and agree to the objectives for the home sale. When does the client need to move? Why are they moving? What are their financial goals from the sale? What concerns do they have about the home selling process?

Many sellers are understandably uncertain about selling their home; it's the agent's job to make sure the client has confidence in their agent's ability to plan their home sale to meet their needs.

PHASE 2: PREPARE AND APPLY HIGH-IMPACT MARKETING TACTICS

A key element in selling a home at the best price is having a carefully crafted marketing strategy for the property. The culmination of tested marketing tactics that Goldwasser provides for its listings attracts more buyers, creates more demand, and ultimately claims a higher selling price for the home.

Goldwasser Real Estate's highly trained marketing specialists play a key role in this phase of a home sale. However, support of the client is important to make sure that all the necessary information is provided to market the home and ensure that their home is in the best condition possible to encourage a quick sale.

Launch Goldwasser Advantage Marketing Plan

At Goldwasser, the agent and listing coordinator set the marketing wheels in motion by launching their listing plan to make sure everything is handled efficiently and professionally. The listing coordinator is in touch with the client on a regular basis to make sure the entire process runs smoothly and remains on track.

Based on the information gathered during the planning stage, Goldwasser's marketing experts develop copy to showcase the home's best features. That information is included on fliers, various websites, an audio recording about the property, and the MLS. Goldwasser's experience and frequent testing of marketing approaches allows them to see which specific methods and tactics help attract the most attention from buyers.

PHASE 3: EXECUTE PLAN TO DELIVER THE BEST PRICE

There are hundreds of elements involved in a real estate transaction. Clients need a team of people who can respond more quickly and handle tasks more efficiently and effectively than one person. At Goldwasser, clients benefit from their agent's personal attention and commitment to overseeing the entire process, plus the speed and expertise of an entire team. All these individuals are focused on getting the client the best price for their home and ensuring a smooth transaction process.

Performance is where Goldwasser Real Estate really shines. Communication is key. That's why throughout the listing process, they work hard to keep their clients informed, offer them the best advice, and follow-through on their promise to ensure a hassle-free closing. At Goldwasser Real Estate, their people make the difference. With a positive attitude and a team atmosphere, they put their clients first and perform at the highest level to sell homes.

Goldwasser Real Estate's client services team is staffed by experienced, full-time professionals who are experts in their respective fields, thus offering clientele the most comprehensive, complete, and timely service available anywhere in the real estate business.

This model of real estate is critical for our economy. The new rise of real estate out of the ashes of the financial debacle and the end of the traditional agent will strengthen the consumer; as a result, our economy will continue to grow and benefit. The sloppy real estate practices of the past created the financial meltdown of the last few years. A more robust real estate model and practices can lead us forward and into a brighter future. For the consumer, this means there will be more money coming back to them from the sale of their properties, and they'll receive professional guidance while buying. This will help our economy heal and get back to thriving. This critical transformation of our economy will allow us to see a return of people building their wealth through one of the greatest forms of investment—real estate.

About Chad and Greg

Chad Goldwasser

Greg Cooper

Chad Goldwasser and Greg Cooper are founders of Goldwasser Real Estate and the Goldwasser Institute. Goldwasser Real Estate is the No. 1 real estate sales team in Austin, Texas, and was the No. 1 team worldwide for Keller Williams Realty prior to the launch of his own independent brokerage in November 2008. Goldwasser Institute is one of the premiere sales and real estate training companies in the world.

Both Chad and Greg remain active in real estate sales as they develop their revolutionary real estate model. A real estate model that's truly unique in the industry and will render the traditional agent and brokerage obsolete within the next 10 years. Where most new brokerages compete to see who has the best profit-sharing model, Chad and Greg have created a platform that allows agents to have tremendous sales success while providing a Nordstrom's level of customer service.

Early in his real estate career, Chad was introduced to the team concept and realized its benefits. His first full year in real estate, he sold 67 homes, which created a solid foundation for growth. The company has now melded the best ingredients of the team concept into a brokerage operation and are they ready to take the concept out nationally to consumers and realtors that sorely need the higher level of service.

Chad, Greg and the company have won numerous honors for their achievements, including Realtor of the Year from the Austin Home Builders Association, ranking as the No. 1 residential real estate team by the *Austin Business Journal* from 2007-2009, and recognition as one of the *lore magazine*/Real TRENDS Real Estate Top 200 Professionals in 2007 and 2008.

Next up for Chad is the No. 1 spot on *The New York Times* bestseller list. His first book, *Some Assembly Required: A Networking Guide for Real Estate,* was published in 2010 with co-author Thom Singer.

CHAPTER 6

Real Estate Problem Solving:
Would Your Agent Go the Extra Mile?

By Adam Briley

On an overcast Saturday morning in October 2010, I found myself sitting in my office trying to figure out how I was going to pay my bills for the next month. I was finally starting to make a name for myself in my real estate market, and now I was on the verge of losing everything. The idea of having to tell my employees, clients and new fiancée that I was now broke and would be forced to close up shop made me physically ill. It was at that point I decided that I was willing to do anything and everything I could to save my business. Any expense that wasn't absolutely necessary was cut, and any revenue I had went back into the business. During this time I had many thoughts of getting out of the business, but it seemed that every time I was close to giving up I was able to help a client in a way that truly made a difference in their life. It was these constant reminders that kept me going when I was exhausted and there never seemed to be enough money left at the end of the month.

I feel very fortunate to have found what I'm passionate about doing at such a young age, and I honestly can't imagine doing anything else. Most people think all real estate agents are in it for the money, and I have to admit that's what attracted me in the beginning. Almost losing everything helped me see that why I truly love what I do is because it allows me to make a difference in the lives of my clients. My favorite phone calls with clients are the ones that happen a month or so after they've moved into their new home. When most of the boxes are unpacked, pictures are on the walls, and it's finally starting to feel like home. I can hear in their voice that all the searching, paperwork and packing was worth it.

There are four questions you should always ask your potential real estate agent. First and foremost, when you're interviewing a real estate agent make sure it's a two-way conversation. There are questions you should ask the candidate, but they should have questions for you as well. If they aren't asking you questions about why you need to sell, how much time you have to sell, and how much you need to sell the home for, that's a red flag. Each transaction I complete is unique, and every seller has different needs, wants and expectations. An agent who comes in and only wants to tell you about themselves and how great they are more than likely has a "one-size-fits-all" marketing approach that may have sold homes at the market's peak but is ineffective in our current dynamic market.

1. *Tell me about a time when you had a financing issue come up on a deal and what you did to fix it?* The mortgage lending industry has changed dramatically in the past five years and with these changes have come many issues for both home buyers and sellers. A huge component of the lending process is the appraisal. I've personally faced many appraisal challenges in my career from undervalued properties to thousands of dollars in required repairs. One example of this is when I was selling a home to a family that had outgrown their existing home and were eager to get into a new home that could accommodate their growing family. We got the appraisal back on their dream home, and it was $5,000 lower than the price they had agreed to purchase the home for. They were absolutely devastated to find this out as with the type of loan they were getting on the home it had to at least appraise for the purchase price, if not more. I knew that the price they had agreed to purchase the home for was more than fair, so I immediately got on the phone with their loan officer to see what we could do. From there I was able to get the contact information for the appraiser and speak with him directly. I was able to provide him with information on some other homes in the neighborhood that sold for significantly more and the final appraisal price that we ended up at was $2,000 higher than the agreed-to-purchase price. This type of situation happens on occasion, and many agents would just

recommend that if the buyer really likes the home they should come up with the money to cover the difference between the purchase price and appraisal price. That's the easiest solution but not usually the most beneficial to you as the client.

2. **Tell me about a time when you had a home inspection or repair issue on a deal and what you did to fix it?** I've never been to a home inspection where the inspector didn't find a single thing that needed to be corrected. The key to a successful home inspection is that both buyers and sellers should have realistic expectations up front. For example, unless you're selling your home "as-is," if there are safety concerns that come up on the home inspection, more than likely the buyer will ask for those to be corrected. Any number of things could come up during the listing as well, from water getting into the basement or trees being damaged after a bad storm. When things like this happen you want to have an agent who's willing to go the extra step to help you. This is what one of my clients had to say after I helped him remove a tree that had fallen during a storm:

> "Adam assisted me every step of the way. From the negotiation to the dropping off the keys, Adam was there. He even went as far to help me to remove a massive tree that was damaged during a storm, just weeks prior to closing. He showed up with his truck, saw and trailer, and went to work. Adam's assistance saved me hundreds of dollars. Ask yourself this important question, Have you ever met another agent that committed to serving their clients? I bet not." —*Jim L. Omaha, NE*

Another issue I had come up recently was when an entire roof needed to be replaced in order for my clients to be able to get insurance on a home they were purchasing. The covenants for the subdivision required all the homes to have shake-style roofs, which wasn't what my clients wanted. They preferred an architectural shingle roof since it's lower maintenance and the price tag was about $10,000 less. I did some research into the covenants and figured out that they could put on the type of roof they wanted with a waiver from the homeowner's association. With the help of the property sellers, we tracked down the right contact person at the homeowner's association and were able to get it approved. It took some extra time and effort, but at the end of the day the buyers were happy to get a brand-new roof and the sellers were thrilled to have their home sold.

3. *How would you rate your negotiating skills? Give me an example of when you used your negotiating skills to get a great deal for your client?* Recently I helped some clients purchase a home for less than half of what it cost to build the home in 2002. The home was built for $1.2 million, listed at $600,000, and I was able to negotiate a price of $500,000 for my clients. I knew my clients loved the house, and I did everything in my power to get it for them at the price they wanted. Many agents will give up when the deal starts to look like a long shot or they hear a couple of no's. You want to make sure you have an agent who's not easily discouraged and who will do everything he can to get you the best deal possible.

Every time I write an offer with a client for substantially less than the price the home is listed at I know we're taking a risk. Some sellers and agents get offended when you bring them an offer like that whereas others are grateful that they at least have an offer to work with. I think a huge part of how they'll react is based on how I present the offer to them initially. It's important that everyone involved in the transaction stay focused on the fact that we're all working toward the same goal: My buyers want to purchase the house, and the sellers want to sell their house.

4. *Can you provide a list of a few past clients I could call as references?* Getting this list of names and actually calling the people on the list to find out what their experience was like firsthand is invaluable. They'll be able to give you a very clear picture of what you can expect the process to look like when you're working with that agent since they've already been through it. It would be good to ask these people about how the agent communicated with them and if all their expectations were met. If anyone of the references who you call has anything negative to say or seems hesitant to recommend the agent I would go back to the drawing board and interview someone else. Every agent should be able to come up with at least four or five clients

whom they've gone above and beyond for who would be willing to sing their praises.

The best piece of advice I can give you about interviewing agents and finding the right one for you is that you shouldn't settle. If you pick three or four candidates and after interviewing all of them and checking their references, you don't have a standout favorite, pick three or four more. Most listing and buyers' agency contracts are for six months, and you don't want to be stuck with someone that isn't a good fit for that long. The home buying and selling process can be very stressful, and you'll want someone on your team you can trust and who you know will do what it takes to get your home sold or to get you into a home you love.

My team's mission statement is: "We believe that we have the ability to change someone's life through helping them buy or sell a home." Whether it's helping a growing family get into a larger home, or helping empty nesters downsize to one that's more manageable we strive to do our best to make a positive change in that person's life. I'm obviously biased, but I believe this is the best way to operate a real estate business. Find an agent you trust and who has a track record of going above and beyond for their clients; they're out there, and you deserve that kind of service.

About Adam

Adam Briley is a real estate agent and team leader at Prudential Ambassador Real Estate in Omaha, Nebraska. In his second year of college he took an entrepreneurship class and decided he would take a break from classes and focus on real estate. In 2006 he started the Briley's Home Selling Team, which now employs seven full-time real estate agents and has sold more than 700 homes. Adam is committed to bringing leading-edge real estate technology and marketing techniques to the Midwest. He has built relationships with top agents across the country to share ideas and strategies about what's working most effectively in their markets. Adam's team's mission statement is, "We believe that we have the ability to change someone's life through helping them buy or sell a home." Adam is passionate about helping others through real estate and volunteering in his community. For more information on Adam and his team, visit www.brileyhomes.com.

CHAPTER 7

Your Trusted Real Estate Advisor:

9 Questions to Ask the Agent Who's Going to Look Out for YOU!

By Jason Secor

With the housing market experiencing so many difficulties in recent years, it can be a real challenge to find a real estate expert who's willing to focus on what your needs are, rather than their own. Today's financial stresses can affect agents just as much as they can affect home buyers and sellers; that's why it's important to have a process in place to find the best possible person to represent your interests in what's likely to be one of the biggest and most important transactions in your lifetime.

I always prize my clients' welfare above any transaction my company might profit from. I like to view myself as a trusted real estate advisor, rather than simply a real estate agent. That trust results in people not only coming back to us when they need to do another real estate transaction but also to refer their friends and family our way.

How can you find your *own* trusted real estate advisor? Well, I'd like to share with you the nine questions you should ask any real estate agent, because the answers will reveal whether that person is, in fact, someone you do business with.

QUESTION #1: HOW MANY HOMES HAVE YOU SOLD IN THE PAST YEAR?

In 2010, the average real estate agent in North American only sold seven homes during the entire year. That's right, only seven homes. Now, you may say, average is OK for you. But you have to consider this fact: An agent that's only selling a few houses a year needs to sell a house *much, much more* than a more successful real estate advisor. For instance, our team sold 60 homes during the past year. I don't say that to brag; I say it because if I see that making a real estate move isn't the right thing for you to do, I'm going to tell you the truth. That's because I'm not desperate to make a commission off you (even though I will work just as hard as that agent who's "hungry").

QUESTION #2: WHAT'S YOUR PROCESS FOR HELPING ME BUY OR SELL A HOME?

If an agent over the phone immediately begins setting up appointments to see homes (or if you're selling, for potential buyers to *look* at your home) and never makes an effort to sit down with you to establish a working relationship, that, to me, is a warning sign. Before you begin working with a realtor, that person needs to know what your objectives are and what your financial situation is.

If you want to buy, the agent needs to know what kind of mortgage you qualify for and, if you're selling, what you need to recoup from that sale. If you're suddenly just caught up in a whirlwind of appointments, it shows that the agent doesn't really care about where *you* are. In contrast, a trusted advisor will ask for a face-to-face meeting at his or her office to decide on the best approach to the process for *you*.

I know this, because I consider myself the "rebound guy." Many home buyers go out with the average agent and get burnt by bad (or no!) advice, and then they end up knocking on my door. I spend an hour to an hour and a half with them in that initial meeting, educating them on the local real estate market, any parts of the process they might not understand in full, and discussing their options. They usually tell me that was the best hour or so they could have spent, and that the other agent didn't talk about any of these crucial matters with them.

QUESTION #3: ARE YOU A SOLO AGENT, OR DO YOU WORK WITH A TEAM THAT HAS SPECIALIZED ROLES?

I started out as a one-man band when I began helping clients buy and sell homes, and I quickly came to see the value in assembling a team of pros who were experts in their particular areas.

That's why our LivingInBirmingham.com office consists of buyers' agents, a client closing coordinator, a client care person and other support staff. In every other industry, there are teams of people working in specialized roles, whether it's a medical clinic, a bank, or any other company you could name. In real estate, however, people sometimes assume a lone agent can handle everything. The truth is realtors that work with great teams have more manpower and can get things done a lot more efficiently.

A team can also accommodate a client's schedule more easily. For instance, if a solo agent has five clients who want to look at a house in one day, that agent is going to be hard-pressed to make that happen. A real estate team, on the other hand, can help cover a multitude of situations more effectively.

QUESTION #4: WHAT ARE THE THREE MOST IMPORTANT THINGS YOU'RE GOING TO DO TO HELP ME?

Now, I'll admit, 20 different realtors might give you 20 different answers to this particular question. But I make it a point to give my clients *these specific answers*, because I believe they cut to the heart of the kind of service that should be provided to them.

The first important thing I do to help my clients is to take a consultative rather than a sales approach. What does that mean? Well, it all links back to what I've already talked about—being a *trusted real estate advisor* instead of a real estate agent. That means identifying their goals and desires and what they really need to accomplish. Again, that may mean they shouldn't even think about buying or selling a home at the moment, depending on the economics involved. I've sat down with many families who, after we did so and evaluated their situation, decided, "Hey, we need to wait a couple of years to do this."

The second important thing I do to help my clients is *negotiate*. Obviously someone selling their home wants to get top dollar, and just as obviously, a buyer wants to get the best price on a home as they can. Because our team knows the local market so thoroughly, we know what kind of offer should be entertained and which isn't worth the time and effort.

The final important thing is we oversee all the details of our clients' real estate transactions, so there's as little stress and worry on their end as possible. From providing effective marketing for someone selling their home to making sure the closing on a purchase or sale goes smoothly without a hiccup, our team is there from start to finish to set up home inspections, appraisals and anything else necessary to the process.

QUESTION #5: DO YOU HAVE PROFESSIONALS WHO CAN HELP WITH ASPECTS OF MY REAL ESTATE TRANSACTION THAT I CAN'T HANDLE?

Trusted real estate advisors also work with other professionals that *they* trust. That includes people who supply homeowners' insurance, home inspections, pest control and other ancillary services. The realtor is supposed to be the expert on these kinds of matters, not you, so they should put you in the right hands when these services are needed.

We have all these kinds of relationships in place to make sure our clients are fully taken care of by reliable and experienced vendors. Sometimes a client will insist on using someone they know for one of these services, and, of course, that's their right. The advantage of using our network of professionals is we trust them and know they'll do the job in the best possible way.

That doesn't always happen when a client uses their own person, especially in the area of mortgages. When they do use their own mortgage person, I would estimate that in more than 80 percent of these cases, the client comes back and says, "Jason, we wish we would have gone through your person; it's just been a nightmare." My point is, there are a lot of people out there in this business and you have to find the quality person who's going to deliver. Our network has already been tried and tested.

QUESTION #6: WHAT KIND OF COMMUNICATIONS SYSTEM DO YOU HAVE IN PLACE—ARE YOU HARD TO GET IN TOUCH WITH?

You're going to want calls returned in a timely manner when you're trying to buy or sell a home because when there's an issue or an opportunity that suddenly makes itself known, you want to react as quickly as possible. If your real estate agent doesn't do the necessary follow-up with you or keep you apprised with regular updates on your situation, you can feel alone and very tense.

Now, for my part, I'll be honest: I get a lot of calls during the day, and I can't answer them all when they come in. When I'm meeting with another client, I consider it rude to pick up the cell phone every time it rings. I want to give the people I'm with my undivided attention. However, I make sure that one of our team members is always there to help if I'm not immediately available during business hours.

Unlike most realtors, we also have a system in place to update our clients on a weekly basis. When something happens relevant to a client's situation, we obviously will get in touch to let the client know the particulars. Beyond that, we also make at least one proactive call each week to let our clients know what's going on with property they want to buy or sell. They also get a minimum of one email a week that either features updates of new homes that might meet their criteria, if they want to buy, or a list of properties that just sold, if they're selling and want to know what's going on in the market.

QUESTION #7: WHAT KIND OF GUARANTEES DO YOU OFFER?

A realtor will sometimes try to lock you into a 90-day, six month or even a 12-month agreement to work with them, but what are they offering you in turn for that kind of commitment? Obviously, the agent wants you to sign the contract, but do you have any kind of protection? Is there an easy exit guarantee that allows you to end the arrangement if you're not happy with the service provided?

Again, buying or selling a home is a huge pressure-packed transaction for you. You should make sure that, if the realtor isn't doing what you need them to do, you have recourse to get out of that contract and work with someone else.

We offer that guarantee on our end; fortunately, no client has ever had to use it. But if ever we didn't live up to our end of the bargain, we would allow a client to cancel (provided they weren't already putting in an offer on a house we helped find them, or in the process of accepting an offer made on their house).

Everyone is human, of course, and everyone makes mistakes, including us. We only ask for the chance to rectify an error if it happens, so we can make it up to the client. We don't require they give us that chance, and, again, happily, we haven't had anyone *want* to break a contract with us.

QUESTION #8: DO YOU PROVIDE REFERENCES?

References from satisfied clients verify that the agent has provided quality service in the past, and they also give you an objective viewpoint of how well the agent in question performs. For example, on our website at www.LivingInBirmingham.com, we provide video testimonials of clients telling how we helped them with their real estate needs. You should look for testimonials in which people share their full names and complete stories about working with the agent. Just beware of one-sentence comments from a "Tom S." or a "Barbara W.," because they just might not be real!

QUESTION #9: DO YOU UNDERSTAND THE LOCAL MARKET WELL ENOUGH TO HELP ME GET THE BEST PRICE POSSIBLE?

If you're moving into an area and need to buy, you most likely have no idea how the local real estate market works or what current conditions are. Even if you live in the area, you may not know whether properties are going for more or less money in recent weeks.

That's why you need a trusted advisor who's very active in the local market, who has shepherded multiple home sales and purchases, and knows where things stand at the moment. Does the agent know the market stats? The average list-to-sale price? The absorption rate? Can he or she provide you with very clear charts and graphs that can instantly show you what's going on?

Your agent is supposed to be the expert educating you on the local market, and you want to choose the person best equipped to give you the relevant information that will allow you to make the best decisions. Knowledge is not only power, but it's also *money.*

It's not enough to just go on Zillow.com and browse current prices and tax records because sometimes you can't even trust an appraisal. An uneducated realtor in these times could end up giving you bad information and cause you to lose money you can't afford to lose.

A real estate agent doesn't set prices; the market does. That's why a trusted real estate advisor will look at the market, not at a home's sticker price, to determine what the real current value is and give you an honest estimate. At LivingInBirmingham.com, we consider this educational process crucial to our work with our clients. Real estate transactions require tremendous financial commitments on their part, and we don't want them to make the wrong move or do anything that will haunt them long after the fact.

Remember, trusted real estate advisors won't be evasive when you ask them these nine questions. They'll answer them honestly and directly. A real estate agent who's seeing dollar signs where your face should be probably won't and, instead, will promise you the moon if you start working with them immediately. *Don't.* Take your time; ask these nine questions and think about the answers carefully.

A trusted real estate advisor can save you tens of thousands of dollars— or prevent you from going through with what could be a disastrous transaction. Choose carefully, and you'll end up with a favorable outcome that will make you glad you worked with the right professional. I wish you the best of luck in all your real estate endeavors.

About Jason

Jason Secor, with The Living in Birmingham Team, consistently sits at the top 1 percent of all Real Estate agents in the Birmingham area based on volume and closed transactions. It was only after a three-year frustration in the mortgage industry, watching clients oftentimes having to literally pay for their realtors' mistakes that led him to become an agent himself and vow to do business better. Jason developed his successful business by simply being committed to helping home buyers and sellers—educating and empowering them to make confident real estate decisions that are in their best interest, even if that means not buying or selling a home with him. Jason has appeared on NBC, CBS, ABC and Fox affiliates as well as in the *Birmingham Business Journal* and the *Shelby County Reporter.* He's a charter member of The National Association of Expert Advisors, received the coveted Certified Home Selling Advisor designation in 2012, and was nominated for the *Birmingham Business Journal's Top 40* Under 40 award. Jason is known for his enthusiastic personality and his relentless pursuit to familiarize himself with the most up-to-date market trends and the most cutting-edge technology for the real estate industry. Jason divides his time in similar capacities as well as other lucrative business ventures. His tireless efforts to better himself by bringing a higher standard of service to his clients have simultaneously raised the expectations for realtors in the Birmingham area. Jason wants to impact the world in a positive way; he just happens to be in real estate.

To learn more about Jason Secor and the Living in Birmingham Team, visit www.LivinginBirminghamTeam.com.

CHAPTER 8

7 Secrets to Sell Your Home for 4.5 Percent More— Money Guaranteed!

By John A. Miller, CRS

Craig and Sara set out to find a larger home when their living room became their children's play room. Sound familiar? Sunday morning 9:17 a.m., after a quick coffee run, Craig is scouring the internet for their dream home. "OK Sara, let's pack up the kids and drive by some of these homes." This was the beginning of a terrible tragedy the couple soon endured. Had they read this chapter first they would have learned the "7 Secrets to Sell Your Home for 4.5 Percent More—Money Guaranteed."

There are two ways to learn lessons in life: You can learn from your own mistakes or from the mistakes of others. Let's see what Craig and Sara could have done differently that literally cost them thousands of dollars. This money could have been used toward retirement, a new car or college tuition!

Craig and Sara tried selling their house on their own, and when that didn't work, they hired an agent. Eight months later their home hadn't sold, and some other family bought the dream house they were hoping to buy.

They should have hired an agent, and not just any agent but the right agent, an expert. Why am I saying this? Well, let's look at the facts. Professional real estate agents have been around forever, and if they didn't perform a valuable function, the profession would have perished long ago. Based on statistics from the National Association of Realtors, agents help home sellers net more money in their pockets than they would if they sold their homes on their own. If that isn't enough, the right agent can sell your home faster, and less time means more money in your pocket.

Here are the seven secrets to not lose thousands when selling your home.

SECRET #1: DON'T HIRE AN AGENT WHO WORKS ALONE

You have two choices: You can hire an agent who works by him or herself or an agent who has a team of expert specialists handling all areas of an agent's job. Say you had a choice to fly one of two airlines: The first one had a team expert for each area needed to get you across the country safely and on time. The team included an expert mechanic, expert pilot, expert baggage handlers and expert flight attendants—all doing their own individual jobs for years and all were excellent at what they did. Or you could fly the second airline where the pilot has to load the luggage, fuel the plane, make and load the food, handle the ticketing, repair and maintain the engines—and when all that's done, they fly the plane! Which airline would stand the greatest chance of getting you to your destination on time and safely?

Real estate agents are similar. When they work alone, they have to prospect for new business, market listings, go on listing appointments, manage their sales that are under agreement, set appointments to show homes, take buyers around to show them homes, provide sellers with feedback and updates, and return emails and phone calls. So you can hire one agent who tries to do all these things himself, or you can choose to buy and sell your home with an agent who effectively recruited and properly trained a team of experts. More than likely, these are individuals who perform at a high level of efficiency because they perform that specific role every day for years. All these people are accountable and work specifically for you and your agent. Also, in either scenario, the fee for service is typically the same. Now which agent is more likely to get your home sold quicker and for the most amount of money? Hire an agent who leads a team of experts, not a jack of all trades.

SECRET #2: DON'T HIRE AN AGENT WHO NEGOTIATES THEIR COMMISSION DOWN

You're probably thinking you want to save money, so you ask the agent to cut his fee. This is the worst place to save money. There are many reasons why, but here are the most compelling. By the way, you should always ask the agent you're interviewing if he'll cut his commission because fees are negotiable. But if the agent says yes, don't hire that person! Think about it for a minute: You're interviewing someone for the job of netting you the most amount of money for one of the largest investments in your life. If you give the job to that agent, you're leaving it in the hands of a weak negotiator. Since they don't possess the fortitude or skills to justify their own fee, they'll be weak when it comes to getting you the highest and best price for your largest investment: your home. You want to hire someone with skills, an expert negotiator to work on your behalf.

There's another reason you shouldn't hire an agent who will negotiate their fee down, and that's honesty. While buying a car, the salesperson gave me a price and said that was the absolute best he could do. Upon leaving, he gave me an even better price. I still chose to leave because I felt he lied when he told me the first price was the best he could do. My opinion is that starting off a business relationship with a lie is the worst thing you can do. So when an agent cuts their fee, it's like he lied when he told you the higher rate. As an expert agent for many years I would often tell my clients that if that small percentage is so important to them, let's add it to the sales price and have me work that much harder to get you top dollar for your home.

Think about it like this: If your boss offered you a higher hourly pay and a bonus if you agreed to work harder and with more enthusiasm, would you do it? In reverse, how would you feel and respond to a cut in pay?

SECRET #3: DON'T HIRE AN AGENT WHO SUGGESTS YOU PRICE YOUR HOME HIGHER THAN FAIR MARKET VALUE

... or leaves the pricing up to you! If you went to a doctor with a broken arm, and you were asked, "How would you like me to set the cast?" I would find another doctor, wouldn't you? You want to hire an agent who can not only tell you about the value of your home but also what's going on with the market in your area and how those statistics affect your

home's value. There's nothing more prevalent in causing homeowners to lose money than pricing their home too high and wasting valuable marketing time because the agent promised a high price just to get you to sign an agreement with him. Pricing higher doesn't get you more money; in fact, even if you were to get a buyer to agree to a price higher than market value, that buyer would have to go to a lender to get financing. As soon as the buyer applies for financing, the lender sends out a professional appraiser. When the appraiser submits the report to the lender and the value is less than what you and the buyer agreed upon, the lender will deny the buyer the loan, causing you, the seller, to either adjust your price to market value if you want to sell, or you'll simply not be able to sell. You see, we can only get fair market value for our homes, so why waste time asking and hoping for more when a buyer can't even get the financing to buy it, even if he wanted to pay you more.

Overpricing is a massive waste of time, and ultimately, you lose money if it takes longer to get your home sold. Consider that mortgage rates could go up, losing more buyer prospects for you and causing you to pay a higher rate and have less affordability when you go to buy another property. You could lose thousands on that basis alone. In a declining market, you can lose equity over time. Have you ever seen what percentage of your mortgage payment goes to principal and how much goes to interest? You could lose thousands of dollars in interest payments. You could be missing out on tax advantages, and you might end up making payments on two houses. Price it right if you want to sell, and especially if you want top dollar.

SECRET #4: DON'T HIRE AN AGENT WHO HAS NO OR FEW OTHER HOMES TO SELL

Activity breeds activity—the more listings an agent has, the more buyers she can attract. The more buyers an agent can attract, the better chance they can bring a buyer to your home. If you had to float across the ocean and your survival depended on you catching and eating fish, which type of boat would you choose to travel in? A boat that has two fishing poles and two pieces of bait, or one that's equipped with more than 40 fishing poles and bait for each. Which boat would provide you with the best chances of getting you across the water alive and in good health? You see listings are like bait that attract buyers—the more your agent has, the better your chances are of getting you across the choppy waters and landing a sale of your home faster and for more money.

SECRET #5: DON'T HIRE AN AGENT WHO HAS NO ACCOUNTABILITY

For years, agents and their companies have been asking home sellers to sign strict contracts locking them in for six to even 12 months long. I've heard countless stories from home sellers saying that when they first hired their agent everything was great. They say, "The agent was enthusiastic, called us every week; it was great. Then after a month or two, the phone calls came less and less. We had no idea what was going on or if anything was happening with regard to the marketing of our house. We received no feedback when a showing occurred, and even those were few and far between. When the listing contract expired, they never even came by to pick up their sign. We don't know what happened? Our agent just disappeared."

I'll tell you what happened. The agent lost enthusiasm after he realized he overpriced the home, and it wasn't going to sell. The agent didn't have the guts or caring to call the seller and tell them the truth. "Guess what? I screwed up and overpriced your home, and that's why you're not getting any showings. No showings means no offer; no offer means no sale. We need to adjust the price to generate more activity."

That's a hard call for an agent to make, so they play the avoidance game, all the while hoping that some sucker will fall off the turnip truck, roll into town, and buy the house for cash. Then they won't have to have such an uncomfortable conversation with you. If this happens to you, you want to be able to get out of that agreement fast and find an agent that will research and find out all the reasons your house is not selling. By the way, there are only three reasons your home isn't selling: In order of importance, they are price, promotion and presentation. And yes, there are entire books dedicated to each of those three items.

SECRET #6: DON'T HIRE AN AGENT WHO ACCOMPANIES SHOWINGS

Keep this major point in mind: Most buyers who look at your home will have their own agent and won't be calling your agent direct to see the house. It's likely that your agent's marketing efforts will attract a buyer to your house, then that buyer calls their very own "buyer's agent," who represents the buyer's interest in regard to price and terms.

You may have heard that agents ask the seller of the home to leave when it's being shown, and I agree that makes a lot of sense. It makes the buyer feel more comfortable and helps the buyer visualize themselves living in the house. Hard to do if another family is sitting in the living room, saying "Oh, don't mind us, go ahead and look around." Ugh, real uncomfortable for the buyer. Sellers, my advice, go away.

Now the irony is the agent tells you to leave, but then who shows up? Ta-da! Your agent, the seller's representative! That's more intimidating and uncomfortable than the seller being there themselves. The buyer's agent coaches the buyer in the car by saying, "If the seller or the listing agent (seller's representative) shows up, don't lead on that you love the house as it won't help us in our negotiating. Keep a poker face if you like it." From more than 20 years of sales experience, I can tell you that when a buyer can't express their emotions, it's unlikely he or she is going to move in the direction of a purchase. Even something as big as a house is an emotional purchase.

The agent for the seller showing the house has no purpose, as there's nothing an agent can say to get a buyer to like a house the buyer doesn't like. If you want to convey valuable information about your house, all that information can be left on the table in an "information book." Conversely, there's nothing an agent can tell a buyer to not buy a home they absolutely love. Truth is, agents don't sell homes; homes sell themselves. A good listing agent will merchandise your home and negotiate the best price and terms on your behalf. You're not hiring a professional to stand and point through the doorway of the smallest room of your house and say to a prospective buyer and the buyers' agent, "And this is the bathroom." Wow! What gave it away? Was it the bowl bolted to the floor or the tub with the shower thingy hanging over it?

You and your agent's goal should be to sell the home for the most amount of money and in the shortest amount of time. Letting the buyer and their agent look at the home without you and your representative will allow that to happen.

SECRET #7: *DO* HIRE AN AGENT BASED ON TRACK RECORD AND WHAT HE'S GOING TO DO TO SELL YOUR HOME

The biggest mistake homeowners make is hiring an agent because they know the person, or the agent gave them a "great deal" on the commission, or promised them more money for the house. All these scenarios end up in utter failure, and you, the homeowner, run the risk of having your house on the market for a much longer time, losing you thousands of dollars. Hire slow and hire the right person for the right reasons. An expert will always make you more money than they charge.

About John

John Miller began his real estate career in 1991 and has worked with major real estate companies as a top-producing agent, ranking within the top half of 1 percent nationally. Being an active member of the real estate community, John has served on both the Professional Standards Committee and the Education Committee with the Board of Realtors. John has also served as a member of the board of directors for MLS PIN.

John became a sales manager, then senior vice president for one of the country's largest real estate companies, where he was the company's top recruiter, recruiting 71 agents in one year. As a regional vice president, John successfully led one of New England's largest real estate companies, overseeing 17 offices with more than 450 agents. He also had a phenomenal opportunity to work as a professional speaker, sales trainer, and director with North America's largest and most "results getting" real estate training company.

John has earned the following accreditations: CRS (Certified Residential Specialist, Highest Designation Attainable), ABR (Accredited Buyer Representative), GRI (Graduate of the Realtor Institute), and CNHS (Certified New Home Specialist).

To find out more about John, call him at (508) 523-8033, email john@JohnMillerRealEstate.com, or visit www.JohnMillerRealEstateExperts.com.

CHAPTER 9

How to Reach Your Real Estate Goals and Get What You Want From Your Agent

By Joy S. Deevy

In today's world, we all have access to so much information that we think we don't need expert help. Just as you need expert guidance from doctors and lawyers, you also need expert advice from your real estate agent to reach a successful outcome. Your real estate agent can provide expert guidance to help you close your home sale successfully. If you follow these five rules, you WILL get what you want from your real estate agent.

RULE #1: KNOW YOUR COMMUNICATION STYLE AND HOW IT WILL WORK FOR YOU

If you like to see details or analyze facts before making a decision, then expressing this important trait to your agent will encourage him or her to help you understand the details of the process. Conversely, if you're a person who prefers to keep the details out and appreciates an overview, then share this with your agent so he or she can better communicate with you. You'll feel like your agent really knows you, and it will help your transaction go smoothly.

RULE #2: BE TRUTHFUL WITH YOURSELF AND YOUR AGENT ABOUT YOUR FINANCES

It may be easier to keep your finances to yourself, but this is one time that sharing your ability to purchase will matter. Your lender and your agent should know what you can comfortably afford to spend and the amount you don't want to exceed. If you're not truthful about how much home you can afford, you may miss out on a property that could fit your needs. The process can also take much longer if you're dishonest about how much money you can spend or how low you can price your home to sell. A buyer can miss out on great mortgage rates, and a seller can end up selling a home for much less.

RULE #3: UNDERSTAND THAT YOUR AGENT IS YOUR ADVOCATE

Some buyers and sellers think their agent only cares about making money. Your agent is your advocate and must work for your best interests. The National Association of Realtors *requires* agents to abide by a code of ethics and to represent your best interests. Tell your agent your likes and dislikes and move toward your goals together. Agents understand that if you're happy, you'll refer people you want to have the same great experience.

RULE #4: UNDERSTAND THE NORMS OF YOUR MARKETPLACE

If you're moving from one state to another, knowing the real estate norms in a new market becomes very important during negotiations. For example, in some states, appliances are included in the sale, while that may not be the case in your state. In some marketplaces, it would be insulting to the seller to offer more than 5 percent off the list price when homes are selling for 97 percent of their value. As a result, some sellers refuse to counter offers in negotiations. Look to your local agent to provide you with typical norms in negotiations, and let the values of surrounding homes guide you to make smart decisions.

RULE #5: TREAT YOUR AGENT LIKE ANY OTHER PROFESSIONAL YOU RESPECT

Your home sale or purchase is one of the biggest investments you'll make in your lifetime. As you go through this process, treat your agent as respectfully as you would treat any other professional. Since you meet your dentist, lawyer, doctor, or accountant during business hours, then show the same respect to your real estate agent and request to meet during his or her business hours. Ask what those hours are at the outset. Many times, buyers and sellers demand an immediate appointment but would not make the same request of any other hired professional. If you behave respectfully toward your real estate agent, he or she will, in turn, treat you with the utmost respect and help you successfully complete one of the biggest transactions in your lifetime.

About Joy

Joy Deevy is a native resident of the Greater Washington area and an experienced real estate agent for Coldwell Banker Residential Brokerage. With 13 years of experience in the real estate industry, Joy has sold more than $250 million of residential real estate. She's one of the most productive real estate agents in the Northern Virginia and DC metropolitan area, consistently placing among the top-producing real estate agents in markets she serves. Joy continues to rank as the No. 1 real estate agent in homes sold for Coldwell Banker in her local market.

As a real estate expert, Joy's mission is to maximize her clients' property values by tailoring a marketing plan that will net clients the most money on their real estate investment. Her excellent negotiating skills, combined with extensive knowledge of the real estate market, ensures each client gets the most competitive contract possible. Joy wants to ensure that every client is a "client for life" and that clients have no hesitation in referring Joy and her team to friends and family in search of an outstanding real estate agent and marketing specialist. Joy belongs to the Northern Virginia Association of Realtors (NVAR), a real estate trade association that has a strong code of ethics by which all members must abide. She has earned the NVAR Lifetime Top Producer designation and has been repeatedly chosen as one of Coldwell Banker's International President's Elite real estate agents. Joy is also an invited member of the National Association of Expert Advisors.

Joy is licensed in Virginia and Washington, DC. She specializes in Alexandria, Arlington, McLean, Falls Church, Fairfax County, and Washington, DC, residential estate.

CHAPTER 10

Anything Worth Doing Is Worth Overdoing!

By Christopher M. Upham

Steven Tyler of Aerosmith and Mick Jagger of the Rolling Stones often described their rock 'n' roll lifestyle by saying, "Anything worth doing is worth overdoing!" But I've found that this philosophy also best describes my approach to helping clients sell and buy real estate.

Look, it's the 21st century…in an age where every year Apple comes out with the newest, greatest, fastest iPhone, you should expect more from your real estate agent. Where last year's iPhone or iPad is so slow and outdated that people can't live without the new release, could you imagine if someone in the cell phone industry tried to sell you a 1995-era brick phone? Unless it was some sort of antique collectible or just a joke to be used as a prank gift, you would just laugh at them, and there's certainly no way they would still be in business today selling old products and services.

But it's astonishing to me that when it comes time for homeowners to sell or buy the single most expensive asset they'll ever own, they think it's normal to hire someone and pay them tens of thousands of dollars to use technologies, tools and methods that are 10 to 20 years outdated.

I don't think the things I'm going to share here are especially noteworthy. In fact, I wouldn't be surprised if when you read them you say, so what's the big deal, this is normal everyday technology I see everywhere. I wholeheartedly agree. The reason why this is noteworthy is because in my own market of the Alexandria, Virginia and Washington, DC, metro area, which has tens of thousands of real estate agents vying for your business, I can count on one hand the number of agents who are using any of the tools I'm going to mention, let alone putting them all to use to maximize your real estate experience. You almost have better odds of winning the lottery than finding a real estate agent who's actually fully operating in the 21st century!

Now, I know that I'm going to feel embarrassed putting these tools, technologies and ideas down in a book. Why? Because in my business we're typically implementing new and improved tools every three months. So by the time this book goes to print six months from now, the systems we're using to help people buy and sell real estate today will have already seen two new generations of technology roll out. But I can guarantee you one thing: Homeowners will still be hiring real estate agents who are delivering 1996 service simply because they're the agents everyone has used for the past 30 years.

What are some of the things you should expect from a 21st century real estate expert advisor?

THE BASICS

- They should be comfortable communicating in real time with 21st century tools. In this day and age, would you believe there's a top-producing real estate agent in our town who until just months ago had their assistant print out the emails received from clients every day so they could handwrite the reply and have the assistant type and email the response the next day? The last time I remember seeing this type of activity was 1960's government bureaucracy, not cutting-edge 21st century professional service!

- They should have an active and impressive online presence and be skilled at using the internet on a worldwide scale to connect buyers and sellers.

- They should feel at ease leveraging social media, such as Facebook and Twitter, to give properties maximum exposure and to connect sellers and buyers

What are the differences you might see with a real estate agent that's operating in the 21st century and delivering cutting-edge service?

THE DIFFERENCES

The bottom-line job of a real estate agent is to give maximum exposure to the seller's properties and get them sold for the best price.

1. *Online media:* It seems amazing to me that as of the publishing of this book, we even have to be discussing these issues. I don't feel like any of the things I'm sharing about our practice are technological breakthroughs. They're used daily in every single industry. What makes it noteworthy and important to discuss is that in so many cities across America, the old establishment real estate agents that have been dominating the market for the past 20 to 30 years do not use these 21st century tools.

- *Old:* Upload a few pictures to the MLS and get a free standard-issue, plain-vanilla slide show. Literally, this is what you get:

  http://slideshow.mris.com/slideshow.cfm?ListingKey =97418503442.

- *New:* First, forgetting that no one will actually fat finger that whole web address into their computer to try to see the plain-Jane slide show, how do you effectively share these pictures. Until now, agents just weren't creative enough with 21st century tools to truly maximize the exposure of their seller's properties. With the New Rise in Real Estate, cutting-edge agents buy custom domain names to replace long URLs with something that's easy to remember and share through multiple venues, such as sign riders in front of the house, postcards, emails, letters, Facebook, Twitter. Here are a few examples:

  - *HGTV-style video (www.208WestWalnutVideo.com):* You-Tube is the fastest-growing and second-largest search engine in the world. A couple years ago, I had a client in Florida sending properties that interested them. One day, instead of sending me an MLS listing, they sent me the YouTube video for the property. At that moment, I knew this was a cutting-edge method to connect buyers and sellers. Some agents say they use videos to market their listings, but really it's just the same dull MLS slideshow set to music and uploaded to YouTube. Since people can shoot videos for free with their handheld cameras, agents don't even spend a few hundred dollars for a lame slideshow video. Going along with my theme of "anything worth doing is worth overdoing," in my business I set aside a huge budget for creating fully produced HGTV-style videos for my sellers' properties. Then I assign an easy-to-use-and-share URL and push the video out through every means possible, providing the maximum exposure.

- *HD 360 virtual tours with custom URL (www.208WestWalnutTour.com):* We pay extra to use high-definition virtual tours to ensure that the biggest, brightest, most vibrant colors and photos possible are used to market our seller's homes. Full professional photo shoots are done, and the tour is set to music with details and links to pertinent information buyers need and want.

- *Interactive floor plan virtual tours (www.208WestWalnutFloorplan.com):* I have the best mom in the whole world. She loves opening her email every day to see the latest listings from my website. My Mom tells me she loves seeing the interactive floor plan virtual tours. Instead of just seeing random photos of a house and not really knowing how they flow and fit together, the interactive floor plan tour allows you explore the professionally produced CAD architectural drawings of the house, roaming from room to room and viewing photos from various views and vantage points. The result is a much better experience that gives the buyers the true sense of how the home would feel if they were living in it.

You would probably expect that if the interactive floor plan virtual tours are so key to allowing buyers to fully experience a home that every listing agent would use them to help market their sellers' homes. But the vast majority of real estate agents don't. It's not that they don't have access to it. Interestingly, many of the top agents in our town use the same professional photographer for their photo shoots. This same firm also produces the professional CAD architectural floor plans. One day after doing the photo shoot on one of our listings, I realized the photographer and I had both forgotten to ask for and complete the CAD floor plans. I asked her why she hadn't thought to remind or ask me about doing the floor plans. Her answer was very telling and highlights my entire point. She said she didn't think to mention doing the floor plans because none of the other top agents she works with ever ask her to do CAD floor-plan drawings for their listings.

- *QR codes and texting to custom mobile websites:* As smart-phones have become an integral part of our daily lives—at the center of how we obtain and consume information—it's no surprise that people want to use their smartphones to access information about real estate listings. It used to be enough to have a custom, single-property website to market real estate listings. We now use QR codes and text-for-info signs and ads that drive consumers to multiple, custom mobile websites. These mobile websites are opti-mized for smartphones, allowing home buyers to view full virtual tours, see all the stats and details on a property, and even schedule appointments for private showings all while standing in front of a house.

My motto, "Anything worth doing is worth overdoing" doesn't ap-ply just to technology, however. In fact, the biggest examples of how we employ this philosophy to maximize exposure of our sell-ers' listings to the market are demonstrated in very low-tech media.

2. *Brochures:* The vast majority of the agents people hire to sell even upper-bracket luxury homes print 50 brochures on the color printer in their office. They're very proud of the fact that their brochure is in color, or that it might even be several pages thick. They're also impressed by their own 1998 newsletter design abilities using Mi-crosoft Publisher to slather a collage of photos of your house into a brochure. Personally, I can't believe home sellers actually pay real estate agents to do this sort of nonsense. To borrow a phrase from a popular ESPN football segment, "C'mon man!"

We believe our clients deserve professionally printed, UV-coated, glossy, 8.5-x-17-inch multipage professionally designed brochures. Furthermore, where most agents might order 50 brochures and only give them to the most serious of buyers, we often spend thousands of dollars to order 750 to 1,500 of these professionally designed and produced brochures. What could one possibly do with all those beautiful feats of printed glory? Well, if you believe in our philosophy of "anything worth doing is worth overdoing," you give them to each one of the 750-plus open house visitors, you mail and hand-deliver door-to-door, full information packages to another 200 to 400 neighbors, influential and well-connected members of the community along with cover letters, driving people to the online media asking, "Who do you know who's looking for the perfect home in your neighborhood?" By reaching out to these influencers, we tap into thousands of people in their networks of friends, colleagues, co-workers and associates, thereby multiplying our opportunities to connect buyers and sellers. Other agents say we're crazy for spending this kind of time, money and effort to market our clients' homes for sale. We just think, "anything worth doing is worth overdoing!"

3. *Open houses:* There couldn't be anything more old school in real estate than open houses. Agents have been holding open houses for years, but it's interesting that so many agents don't do them anymore for their sellers. Mind you, I was one of those agents myself. I would tell my sellers that the behind-the-scenes secret is that open houses are just the agent's way to connect with future clients. While it certainly does happen that good agents gain clients when they interact with buyers and sellers, when a home seller wants to get the best price for their home, why wouldn't they want to expose it to the most people in order to find a buyer? It used to be that the secret weapon agents would use for a successful open house was to bake cookies. Let me tell you, after years of trying the old school methods of offering cookies, chocolate, drinks, etc. at open houses, I found that visitors never even took the treats. Instead, I was the only one eating the sugary delights—and getting fatter every week!

After realizing the old methods didn't work for bringing in tons of visitors to an open house, I decided to apply our philosophy, "anything worth doing is worth overdoing" to open houses. Agents usually have a couple open house signs they set out on the corner and in front of the house and maybe blow up a couple balloons. Consistent with my theme, we set out to put an open house sign on every street corner in the city, creating a strategically placed network of signs, requiring a map to keep track of everything, all leading people through town like ants in a colony directly to our open house. The result is every single week when many agents have three to five open house guests, or think that 12 visitors is a busy day, we often see 45 to 60 visitors week after week at the open houses we hold for our sellers. Thirty-five visitors, or three times the average agent's good day, is actually slow for us. All week long we hear people talking about how they saw our signs all over town on Sunday. Why is this important? Simple…it connects more home buyers and sellers.

Listen, we're well into the 21st century now, and you should really expect more from your real estate agent. When it comes to selling or buying the most significant investment of your life, "good enough" or "this is the way we've always done it" is a dangerous path to take. Make the smartest decision of your life and ask your real estate agent if they believe in the Upham philosophy of "Anything worth doing is worth overdoing!"

About Chris

Chris Upham, located in Alexandria, Virginia, is a nationally ranked real estate agent serving the luxury real estate market in the Washington, DC, metro area. A member of the National Association of Expert Advisors, Chris is dedicated to going above and beyond his clients' wildest expectations to deliver the absolute best real estate marketing, service and experience available. As a former military officer, engineer, architect and project manager, Chris knows that every single home buyer and seller will make the decisions that are best for their situations, when the timing is right, and when they feel they have seen all their options. Chris's job is to simply facilitate that process for his clients by building trust in a no-pressure environment. To view Chris's video series or download the free report, *Top 5 Most Costly Seller Mistakes* and *Top 5 Most Costly Buyer Mistakes,* visit www.UphamRealEstate.com.

CHAPTER 11

How to Sell Your Home Using Online Methods

By Jared Chamberlain

Selling your home using online methods is the best way to find qualified buyers and have that firm sale before you know it! However, it's not just the online "stuff" alone that makes this method of selling homes work so well. There are many steps that need to be completed first in order to get the maximum exposure and response you're looking for before we even go online.

Back in the day, buyers would have to actually physically see your home in order to tell if they liked it or not. Now, they'll look at what's available to them online and have a gut reaction to what they see, thus pushing them to see the home or to pass for a possible other day if they can't find anything else.

There are so many things in the market that we can't control, so we must control what we can. The only items that we are truly able to control is how the home presents and is prepped along with how it's perceived on the market. Everything else, from the neighbors and general market conditions to the future unpredictables are basically out of our control.

I would like to introduce you to Catherine and Josh. They were looking to make a change. They simply couldn't make their current home work for them anymore. Life had brought some amazing changes, and they were expecting their second child in the coming months and knew that where they were living currently just wasn't going to work.

Let's take a couple of steps back. Catherine and Josh met a couple years ago when they were doing their orrientation to their new jobs at the time.They both had gone to the same university for the same degree but never knew eachother or met during their schooling. Both Josh and Catherine ended up working at the same job as engineers and were very excited about it. Josh continues to work at the same job in the downtown core, and Catherine just completed her last maternity leave and has gone back to work. About two months ago, they found out the great news that their little boy was going to be a big brother!

They moved into their current home when they first got married and have loved the townhome complex they live in. They purchased a quality property a couple blocks from their current job in the downtown core, but with only two bedrooms in their townhome, it wasn't going to cut in anymore.

I met with the couple, and we discussed how we were going to make this transition. I walked them through all the different steps on how we were going to market their home online and use the internet to their advantage.

I explained to them that the number of buyers who are looking online for their new home was nearing 90 percent of all buyers, and we must have their home found and visible where the buyers are hanging out and searching. It's not enough to simply hang a sign in the online world and hope a buyer finds us; we need to be proactive and actively make ourselves be found! I also made it very clear that we can have the best places to hang that virtual sign, but if the home isn't ready to be sold and showcasing itself to the nines, it's a waste of time and effort on everyone's part.

Here is what else I told them:

1. USE THE MLS: DON'T HOLD BACK!

Using the MLS is the best way to get the most exposure for your listing as it's the most widely used site out there for selling a home. I explained that the key is what we do with the MLS. If we're just throwing up dark photos and have a written description that we took off a cereal box, we're not using this powerful system to its potential.

The key is to bear it all. Don't hold back anything. We must give them links to our website so they can see all the details like floor plans, feature sheets, extra photos, maps etc. Show everything!

"Wouldn't this be too intrusive and give too much info to the buyers? Shouldn't we have something in our back pockets so we can get them to call you?" said Josh. I explained that long gone are the days of withholding information and waiting for the buyers to come to you. They want to know the info, and they want to know it now!

This generation, which is now the majority of buyers out there in Calgary, are briliant at many things, and one of them is not remembering lots of info but rather knowing where to find info when they need it. They expect to be able to research questions and addresses and find exactly what they're looking for. It's an absolute must that we give them what they need and in most cases *more* than what they need!

Josh still seemed a bit worried with that answer, and upon further investigation he wanted to ensure that he wasn't allowing his family to be a target of burglary. I totally understood and explained that if there were items that were of great value, which were best to not have photos of, we can do that and not post those items online, or it may be best to just have them removed from the home while the sale process is happening.

2. HIRE A PROFESSIONAL STAGER

I didn't want to offend Josh and Catherine as their home was in amazing condition; however,we all know that having kids in the home can bring a whirlwind of trouble to a home and take out the "wow" factor quickly. So I showed them how we work with a professional stager who comes into their home, walks through the house, and ultimately gives them a checklist of all the to do's that need to be done prior to photos being taken.

The reason we do this is extremely simple:

- We want to maximize what you already own by moving it around and using the space to show it off.
- To explain to the buyers in a clear picture the features and functionality of the home.

Did you know that homes that are staged bring in about 7.6 percent more in a sales price than those that aren't. To really maximize our short time on the market that we're expecting to have, we need to have the home appeal to the specific buyers who will be looking for the home.

In doing so, we need to know who the buyers are for this area. We need to know what they like, love and hate, and what superstitions or specific cultural and religious sensitivities they may have and appeal to them. Working with a professional stager takes all the guessing out of this and lets us know exactly what we need to do.

3. PHOTOGRAPHY: LETTING IT ALL HANG OUT!

Having professional photos is an absolute must and non-negotiable in my books. I explained to Josh and Catherine that when buyers are looking online, they'll be able to see everything we expose of the home. This can essentially be viewed as the first showing, as they're looking at the home and are able to see everything.

Because of the online methods we use, having the photography to back it up must show what your home is really like. We want to be able to draw out the emotions of the buyers when they're looking at the photos and give them an experience that gets them to book a showing. Using quality photography that showcases the home in its best fashion is going to bring in many more buyers, and action to the listing guaranteed!

In conjunction with the photos, we need to have extra photos above and beyond what's on the MLS as well as a virtual tour that the buyers can find easily. Again, it all goes back to giving the buyers more info than they expect to find, and in turn having them fall in love with your home because they can truly see what it is.

4. GETTING TRUE EXPOSURE: PUT THE LISTING ON SITES THAT ARE BEST FOR YOUR AREA

This is probably the tactic that most agents don't use and in my mind is the big secret!

I explained to Josh and Catherine that we could do the same thing as many other agents in Calgary and use some online systems to have the listing sent to hundreds of other sites just like every other listing out there. But I explained to them that money doesn't flow to similarity but rather to differentiation, so we need to be different in how we get your home found.

What we do is we only use about 15 to 17 websites that we've hand-picked from literally hundreds. How we did this is we looked at the top sites that were ranking when we searched certain terms in Google, which many buyers were using. We looked for sites that allowed us to sell real estate like classifieds or specific home listing sites. From there, we then did some research and back-end work to see what the stats were on these sites and how they performed. Once we have determined what the sites are, we then would manually input the listing into these sites and maintain the listings to ensure the info posted is correct and up to date. We input any photos if it allows, and again put as much info on the home out there as we can. Once this happens and takes effect, we'll start to see some top rankings for the address of your home.

I then pulled out my iPad, did a quick Google search of a random listing of ours, and—*violá*—there on the first page were multiple results of our postings, which gave the client the right info for that home.

5. BECOME SOCIAL

A big part of getting great exposure to your listing is sometimes not selling them at all.

Let me explain: We've built an online network and sphere of its own. I've had people say to me that when they think of Facebook or are on there, they always see us on the site. The key to this is that I'm being real and myself and *not* selling homes to them.

We host multiple photo contests throughout the year for different types and demographics of people, make every attempt to turn online interactions into in-person meetings, and so on. My online friends know what I do, but that's not who I am. They know if they want to deal with an honest and outstanding realtor that they can get in touch with me.

We've also created a community group on Facebook called Living in Calgary. This group has just passed the 6,200 member mark and is continuing to grow daily. Having a group that's focused and loves on our incredible city is a huge asset to getting our name out into the community and being known as the guy to go to for questions about the city!

Ultimately, buyers will drive by the homes that entice them with what they see online. If it doesn't look good and it's not grabbing them in a personal way, they won't see your home and simply drive on!

What this all boils down to is we have to sell your home three times:

1. We have to sell the home and give the buyers the right impres-

sion and emotional connection online.

2. We then need to get the exterior of your home in perfect shape because the buyers are going to drive by, and they need to fall in love with your curb appeal.

3. Finally, we need to have the home in show-home condition when they physically view it, as this will make them either love the home or pass on it.

Nothing can replace the physical walk-through of a home where the buyers can touch, feel, sit down, and get a sense of the physical space. But what has changed is that buyers are now basing a big part of their decision—before they even get into the home—on what they see online!

We need to be found online, and the buyers need to love what they find!

About Jared

Jared Chamberlain is a real estate expert in Calgary, Alberta, Canada. He leads a team of highly trained and passionate agents who are all at the top of their game! Jared has honed and developed his online marketing skills over a number of years and has sold homes for more than 800 clients in his career. Jared works closely with his wife, Rebecca, in their business.

To get more information and specific sites to use when marketing your home online, go to: www.tcgroup.me/BookDownloads. (This page will be updated as we find new resources to use.)

If you're considering working with The Chamberlain Group or would like more information, head to www.ChamberlainGroup.ca.

CHAPTER 12

What Your Agent Won't Tell You:

6 Insider Strategies to Get Your Home Sold

By Lars Hedenborg

In 2005, everyone was convinced that the place to make your fortune was in real estate.

After 2008...not so much.

Back "in the day," however, it was easy to get a mortgage covering the entire cost of a real estate purchase. After you bought the property, all you had to do was wait a couple of years, then sell it at a tidy profit. Then just rinse, repeat, and make even more money.

Well, as you're probably more than aware, times have definitely changed. These are volatile economic times, which makes real estate more unpredictable than ever. Prices and interest rates might be going one way or the other—you never know.

What you *do* know, however, is that all that uncertainty makes selling your home a much more difficult task. At the end of 2011, 1 out of 4 properties were underwater; in other words, worth less than their mortgage value. Today, more than ever, you have to make sure you're getting *maximum value* for your home sale to make a decent profit, or just to avoid taking a loss.

That's why, in this chapter, I'm going to share six insider strategies that can help you overcome a slow economy as well as a slow real estate market. These strategies are proven. I know, because I've used these them to help hundreds of families successfully sell their homes, despite the market or the economy. These methods enable our clients to sell their homes for up to *18 percent more* than traditional real estate methods. I'd like to see you obtain the same awesome results.

INSIDER STRATEGY #1: ONLINE IS WHERE THE ACTION IS—AND WHERE THE BUYERS ARE!

These days, sticking a "for sale" sign on the front lawn and putting a listing on the MLS just isn't enough to sell a home. Traditional advertising produces little interest because more than 90 percent of home buyers are searching *online* for their dream house.

That's why you must use today's most cutting-edge online marketing strategies to make your home "pop" to the internet buyer. For example, you have to make sure your listing is on the most heavily visited real estate sites and prominently placed in a premier position on those sites. You must have it featured on virtual online tour sites, such as Obeo.com, and you also need exposure on the heavily used *non*-real estate sites by using the most effective social media tools out there. That means getting it on Facebook and Twitter, as well as hugely popular video sites, such as YouTube and Viddler, so your home is seen by the largest pool of buyers possible.

Many real estate agents *still* don't recognize that online marketing is vitally important in today's real estate market. Hands down, it's the best way to increase visibility and demand. When you use online resources to maximize your home's marketability, you're able to attract the most buyers and, in turn, that drives demand for the property. When you attract more than one buyer, they compete with each other and drive up the price. When you only attract a few buyers, they just end up competing with you! That's not a contest you can usually win.

INSIDER STRATEGY #2: BOOST YOUR HOME'S VALUE—AND IT'S PRICE!

When car dealers want to sell a vehicle, they know how to get top dollar. They get the car meticulously detailed, make all necessary repairs, offer a solid warranty and an incredible financing package.

Since most homes are worth at least 10 times the price of a used car, isn't it worth going to the same effort for your property before you attempt to sell it?

Of course it is, especially since the real estate market in most places is overflowing with inventory. You want to do everything you can to make your home stand out from the rest.

Most important, you must improve the condition and appearance of your property. We find that the number-one reason some homes sell faster than others is simply because the seller took the time to make the property look as good as possible. You have to realize that the average buyer is going to look at around 15 to 20 properties and directly compare them to yours. This is one beauty contest you want to win because the grand prize is a swift and profitable sale. Unfortunately, most agents don't spend the time to make sure this essential element is taken care of, or they're afraid to ask the seller to step up and spend the money to do it right. This usually means they lose a lot more money on the sale itself, because the property doesn't show as it should.

Returning to the car dealer scenario, we like to market our homes as if they're certified pre-owned (CPO) vehicles. Recently, I paid $16,200 for a car that, if it had been a CPO, would have cost me $22,000 to $24,000. On the auction lot, the car wouldn't start (bum battery), the transmission fault indicator was on, the interior was dirty (including stains on rugs), and the exterior was just plain filthy. If the seller had spent about $800, as I did once I owned the car, to restore it to good condition, he could have sold it for $6,000-plus. That meant I got a terrific bargain.

You *don't* want your home to be a bargain, though—to drive demand, you need to have the best home for the best price. For example, I recently helped someone who already had listed his home with two other agents in the past year. He was asking $200,000, but the house didn't look like a $200,000 house. I told him exactly what he needed to do to sell the home at the price he wanted, so he ended up spending about $4,000 on painting, lighting fixtures and remodeling the kitchen and bathrooms (we know how to take our clients' dollar far!). We then went out and relisted the home for the same $200K price. It sold at 97.4 percent of that asking price in less than a month and a half.

As a seller, you also have to make sure the buyers feel as secure as possible about the large investment they're making by purchasing your property. Offer a home warranty that covers anything major that might go wrong, which is seen as a big gesture of good faith. Also, get the property preinspected and make all the repairs. Buyers are going to find out about these items anyway, so nip it in the bud and get them taken care of ahead of time.

Moral of the story? You spend a little money to make a lot more.

INSIDER STRATEGY #3: BEFORE YOU SET YOUR PRICE—DO YOUR HOMEWORK!

If you expect to get the best price for your home, you need a plan in place to achieve that goal. That means establishing a sound pricing strategy before you list your home. Your price is a signal to potential buyers of the absolute maximum amount they'll have to pay for your home. You need to be careful not to price the home too high, or you'll scare off buyers and agents from even coming to preview your home. Of course, if you price too low, you risk having to settle for much less than you were hoping to get.

Most traditional agents will only look at comparable home sales to determine where you should price your home. If done properly, your pricing strategy should include an in-depth analysis of other factors, such as the local and national economy and interest rates.

The right real estate agent should have his or her finger on the pulse of the market and know about where your list price should fall. The right pricing strategy is critical, so you want to make sure your agent is a true expert and selling a lot of homes. That way, he or she really knows the market from the inside out.

INSIDER STRATEGY #4: DON'T BE A ONE-MAN BAND—GET HELP FROM AN EXPERT!

Many homeowners who need to sell are afraid they're not going to get what they want for a purchase price, and the last thing they want to worry about is cutting into that amount by paying a realtor as well. So they go the "for sale by owner" route. But now, more than ever, that's a road you don't want to take.

Just as you wouldn't perform surgery on yourself or go to court without an attorney, you shouldn't attempt real estate without the right professional in your corner, giving you the advice and guidance you need. With the glut of homes on the market and all the complex variables that have to be handled, you need a team of professionals to help you through the process.

The people who've tried to do it themselves are in agreement. According to a survey of people who sold their own homes by the National Association of Realtors, nearly two-thirds of them *wouldn't do it again.*

You don't want to come out on the other side of a real estate transaction filled with regrets; you want to feel satisfied that you did the best you possibly could. That's why a real estate pro is essential to help with such tricky issues as setting a price, marketing handicaps, liability concerns and time constraints.

The other bigger issue is that properties that owners attempt to sell themselves have difficulties attracting buyers. Without the professional marketing a true real estate expert can provide, your home just won't stand out from the rest of the homes on the market.

Choose carefully when picking your agent. Interview at least two or three different ones, because all realtors aren't created equal! The *right* realtor will know the local market inside and out, won't promise you the moon, or throw around unrealistic prices. The right agent will be handling current listings, have an effective multileveled marketing campaign for your home and won't be afraid to give you their background or references. Go with someone you trust and feel confident about working with, and you'll be in good hands. Also consider using an agent that has a team of professionals behind him. The days of the "do it all" agent are over because real estate is just too complicated to rely on a single person. Go with a great team, and you'll get great results!

INSIDER STRATEGY #5: WHAT'S YOUR MOTIVATION? *KNOW* WHY YOU'RE SELLING!

There's a phrase coaches often use with athletes who aren't performing at the level they should: "You have to *want* it!"

To find success in just about any endeavor, that's the case—you have to want it. That's no less true in real estate; your motivation to sell is the determining factor as to how you'll approach the process. It affects everything, from how you set your asking price to how much time, money and effort you're willing to invest in the effort to prepare your home for sale.

The plain truth is that you must be highly motivated to sell your home. This is a buyer's market, and if you're not ready to give the sale of your home a "full-court press," you might want to wait until the market turns around. My personal experience is that, when I've had difficulty selling a home for a client, I find out after the fact that the client wasn't really motivated. This is a waste of time and energy for both me and my team as well as the seller, and everyone is unhappy in the end!

INSIDER STRATEGY #6: NEGOTIATE THE BEST DEAL— DON'T SETTLE WHEN YOU DON'T HAVE TO!

If you and your agent have effectively executed a sound plan for selling your home, you'll most likely see some offers coming your way, but the offers will almost always be below what you (as well as the potential buyer) know it's worth.

That shouldn't throw you or cause you to be upset; it's just how negotiating works. Evaluate the offer objectively with your agent's help, and look at it as a starting point for the negotiation. Counter a low offer, or even an offer that's close to your asking price. That lets the buyer know that the first offer wasn't acceptable. If that buyer is really serious, he/she will come back and negotiate further. Use hard facts and little subjectivity so the buyer has to see things from your point of view.

When it comes to negotiating, I often push sellers more than they want to be pushed. For example, I recently had a seller get an offer on his home for $440,000. He wanted to take it, but I said we could do better—and we did. I was able to get the buyer up to $472,500. Of course, my client was scared to death the whole deal would fall through, but that fear turned to ecstasy when we got him an extra $32,500 for his home!

We all know that selling a home can be nerve-wracking. It's a major event in your life, and one that you can't approach with less than a full effort. That's why you *must* align yourself with the right real estate team to expertly manage the process on your behalf. Don't kid yourself and think you can do it on your own. Do yourself a favor and work with the pros to obtain the best possible results.

About Lars

Before starting in real estate sales in 2007, Lars Hedenborg worked in various corporate roles, including engineering project management for a utility company, corporate finance analyst for a New York City investment bank, and acquisitions and strategic planning for an aerospace company. Lars is currently broker/owner of RE/MAX Real Estate Experts in Charlotte, North Carolina. In four short years, Lars achieved Hall of Fame status with RE/MAX by earning in excess of $2 million in gross commissions. Lars leads a team of agents with combined 2011 production of 180 transaction sides and $43 million in sales volume. The team consists of two listing partners, five buyer specialists, two inside sales associates, and three administrative professionals (listing manager, closing coordinator and marketing manager). Lars graduated from the Stevens Institute of Technology in 1995 with a Bachelor's of Engineering and from Duke University's Fuqua School of Business in 2004 with Master's of Business Administration. Lars admits that he owes much of his success to standing on the shoulders of giants (his coaches) and humble implementation. While Lars loves the real estate business, his true inspiration is his family; he and his wife, Julie, have two children: Anders (4) and Kendal (almost 2).

CHAPTER 13

Certified Home Sales:
A Little-Known Secret to Sell Your Home Faster and for More Money

By Kevin Clancy

It's no secret that the real estate market has changed dramatically over the past several years. The days of multiple offers over asking price the first day on the market are, for the most part, gone. In 2011, in the upstate New York market, over 50 percent of homes listed for sale didn't sell during the first six-month listing period. Homes languishing on the market for 12 months or longer are increasingly common. Our specialty has become selling homes that have been listed by other firms and have failed to sell. We can easily document the number of homes that failed to sell with other firms in six months that we sold in less than 30 days for top dollar. Despite the down market, this year has been our best ever! Our success in selling the tough ones can be attributed to a variety of systems we employ. However, one system we use takes advantage of two fundamental marketing concepts: risk reversal and differentiation. This little-known "secret weapon" to sell homes quicker and for more money has been the use of "Certified Home Sales."

The value of this concept was driven home the last time I purchased a car. Because I drive so much as a realtor, I always buy preowned cars. As I looked at cars, I noticed most of the cars the dealers offered were "certified preowned." I was able to find almost identical cars I wanted both in a private sale and on a dealer lot. However, the private sale vehicle was roughly $5,000 cheaper than the dealer-offered vehicle. Easy choice, right? Save $5,000 and buy the same car the dealer has. Guess what? I paid the extra money and bought the car from the dealer. Here's why: Like most consumers I'm risk adverse. The thought of getting stuck with a $30,000 lemon isn't very appealing. The dealer offered me a "certified car" for more money, but it took away many of my concerns and risk. The dealer inspected the car, cleaned it up, and offered an extended warranty. The removal of this risk was worth the extra money to me.

Car manufacturers have millions of dollars to spend on market research and marketing. I'm sure the certified car program was introduced after a huge investment of time and money on their part to find a way to compete with private sellers and small mom-and-pop car lots. It's now used throughout the industry for one reason—it works. Consumers will pay more to a dealer over a private seller simply because they have an aversion to risk, and it differentiates the products that the dealer offers from that of private car sellers. As I thought about it, I pondered why the real estate industry didn't do the same thing with homes.

When you're making a retail purchase, what's one of the first questions you ask? Isn't it: What's your return policy? As consumers, we're risk adverse. If you're worried about making a mistake buying a $50 coffeemaker, how do you think buyers feel shelling out hundreds of thousands of dollars for a home purchase? After being involved with thousands of real estate transactions over the past two decades I can tell you that home buyers are worried about making a mistake. It's true more in this market then in any of the past markets I've been involved in. It's marketing 101; remove buyer risk and you increase sales. Just like the car dealers, the answer in real estate sales is the certified home.

I truly believe that certified home sales, which are almost unheard of in the real estate industry today will quickly become the norm within a few short years. Today, they're the exception and not the rule, which gives a certified home a huge competitive advantage. Money flows to difference and in a market full of sameness with standard real estate listings, certified homes standout. Here are the five easy steps we take to certify a home before we list it for sale, which results in shorter marketing times and higher sale prices.

First, we have the home **inspected** prior to listing by a certified home inspector. This includes a radon gas test, well, and septic test, if applicable. Any items indicated in the report are addressed by the homeowner prior to listing the home for sale. The inspector's report and documentation on any work the seller completed is left on the kitchen counter for the buyer to see. This puts buyers at ease as they know the seller is proactive and a professional has already inspected the home. Often the buyer will forgo their own inspection and can save $500 by relying on the seller-provided inspection if they choose. For first-time home buyers short on a down payment, this can make a significant difference in affordability. In addition, it alleviates the problem of getting a home under contract, taking it off the market for several weeks only to have the deal fall through for a defect indicated by a buyer home inspection.

Second, we put a **home warranty** on the home. What if something breaks or the home inspector misses something? Home buyers are always worried that the smaller things in the home will break right after they buy it. Likely they've put their life savings into a down payment and closings costs. If the dishwasher goes they aren't going to have the money to repair it. If buyers are worried about repair costs on smaller items, a problem with a big-ticket item after they move in, like a roof or boiler, could potentially cause a major financial strain. The answer to alleviate this concern is a home warranty program. Home warranties are reasonably priced and typically cost $400 to $600. However, they're bargain as they generally cover the cost of repairs for all the major systems in a home, including roof leaks, appliance repairs, heating systems, electrical and plumbing issues for the first 12 months of home ownership. Just like the car dealers extended warranty, this puts buyers at ease because they know they won't have to make any out-of-pocket home repairs for at least the first 12 months. Based on one study, homes with home warranties sell for up to 3 percent more than homes without them, yet they're only used on a small portion of the homes sold today.

Third, we have the home **appraised** by a professional bank appraiser. Along with the inspection report and home warranty information, this is left on the kitchen counter. Buyers aren't experts on home evaluation. On average, they'll look at about eight homes before they make a purchase decision. They often rely on their buyer agent to determine if the price is right. Buying a home is a process, not an event, and it's rare that a buyer purchases the first home looked at. This isn't because the buyer isn't motivated. It's because the buyer simply hasn't moved far enough along in the buying process and hasn't seen other homes for comparison.

Being the first home a buyer looks at isn't a good thing. Over my career I've probably heard the same feedback from buyer's agents hundreds of times: "This was the first home we looked at; they aren't ready to pull the trigger." The buyer isn't ready to make an offer because even if the home is perfectly priced, the buyer doesn't realize it because they've only viewed one home. Having an appraisal completed and available for the buyer lets them know the home is priced right for the market and helps move them along in the process, even if it's the first home they look at. In our market, homes sell for about 95 percent of list price on average. This simply means if you want to sell your home, you need to price it within 5 percent of the perceived market value. The appraisal provides that value, and we price all our certified homes within 5 percent of the appraised value. It puts the buyer at ease that they're not overpaying for the home. It also helps eliminate the problem of a low appraisal when it comes time for bank financing.

Fourth, we have the **home staged** by a professional home stager. Home staging is important because it presents the home in the most positive way possible. Sure you may love a purple kitchen, but it isn't about your preferences. It's about making the home appealling to the current market, and home stagers have the expertise to do this. Often, this is as simple as cleaning, decluttering, rearranging and removing furniture, and making sure each room has a purpose. The home stager will go through a home from top to bottom and provide a detailed checklist of items that need to be addressed. These are items that generally have a minimal cost but will return many multiples of the investment when the home is sold. It's still amazing how many homes are on the markets that simply aren't in presentable, saleable condition. Pet odors, clutter, dated furniture, worn carpeting, etc. all have a major impact on a home's value. Based on statistics provided by the home staging industry, a staged home will sell up to 80 percent faster than a home that hasn't been staged, and it will sell for a higher price. On average, home staging is reported to return up 586 percent on the money spent. Our own experience with home staging supports these claims, yet still only a small portion of realtors and home sellers will use the services of a home stager.

Finally, we offer a **"return" policy**! Buyers in the current market are still worried and skittish. Not only are they worried about buying the wrong home, but they're worried about economic conditions and job security. What if they buy the home and lose their job a month later and have to sell? What if they get transferred? What if they find out they can't afford the home after they get in? To eliminate this final buyer objection, we developed our own return policy. If a buyer purchases a certified home from us and decides to sell for any reason within 12 months we'll sell the home for free! Again, by removing the risk of purchasing a home we increase the likelihood a buyer will make an offer. How many times have seen a 30-day money-back guarantee offered? It's offered because it increases sales by removing perceived risk, yet only a small portion of purchasers ever return the item.

So now you have a home that's inspected and defect-free, covered by a warranty, priced at market value, staged and shows better than competing properties, and offers purchasers an easy exit plan in 12 months if they're unhappy. Money flows to difference and in a sea of sameness these features separate a certified home from the rest of the homes sitting on the market. If you're a buyer deciding between two homes, and one is certified and one isn't, which one would you buy? Assuming all other things are equal, choosing the certified home becomes an easy choice, just like it did for me at the car dealership. Employ the use of a certified home sale when you sell your home, and I guarantee you will sell it quicker and for a higher price. Get your home certified and starts packing!

About Kevin

Kevin Clancy has been licensed to sell real estate since he was 18. He has a degree in marketing from Siena College and an MBA from the State University of New York at Albany. Clancy has spent the last two decades working as a state certified real estate appraiser and real estate broker. He has personally been involved in an estimated 10,000 real estate transactions during that time period, both as an expert consultant and real estate broker. Currently, he heads a top team of real estate agents specializing in selling tough to sell homes with innovative marketing techniques. Clancy and his team are consistently ranked among the top individual brokers and brokerages in the Capital Region of New York. Clancy is the founder of www.clancyrealestate.com and www.certifiedhomesale.com He's also the founder and author of the inspirational blog *The Monday Morning Mojo With Kevin* that can found at www.Ineedmymojo.com. He can be reached in the office at (518) 861-7016, ext 104.

CHAPTER 14

The Ebb and Flow of Real Estate:

How Cycles Affect Buyers and Sellers

By Patricia A. "Tricia" La Motte

The woman sat in my office telling me that she had been approved by her lender friend for a $400,000 loan, no money down, stated income, with an interest-only option ARM loan, and that she *must* have granite counters, large walk-in closets, and all the other things everyone else she knew also had to have. When I explained the current market cycle and why she should seriously consider some other options, she told me, "There was no need to be concerned because homes appreciate $100,000 every year." I was stunned and asked where she got that information. Well, of course, she just "knew this was the case due to the widespread increase of home prices prevalent at that time." This was in 2006. Unfortunately, she didn't listen to me or her husband or her mother, who apparently were just along for the ride.

If you don't understand that there are cycles in real estate, you could make the same mistake this couple did. By the way, I never heard from her again after our initial consultation. No doubt, she went on to become one of the vast number of homeowners who went through a foreclosure when the market corrected, or shall we say, fell.

Have you ever stood at the edge of the ocean and looked at the waves coming in? Recently I was at a family gathering at a spectacular Central California coastal city watching the waves break on the shoreline. It made me think of the cycles of the real estate market. Some waves are low, some high, some are tossed by the wind, and some appear to be full of bubbles. A swimmer would do well to ascertain from the locals what lies underneath the surface—rocks, barnacles, an undercurrent or a dangerous riptide—before jumping into an unknown sea. Real estate also has highs and lows, and as we've recently seen…bubbles. When you look at the surface, there's so much that can't be seen. A "new rise in real estate" indicates there were previous rises in real estate, and along with them, falls. This constitutes a cycle.

To really understand the real estate market and be prepared for the highs and lows that inevitably come, the undercurrent must be analyzed—the big picture must be viewed.

Different elements can have an effect on the ocean waves: winds, the cycles of the moon, or perhaps an unseen whale below the surface. This would all change the exact way and timing of that wave hitting the shoreline. This is how the real estate market is. Cycles in nature are everywhere, and they are interdependent. The real estate cycles are also interdependent, and among the most important markers in a real estate cycle are gross domestic product, inflation and unemployment. Some of the important drivers of the real estate cycles are demographic demand, human psychology, credit, government's role in the cycle, and the global real estate cycle.

Real estate cycles have been a significant underlying reason for the financial successes and failures of real estate investments throughout history. There have been a number of studies done on the importance of the cycles of the real estate market, one of which is the classic study done by Homer Hoyt. The movements of the real estate cycles appear to change over time; nevertheless, the undulations of the housing market in the United States have shown some regularity over the past decades.

The rise and fall will continue—it's just one of the attributes of a market—like the ebb and flow of the sea, or the waxing and waning of the moon.

What can buyers and sellers glean from the fact that the real estate market is cyclical?

WHAT REAL ESTATE CYCLES MEAN TO HOME BUYERS

It's always a good time to buy a great piece of real estate, and this is especially true now. Homes are more affordable than they have been in a generation, and mortgage rates have been at a historic low. When inflation picks up again, the rates will head up as well. Historically, the top four reasons that buyers give for buying a home are:

1. *Affordable home prices:* The U.S. government has interesting statistics on prices if you're interested in numbers. Suffice it to say, prices have decreased in almost all U.S. cities. In Los Angeles County, we're back to 2002 home prices. If you think you missed out on a good time to buy in the past... think again!

2. *Low mortgage rates:* When I started selling real estate in 1981, the rates were 18 percent, in 1989 rates averaged 10 percent, and recently they've been around 4.5 percent. With rates this low, most people believe there's only one way they can go...up.

3. *Affordable family purchase:* Affordability is indicated by how much of a family's income is consumed by the mortgage. In 1981, it took 36 percent of a family's income to pay the mortgage. Today, it takes 14 percent—a historic low.

4. *Tired of paying rent:* There will always be people who want to have their very own home; we'll talk about Fannie Mae's recent study in a moment.

We're currently experiencing the first two conditions that cause people to buy—affordable prices and low interest rates; and if a first-time buyer is tired of paying rent, then there are ways to help with the third reason—being able to afford a purchase.

As a potential home buyer, you're advised to get in contact with an expert real estate advisor months before planning on making a purchase. This preparation could save you tens of thousands of dollars and enable you to afford that purchase. This isn't new advice. However, due to the increase of FICO scores necessary to be approved by Fannie Mae, Freddie Mac and FHA loans, it's even more important for the savvy buyer to have ample time to increase a FICO score, if necessary, and be in the best position to qualify for a loan with the most attractive rate and the best loan for their situation. Even if you're paying cash, you still need to consult with an expert advisor so you understand the market and get the best home, in the best area for your needs, and the best deal possible.

There are basically two types of real estate buyers: owner-occupied purchasers—the classic homeowner—and investors. Within those two groups, there are additional groups. For instance, among the owner-oc-cupants there are those who are looking for a reasonably long-term stay in their home for at least seven years. These homeowners are a prime example of the recent Fannie Mae study, which cites the results of a survey listing the top four reasons people purchase homes:

1. It means having a good place to raise children and provide them a good education.

2. You have a physical structure where you and your family feel safe.

3. It allows you to have more space for your family.

4. It gives you control over what you do with your living space, like renovations and updates.

Another type of home buyer may be looking ahead with the idea of only living in their home for two years, then possibly renting that property and moving to a larger home, thus building an investment portfolio as they go. Done correctly, this has worked well for many property owners.

WHAT REAL ESTATE CYCLES MEAN TO INVESTORS

"Ninety percent of all millionaires became so through owning real estate." —Andrew Carnegie

The residential real estate market offers many opportunities for inves-tors. This second class of real estate buyer also has more than one type: the first-time investor, the move-up investor, the portfolio investor, the performance investor, or purchasing for rehab and resell. Depending on the current point of the cycle, there can be great potential for all these investor types. Currently, many first-time investors are seeing the ad-vantage of using a self-directed IRA to invest in real estate.

A true investor is looking to increase their present and future portfolio; perhaps with the goal of paying for their children's college education, or their retirement, to finance a charity, to leave a legacy to their family, or any number of reasons. They could be seeking cash flow or appreciation. There are many opportunities for the buy-and-hold investor today. Due to the number of previous homeowners who've lost homes through foreclosure or sold through a short sale, these people will be renting until they can buy again. This presents an opportunity to provide good rental homes in areas where previous homeowners still want to live and go to school and work. Properties smartly purchased in desirable areas can present cash flow to the investor. This usually presents a more attractive investment than CDs, T-bills, mutual funds or stocks.

There's a time and a season for any type of real estate investment, and it's important to know the strategy to use at the right time. For someone wanting to get started in investing, begin with a consultation with an expert advisor who's trained in real estate investments. Learn from their experience. There's no reason to "go it alone." Experience a rise in your investment portfolio the smart way.

WHAT REAL ESTATE CYCLES MEAN HOME TO SELLERS

There are three initial things that sellers can do to be best positioned in any real estate cycle:

1. *Really understand why you're moving.* If you're not motivated, then you're really not a true seller. This may absolutely be the best time to sell. Perhaps you've wanted to move to a nicer neighborhood, better school district, larger home, or retire out of the area, etc. Due to the current lower prices, you can take advantage of a lower price range when you *purchase,* which means that your monthly payments and property tax base will be lower than if you purchased when home prices are higher. Approximately 25 percent of current homeowners have substantial equity in their homes. The current cycle may afford them an excellent time to make a move—perhaps one of the best we've seen in a long time.

2. *Understand the current local market cycle.* Know the absorption rate, the average sales price, the average days on the market, number of homes currently on the market, etc.

3. *Consult with an expert advisor who knows the local numbers.* Find one who will work with you to uncover the answers to these questions and many other vital issues in timing your sale.

If you're a seller, the best way to be positioned in a cycle is to sit down with an expert real estate advisor and look at what the absorption rate is, the average price range, the average time on the market. Look and consider the comparable sales. For instance, if it's taking four or five months average time to sell in your area and the prices are going down, then you need to price your home accordingly. You can't price your home at what you think it will sell for *now*. It needs to be priced at the projected sales price four or five months out. This will enable you to be priced competitively for the current market, with the result of actually getting your house sold for the best price, with the quickest sale, and less hassle to you. An expert who knows their numbers can interpret the statistics and graphs.

Real estate has always been local; the newspapers and news media generally report the national real estate market—you need an expert who will interpret that information along with the *local* market.

WHAT THESE CYCLES MEAN TO REAL ESTATE PROFESSIONALS

I believe that there is, and will be, an even greater rise in the quality and dedication of real estate professionals. The very nature of the expansion of technology and available information gives experienced real estate professionals who possess and act with wisdom, integrity, and the determination to stay on the cutting edge of their field the ability to shine. Most important, the best of these agents will have a true heart for their clients—to give them expert advice based on *their clients' needs*. I've seen far too many agents go by the wayside because they weren't willing to obtain the knowledge, apply the systems, and adapt to the current cycles in the real estate market with a strategy that brings the best results for their clients. Now's the time to bring all these elements together and experience the new rise in real estate.

To learn more, visit these websites:

www.TriciaLaMotte.com

www.SantaClaritaHomeMarket.com

www.SCVHomePro.com

About Tricia

Tricia La Motte, known as the "SCV Home Pro," specializes in getting her buyer clients the properties they really truly want and love at a better price than they thought they could afford, and for selling homes fast, giving her seller clients "Expert Advice with Guaranteed Results."

As a Southern California native and having lived in the Santa Clarita Valley for the past 40 years, Tricia has a unique perspective on the area—seeing and experiencing the changes in the local Santa Clarita community over several decades.

Tricia has earned numerous awards and recognition for her Santa Clarita real estate production and dedication to learning and continually striving to improve her real estate practice. However, the most important recognition to Tricia is receiving the thanks from her loyal real estate clients for a job well done: "I take the time to listen and act upon my clients needs, and I genuinely care for the people whose lives are being touched by moving to or from their home."

Tricia's goal is to continually remain at the forefront of knowledge in her field so she can provide the best service for her clients. Tricia is smart and uses knowledge and wisdom with all parties in a transaction to create an environment where everyone feels good; however, she does not forget who she's working for—her client.

Tricia specializes in Santa Clarita residential real estate, from condos to luxury homes, foreclosures, short sales and investments. She has been serving the Santa Clarita Valley in North Los Angeles County, California, since 1981, and is a consistent top agent in the Santa Clarita Valley, as well as a Keller Williams International Triple Gold Winner. Tricia is a Certified Residential Specialist, a Certified Negotiation Expert, a Certified Investor Agent Specialist, a Certified Distressed Property Expert, and a Member of the National Association of Expert Advisors.

For free reports on home buying and the Guaranteed Sale Program, visit www.TriciaLaMotte.com, or to search for homes and neighborhoods, visit www.SantaClaritaHomeMarket.com.

CHAPTER 15

Eliminate Your Debt at No Cost:

Hire a Top-Notch Real Estate Lawyer and Broker to Short Sale Your Home

By Joe Hochman

Many homeowners are struggling to make their mortgage payments in today's economy. Our law firm and real estate brokerage receive many inquiries from homeowners and investors who own properties that are worth less than the mortgage balance. These property owners are "underwater" and have experienced a variety of hardships. Some have lost their jobs, are going through a divorce, took a cut in pay or lost their business. Others found the interest rate on their mortgage loans recently increased to an unsustainable level, incurred uninsured medical expenses, went through a family tragedy or a serious illness. As a result, they can't afford to meet their monthly mortgage obligations. When such hardships strike, people generally act in one of two ways: 1) They ignore the financial reality and hope or pray the situation will resolve itself or simply go away, or 2) they actively seek help. In all honesty, most people who ignore the reality of their situation either never seek help or ask for assistance only when it's too late.

I vividly remember all the phone calls and email messages received over the years from people who contacted us for the first time only days before or after a foreclosure auction. Each time, they asked the same question: "What should I do?" Although I try to help them realize the gravity of their situation and the need to take immediate action before they're forcibly removed by law enforcement officials, I can't help but wonder why they waited so long before calling anyone for help. The best time to seek help from a skilled professional is as soon as an issue arises relating to your mortgage debt. In some states, law enforcement officials can forcibly evict residents from the property after a foreclosure auction and prevent the former owners from taking any of their worldly possessions until their belongings are either put out onto the street or placed into a locked storage facility. To parents, I always ask: "If an armed sheriff gives you five minutes to leave the house or be arrested, then what are you going to grab with your two available arms -- your kids or your photo albums." The answer is always the same: "I'm going to grab my kids." I'd do the same thing.

Fortunately, those calls are the exception. Most of the people who contact my law firm or real estate brokerage are highly motivated to find the best way to avoid foreclosure and prevent bankruptcy. I realize that most homeowners hesitate to seek professional help because they either don't have the financial resources to hire the best real estate lawyer or real estate broker in their market or they don't know where to look. The purpose of this chapter is to provide you with the tools to locate and hire a top-notch real estate lawyer and exceptional real estate broker who can convince your lenders to approve your short sale and settle your debt, all at no cost to you.

As you can imagine, not all lawyers, short sale negotiators and real estate agents are alike. The key to ensuring that your legal and financial interests are best protected is to select a licensed and savvy legal expert who can lead you through the short sale minefield. There are 10 steps to follow before you hire anyone to list your property for sale or negotiate with your lenders:

1. *Honestly assess your situation and needs.* Do you have a verifiable hardship that makes it impossible for you to continue making your mortgage payments, or do you simply want to sell your property because it's underwater? Virtually all lenders require that their borrowers prove a verifiable financial or other hardship as a precondition to considering a short sale. Without a verifiable hardship, your chances of getting a short sale approved are slim.

2. *Research and consider your options.* If you need or want to stay in your home, then a short sale isn't right for you. If your goal is to sell your property and eliminate your mortgage debt forever, then a short sale is likely your best chance of negotiating full debt relief with your lender without a devastating hit to your credit score. Through the short sale process, sellers have the chance to be released from all financial and legal obligations by every single mortgage lien holder. The same opportunity doesn't necessarily exist in a loan modification, deed-in-lieu of foreclosure, bankruptcy or foreclosure.

3. *Find a top-notch real estate lawyer who specializes in short sale negotiations.* Ask for referrals from trusted friends, neighbors and colleagues. In order to get help, you need to ask for it. Search the Internet for real estate lawyers who concentrate on short sales in your area. Confirm that the individual is an actively licensed and practicing real estate lawyer. The Internet is filled with individuals who may have once practiced law or who concentrate on criminal, personal injury, family law or other areas that aren't relevant to your real estate issues. If you find an actively licensed and practicing real estate lawyer, then determine whether the attorney is also an actively licensed real estate broker who has his or her own real estate company. That way, you'll receive the best of both worlds by having a common umbrella of protection. Check the lawyer's rating and reviews on websites like Avvo.com. Thoroughly review the attorney's website for testimonials and information that can help you become an informed consumer. Remember, you're looking for an experienced and knowledgeable legal expert with a proven track record of success for her or his clients. Don't settle for average. You should be looking for a preeminent lawyer who has obtained meaningful results for clients, including significant debt relief.

4. *Ask tough questions and insist on straight answers.* This is where most people fall short. Realizing that most people don't know what questions to ask, I always help prospective clients ask me tough questions. People are searching for a lawyer whom they can trust, ask questions, and receive honest and meaningful answers without being gouged financially, even if the answers

aren't always what they want to hear. I don't pull any punches during consultations for our No Hassle Short Sale Program. As a result, people leave the consultations armed with information that will allow them to make significant decisions that impact their finances, homes and lives, even if they don't become one of my clients. Questions you should consider asking include: What exactly do you do to represent my interests during a short sale; who will be negotiating with my lender, a lawyer or staff; on average, how long will it take to get the short sale approved; what is your success rate; have you negotiated with my specific lenders in the past and what were the results; on average, how often are you able to obtain full debt relief for your clients; can you provide references of past clients whom I can contact; why should I hire you vs. another lawyer or non-lawyer negotiator.

5. *Learn the out-of-pocket costs to you.* If you feel comfortable with a particular attorney and law firm and think they might be the right fit for you, then it's important to ask about costs and fees. Do they charge an upfront fee? If so, then consider whether you're willing or able to pay such a fee. Are the fees contingent upon a successful result? This is the ideal situation because it creates the most incentive for the lawyer to work hard to get the short sale approved and closed. Who pays the fee: you, the real estate agent, your lender or someone else? Is there a refund policy or guaranty? Do they require an in-person consultation and a consultation fee? If so, then think twice about that particular law firm. In all likelihood, their real motivation is to collect your money up-front and lure you into a sense of obligation to move forward through their "preferred" vendors. Instead, seek legal professionals who don't mandate a consultation, yet who may offer a 30 to 60 minute in-person or telephone consultation at a reasonable cost and only as an option. Does the law firm require that you and buyers use a specific title or escrow company? If so, then be concerned that the law firm may be exposing you to legal liability under the Real Estate Settlement Procedures Act (RESPA). In addition to any legal fees, who will be responsible for paying real estate commissions, closing costs, real estate excise or sales taxes, homeowners association transfer fees and the like? In our No

Hassle Short Sale Program, our clients pay no legal fees, real estate commissions, closing costs or sales taxes. We put it in writing so our clients know what they're getting in advance.

6. *Understand the limitations on any legal representation.* Don't expect that your short sale attorney will also help you form a new company or handle your divorce as a part of the engagement. Instead, you want your real estate attorney to concentrate on negotiating with your lenders, getting your short sale approved and settling your debt. Hire separate counsel to handle any other matters. If there are limits or restrictions on the legal representation, then make sure they're clearly disclosed in writing. Some law firms serve only as a neutral third-party negotiator and don't actually represent property owners during the short sale process. In those instances, there's no attorney-client relationship and the protection for sellers is limited.

7. *Hire a respected lawyer before you list your home for sale.* The key to ensuring that you're legally protected at every stage of the process is to hire a legal professional first. Real estate agents aren't allowed to provide legal advice or opinions about the legal issues that impact your life, property and money. Doing so constitutes the unlicensed practice of law and can result in civil and criminal penalties. For that reason, you should rely on the advice and opinions of a knowledgeable real estate lawyer and short sale expert who will answer your questions.

8. *Don't do it yourself.* Let's say you needed to have surgery to remove your appendix. You know it's a serious matter that necessitates expert care by a trained and skilled surgeon. Would you insist that an experienced professional perform the surgery, or would you do some research on the Internet and try it yourself? Even the most knowledgeable and capable surgeon wouldn't operate on herself. The same is true when it comes to selling your house, trying to convince your lender to approve a short sale and settle your mortgage debt. Your best chance of getting your lender to accept less than your remaining loan balance and to forgive your debt is to have a respected and talented real estate lawyer handle the negotiations on your behalf. A skilled lawyer will act as a buffer between you and your lenders. That

way, there will be less chance for you to say or do anything that might hurt your chances of getting your loans settled. A skilled lawyer will also be able to get your lenders to stop calling you at home, work or on your mobile phone.

9. *Your lawyer should never accept "no" as an answer.* Most people, including lawyers, don't have the stomach for short sales. They're hard work, requiring dedication, experience, specialized skills and perseverance. It's critical to know when to push a lender hard and how to contact decision-makers who can approve the transaction when roadblocks arise. Lenders love to say no to their borrowers, real estate agents and lawyers. Most short sales fail to get approved because unskilled negotiators lack the willpower and initiative to continue pushing for a "yes." My law firm and I have successfully negotiated short sales for years. As a result, we've found valuable contacts at every major lien holder. When a low-level bank negotiator is unable or unwilling to move the short sale forward, we'll routinely escalate to highly positioned decision-makers, including executive officers. Without such contacts, you're left to chance. In addition to having specific expertise, knowledge and highly tuned instincts, your short sale lawyer should never give up on you or the transaction.

10. *Create an incentive for your lender to approve the short sale and settle your debt.* Your house or investment property is collateral for your mortgage loan. Why would your mortgage lender agree to accept less money than you owe and release its interest in your collateral? Unless your real estate lawyer can clearly articulate how a short sale will result in more money for your lender than a foreclosure, your lender will choose foreclosure every time. Calculating the net proceeds that your lenders will receive from a short sale compared to foreclosure is a science, not guesswork. To get positive results, your real estate lawyer must be able to clearly articulate the financial benefit to your lender. If your real estate lawyer is armed with the same software and tools that lenders use to calculate net returns from short sales vs. foreclosures, then you'll be able to determine right away whether a given purchase offer has any chance of being accepted by your lender. By using the same software

that lenders use, my law firm can quickly calculate the precise amount that a lien holder will net from a given short sale. By showing the lenders that we possess their same numbers, our negotiations are streamlined.

According to one statistic, short sales have an average success rate of only around 18 to 24 percent. In other words, lenders deny 76 to 82 percent of all short sales, resulting in foreclosure or bankruptcy for homeowners. When I talk with real estate agents, lawyers and others who attempt to negotiate short sales with lenders, I understand why those numbers are so abysmal. Most people simply lack the knowledge, drive and fearlessness to engage in intensive and meaningful negotiations with lenders and the skills to overcome their many hurdles. My law firm and I currently have a success rate of 92 to 95 percent. We get short sales approved and closed on a regular basis because we know the tricks of the trade. In addition, we routinely obtain full deficiency waivers and significant debt relief for our clients in the process.

Lenders and loan servicers are represented by legions of lawyers who are singularly focused on collecting money from you. You should also be protected by a determined and experienced legal professional, who can get your short sale approved and your debt settled, at no cost to you. You now have the tools to locate and hire a great real estate lawyer and real estate broker who can short sale your property, negotiate with your lenders, protect your legal interests and eliminate your mortgage debt. Because preventing foreclosure is often a race against time, it's important to act quickly and before it's too late.

About Joe

Joe Hochman is unique in the real estate industry. Combining more than 20 years of experience as an actively licensed and practicing real estate lawyer and real estate broker, Joe is frequently referred to as the "Short Sale Guru" by clients, colleagues and industry professionals. Joe is a recognized and sought-after public speaker regarding short sales, real estate, foreclosures, legal, business and mortgage lending issues. Having taught short sales to hundreds of real estate agents, lawyers, loan originators, title and escrow providers in many states, Joe always strives to instill his positive and "never take NO as an answer" attitude to everyone he meets who wants to try their hand at short sales. Licensed to practice law in Washington and Arizona, Joe is also a member of the National Association of Realtors and a contributing author to legal and real estate sources. Joe has been rated as "Excellent" by the internet's largest expert-only lawyer rating service.

Known for his ability to get "impossible" short sales approved and closed, Joe and his team are routinely able to obtain debt relief for homeowners totaling hundreds of thousands of dollars. He is also the go-to short sale negotiator for real estate investors and buyers who want to save thousands of dollars on their property purchases. Through his innovative No Hassle Short Sale Program, Joe offers property owners the opportunity to receive complimentary legal representation by a respected real estate law firm and the chance to pay no real estate commission, closing costs or real estate sales taxes. His focus is on helping clients achieve freedom from their mortgage loans while avoiding foreclosure and bankruptcy.

Joe is the Managing Attorney of Hochman Legal Group, PLLC and the broker-owner of Avanti Realty, LLC. To learn more about Joe Hochman, the No Hassle Short Sale Program, and how you can obtain mortgage debt relief and complimentary legal representation from an accomplished Real Estate Law Firm,
visit www.HLGLAW.com, email info@HLGLAW.com or call (425) 392-1548.

CHAPTER 16

The Short Sale:
Your Best Long-Term Solution?

By Jeremy Mellick and Jeremy Eide

During the housing boom you probably never even heard of something called a short sale. Now you can bet that between 40 to 70 percent of the homes for sale in your neighborhood, depending on where you live, are either a short sale or bank-owned listing. As house prices continue to fall, more and more Americans face a decision they never thought they would have to make: short sale or foreclosure.

The housing market has obviously changed dramatically since the 2008 crash, and the plain and simple fact is that more than 10 million homeowners are "underwater." That's currently the situation with an unbelievable 1 in 5 mortgages in America. In the beginning of the crash, homeowners did everything in their power to keep their friends and neighbors from knowing they were doing a short sale. Now it's not un-common to find them talking about it on the most popular social media sites.

Some families have suffered a loss of income that made the home they purchased unaffordable, while others have simply decided that they no longer want to *throw good money after bad*. Everyone has a different story, but we'd like to start this chapter with a typical one that illustrates just how millions of Americans fell into this predicament—and how they might be able to climb out of it.

PAUL'S STORY

In 2005, the housing market was booming. Interest rates were in the low 5 percent range, and property values kept going up and up. Paul thought he would be crazy not to take advantage of this opportunity for his family to live the American dream and buy a home. Plus, he discovered that getting approved for a mortgage would be easy—he wouldn't even need a down payment.

Paul had it all figured out. They would buy a good starter home, stay there for a few years, sell at a profit, then move to a bigger house when he and his wife had more children. In the meantime, he'd get a nice income tax deduction on the mortgage interest while he watched his home value rise and rise. Melinda, his wife agreed...how could they *not* buy a house with all that going for them?

In August 2007, they celebrated their second anniversary in their new home, as well as the fact that Melinda was pregnant with their third child. It was time to trade up, but there were storm clouds on the horizon. The real estate market was no longer on the way up—it was headed in the other direction. Paul and Melinda decided the best thing to do was to quickly try and sell the home for a price that would at least pay off the mortgage. They could then just rent a larger home for awhile.

Paul and Melinda discussed their plan with their real estate agent, who ran the numbers for them, based on current local market prices. The agent then delivered some bad news. After the expense of selling the home, Paul and Melinda were going to be short about $20,000.

Their house was "underwater."

The couple was shocked. They asked the agent what she thought they should do. Her answer was also a little shocking: "There's nothing you *can* do. You're just going to have to wait it out." They took in the situation and decided to sit tight; after all, there was no reason to panic.

Suddenly, there *was* a reason. The economy really crashed in late 2008, and in early 2009, Paul discovered his company was suddenly no longer authorizing overtime for any employees, effective immediately. Paul had consistently been paid a lot of overtime; in fact, it was one of the reasons he had decided he could afford to buy the house in the first place. Without that extra pay, he wasn't going to be able to handle the

$2,200 monthly mortgage payments.

There was still another possibility. Paul had heard that the federal government had begun a program to help homeowners like them stay in their homes; under the program's guidelines, their mortgage company might reduce their monthly payment to an amount they could afford.

Paul decided to give it a try. A customer service person at the mortgage company said she would mail him some forms to fill out for the loan modification program. She also told him that they should make trial payments of $1,600 per month for the next six months. If they made those six payments on time, they would be considered for a permanent loan modification.

They filled out the forms and successfully made the six lowered payments. However, it didn't end up mattering; the mortgage company mailed them a notification that their request for a permanent reduction was denied. To make matters worse, because they had been making only partial payments, they now owed $6,350 to make up the difference for those past six months, which was due immediately. If they didn't make that lump-sum payment, they faced foreclosure.

Paul and Melinda were devastated; they didn't have that kind of money on hand. When Paul went to work, his friend Jim could see he was upset and asked what was wrong. After Paul told him, Jim revealed that he himself was in the same situation, but his house was now on the market.

"Whoa," said Paul, "Aren't you upside down? How can you afford to sell?"

"Simple. I'm doing a *short sale*," replied Jim.

Paul had no idea what that was. Jim explained that if Paul worked with a real estate agent who specialized in short sales, the agent would list his home at an attractive price. When he got an offer, the agent would then negotiate with Paul's mortgage company to reduce the amount that he owed to the point where he could sell the house and walk away free and clear.

It seemed like the perfect answer. Paul called Jim's real estate agent to get the process started. After about a month, they had an offer, and the real estate agent successfully negotiated with Paul's mortgage company to accept the sale price. Not only that, but Paul and Melinda also received $3,000 at closing to help with moving expenses. Finally, they had some relief.

Afterward, Paul and Melinda moved into a rental that was almost twice as big as their previous home—and cost about $700 a month less than their mortgage payment had been. They could actually put some money away. The real estate market continued to drop and, in 2011, they were able to buy a home that was big enough for their family, just as Paul had originally planned back in 2005.

If it hadn't been for the short sale, it wouldn't have happened.

NO HARDSHIP REQUIRED

As Paul and Melinda's story illustrates, many good, well-meaning people found themselves "house-poor" as a result of the massive crash in the real estate market a few years ago. Caught between owning a home worth less than the mortgage and not being able to afford the payments because of the bad economy, these homeowners were clearly stuck between a rock and a hard place. To make matters worse, the government's loan modification program didn't work for most. That's why the short sale soon became the only viable escape route for many.

There are plenty of reasons why someone would consider doing a short sale: divorce, loss of income, reduction of income, illness, job transfer, military obligations, and incarceration are just a few. However, there doesn't necessarily have to be a dramatic hardship situation for your mortgage company to consider allowing you to short sale.

Sometimes, the choice to do a short sale comes down to it being the best *business decision* for the homeowner. Many homeowners are facing a situation where it could take their property more than 10 years to move back into the black, assuming that another generous rise in real estate takes place. A short sale, however, could enable them to buy another home in two to three years at current prices.

Below, you'll see a graph showing an example of the financial considerations a typical homeowner might face in today's real estate market. The home that's being represented is currently worth $200,000, but the mortgage on the property is $290,000, leaving the homeowner $90,000 in debt should he attempt to sell at this moment.

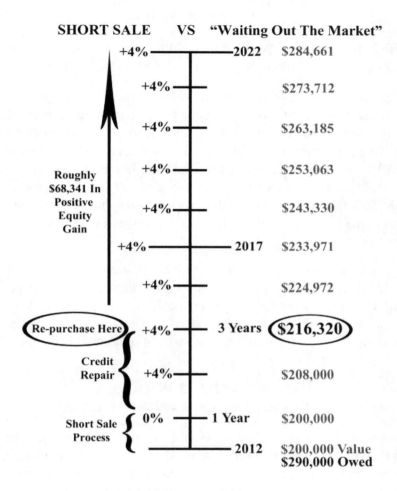

What if the homeowner decides to wait as long as 10 years to sell? He'd make back his money for sure by then, right? Probably not. Even taking into account an optimistic forecast of 4 percent gains in property value per year, the homeowner would *still lose money* if he were to sell in 2022.

With a short sale, however, the homeowner could possibly repurchase a similar home in about three years for around $216,000. Not only has he eliminated his negative equity, but he has also put himself in a position to *build roughly $68,000 of positive equity* in the home, as he's bought it at current market prices, not the inflated prices of a few years ago. That's why a short sale can make so much financial sense to an underwater homeowner.

WHAT'S IN IT FOR THE BANK?

You might be thinking, "Wait a minute. Why would a bank actually take $90,000 less to pay off a mortgage? How is that smart for them?"

To begin with, you have to understand a few facts about the mortgage industry. The company you make your house payments to is rarely the "investor" who actually advanced the money toward your property purchase. That company is usually only the "servicer" for the loan. Investors will look at an underwater property that homeowners want to get out of and quickly see that they'll get X amount of dollars for a short sale and X amount of dollars if the property goes into a foreclosure. In the vast majority of cases, they'll lose more money on a foreclosure than a short sale.

A large number of homeowners have already demonstrated they would rather have their homes go into foreclosure than continue to pay off a mortgage that's a money-losing proposition on their side. Investors know that and would rather allow a short sale. Just like it being the best *business decision* for the homeowner, most of the time it is for the investor as well.

THE SHORT SALE PROCESS:
THE GOOD, THE BAD AND THE UGLY

What's required to make a short sale work for you? When it comes time to negotiate with your mortgage company, you'll need to provide your agent with some financial documents, such as tax returns, pay stubs and bank statements from the past two months. Your real estate agent will need the authority to negotiate with the mortgage company on your behalf.

Most short sale experts will guide you smoothly through the process, beginning with giving you a packet of paperwork to fill out *prior* to listing your home for sale. If they have you list your home *before* filling out this paperwork, that's not a good sign, and you should probably consult someone else to assist you with your short sale.

Why is having a short sale expert in your corner so important? That's where the "bad" part of "the good, the bad and the ugly" comes into play; there are things that can go wrong if the proper precautions aren't taken. You might have tax consequences, or you could end up owing the difference between what your mortgage company *nets* from your short sale and what you actually owed them (an amount known as "deficiency"). If your agent isn't experienced in this type of transaction, you could end up with more liability than you would in a foreclosure.

You can avoid all that if you have the right expert handling your short sale. Here's the *ugly* part: *More than 70 percent of homeowners who end up losing their homes in foreclosure never seek help from a professional, even though it would cost them nothing. Most of them don't even know they have other options.*

But let's focus on the *good*—the fact that a successfully negotiated short sale will allow you to move on with your life and not be haunted by the consequences of a foreclosure. Those consequences can last for years and prevent you from buying another home for five to seven years. When you *do* apply for another home loan, you'll have to disclose that you've suffered a foreclosure in the past.

On the other hand, most of *our* clients are able to get their credit back to the point where they can repurchase a home within *two* years. And you're generally not asked if you've ever done a short sale when you apply for another mortgage.

With a foreclosure, you can feel completely helpless as you wait for your family's home to be forcibly taken by the bank and watch it possibly fall into complete disrepair after the fact. You'll also be stigmatized by the infamous "F-Word"—FORECLOSURE—on your credit report and probably in your social circles as well.

With a short sale, you put yourself in control, not the bank. It also allows you to negotiate with the mortgage company to have them possibly waive any rights to collect a deficiency balance from you down the road. You walk away from your home with your head held high.

However, you *must* act quickly if you're in danger of foreclosure. A looming foreclosure date can limit the time you and your agent have to market your home and negotiate the short sale. Simply waiting for the foreclosure ax to fall is never the best choice for a homeowner in trouble. A short sale could be your best long-term solution, but you'll never know if you don't look into it.

For the long term, a successful short sale negotiation eliminates your loan deficiency and puts you in the best possible position to purchase another home down the line. If you're a homeowner who's underwater, wouldn't it be a great feeling to be able to drain away your debt and swim off to a more secure financial future? Consult with a short sale expert and see if it's the right option for you.

About Jeremy and Jeremy

Jeremy Mellick

Jeremy Eide

Jeremy Mellick grew up in a suburb Southeast of Seattle. From childhood his entrepreneurial spirit was evident. He constantly searched for a way to take business opportunities to a higher level. Instead of having the standard lemonade stand when he was a child, Jeremy stepped it up a notch and ran an Italian soda stand. Whether it was selling baseball cards to his friends or standing outside the grocery store selling newspaper subscriptions, Jeremy outsold nearly everyone else. His sales skills followed him into high school where he proved that carrying a bag of candy bars that he bought in bulk and resold could be a very lucrative business.

In 2003, Jeremy decided to enter the world of real estate sales. Within one year, he was among the top agents across the country. In his second year, Jeremy was honored as being in the top 10 percent of agents nationwide, and he hasn't looked back. Now the owner/CEO of Excel Real Estate Experts, Jeremy is focused on giving back to the real estate community. He does this by facilitating classes for local agents, teaching them the skills that have made him so successful.

Jeremy Eide was also born and raised in the Seattle area. He's a former Marine who has been married to his high school sweetheart for 13 years and has three wonderful children. Since 2007, Jeremy has made it his goal to help as many homeowners as possible avoid foreclosure. By guiding them through a successful short sale, he has been able to help homeowners move forward with their lives and start fresh, with confidence to purchase a home in the future. Throughout the years, Jeremy has negotiated more than 135 short sales and has worked with all the major banks as well as most of the local banks and credit unions.

Understanding *the get more when you give principal,* Jeremy has instructed many local agents on the process of successful short sale negotiations. With only 10 to 30 percent of short sales being successful nationally, Jeremy realized that in order to help the greatest number of families avoid foreclosure, he needed to extend this reach through other agents. By teaching other local real estate agents how to successfully negotiate a short sale transaction, Jeremy's hope is that those agents will then have the skills to successfully help more homeowners.

Jeremy and Jeremy combined forces in early 2011, forming one of the Northwest's most dynamic and fastest-growing real estate teams. Knowing how important specialization is in being successful, Jeremy and Jeremy have taken separate roles on the team. While Jeremy Mellick specializes in marketing and selling homes in traditional transactions, Jeremy Eide is in charge of the short sale department.

When it comes to *traditional* sales, Excel Real Estate Experts is known not only for their ability to get homes sold quickly and for the most amount of money possible, but they also put their money where their mouths are. If they can't sell your home, they'll buy it themselves, guaranteeing that their clients will sell their home.

For more information on the short sale process, go to www.HomeSolutionsNorthwest. com. If you need help with a traditional real estate transaction, go to www.Excel RealEstateExperts.com, or you can call them any time at (206) 319-5200 or toll free at (800) 460-9191.

CHAPTER 17

We Interrupt This Book With an Important Message About Short Sales— No Fear/No Shame

Don't do anything until you read this important chapter!

By Woods Davis and Jeremy Bowman

Until 2008, Lisa and Greg were typical homeowners, both with good-paying jobs, a little savings in the bank, and a bright future ahead of them. They had three children, a cat named Inkie, took vacations once a year, had dinners out a couple of times of month, and anticipated redoing their kitchen because they loved to cook and entertain family and friends. Then it happened—the unexpected event that changed their good life into one that was filled with dread. Greg's company downsized. The economy had impacted his firm significantly, and although he had worked for them for more than 15 years as a manager, in order to remain viable as a business, the company had to eliminate nearly 30 percent of its jobs, many of them in management, including Greg's.

At first, Greg spent most of his time looking for a new job in his field—through an employment agency, job fairs, networking and online career websites—and he was pretty confident he would be able to find something that would pay the same salary or close to it. But after a few months of collecting unemployment and dipping into savings to make up the deficit between his former pay and what he got from unemployment, Greg and Lisa began to fear what might happen to them. He couldn't find a job where his experience and skills would apply, and he was told frequently by potential employers that he was "overqualified" for the other positions that were available. Lisa's income barely covered food, utilities, car payments and insurance. They had already borrowed from both sets of parents to put a sizable down payment on their home in 2004, but the difference between what they paid for it and what it was worth in the current market was sobering—their house had lost about 40 percent of its value in those three years.

They spent many sleepless nights talking about all their options, trying to choose one that would allow them to remain in their house, but their application for a loan modification had been denied, they were quickly running out of money to pay their basic bills, and they had no funds to pay their mortgage (which had reset at a higher monthly payment just three years after they bought their home). Lisa and Greg had heard what some people were doing in their position, where they couldn't sell their house at a high enough price to cover the balance owed to the lender—they were bailing out of homeownership. Some were just neglecting the obligation they had made to the lender when they bought the house. Others were jumping ship because they felt the lenders had misled or talked them into buying a house they really couldn't afford or would easily lose if something unforeseen happened like job loss, medical expenses or home repairs. Everyone, it seemed, was abandoning their homes and causing major damage on the way out, feeling that their actions were warranted by their anger and disappointment. Greg and Lisa knew that neither of these options were something they would do, despite their difficult circumstances. They thought about the effect a foreclosure would have on their personal integrity and credit. They had witnessed how foreclosure affected their neighbors, lenders, and everyone involved in the home buying or selling and related industries in their community.

Lisa and Greg decided to meet with a real estate professional who had been recommended to them by a close friend—someone who knew their situation. Someone who knew they needed professional guidance about what to do next. The real estate agent who showed up at their door explained to them that there were legitimate options available to resolve their situation. He was a Certified Program Specialist with Program HR 3648, a nationwide initiative to help homeowners avoid foreclosure. As a Program HR 3648 Specialist, he had volunteered his time and resources to help dozens of homeowners and lenders successfully complete short sale sales to resolve their mortgage problems. He gave them a website: www.programhr3648.org/ where they could listen to other homeowners tell their stories and describe how they'd been helped completely for free. For the first time in many weeks, Greg and Lisa felt they would have an honorable way to handle the sale of their home—a way to make the most of their difficult and troubling situation.

Lisa and Greg's circumstance is typical of individuals who find themselves unable to handle their mortgage payments. Sometimes homeowners have lost jobs, had cutbacks in hours, a demotion, pay cut or major medical bills. Some have been relocated by their company or the armed services and can't sell their house for the amount owed to the bank or rent it to cover the cost of the mortgage, taxes and insurance. There's no shame in finding yourself in a hardship situation. The only shame is that many homeowners don't know what their options are, or that they even have options other than foreclosure. And many have only heard negative comments about short sales and don't realize that this can be the best option to completely resolve their situation, when handled properly.

With today's economy, the number of homeowners struggling to stay above water continues to increase, and according to many experts in the housing industry, this trend will continue for the next several years to come. The increasing number of distressed properties for sale is depressing home prices, which in turn, creates more distressed properties as more home mortgages fall underwater. Foreclosures have the most damaging effect on home values, averaging 32 percent below the average sales price of homes not in foreclosure, according to the *RealtyTrac 2011 U.S. Foreclosure Sales Report.*

Pure and simple, foreclosures are devastating. The homeowner is forced out of his or her home, the house is either sold or reclaimed by the lender where it must be maintained or refurbished to compete with other properties that are for sale, and the property can become a blight on the neighborhood. Foreclosed homes also affect neighborhood home values, can become an attractive nuisance and target for vandalism, and the lender will both spend and lose more money on a foreclosure than on a short sale.

If you're facing a foreclosure, you're not doomed to be a part of the problem. You have options, and you can be a part of the solution! A Certified Program HR 3648 Specialist can give you the facts about what will work best for you and how to handle the emotional trials that many experience during financial struggles. You may have feelings of disappointment, fear, anger, guilt, depression, and helplessness as you recognize that keeping your home isn't an option for you. You may feel that you're giving up your dream. Making the decision to be pro-active in handling your circumstances in the most positive and honorable way you can is both life-affirming and a confidence builder. Taking action rather than being acted upon will do more to change your attitude and make what's a very uncomfortable and difficult situation become an opportunity for a fresh start and a brighter future.

It's important that you don't act in haste or anger. Some homeowners feel betrayed by their lenders because they were unable to get the loan modification they applied for or because their loan payment reset at a much higher level than they could afford, or they feel misled by the "easy money" offered to them when they received an approval for their home purchase. Or worst of all, they just can't get anyone at the bank to help them! Some homeowners use these negative, victimized feelings as a rationalization for damaging the house they're leaving behind as one last way to "stick-it-to the bank."

We advise you to use that negative, emotional energy and turn it into a positive application to find a Certified Program HR 3648 Specialist, and then cooperating with that real estate professional to get your house listed and approved as a short sale. That will include providing financial documents, such as bank statements, pay, pension, retirement or unemployment statements; a hardship letter that explains why you're no longer able to meet your financial obligation to the lender(s) involved; financial worksheets; and other similar documents, as well as continuing to provide financial documents that the lender requests. But don't worry, your Certified Program HR 3648 Specialist will simplify this entire process and handle all the work with your lender for you. It will require patience with the process—don't forget that the lender (and investor who supplied the money to your lender) is making a sizable financial concession by accepting an offer and payoff that doesn't cover the balance owed on your mortgage loan. The lender isn't the "bad guy" in a short sale. Like you, the lender is the institution that's also picking up the pieces and trying to make the best of a situation that has a sizable downside for them. Also, know that the term "short sale" doesn't relate to the amount of time it takes to list, sell and close on a property; it refers to the fact that the payoff to the lender(s) is a "short" payoff because the bank won't receive what's due on the balance of the mortgage or lien.

By cooperating with your Certified Program HR 3648 Specialist and the lender(s) involved in your short sale, you're being proactive, positive and principled in handling your situation. That pays off in several ways so you can feel good about your efforts. You'll feel confident that you've done everything possible to turn a negative into a positive for everyone involved: the lender, your neighbors and yourself. You'll know that you've made a decision that will benefit you, long-term: Your credit score will be affected for a shorter period of time than if you'd been foreclosed on, you'll be able to qualify for another home loan in as little as two years, and you'll avoid public judgments that can damage your reputation.

Program HR 3648 doesn't advocate choosing a short sale if you have any other viable, long-term options to honor the obligation you made the day you signed the papers to purchase your home. However, we do believe that, if you find yourself in a position where you're not able to meet that original obligation, you can make a choice that will ease your conscience, let you sleep at night, and help you begin to get your life back on track. Deciding to do a short sale shouldn't be a choice you make just because your house is upside down, and your mortgage payment is inconvenient. Before you decide to cavalierly walk away from your obligation, please consider how it affects everyone else—the lenders, the neighborhood, the real estate market, the local economy, and ultimately, your own integrity. On the other hand, deciding to do a short sale because it's best for you and your circumstances should be a decision that has been carefully considered when all other options have been eliminated.

Let us be your advocate in this process. Choosing a short sale can be the first step in the right direction, and with the right real estate professional—who's Certified as a Program HR 3648 Specialist—we'll be there with you every step of the way. In partnership with your agent/ broker and with our support and efforts with your lender(s) to get your short sale approved, you'll be able to move forward in confidence with the rest of your life.

About Jeremy and Woods

Jeremy Bowman

Woods Davis

Jeremy Bowman is the co-founder and president of RealPrompt Real Estate Services, home of Program HR 3648. RealPrompt is America's leading, comprehensive short sale system for real estate agents and brokers. Program HR 3648, America's Free Non-governmental Foreclosure Option, has helped real estate professionals assist thousands of homeowners across the nation avoid foreclosure. Jeremy began investing in real estate in 2002, and by 2005 he helped create RealPrompt's proprietary model that now serves agents, brokers, lenders and homeowners in every market in the United States. Prior to real estate investing, Jeremy founded Pilot Home Technologies, a regional home technology company. Within a two-year period Bowman grew the company to 250 employees across five states and sold Pilot to a venture capital firm. Jeremy has a Bachelor's degree in Political Science, with a minor in Economics from the University of Louisville. He currently resides in Gilbert, Arizona, with his wife and five children.

Woods Davis is the co-founder and Vice President of Marketing at RealPrompt Real Estate Services, home of Program HR 3648. Woods has developed direct-response marketing campaigns and sales funnels that have helped generate more than $35 million in additional real estate commissions for RealPrompt's agent and broker partners. Woods is also one of the top internet marketers in the real estate niche, personally selling more than $9 million in products and services online. Woods's background in real estate investing includes residential building and development, financing and short sales. Woods has a Bachelor's degree in Marketing and Business Management from the University of Kentucky. He currently resides in Gilbert, Arizona, with his wife and two daughters.

To learn more about partnering with RealPrompt Real Estate Services to help homeowners avoid foreclosure and earn lender-approved commissions visit www.RealPrompt.com. To determine what FREE programs are available to help you avoid foreclosure and how you may be able to benefit from Program HR 3648 visit www.ProgramHR3648.org.

CHAPTER 18

Using the 1-2 Punch to Sell Your Home— Pricing and Marketing

By Dionne Malush

After working as a graphic designer for 19 years, I was ready for a change, and the challenge and excitement of the real estate field intrigued me. However, I couldn't begin to imagine working with complete strangers, discussing the positive and sometimes even a few negative factors about their home and then finding the right person to buy this home. How would I go about promoting a home that I had only been to once or twice? How would I promote a home that I didn't have a personal connection to? How would I sell this home quickly so that in the end I not only had a happy seller but also a happy buyer? The task was daunting, but I was determined to become a Top Listing Agent in my field, so by using the tried-and-true method of trial and error, I set out on an adventure that would earn me the title of a Top Listing Agent!

The trial and error was learning how to market a home successfully in order to reach as many potential buyers as possible, whether it's a $50,000 home or a million-dollar home! What I discovered is that the two fields of real estate and marketing go hand in hand! There's no doubt in my mind from what I've learned through the years that my strategy of marrying these two industries has helped me create my niche in this very competitive field. It wasn't an easy process, and, in fact, it was costly, as I've tried countless marketing strategies in an effort to find the absolute best ones that are user-friendly, have proven success rates, and attract the highest number of potential buyers.

Although I place marketing as a key factor when selling a home for a client, marketing alone isn't enough. Ultimately, in order to get every home you list sold, the most important techniques that your agent should be using to stay ahead of the curve are pricing, marketing and condition. In this chapter, I'm going to focus on pricing and marketing.

PRICING YOUR HOME

Here's a recent example using pricing and marketing: A home had been on the market with a local real estate company for six months and didn't sell. The sellers, after watching my local advertising efforts, decided to call and list their home with me. I was able to show them through analyzing the market that the price was too high for the area, even though they had invested more money in the home than the area could offer. Throughout the listing process, we strategized on pricing and I continued all my marketing efforts. With a bold move, we dropped the price dramatically under market value and had three offers in 24 hours. This example shows that even if we contract the Goodyear blimp or the President to hold an open house, pricing is still the most critical component to selling a house. Pricing slightly less than market value, many times over, gets you slightly more in your pocket. *I always say that the price will cure all ailments of a home (steep driveway, no yard, small kitchen, etc.).*

Essentially, in most markets only 50 percent of homes sell the first time that they're listed. Your second chance to sell your home is to hire the best marketing/listing agent you can find, even if he or she is not in your neighborhood. It takes time to find a good agent. If you hear of an outstanding agent that's located in another part of town, don't shy away from making that call. After all, do you want to get your home sold, or do you want the agent located right down the street who may be a part-time agent to sell your home? Does it really affect where that agent is located?

Take the time to meet and interview your agent, ask questions about what techniques they'll use to get your home sold. If you call your local real estate office and an agent answers the phone and says they can come right over, chances are that the agent answering the phone has too much time on their hands. A busy agent is a productive agent, and a productive agent is working hard to sell your home every day.

I believe that if I want to sell my client's home within a reasonable amount of time, then the road to get there begins with the pricing of that home. When it comes to pricing, professional appraisers seem to sum this aspect up best using just three words: "Buyers Create Value." Your home is worth as much as a member of the buying public will pay for it. After it's been on the market for months, you've been given a clear message that the property may not be worth your asking price. This is particularly true if there haven't been many prospects coming to see your home; if it has been shown a lot, your agent should be providing you with feedback so you're aware of what the buyers like or don't like. What you do at that point depends on whether you really need to sell, and whether you're working with a time limit. If you're not really motivated to move soon, you can always wait—years if necessary— and hope inflation will catch up with the price you want. The problem is that in that time, your home begins to look and feel shopworn. Buyers become concerned about a house that's been for sale for a long time. Unfortunately, even though the reason may simply be a price issue, buyers will begin to imagine all kinds of other reasons, such as a condition or structural problem, some sort of damage, or maybe that it was built on an old cemetery. Don't allow a potential buyer to question anything about your home. Be knowledgeable about your neighborhood and price accordingly. The buyers make the value, so do everything you can to showcase the value of your home! There's no point in saying, "We simply can't sell our house." Anything will sell if the price is right.

MARKETING YOUR HOME

After setting an appropriate price for your home, it's time to begin marketing it.

I've compiled a list of my "Top 10 Selling Tips" that you should make sure your preferred agent is using in order to get your home out to the maximum number of potential buyers in the most successful manner.

1. *Front of the home photo:* Since most buyers begin their home search online, appealing and captivating photos that really capture the beauty of your home are crucial. Buyers shop with their eyes first and if the picture of your home catches their eye while

they're browsing literally thousands of listings, then they'll read further. Listings without a photo will almost always be ignored and overlooked—think about that, what have you ever purchased sight unseen? Pictures are critical to capturing a buyer's attention! Here are a few ideas to make that exterior picture most appealing: Crop out sidewalks and streets that take up too much space on the photo, remove vehicles and toys from the driveway or front of the home, shoot up close and angled photos (take a few pictures so you can choose the best one), avoid shade on the home, make sure the path to the front door is clear and free of any overgrowth, and finally make sure your agent takes the maximum number of pictures that your multi-list allows.

2. *Exterior photos:* If your home doesn't have a yard, be sure to highlight all the other great features of your home. Take pictures of clubhouses, pools, spas or tennis courts. However, if you do have a yard, potential buyers will want to see it, and they need to be able to picture their family using it. With that being said, be sure to mow the lawn and trim the bushes, put away toys, remove any evidence of pets, find the best angle to give the most flattering picture that will emphasize the space, and avoid shooting into the sun. Always remember to take a picture of the back of the home; this technique has helped me in selling many homes.

3. *Interior photos:* Take pictures of every room! Again I have to emphasize that buyers are visual—when they're looking online, they'll want to see plenty of pictures! A few pointers: Open the drapes and blinds, turn on the lights, remove trash cans and close toilet lids, keep decorative items to a minimum (maybe a floral arrangement in the kitchen and dining room), and pick the main focal point of each room for your picture.

4. *Virtual tours:* Everyone loves a virtual tour no matter how long or short it is. The virtual tour allows the buyer to do their own private walk-thru of the home without any pressure. Ideally, adding a personal story to the tour will really hit home! Did something funny, touching, surprising, or even wacky happen in your home? Then let the agent tell that story to everyone that's viewing your home. With an actual story in place that occurred

at your home the buyers can begin to picture themselves creating the same kind of memories there.

5. *Signage:* "For Sale" signs encourage potential buyers to call that number immediately. Placing a "For Sale" sign in your yard is free advertising! If you have a corner lot, use two signs. You never know who might be driving through the neighborhood—maybe somebody is lost or visiting or even making a delivery. If there's no sign, then those people won't know your house is for sale and who knows, they may be in the market for a new home!

6. *Print advertising:* Print advertising is only effective for those people who read the newspaper. With all the technology available today, more than 90 percent of buyers will look online first! Keep in mind that this is something they can even do at work, and they'll have the advantage of large, clear ads and full-color pictures. There are multiple real estate websites; many are free, but some can only be accessed by a brokerage company, while others charge the agent a fee to list their properties. Ask your agent what websites he or she uses.

7. *Direct mail:* "Just listed" postcards or other forms of direct mail advertising can be effective. Mail these items to neighbors who can easily pass them on to someone they know looking for a home, agents representing buyers in your neighborhood, and buyers living in other locations that often relocate to your area.

8. *Open houses:* Sellers love the idea of an open house; buyers not so much. Statistically, only 1 percent of homes sell nationwide at an open house. You might think the open invitation to come and tour your home would be appealing, but most often it's only the homes in high-traffic areas that buyers swarm to. It's no different than walking into a car dealer or furniture store, you immediately feel pressured and you just know that salesperson is watching you from a distance. Buyers don't want to be pressured or uncomfortable, so they most likely will pass on the open house and do their search online!

9. *Broker and agent tours:* These can be more effective because you're asking the people that will be bringing the buyers to your home to come and take a look around. Agents don't need to feel

pressured or uncomfortable because they're not the ones buying your home, but by seeing your home in person then they'll know exactly which of their buyers is looking for the qualities of your home.

10. *E-fliers:* Technology has made it so easy to send electronic fliers, and you can send them to literally hundreds of people. What better way to get the word out that your home is for sale. Make sure you include some great photos and plenty of details. Don't forget the address, the price and contact information! Take full advantage of the power of Facebook and Twitter. Make sure your agent is on at least one of these sites, and make sure they have lots of "friends." If your agent has 1,000 Facebook friends, then 1,000 people could potentially see your listing!

In summary, you as the seller have the upper hand. After all, you'll decide which agent will list your home, so choose wisely. Be sure to interview agents to find one that's dependable, reliable and aggressive in their approach to selling your home. These agents will price your home competitively and market your home aggressively using their established web presence as well as all resources available to them through their office. You may not like it when your agent suggests a price reduction, but you need to decide if you want your home sold quickly, or do you want it to sit for six months or more and then hopefully get your original asking price. Add up the expenses you've incurred in those six months, and you'll see that had you started at a competitive price, then chances are your home would have had more showings, more offers, and quite possibly a quicker sale! In marketing your home, a realtor is making an investment of time, effort and money in your property. It's in their best interest to see that your home is sold in a timely manner and for the best price possible. Don't forget to ask your realtor what they do to market a home—you might be surprised at their response.

Buying and/or selling a home may be one of the most important and stressful events of your life, but it should also be enjoyable! It shouldn't be intimidating or overwhelming. A good agent will keep you informed and up-to-date, will always be in contact with you throughout the entire process, and will help you navigate this course from start to finish. Your agent's job is to sell your home, so allow them to do their job. Ask questions, provide input and make suggestions, but don't try to control every aspect of this process. Build a relationship with an agent that you are comfortable with, and work as a team. The agent/seller relationship is crucial to a successful sale. Everybody wins when a home is sold, and if you and your agent can employ the techniques of pricing, marketing and condition, then the steps you've taken should achieve the desired outcome quickly and successfully! You'll have acquired a trusted source you'll go back to time and time again, and the agent will have gained not just a seller but a valuable and important lifelong client and friend. Best of luck in selling your home!

About Dionne

Dionne Malush is a listing and marketing specialist in the Pittsburgh area. Just eight years in the business, she's well known in her market and keeps herself in front of the consumer. She calls herself "The Almost Famous" Realtor. With a creative background (more than 20 years as a graphic designer), she has been able to climb to the top in her market using her artistic ability. Dionne is a 1989 graduate of the Art Institute of Pittsburgh. Since starting her real estate career, she has been coached by many of the top coaching companies, including Mike Ferry, Buffini & Co., Rich Levin, Real Estate Champions, Jerry Bresser/Donna Stott and Anthony Robbins. Her design background and many years of training help set her apart in an industry where anyone can become a real estate agent, but becoming a successful Realtor® is a much bigger challenge.

She has achieved the prestigious Centurion Award from her five years at Century 21 Frontier and is climbing the Coldwell Banker ladder, too. She's ranked in the top 3 percent in sales at Coldwell Banker Pittsburgh, among more than 1,000 agents.

Working with her assistant, Kim, she's able to dedicate her to time to focusing on what she needs to do daily to get a house sold. Dionne studies the Law of Attraction daily and maintains goals in writing to help her get to each level of her success.

Dionne lives about 30 miles south of Pittsburgh in the small town of Belle Vernon. Feel free to contact Dionne anytime by visiting her website at www.malushrealestate.com.

CHAPTER 19

Property Not Moving?
The Reason Homes Don't Sell

By Brian Flynn

It's not the price; it's your marketing plan. That's right! The only reason a home doesn't sell is due to an ineffective marketing plan. Many real estate agents are fooled into believing that price alone is the reason homes don't sell. But successful home sellers, those who take pride in leadership and forward thinking, understand that many other factors beyond price are at play.

The obstacles to sellers not realizing their desired results are ineffective marketing techniques, poorly planned staging, unsuccessful negotiation skills, and inadequate use of information technology.

MARKETING PLAN

Prospective agents must possess all-important marketing skills. Marketing-related questions for an interview must include:

- What is the difference between your marketing plan and your competitors'?
- How do you market to traditional as well as internet venues compared to others?
- How do you market to other real estate agents?
- How do you customize the marketing of specific properties?

HOME STAGING

"We only get one chance to make a first impression." No where is that cliché more obvious than in selling a home. Real estate staging is a key element to successful marketing. Prospective agents need to be able to respond to the following questions to demonstrate their expertise in the property preparation:

- What staging can be done to add to the value of our home?
- What visual problems might the presentation of the property have on prospective buyers?
- Is there anything that can be done to address these problems through effective staging and visual enhancements?

PRICE NEGOTIATION BASED ON SOLID RESEARCH

Successful sellers must be able to demonstrate an understanding of re-evaluating proper pricing strategies. Your prospective agent must be able to prepare an accurate and current market analysis. Make sure the candidate is familiar with details of current pricing trends for your over-all marketplace, including:

- Days on the market for properties in your specific price range
- The list-to-sales price ratios for homes that have sold
- Square footage cost
- The number of homes currently active in your price point

NEGOTIATION BASED ON INCENTIVES

Qualified real estate agents know a successful sales approach always includes skillful give and take. Make sure your prospect can discuss the following incentives:

- Offsetting closing costs
- Buying down an interest rate
- Closing date flexibility
- Home warranties

INFORMATION TECHNOLOGY PLAN

Your potential agent needs to demonstrate an up-to-date proficiency with information technology. These questions will help you assess this proficiency:

- How do you provide properties with greater shelf positioning?
- How many websites will you use to market our property?
- How do you generate consumer traffic for our home on the internet?
- How do you plan to create a marketing strategy for the property using photographs? Be specific regarding types of pictures to be taken, the suggested order to be displayed, and identification of certain rooms to be featured in multiple photographs.
- Are you familiar enough with technology to be able to produce a virtual tour or video of the property?

SALES TRACK MANAGEMENT AND DOCUMENTATION

- How will you manage our transaction from contracts to closing?
- How will you provide us with necessary feedback?

THE DONOVANS: A SUCCESSFUL CASE STUDY

The Donovans were an elderly couple from a nearby Boston suburb who were eager to move on to the next stage of their lives without delay or worry. When they contacted The Flynn Team, their home had expired with another realtor. We offered them a detailed marketing plan, and we promoted ourselves as experts in successfully moving expired properties.

- *Marketing Plan Item #1: Staging.* We made certain the house was neat and uncluttered and the furniture carefully arranged. Presentation is everything. We pulled the kitchen table away from the wall to show an attractive eat-in kitchen. Next, we removed the big recliner chair from the living room entirely to suggest a more roomy living space. Then we added attractive plants and flowers, trimmed hedges and cut grass to create a positive first impression for prospective buyers. We achieved these visual improvements for little or no cost.

- *Marketing Plan Item #2: Exposure.* The previous agent had the property listed only on the MLS and its own web page. We went to work immediately to broaden the exposure of this property by listing it on more than 100 search engines, such as Realtor.com, Boston.com, Trulia.com, Zillow.com, etc.

- *Marketing Plan Item #3: Photographs and virtual tour.* Next, we decided to dramatically increase the number of photographs of the property from three shots to 25. Our experience has demonstrated that exterior and interior photos and adding an internet virtual tour are extremely helpful techniques in moving our properties.

- *Marketing Plan Item #4: Research.* We were happy to show the sellers important market trends, such as days on the market, list-to-sales ratios by town, and the number of homes for sale within their asking price point.

- *Marketing Plan Item #5: Price.* Armed with the benefits of these marketing elements, we were able to convince the seller to agree to a 10 percent price reduction.

- *Marketing Plan Item #6: A successful open house.* The preliminary diligence of the steps outlined above allowed us to stage a successful open house with confidence. Twenty-five parties arrived for the first open house, and the sellers received three bona-fide offers.

- *SOLD!* In less than a week, the Donovan's home sold for 99 percent of the asking price. We're convinced that by following these simple common-sense marketing rules we can effectively market and sell expired properties in the shortest time at the highest price.

About Brian

Brian Flynn, the broker/owner of RE/MAX Results, based in Medford, Massachusetts, is a top performer living up to the RE/MAX LLC legacy. The Wall Street Journal ranks him and his team as one of the top 100 of residential sales teams in terms of volume and gross commission. They were also voted best real estate agency in Medford by the consumers. Brian's team serves all of Eastern Massachusetts and produces more results than their average competitor. Brian's websites are a clearinghouse of all things related to Boston Real Estate, complete with blogs, articles, reports, multimedia, and social networking. Brian covers such topics as "how to sell a house that didn't sell" and "how to stop paying rent and own your own home." Buying, selling, remodeling and negotiating are other topics covered in the bounty of resources. From the most inexperienced to long-term investors, Brian and his team point customers in the right direction with the facts. With the motto of "saving the American dream," Brian warns customers to pause before opting for foreclosure by pointing out the scar on their credit report, the possible litigation from lenders, and perhaps even being passed over for a job. While Brian can walk you through the foreclosure, the firm ensures it is the last resort. Short sales, bankruptcy and refinancing are a few examples of alternatives him and his team can talk you through before making such a significant decision. Brian also represents 20 years of expertise and holds such designations as Realtor, Certified Distressed Property Expert (CDPE), Seniors Real Estate Specialist (SRES), Accredited Buyer's Representative (ABR), and Certified Residential Specialist (CRS). You can reach Brian by email at bflynn@remax.net or telephone at (781) 395-4000.

CHAPTER 20

Reverse Offer:
Creating a Seller Advantage in a Buyer's Market

By Jeff Cook

In a buyer's market, sellers look specifically for skillful tactics to get their home sold in the shortest amount of time and for the most amount of money. They normally look to their realtor for the latest and greatest sales technique to help them accomplish this goal. One of the tactics that has been especially helpful is known as the "reverse offer." The reverse offer is defined as "a seller making an offer in reverse to a buyer to engage that buyer into an offer negotiation that otherwise may not have been consummated onto the seller's property."

The biggest hurdle a seller faces in today's real estate market is the lack of consumer confidence from the buyer. There isn't a lot of certainty that the buyer is confident that they've negotiated the best deal or even in thinking that they've selected the best home, or what options may be available had they waited to see what comes on the market tomorrow. Buyers are reluctant to get out their checkbooks and make the seller an offer until their emotional hot buttons have revved up. This reverse offer assists in getting the buyer emotionally connected to your home.

Let's reverse the role for a moment and say that you were in the shoes of the buyer, and you've just received a job transfer to the area in which you currently live. If you're like most home buyers, you would get onto some home-search website, inquire about homes, locate a realtor, and begin the shopping process. From the buyer's vantage point, there are several challenges in this process to be aware of. Consider having to narrow down the search to a specific area within a city where you've never lived, locating a home that has the amenities, shopping and the lifestyle you're accustomed too, but also staying within an affordable price range. Unless you're paying cash, the tightened qualifications set forth by most mortgage companies must also allow your "taste" to be financeable into a cozy monthly payment with decent mortgage terms.

The buyer in today's market faces all these hurdles before they ever step foot in your home for the first viewing, and since inventory levels are at an all-time high across most of the country, the number of homes that these buyers want to view before making their decision is also at an all-time high. Therein lays more frustration for the buyer: 30 to 40 percent of the homes on the market today are unsalable and aren't clearly labeled as such. The inventory must be thoroughly examined to determine which homes are ineligible from the onset. Examples of this would be a home that's listed at $260K but only worth $250K, and the seller has a mortgage balance that requires them to sell at the $260K. The home is unsalable because your banker is going to require an appraisal that will result in the bank only honoring a contract amount at the $250K, in which you nor the seller now has the ability nor desire to cover the $10K difference. Even worse, say that seller has no ability to bring money to the table (upside-down home) and a mortgage balance that won't allow them to go below a $275K asking price—again because the home is only worth $250K, which means the seller must apply to their bank for a hardship package, modification, or a short sale that may take months to get approvals or declination. The buyer may be getting tricked into thinking these homes are good bargains at ridiculously lower than achievable listing prices (i.e., the seller lists at $200K, hoping a quick offer will come that they can present to the bank, quickening the turnaround time that the bank will unveil their lowest acceptable sales price, which most times is much more than the $200K list price that you were presented initially).

After the buyer has eliminated "the unsalables," the challenge begins to then narrow down the remainder into their top picks, which is where the reverse offer comes in handy. Because inventory levels are so high across the country, buyers are paralyzed by the number of choices. Typically, we see a buyer add a home to their favorites because it matches certain emotional hot buttons and then add another home because it satisfies a different budget comfort, and often Mr. Buyer will choose a different top pick than Mrs. Buyer. As a result, buyers typically have four to five prospective homes in their top choices, and oftentimes we see that there isn't one clear consistent front runner among the buyers.

Part of the reason why we developed the reverse offer was to eliminate the buyer's agent having to be an excellent negotiator or that agent having to convince their buyer that your home is indeed the best choice through traditional methods. The average realtor in most markets sells three to five homes a year, and since regulations, realtor law, and the mortgage industry changes daily (interest rates two to three times a day), it's not a good idea to leave the successful sale of the seller's home into the hands of the average realtor.

The traditional method is that a seller sits and waits and hopes that a buyer likes their home, and that buyer would have their agent execute a written offer to purchase the seller's home. This traditional method is still effective, but if you're the seller in the transaction, the wrong person is in control of the negotiations. By virtue, the reverse offer puts the seller in control of the negotiations. There's nothing in the rule books that says a seller must sit and wait on the buyer to make a decision on their home, so why not make the offer in reverse and entice the buyer into your home by making certain concessions to them? In most states, realtors are mandated by state law to present to their client any offer that's received or concerning their client. When the buyer's agent receives this offer from the seller's agent, the buyer's agent is legally bound to submit that offer to the buyer, and have that client approve, reject or counter the offer. Oftentimes, this sudden negotiation propels our clients' homes to the front-of-mind awareness in a buyer's decision process. Communication with the buyer's agent here is effective to determine what concessions to the buyer are important, and the seller then inserts those items into the reversed offer to the buyer. Oftentimes, because the buyer's agent is informed and playing along with the seller and seller's agent, they've bought into the idea that this is their best shot at getting their buyer off the fence to make decision, which results in a harder push to get the buyer to accept the terms of the offer. Oftentimes, we hear buyer's agents giving us feedback that their buyer decided to go ahead and take the offer because it "must be fate" or "at least we'll negotiate with them first to see if we can make a deal," since this particular seller's home came up first on their radar. After all, if Mrs. Buyer had any inclination that this home could possibly have been "the one," then Mr. Buyer would be foolish to not make mama happy in their brand-new home!

If the buyer just went through an extensive house-hunting process to successfully jump through all the necessary hoops and selected their top three to five homes, and they've determined they're the only buyer interested with no other offers on a home, they're more inclined to offer the seller a much lower price, sometimes cheating the seller out of tens of thousands based on the principle of the buyer's market. When we started using the reverse-offer technique, the sole intent was to get the buyer to play ball with our seller client, but what we quickly realized was that when our seller made the initial offer, he/she maintained control of the negotiation process, which resulted in much higher list-to-sale-price ratios for our sellers. After the reverse-offer technique was fully implemented, receiving low-ball offers were a thing of the past, and by maintaining control, our seller clientele's list-to-sales ratio immediately improved 2 to 3 percent, and overall 6 to 8 percent higher than many other realtors in our marketplace, which virtually covered the entire real estate commission with this one technique.

One obstacle early on was the buyer's opinion of the home value being different than our own, and therefore, the buyer challenging our price in the reverse offer. We successfully overcame this hurdle by conducting appraisals and home inspections on all newly listed homes and disclosing them to the buyer at the time of our reverse offer. This created a win-win scenario with the buyer and the seller—and eliminated the need for pointless concessions from the seller.

The biggest advantage of the reverse-offer technique is using it to create a multiple-offer situation for the seller client. Let's say buyer A views the property on Saturday, and buyer B views the property on Sunday. Our seller makes a reverse offer to buyer A on Monday and gives them 14 days to determine if they like the offer terms and also makes that offer contingent on not having accepted any other offers on the home during that 14-day review period (a non-binding letter of intent to the buyer will also suffice, depending on the state that you're in). On Tuesday, we notify buyer B that we are working an offer on the property that they've viewed, and if they're interested in the property, they should submit their highest and best offer immediately for review. The beauty of this real estate transaction is it functions exactly like a group of kids in a toy store: There may be hundreds of toys, but most all the kids like the one toy that the other kid is already playing with. Oftentimes, this technique will result in a multiple-offer situation on the seller's home in a buyer's advantage market. We've witnessed dozens of times that one of the two competing buyers will pay at and in some cases above full price for a home that their fellow buyer has an interest in. Moreover, if buyer B isn't interested in submitting an offer, any other buyer that views the property over the next 14 days is made aware that there's an offer pending review, and it's in that buyer's best interest to quickly submit their highest and best offer.

About Jeff

Jeff Cook is a real estate broker in Charleston, South Carolina, and is part owner of the second-largest realty company in the Charleston Metro area, The AgentOwned Realty Co. Jeff was laid off in 2002 in the corporate America environment for being among the best sales associates, when the company eliminated commission-based sales agents and paid them their average hourly wage. Jeff rebounded in 2003, graduating both with a bachelor's in business from the University of South Carolina and also from Real Estate University, both within a week of each other. Jeff went on to open his own small business, where he could be rewarded for his honest, hard work and provide a safe goal-oriented work force within his organization. In 2011, Jeff was the No. 1 residential resale agent in the Charleston, South Carolina, market (non-REO and non-new construction) and is frequently sought out by local media publications, talk shows and local radio stations for his real estate update. Jeff is married to the lovely Sarah Cook, and they have a husky-shepherd mix named Johnny. For more information or to sell your Charleston, South Carolina, area home, Jeff can be reached at (843) 261-2069, JeffCook@JeffCookRealEstate.com or www.JeffCookRealEstate.com.

CHAPTER 21

Move Your REO Administrative Staff Overseas to Exceed Expectations and Stay Profitable

By Henry Benito

This chapter can help any small business compete and offer services you generally can't afford. In my case, I will show you how I did it with my real estate brokerage and specifically managing and selling foreclosures for major banks, servicers, hedge funds and GSE's. In my market area (Miami-Dade) REOs (real estate owned) comprise almost half of all sales. I'm in the top five in units sold with a real estate board of more than 20,000 members. I attribute a major portion of this success to our use of outsourcing overseas.

I've been doing limited REO work since the late '90s while I operated an investment company that bought, renovated and sold homes. Back then REO assignments from lenders were few and far between, especially during the real estate boom. People in my market jumped on the pre-construction train. Most agents didn't know the difference between an REO, short sale, or a Brokers Price Opinion. They didn't have to, since all they had to do was find eager buyers and get them easy loans.

In early 2007, an old client approached me with 30 new REO assignments. This mega-lender might have given me five properties per year at most during the boom. At this point my investment company had been operating in the red for the last two years when the market turned, so I decided to drop my investment activities and just liquidate any remaining properties I had.

It was all up to me. I couldn't count on any of my agents because they didn't have the first clue of what needed to be done. So I started working 15 hours a day. I'm a control freak so this was in my comfort zone. I was checking occupancy, negotiating relocations with occupants, getting properties trashed out, BPOs, inspecting, supervising repairs, listing, negotiating offers, following up on closings, and submitting reimbursements. Everything I'd done in the past but at 10 times the pace. I could easily manage 30 to 40 assets by myself, probably faster than a team, but I started thinking, Can I keep up this pace?

Also, the mega-lender was dumping more assets on my lap. I figured out I better get some help and fast. So I went out and did what most brokers in my position do. They get one of their inexperienced agents, hand them the file, tell them they'll be helping me with the property, and put them on a split. I did that for a few months but didn't like the results. It was difficult to mold an independent contractor into an employee. By this time, servicers were using web portals to load up all their assets and communicate with all parties to move them quicker. Agents had tasks and were being graded on how fast we completed them. I couldn't rely on one of my agents to work at the same pace I could, so I took over all the files.

As fate would have it, author Tim Ferriss came out with a book called *The 4 Hour Workweek.* I'm not an avid reader, but I devoured the book in two days. This guy was working four hours a week while I could barely get four hours of sleep a day. He had virtual assistants around the globe doing everything for him. This guy is a business-lifestyle stud, I thought to myself. The light bulb went off, and I decided I was doing the virtual assistant thing pronto, and I was going to make it work.

The land of boxer Manny Pacquiao was my first target. I saw Filipinos work while in the Navy and knew these people had a strong work ethic. I also started doing research on what admin or call-center people get paid in that country. There was no reason I couldn't hire at least one to train to start. I opted to contact and interview call centers and found one that would charge me double to triple of what I would pay hiring someone direct. I went that route because I'd rather have some supervision of the person I'm hiring and I was brand new to this.

During that time more and more tasks were being done from a web portal, and there was a lot of data entry to do. I started using software where the VA can see my screen, hear me, and I can record a video to go over step by step how to fill out a report and where to gather the information. I was quality controlling the final product to the seller, but I freed up a few hours of my time by not working on data entry.

REO volume was steadily increasing and due to our strong performance metrics on the web platforms, new clients approached me with more properties. Work hours were steadily increasing as I fought to keep up. I started bringing on more VAs and local employees at a controlled pace.

Along the way I hired VAs in the Philippines and quickly terminated them when I saw consistent performance problems. There were just too many people looking for this type of employment so I needed to look for the sharp ones. Eventually, these people started identifying themselves, just like when you hire local employees.

Every facet of the REO operation was growing exponentially, so I figured out that if my clients (which had more properties than I did) have different departments, then I needed to mirror our operation like theirs. The vast majority of real estate agents can't afford 10 to 15 different local assistants. REO sellers were expecting more and more from their listing brokers, with reduced compensation on the listing end being the trend. Several listing brokers I knew either stopped servicing accounts because they were losing money or tried to service the listing as best as they could and hoped the client didn't figure out how many things were falling through the cracks.

OVERSEAS LEVERAGE

You can hire 7 to 10 overseas people to every 1 American. That puts me in a position where I can afford to hire dedicated staff for each department to provide an optimum service level to the banks that a traditional agent can't. That person can be trained to become a specialist by doing the task day in and day out. I have about a 50/50 ratio of local assistants to overseas. I figured out that ratio works the best for me, and I have licensed agents doing the work they're supposed to do. They all work in an assembly-line format, pushing the property through the motions. The property sits in a certain department until something triggers it to move to the next stage. We have field, premarketing, marketing, accounting and buyer's agents working in tandem.

Another benefit of having people on the other side of the world is you can have your business working day and night. Clients send us a message at 10 p.m. or assign a new property at 2 a.m., and someone on our staff responds right away. They're amazed we can reply this quickly at all hours, and our back-end tasks are being addressed in the evening/early-morning hours. What real estate office works those hours?

The last benefit of using this concept is you can apply redundancy to your operation, which is critical as a small-business owner. I first learned this concept in the U.S. Navy where I operated nuclear power plants. Every system on a nuclear engine room has at least two components just in case one fails. Sort of crucial when you're in a submarine a few hundred feet under the water and you need propulsion, or you'll sink to the bottom of the ocean. In your business, each staff member needs to be cross-trained to be able to support another one when it's really busy, someone is absent, or you just need to let someone go.

You might ask what can a person on the other side of the world do in the REO business? I'll be frank....in many cases, more than the local staff I've hired. People in developing countries treat being hired by an American firm as winning the lottery. My overseas staff puts in extra hours without being asked if tasks need to be done. They get rewarded for that extra effort by pay increases, employee of the month bonuses, and flexibility with their schedules. I'm not sure what I would do without them. I understand that hiring U.S. workers is what this economy needs, but ironically by hiring overseas personnel in my business I've taken away market share from other REO agents because we can outperform them, and with more volume, I can afford to hire more local staff that I require for some functions.

Overseas leverage has allowed us to grow to the point that in 2010 we built a brand-new state-of-the art 1,600-square-foot REO operations center in Miami. The local staff can communicate easily with our overseas staff via group chat and video. We have time-zone clocks and workstations positioned in the same way our assembly line is. We're also green and have to since we collaborate with overseas staff via the web. There are several web-based REO agent management programs, and I recommend you implement one as soon as you get to 50 assets managed. Not using one to hold your data will just set you up for failure since the programs help you and your staff with tasks and communications.

You might ask how do I find how to hire the staff and board them initially to ensure they become a productive member of the team? At first, I recommend you find a call center or a company that specializes in "Business Process Outsourcing." It's just easier at first to have them assign you the right person. They can also easily replace the person with someone new in the event the first hire doesn't work out. They also handle all the regulatory procedures in that country for you.

After you get some experience under your belt, a great resource to hire VAs directly is ODesk.com. I suggest you use an online application questionnaire to prescreen your applicants. Have the prospect tell you a little more about themselves and attach their CV. By doing so, you can get a better grasp of their English comprehension and writing ability. An excellent online form- and questionnaire-building service I use is wufoo.com.

You also need to have your prospect perform an online personality assessment. I have the applicant fill out my questionnaire and when they press submit, it's redirected to my company's personal testing site from an outfit out of Texas called hireMAX (www.hiremax.com). The employee is prompted to complete the exam, and I only interview the applicant after I like what I see on the questionnaire and exam results. This saves a lot of time. The great thing with hireMAX is if I don't like the responses an applicant gives me or the CV, then I don't have to grade the exam and, therefore, pay for the testing. Speak with Norm Bobay at hireMAX and tell him to set you up with the same program he's using for me.

After you start working with your first VA, be sure that you're recording all trainings and setting up what's called an SOP (standard operating procedure) manual. Remember, you're trying to set up a business that will run by itself, and it needs to start with the first person. I use the recording function of GoToMeeting.com to have the VA watch my screen while I go over the procedure and slides I create for the training. That video can be saved on a virtual drive (for example, a service like Dropbox.com) so your assistant can have access to the training in the future. Most important this will be a resource for future team members. Start with outsourcing what's taking up the most time. I suggest BPO, MSR, and MLS data entry to start.

Also, there are many general REO online educational training programs, available from companies like Default School, Five Star, and REO Training Solutions. Even though your VAs might not be doing 80 percent of what's in the training, it gives them the big picture. Also, this is a great time to evaluate their online work habits without wasting a lot of effort on someone that might not work out. Not everyone can work remotely independently.

Chat software is vital for communications. I started with Google Apps for business that provides chat, but when things got bigger, we started using HipChat.com.

Your prospective employees will be checking you out as well before they come work for you, so having a professional website is money well spent. I prefer to not use run-of-the-mill websites sold to agents because it makes me look like every other real estate agent. I also don't want to spend an ungodly amount of money to start or maintain a site. I've found a company called ubertor.com out of Canada as the best fit to develop a customizable site at a really low cost. Check them out.

I also demand my VAs use Microsoft Outlook, and we share the same branded email signature. I use the virtual PBX service Grasshopper. com for my business number to give my staff an extension (local and overseas). Calls come into our office and are then redirected around the world to the VA.

Finally, I want to leave you with the thought that using overseas staff can transition you from agent/broker to business owner. When I started building my team, I worked 15 to 16 hour days seven days a week. It was only a matter of time before my health was going to fail me with that schedule. With my beautiful wife and two small boys I'm responsible for, I had to do something different and not follow the crowd. Along the way, as I moved more responsibilities onto my new staff, I was able to reclaim my life back.

I still oversee my people, but with a competent staff I have time to work on the business and just make it stronger. When you have time to dedicate to working on your business, then you start finding better ways of running the whole thing, expanding, training your people, and bringing on new talent as you need it.

I hope some of this information will help the thousands of agents already in the REO business or looking forward to entering it. It has gotten me to the point where the business can run without me, I can stay profitable, and have time to do the things I want to do like share some knowledge with you!

About Henry

Henry Benito is a real estate broker and REO default professional who specializes in the South Florida real estate market. He opened his boutique real estate firm in 2001 to specialize in distressed assets exclusively. He's sought after as a consultant on outsourcing administrative work overseas and setting up REO teams to operate efficiently. He's also in the top five in closed sales of all REO brokers/agents in the Miami-Dade market. Henry has various REO certifications, is a certified Luxury Home Marketing Specialist, is a member of the Mortgage Bankers Association, and is a certified veteran and minority-owned business.

If you're a corporate seller looking to add coverage to your agent network, visit our website www.BenitoREO.com to request a special report called "Leading REO Agents—Miami-Dade County Edition." This report will list the top 20 agents in the Miami-Dade market in 2011 in units sold, average DOM, SP/LP ratio, and percentage of properties sold in-house based on MLS data. Just send your request via the Contact Tab.

CHAPTER 22

The REO Revolution in Real Estate:
The Rules Have Changed

By Jonathan Modene

What's REO real estate? It's "real estate owned" by the bank, which typically means foreclosed or soon-to-be foreclosed (in the case of short sales) real estate. Banks don't like owning these assets. In fact, banks *hate* owning, caring, managing, repairing and paying the taxes and utilities on these assets. They're a bad part of the lending, banking and loan servicing business that banks make their money on.

Today, there are no better buys than purchasing REO properties, whether it's for your first home, an investor looking to add real estate to an investment portfolio, a buyer getting their next home, or even a hedge fund looking to make money. But the rules for playing this market have changed since the '90s real estate boom. Here are the rules for the new REO market:

RULE #1: THE OLD MARKET IS GONE, GONE, GONE

Most people don't like change, but change comes—and in business, it comes fast. In the American residential real estate market, change has come—and come fast. And it's not going back to the way it used to be. Why?

- *The old banks are gone.* In my city, 20 years ago, a great savings and loan operated. They did things one way: their way. They operated however they wanted to, and then—poof—gone. A whole new panoply of lenders, loan originators, mortgage brokers, and new banks moved in... and they did things how they wanted to. Now, most are gone. The regulatory rules and legal overhead is crushing for a smaller mortgage broker or small local bank. The banks that left, the savings and loans that closed—they're not coming back.

- *The old loan programs are gone.* Love them or hate them, but they're gone, gone, gone. I'm talking, of course, about the "liar loans" of the '90s and '00s. Remember? You "stated" your income on a piece of paper, and no one checked or verified what the borrower wrote down, so they became known as "Stated Income Loans." They're gone—crashed with the stock market and the real estate market, and the other fast and wild ways of 10-plus years ago. Gone too are the other exotic and esoteric loan programs for people who didn't have money to buy houses they couldn't afford at prices that didn't really make sense, and they're not coming back.

- *The old mortgage brokers are gone.* Vanished, vanquished. The great mortgage brokerages have largely vanished in the Midwest. In their day they were glorious to behold—titanic machines spitting out loans and loan packets, bundling the completed packages of loans to German investors and Japanese insurance companies. But then the market turned. The tranches of pooled "Grade A" risk were exposed in the harsh light of day for what they really were—pools of putrid risk; pigs with bows and ribbons festooned about them, but they were still stinking pigs. The mortgage brokers who did this? Gone, and they're not coming back.

- *The old appraisal rules are gone.* In the "old days," five or so years ago, if a house wouldn't appraise, you would—and I'm serious here—just get another appraisal. See how simple that problem solved itself? The loan officer would simply call "his favorite" appraiser to make sure it was "properly appraised." Imagine that! (Common sense would tell you if a house doesn't appraise for what you're paying for it, you shouldn't buy it at that price!) But I digress. The appraisal rules of today are rigid. They're rigorous, and they have teeth behind them. Appraisers are reviewed, graded, and subject to state and federal regulation. The old appraisal rules are gone, and they're not coming back.

- *The old buyer/seller tricks are gone.* It happened. The buyer got his downstroke from the seller (wink/wink). The seller got a special secret mortgage back from the buyer. The buyer got new furniture. The seller paid for this. Back and forth the money flew—all under the radar. Off the books. Under the table. At its simplest, it was just the seller paying the closing costs for cash-poor buyers, with a "carpeting allowance" or a "redecorating allowance" covering the action up. At its worse, it was sophisticated legal/criminal acts designed to defraud the lender. It's gone, and it's not coming back.

- *The old values are gone.* They are. If they aren't in your market or your country yet, they'll be gone soon. The bubble has/is/will be popping. Sorry, but the game is over. The string has run out. The fat lady has sung. The gig is up. And a seller who's certain that waiting for prices to come back is a matter of time is right, but your kids or grandchildren will be the ones who see it come to pass. The old peak real estate values are gone, gone, gone, and they're not coming back.

RULE #2: THE NEW MARKET IS ABOUT INFORMATION

In real estate, before you look, negotiate, close, and move in, you must have information. Information make makes everything work better. No money? You can still buy if you have the best information. Special needs? You can get a great house, if you have the right information.

- *The internet has changed everything about real estate, and the party with the most information usually wins.* In real estate today, the best source of readily accessed real estate is found online. So you *must* learn about your local market or the market you're buying in, and you can only do it right with online data sources. Find the county auditor. Learn to look and navigate that site well. Learn how to download and access the comparable pricing data that's available. See about accessing other data sources for sold information on the market times, price reductions, and environmental, zoning and governmental issues that affect real property where you're buying. Why?

- *The right information gets better terms, better deals, better prices, and helps you make a better decision.* In every case, in my experience, in this new market, the buyer with better information gets a better price. A better house. A better deal. Information crushes every other mitigating factor. Under all is the land. But overall is intelligence. Actionable intelligence. So above all, get the best intelligence on the real property you want to purchase. Get help. Pay for it. Borrow it. Beg for it. But get it.

RULE #3: THE BEST BUYS AND THE BEST DEALS TAKE PREPARATION AND WORK

Things that are worth having are usually worth working at. REO real estate deals are definitely worth working at!

- *Tactic #1: Find the bank-owned bargain.* This is simple: The best bank-owned bargain is the house you can actually buy today. Many foreclosures are in "unable to market status." They're foreclosed but not for sale. Or they're in a terrible state of limbo—zombie-like houses that are haunted with sellers or tenants who can't move on, and buyers who can't move and get clear title. Each state has a different foreclosure-time horizon, so here's a simple rule: Worry about, care about, and learn about and work for the property that you can actually buy—that the bank is marketing for sale.

- *Tactic #2: Find the seller in trouble with means to get out.* Hard to do but a great thing to pull off when you can. How? A seller who's mobile, gainfully employed, and who doesn't want to go through the trauma of having a foreclosure or short sale on their credit history. Someone who's upside down and owes more than their house is worth, and knows it. They need to have moved out of denial to acceptance. And they have to be able to write a check or satisfy the bank for the pain they're experiencing. If you find this seller, get a great deal and a potentially safe house.

- *Tactic #3: Find the seller who's in trouble but whose one best buy is working with their bank.* This is a "short sale." The seller will be "short" when the house is sold and not able to pay the mortgage. But if the bank accepts *all* the money and if the seller agrees to either walk away with nothing and/or sometimes pay more later, then you, the buyer, get the best deal of all: a below-market-priced home without the damage or unknown issues that a cold/empty/vacant/ distressed bank-owned home can bring. Find a great short sale bargain, and you're most likely getting the absolute best REO buy in your market.

RULE #4: THE SMART BUYER SHOULDN'T BE AFRAID TO NEGOTIATE

This is where money in real estate is made. Only here—on the front end. When you buy. When you negotiate.

- *The bank wants to sell—and their only way out is to sell.* Understand this. They're not going to keep this house. Be patient. Be informed with great information (see above). But don't be hasty. They have to sell this house. You can buy any house. And if you pay too much? That money is gone forever. So understand their motivation and position and be patient.

- *The bank needs to sell because only bad things happen to empty houses.* Lenders and REO management companies have figured this out. The value will go down, not up. The mold will increase in mass and coverage area, not dry up and blow away. The vandals won't gently shut the door on their way out with the copper, the HVAC system, and the siding. Nothing good happens to empty houses. That's what's in your favor.

- *The bank must sell, but only if you're "their" kind of buyer, so make it very, very easy for the asset manager to work with you.* The bank makes the rules. Obey them. Cheerfully. Even if they're foolish. They want blue ink? Give them blue ink. They want you to be "pre-approved for a loan" by their own mortgage division? Sure! Great! They want their addendums filled out? Yes! Happy to! They want earnest money in Indian Rupees? Yes! Happy to go to the airport and exchange my dollars for rupees! The goal is to get the right house at the best price. And the path to this is to the follow the rules, play by their rules, and show them that you're a serious and easy-to-work-with buyer. It's that simple.

RULE #5: THE BUYER MUST BEWARE

So you find the house. You get the information. You negotiate the deal. The contract is signed. Now it's time to verify.

- *No one can tell you what's wrong.* If they say they do, they're guessing. They didn't live there. So if you *must* have all the facts known, then you shouldn't buy a bank-owned house, because no one in the transaction knows.

- *Your new, putative neighbors may have issues/motives you don't know.* They may not want you to buy it, so they'll "talk the dog" on the house. They may want you to buy it but not tell you what they think they heard the foreclosed owner tell them about the leaky basement because it's not any of their business. You just don't know! So you can't—at least at this point—trust the neighbors.

- *Your home inspection is simply a safety check, not a guarantee.* You can only trust the inspection for what it's worth. It's not a guarantee; it's a snap shot—a best guess by a hopefully trained and credentialed inspector. But they miss things. Things are patched and hidden. Houses are often sophisticated systems that evade easy answers. Water moves sideways! Walls are covered, hiding cracks. You just don't know.

- *Many flaws and details can remain hidden—that's why you pay what you're paying.* In the final analysis, you have to get an "REO discount" to overcome the risk of buying distressed, undisclosed, vacant and risky property. And that REO discount has to be greater than the risk you take. Pull it off and you'll get a great house at a great price. It will be cheaper than renting. It will be cash flow. It will be flippable.

It's the new REO Real Estate Revolution!

About Jon

Jon Modene has been setting the standard for real estate sales and marketing excellence in Toledo, Ohio, for many years. He earned his MBA from the Fuqua School of Business at Duke University and then worked in sales and marketing for IBM. Transitioning to real estate, he's the CEO and broker for RE/MAX Masters in Toledo. Last year he sold more than 300 houses in a market where the average agent sells just three. Jon specializes in real estate marketing and sales.

If you're reading this, you probably understand the value of real estate, and you most likely own a house. And, of course, you know that it's not too hard to sell a house if you price it low enough. But dumping a house like that dumps your family's equity—and that's not fun. Any agent or owner can do that. What's more difficult is delivering the right buyers to a property. Quickly. Easily. Especially buyers who are interested in your house and can also close the deal.

If you're a seller, here's what it's all about: properly pricing, staging, negotiating, and marketing your house.

Jon works with private homeowners, banks, asset managers, hedge funds, "for sale by owners," local governments, nonprofits, and people who owe more to the bank than their house is worth. He then finds the right person at the right time in the right way to purchase their real estate. Jon creates the result: a closed deal.

In the end, it all comes down to earning that slogan that Jon has been using for 20 years: "A Tradition of Trust in Northwest Ohio Real Estate"... One sale at a time.

To learn more about Jon and his team of experts, visit www.Modene.com, his award-winning blog, www.PerrysburgBlog.com, or call (419) 466-7653.

CHAPTER 23

Military and Veterans Housing:

The Opportunities for Those Who Served (and Civilians Too!)

By Jose L. Segarra

In 1944, as part of the Serviceman's Readjustment Act (more commonly known as the G.I. Bill), those who served in the military during World War II received many life-changing benefits for the first time. They were given the means to go to college and also a weekly stipend of $20 until they found jobs in the private sector.

But one of the most important aspects of this legislation was that, for the first time, it granted low-interest, zero down payment home loans for servicemen. This new program affected not only the futures of these brave veterans but also the future of the entire country. It resulted in millions of American families moving out of urban apartments, creating the rapid rise of the suburbs in the '40s, '50s and '60s; prior to the bill, only upper-income people could afford good-sized homes outside of cities.

How much of an impact did this program make? Since it was created, *over 18 million home loans* have been guaranteed through the Department of Veterans Affairs (the VA, for short).

As the owner of Exit Homevets Realty, where I also act as a broker and agent, 70 percent of my clients are veterans or those currently serving in the military, who take advantage of this great government program.

That's because my business services the residential area around Fort Hood (located in Texas between Waco and Austin), which is the largest military base in the free world.

I'm proud to work with my clients who have served America to the greatest extent possible, and it's easy for me to relate to them, having served in the Army for 10 years myself, which included being a part of the first Gulf War. I understand what they've gone through and what they need to do to protect themselves in a real estate transaction, so I look out for them. My last duty station was here in Fort Hood. After my discharge, I decided to stay in this community and work in the real estate industry, which is exactly what I've been doing for the past 17 years.

During that time, I've been fortunate enough to serve as the president of the Fort Hood Area Association of Realtors from 2005 to 2007, which is the local real estate board with almost 1,000 members, as well as serving from 2008 to 2010 on the Executive Board of the Texas Association of Realtors as regional vice president, an organization with over 80,000 members and the largest professional-membership association in the State of Texas. I enjoy assuming these leadership roles, but I gain a greater satisfaction out of helping my fellow soldiers with their real estate needs. For soldiers who don't know where they might be headed next, having a decent place to stay for themselves and their families is vital to their peace of mind.

At times, helping active members of the military buy a home can be a lot different than the conventional real estate process. Imagine fighting in the war in Iraq and taking time to email your real estate agent to go over details of a pending home purchase. That's exactly what many soldiers have done with my staff and I while they were overseas. And now that the war in Iraq is winding down as of this writing, we'll soon have 12,000 military personnel back here at Fort Hood looking for housing. We expect to be very busy!

But the VA home loan guaranty program is one that many veterans and service people can take advantage of anywhere, not just here where our offices are, so in this chapter, I'd like to explain a little more about what this wonderful program is all about. At the end of the chapter, I'm also going to reveal some awesome opportunities that this program actually provides to civilians as well!

HOW THE VA HOME LOAN PROGRAM WORKS

VA home loan guarantees were created to help eligible service members, veterans, reservists and certain unmarried surviving spouses obtain home loans. If you qualify for this program, you should definitely take advantage of it—it's a fantastic way to get into the housing market.

What the VA program does is protect lenders from loss if the borrower fails to repay a home loan. That makes it easier for the service member or veteran to get the necessary credit to purchase a home. The VA guaranty can be used to obtain a loan to buy or build a home, buy a condo or cooperative housing unit, as well as to repair or improve a residence already owned by a veteran and being used as a primary residence. Loans to buy a manufactured home or a lot are also eligible, and the VA guaranty can even help refinance an existing loan. It can also be used for a loan to install a solar heating or cooling system or other energy-efficient improvements.

Because lenders are able to have this government guaranty of generally 25 percent of the principal loan amount, a borrower is *not even required to make a down payment*. That's big to service people who might be living paycheck to paycheck; it makes home ownership much easier and more attainable for the valiant men and women who are serving or have served in our armed forces. The borrower also won't have to pay for the expense of mortgage insurance, since the government is guaranteeing such a large portion of the loan; this means significant savings on monthly mortgage payments.

Who qualifies for the VA program? First and foremost, the person who intends to buy the home must also intend to *live* there. In other words, it can't be an investment property or a home for someone else you know or are related to (by the way, if the person is only refinancing a loan, they only have to prove they *have lived* in the home or unit).

Next, the person must have served on active duty for at least 181 days in a branch of the armed forces. If you're no longer on active duty, you must have been discharged for other than dishonorable conditions. The only way you can be eligible for the program if you've served less than 181 days is if you were discharged for service or served at least 90 days and were in the Gulf War.

Even though this is a government program, the home loans are still made by the same lenders, banks and mortgage companies that provide financing for other non-VA loans. You still go through the normal application and approval process, although, obviously, the VA guaranty makes your chances of being approved much, much better. But it also means that you should have a good credit record in place as well as a steady income that you can prove.

The VA loan guaranty will insure the amount of a veteran's basic entitlement—usually $36,000—on a home loan. That usually means the borrower can take out a loan of up to four times that entitlement amount (in this case, $144,000). Again, the veteran's income and credit score will determine how much he or she will be able to get.

FINDING YOUR NEW HOME

If you're currently serving or have served in the armed forces, and want to make a home purchase, here are a few important things you should know about working with the VA home loan program.

First, consider the amount of time you'll be living in the home you want to buy. You'll want to discuss your situation with a real estate professional who really understands the local market. Why? Because you'll want to be able to estimate how long you would have to live in the home to build up some positive equity so you can safely sell when you'll be moving and avoid losing money on the transaction. If the market outlook isn't good and you're looking at living in your new home less than three or four years, you might want to rent instead of buy. I never want to see one of my clients end up "underwater" (i.e., owing more than the house is worth), so I'm careful to counsel them about this unpleasant prospect.

When you do find a home you want to buy, you're required to have a VA-approved appraiser do an appraisal on the home. If that appraisal ends up less than the sales price, the VA won't guarantee that loan, because they don't want to see a soldier pay more than they should for a home and end up in trouble.

Finally, remember the VA program does allow the seller to contribute closing costs. If you can successfully negotiate that point with your seller, it's a big win for you. It means that not only are you not making a down payment, but you don't have to come up with much, if any, in the way of closing costs. Yes, you can actually buy a home without bringing any money to the table!

THE UPSIDE FOR CIVILIANS

As I mentioned earlier, there's a way that civilians can take advantage of the VA home loan guaranty program in a big way. As we all know, a skyrocketing foreclosure rate has been an unpleasant fact of life in much of America over the past few years. Home values plummeted so hard so fast that the value of many homeowners' properties fell as much as 50 percent. That meant many people could no longer afford to make payments on their inflated mortgages due to the downturn in the economy.

Many homes that were bought under this VA program were no exception to this overwhelming situation. They also fell into foreclosure, but when that happens, the VA is responsible for selling these homes. And that's where you can take advantage of the VA program, even if you never served a day in the military.

When you buy a VA foreclosure, you too are able to get a loan without a down payment (if you're going to live in the home), with a portion of the loan guaranteed by the VA and at a good competitive interest rate. Your local real estate professional will have a list of these properties that are currently available. Naturally, most of these available foreclosures are in areas such as the one I serve, where a large percentage of the homes were bought with a VA loan guaranty.

The best opportunity that a VA foreclosure offers is when you buy one that you *don't* intend to live in—as an investment. You do have that option with a VA foreclosure; the difference is that you have to make a down payment, but at 5 percent, it's a very small one.

There's more good news: You can also buy as many as you qualify for. Obviously, prices are great right now, and because many troops are returning from overseas, there's a constant need to provide them with rental homes back here in the states. That means you can buy a VA foreclosure with a very low down payment, rent it out to make a consistent income, then wait for property values to rise again and build up equity.

Best of all, if you use the VA Vendee Financing Program to buy the homes, you'll find they have looser guidelines than conventional mortgages. Your credit isn't determined as much by the usual credit score that banks use. That makes it easier for anyone to buy these properties. An appraisal isn't even required.

That's why people from all over the country are investing in VA foreclosures here in the Fort Hood area. They know this is an awesome rental market. Many soldiers aren't here for all that long, so it's a lot more transitory that regular cities. When the investors don't live in the area, they simply hire a local property management company to handle the rental properties in their absence.

The VA loan guaranty program is a giant help to servicemen and women, as well as veterans. It makes home ownership a real possibility for millions who otherwise might not be able to share in the American dream. I find fulfillment in helping my clients take advantage of this great government program. They've sacrificed enough—it's good to see them get something back.

About Jose

Jose Segarra is a broker and owner of Exit Homevets Realty in Killeen, Texas, and has more than 20 real estate agents. He's a 10-year army veteran and has been in real estate for more than 17 years. He's an expert in helping military families sell and buy real estate. His office is located just outside the largest military base in the free world, Fort Hood, Texas. He has served as the President of the Fort Hood Area Association of Realtors and on the Texas Association of Realtors Executive Board.

CHAPTER 24

Bet Your Bottom Dollar:
Using Guaranteed Programs for Buyers and Sellers

By John K. Mikesh

I remember the first time I heard a *guarantee* used in a real estate promotion. I thought, "Wow! That's amazing. I wish I could do that." It was big, it was bold, and it certainly got my attention. It made me realize that if I were buying or selling a home, I would definitely want a guarantee from my agent. However, as with most things that are new, it's use seemed out of my reach. Fear started to set in as I contemplated offering such a program myself. How could I do it, and how much would it cost me if it didn't work?

I knew the concept would be a huge asset to my business; I just didn't know how to wrap my head around it so I could incorporate guarantees with what I was already using. However, with proper training and coaching, I did, and it has made all the difference!

I soon learned that not all guarantees had to be big in order to generate the same amazing results. Guarantees of all shapes and sizes exist in our world today, and when used effectively, they can be the deciding factor between you and a competitor.

Take Dominoes Pizza, for example. They've become one of the largest pizza restaurant chains in the world because they offered a simple guarantee when they launched their brand. You've heard it, "Delivered hot and fresh in 30 minutes or less, or it's FREE!" They're still known for this guarantee today, even though they stopped offering it in 1993—

THE NEW RISE IN REAL ESTATE

proof that the power of a simple guarantee is huge!

Like Dominoes, I started out small, with something I believed in whole-heartedly. I told sellers I could sell their home in 39 days, or I would sell it for FREE! I was willing to put my money where my mouth was. If I failed, I didn't make a penny for all my work. This made me very motivated not to fail, and my sellers both respected and appreciated this.

The program worked fantastically! If you can believe it, sellers actually started calling me. Curiosity had taken hold. They just couldn't believe how in the world I could make such a claim, especially in a down market. Sellers were calling me wanting to know how it worked, opening the door to more appointments. Each additional appointment was another opportunity to discuss my value proposition and all the great marketing strategies I had to sell their home. As my success grew, I began to increase my guarantees, thus further increasing my audience and adding to my success.

Time after time I found myself meeting with sellers who were stricken with fear and unsure of what to do or how and when to do it. Market conditions can be an excuse or an opportunity; it's all in your perspective. Those who continually speak doom and gloom convey the wrong message to the client—one that says all they want to do is drop the price so they can make the sale. C'mon people, let's take some responsibility here! I believe there's more business in my area now than there was at the height of the market in 2007. I know you're thinking I'm crazy, but let me explain. If the number of sales in any given market are down 20 percent, but there are 40 percent less realtors competing for the remaining business, doesn't that leave more market share per agent? Not to mention that the majority of remaining realtors have already concluded that the market is so bad, they'll have a down year, making that share even greater. What you believe, you'll achieve, and I'll guarantee you that, too!

I also found that the most common complaints sellers had regarding their previous selling experience was a lack of communication and what they felt was a lack of effort on the part of their agent. So I started offering a communication guarantee as well. The guarantee was simple. It stated: "My team will call you every week on Tuesday at 3 p.m. guaranteed, or you can fire me!" In communicating with my clients on a regular basis, I share the results our marketing campaign is having with concrete numbers. By working with the sellers and bringing them in on the processes, they can see for themselves what actions we need to take in order to get their homes sold.

Another key ingredient to successfully using guarantees is setting expectations. Obviously I can't guarantee to sell a house worth $200,000 for $400,000 in one day, so setting expectations up-front is critical. Clearly articulating current market dynamics is a necessary skill of any expert advisor. If an agent doesn't have this basic skill, then how can that agent expect to lead someone through one of the biggest financial decisions of their life. I can't tell you how upsetting it is to walk into somebody's home to discuss their circumstances, only to find they put 100 percent of their trust into an ill-informed opinion of the market when purchasing or trying to sell, resulting in a substantial loss of money.

On the flip side, what if we ran our business like professionals and explained the market data clearly while putting together a strategy we backed with our personal guarantee? When we make a personal guarantee, we put our own financial interests on the line, which is much more reassuring than simply stating to our clients, "I have your best interests at heart." Are you starting to see the point? Who would you rather have working for you?

As I continued implementing my guarantees, they not only generated calls, but they were generating sales. This success enabled me to expand beyond myself and build a real estate team. Today, our strongest guarantee is: "Your home sold Guaranteed, or I'll buy it!" Yes, you read that correctly. We'll actually buy your house for a price acceptable to you so you can look with confidence for your new home! All the terms and pricing are determined up-front before you ever sign anything. No hoops, no pressure, just one decision: Do you want an agent with a guarantee or an agent without one?

How does it work for the buyers? Currently, we're getting one of several common emotions from buyers. Prices will get lower, interest rates will continue to drop, and now is never a good enough time to buy. To them, the market is always dropping, interest rates are always going to reaching new historical lows, and the agent is always saying that now is the time to buy, just to make the sale.

Buyers are paralyzed by uncertainty. They're unsure about their employment, the stability of pricing, and whether their agents are sincere when they tell them, "I would buy this house myself!" or "It's a great deal." So we came up with "Buyer's Remorse Guarantee" to help buyers regain confidence in both us and the market. Simply put, if you buy a home with us, and for any reason you're not satisfied with your purchase within a 12-month period, we'll buy it back from you at the price you paid, guaranteed!

But let's not overlook one other obstacle some of our buyers are facing. How do I sell my existing home to take advantage of the deal I've found today? Enter our "Trade-Up Guarantee," which states that if you buy one of our listings, we'll buy your house for cash! The biggest dilemma when considering purchasing another home is deciding whether to buy first or sell first. Either way it's risky: You don't want to get stuck owning two homes, or having no home at all! The "Trade-up Guarantee" gives you perfect timing on both. Plus, this guarantee benefits both the buyer and the seller.

I've touched on many topics, all of which stem from the use of our guarantees, attitude, expectations and perspective. I couldn't portray this any more clearly than though the following example: When meeting someone for the first time, the conversation inevitably comes to what I do for a living. I tell them I'm in real estate, and you can't believe the reactions I get. It's almost comical. I watch how their countenance changes; they get this expression on their face like they feel really sorry for me. Meanwhile, my business has grown over 200 percent in the last two years! Could it be that the market has provided the perfect environment for the use of guarantees? I believe the answer is yes.

If you would like more information about our guarantees and programs, visit www.JohnMikesh.com.

About John

Originally from New York, John Mikesh has always had a passion for all things stemming from the "home." John has worked in construction, interior design and the architecture fields before settling into his real estate career in 2003, just after returning home from a two-year mission trip to Mexico.

He instantly fell in love with the profession, finding that it was natural fit for his personality and complimented with his ability to understand peoples' needs, even when they themselves may not. In addition, it used his past experiences, while quenching his passion and interest for all things relating to the home.

After deciding he wanted to provide more for his family, John and his wife decided to relocate to a more vibrant market with greater opportunities. In 2006, he settled on the Lake Norman area, just outside of Charlotte, North Carolina. Since then, John has practiced real estate, quickly carving out his share of the market. Year after year he continues to be one of the fastest-growing realtors in his marketplace. Along with being top 10 in the state for RE/MAX International as a single agent, his team now resides within the top 25 on a regular basis. He has also been featured in multiple issues of *Charlotte* magazine as a "5 Star Professional," holds awards from every training program he has been associated with and continues to set challenging goals for the future.

One of his favorite quotes is from Abraham Lincoln: "Good things come to those who wait, but only the things left over by those who hustle."

John, his wife and children currently reside in Mooresville, North Carolina, and enjoy being involved with their local church and many outdoor activities.

You can connect with John at: john@themikeshteam.com
www.JohnMikesh.com
www.facebook.com/john.k.mikesh
www.LakeNormanRealEstateSearch.com

CHAPTER 25

Movin' On Up:
Upgrading to the Home of Your Dreams

By Joseph A. Schlager Jr.

I remember a time, not so long ago, when I would put a "For Sale" sign in the front yard of a client's home—and it would be sold by the end of the week. No one felt any sense of urgency about whether their home would sell or not. Instead, the big challenge was nailing down their next home as soon as possible in order to avoid competing with multiple offers from other buyers.

As I said, that time was not so long ago, but it's starting to feel like it was about a hundred years since that was the case. Now the big question is, "Do I even *try* to move?" With real estate values and sales down, many homeowners fear the prospect of not being able to sell their homes for the price they need to get.

That's a shame for those who are ready to trade up to a nicer home. America should be a place where people should always be "Movin' On Up". . .but the stress of today's real estate market is preventing them from even considering that kind of upgrade.

Well, there are ways to still "move on up" and have it go as smoothly as possible, even in a slow market like the one we're currently experiencing. The key is that now, *more than ever*, you must choose the right real estate agent to help you reach your goal. A realtor could either save you—or cost you—thousands of dollars; that's why you want to be sure you have the right person in your corner.

As the No. 1 RE/MAX agent in Virginia—and one of the top 70 in the world—I believe I know the real estate business as well as anyone. That's why I can reveal just how "Movin' On Up" in today's real estate market *can* be done—and how you can accomplish that trip to a new dream house as smoothly as possible. At the end of this chapter, I'll also tell you my special secret of how I enable my clients to move on up! So read on!

MOVIN' ON UP TIP #1: NOT ALL REAL ESTATE AGENTS ARE CREATED EQUAL!

As I just mentioned, a real estate agent can either make you money or lose you money. There's a big difference in what they deliver to their clients, and that's why you need to make the right choice. Here are some ways to make sure you've got the right person:

- Does the agent work alone or has he or she incorporated a "team" concept? A real estate team has specialists and resources that far surpass a solo agent's capabilities, which means they can do a much better all-around job for you.

- Have you interviewed at least three real estate agents before making a choice? It's important to see a few of them so you can evaluate each of their advantages and disadvantages.

- Make sure the agent is doing real estate full time and not as a sideline. You want someone that's completely plugged into the market and makes their living from it, not someone who just picks up a few extra bucks every now and then when they sell a home.

- Find out how many homes the agent you're interviewing has sold in the past year. In the United States, that number is between four and eight for the average real estate agent, but you want someone who does a lot better than that. Also, find out what their average list-to-sale ratio is and their "average days on the market" for their listings, then compare those numbers to the averages from the local real estate board.

- Ask agents how they differentiate themselves from other realtors in the marketplace. See what they have to offer you and why they might be better (or worse!) than someone else.

- Get their take on the local real estate market. Compare notes with what other real estate agents have told you and judge the accuracy of each one's information.

MOVIN' ON UP TIP #2: CONSULT WITH A REPUTABLE LENDER OR LOAN OFFICER!

Just as the right real estate agent makes a huge difference, so does the person who will handle your mortgage needs. If you don't already have someone you're comfortable working with to secure a home loan, find one now—and sit down for an honest consultation to determine what you qualify for and, just as important, what you can afford.

This isn't a point at which you want to put on rose-colored glasses and get in over your head with a new home. Our hearts tend to speak louder than our heads, so it's best to make sure your dream house doesn't turn into a nightmare down the line when you find it a struggle to make the payments.

At this juncture, you should also make sure to get preapproved for a mortgage before you start looking at homes. You'll not only know what your price range is, but being preapproved makes you more desirable as a buyer—and gives you more leverage when you negotiate with a seller.

MOVIN' ON UP TIP #3: AVOID OWNING 2 HOMES (OR, EVEN WORSE, NONE AT ALL!)

If you're planning on trading up to a better house, usually you'll be faced with a potentially difficult situation on one end or the other. For example, if you sell your current home first, there will be instant pressure to find your next home quickly, and you may end up settling for less than you wanted (or being afraid to negotiate a price down for fear of losing it). If you don't find a new home in time, you'll have to put the bulk of your belongings into storage and rent for awhile—and then move all over again when you finally do find a house you like.

On the other hand, if you buy a new home first, your obvious problem will be scrambling to sell your current home as fast as you can, so you don't end up with two mortgage payments every month. That could force you to accept a price for your existing home that's less than you would have otherwise.

There is a way to avoid both scenarios and approach this process in a more relaxing manner. That's something I'll reveal at the end of this chapter, so, again...read on!

MOVIN' ON UP TIP #4: TAKE YOUR HOUSING MARKET'S TEMPERATURE, SO YOU DON'T GET BURNED!

Remember when I said to make sure your real estate agent knew the local market well? This is why: If you don't understand what's really going on with prices—whether they're going up or down —you won't know the best moves to make with either selling your existing home or buying a new one. This is crucial, since you'll be attempting both types of transactions, and you'll be both buyer *and* seller.

When you know whether it's currently a buyer's market or a seller's market, you'll know on which side you have the most leverage—and where you should be careful. In a seller's market, the inventory of homes is going to be lower and demand will be greater. In a buyer's market, the inventory will be higher and there will be a lot of home choices available.

MOVIN' ON UP TIP #5: SECURE YOUR STRATEGY AND SAVE!

Let's talk in further detail about the buyer's market and the seller's market, and how each should affect your buying and selling strategy.

Seller's Market Strategies

First, if it's a seller's market, then you should consider buying your next home before selling your current home. It's going to be easy to sell your house in a seller's market, but it will be more difficult to buy the house you want, due to high demand and the possibility of multiple offers competing with yours. By lining up your next house in advance, you can avoid being homeless for months after closing on your current house.

To do this, however, you *must* secure financing or cash to buy that new home without having to sell your current one. A good lender may be willing to grant you what's called a "bridge loan" to enable you to move forward, or you may have friends or family members in a position to help you with the financing.

If you're unable to obtain the financing to buy the new house first, then you must sell your home first. Luckily, there's still a way to make this work without you ending up out on the street. When you *do* sell your home, have your real estate agent structure the deal with the buyer so that closing is contingent on you finding the new home of your choice. That will protect you from being left out in the cold—literally!

Buyer's Market Strategies

Your problem in a buyer's market may be in selling your home. In this case, you don't want to be stuck with two homes and two mortgage payments, as mentioned earlier. That means, when you find a new home you want to buy, you should have your agent structure your offer so it's contingent on you selling your existing home. That means if you can't sell your home before closing on the new property, you don't have to go through with the purchase. If it truly is a buyer's market, the seller of the new property will be glad to have *anyone* making an offer, so you should be able to make this work.

Of course, if you can obtain the financing to handle the two homes at once, you won't have to worry about selling your current home first. Still, if you don't want to get stuck with your former house for any extended amount of time, you'll want to at least attempt to structure the new offer on a contingency basis.

MOVIN' ON UP TIP #6: WORK WITH A GUARANTEED SALE PROGRAM!

Here's the secret I've been promising to reveal throughout this chapter. If you really want to proceed with peace of mind toward Movin' On Up to a bigger and better home—without having to worry about owning two homes at once or no home at all—you'll work with a realtor who has a "Guaranteed Sale Program," like I do.

If someone decides to trade up to a home that I'm representing for sale, I will, in turn, buy their home for cash. Also, if one of my clients is selling their home—and a person who wants to buy it needs to sell *their* home first—I will buy *that* home for cash as well.

As this is currently a buyer's market, my Guaranteed Sale Program is a big relief to my clients. For example, I had as clients a couple who were engaged to be married. They were both individual homeowners who wanted to buy a new home together for their forthcoming married life.

That meant they had a double dilemma: They had to sell *two* houses to get a new one.

My program guaranteed potential buyers of those two homes that I would buy their existing homes. It made the couples' properties much more attractive and enabled them both to sell in a reasonable amount of time. In this market, that was an awesome outcome!

You, too, can have that kind of awesome outcome when trading up to your dream home—if you follow the advice in this chapter and work with an agent who has this kind of guaranteed sale program in place. I'm proud to offer it to my clients and enable their real estate ambitions to be fulfilled. I hope yours are as well.

About Joey

Joey Schlager and The Richmond Realty Team have been serving Central Virginia in spectacular fashion over the past six years, having been named the No. 1 RE/MAX agent in the entire state of Virginia, as well as one of the top 70 RE/MAX agents in the world. That level of success comes from Joey's commitment to providing the best possible service to home buyers and sellers, as well as his groundbreaking guarantee of "Your house sold or we'll buy it for cash!"

Joey's two previous careers were a bit more rough-and-tumble than the real estate industry. He spent eight years in the U.S. Marine Corps, followed by 14 years as a police officer. During his final two years in law enforcement, he worked part time in real estate and enjoyed it so much, he decided to make it his full-time career, a move that he hasn't had reason to regret.

Joey is a native of Virginia's Chesterfield County and currently lives in Hanover County; he also enjoys working in and being a part of the Richmond metro area. He's married to his high school sweetheart, Michelle, who's an indispensable part of his real estate team; together, they have a beautiful 10-year-old daughter, Kristen. Joey loves the outdoors, and, aside from spending time with his family, counts fishing as his favorite pastime.

If you're interested in working with Joey and The Richmond Realty team, contact him at joey@joeyschlager.com, or call him direct at (804) 559-0704 for a free consultation.

CHAPTER 26

Be a Game Changer
And Dare to Be an Agent Who Thinks Outside the Box

By Erin Catron

A new type of thinking is essential if mankind is to survive and move to higher levels.~ Albert Einstein

Remember the grade school game follow the leader? Everyone stands in a line and does exactly what the person in front of them does? This game can go on forever and is a childhood favorite. Unfortunately, some real estate agents have adapted this mindset in their everyday business. We continue to use the same ideas, techniques and weak systems that have been used for years. Many follow the same examples of those before, and on and on and on it goes!

Agents send recipe cards, calendars, refrigerator magnets, show dozens of homes, and put their pictures on their business cards because someone before them said it was a good idea. How many homes are sold from your favorite recipe? How many sellers have called and said that the cherry pie they cooked was so delicious that they just had to sell their home with you. Did a buyer have so much faith in the magnet that held up their child's picture on the fridge that they were compelled to trust you with finding them the best home for their family? The answer is no. Buyers and sellers are looking for an expert to guide them through uncharted waters of buying or selling a home.

Real estate agents must be the experts. We must be the exception, not the norm. Unconventional thinking is imperative to survival and success. Real estate professionals can no longer do the same old thing and expect to thrive. Buyers and sellers need and expect to receive expertise and service. In this new and ever-changing real estate market, buyers and sellers are craving guidance and results. Terms like short sales, REOs and foreclosure are intimidating, and many times overwhelming to buyers and sellers. We must be the educators and leaders, but most important, the experts. I've committed myself to continually being the expert and also offering my clients an unconventional approach as well as unconventional options. Here are six ways my team offers alternatives to the conventional real estate experience.

APPROACH #1: GUARANTEED SOLD PROGRAM

The first unconventional approach is our Guaranteed Sold Program. I literally offer a guarantee to my sellers that I will sell their home. I work with the seller and use the best market data and technology as well as our marketing approach to obtain a reasonable marketing price. Together we determine the value of their home and compare other homes sold to agree on a list price. This price must be competitive with other homes listed as well as homes that have recently sold. I use Bank of America and Chase AVMs, as well as tax records and sold homes from the MLS. The homeowner then lists their home as a full-service listing, at the recommended price. Then we go to work to sell their home. If we fail to obtain a contract after 90 days, we offer a buyout at an agreed price or we waive our commission when the home closes. This not only leads to happy sellers but also listings that are well-priced and positioned to sell. I've been offering this program for more than a year and have not yet bought a home or forfeited my commission.

APPROACH #2: IMMEDIATE BUYOUT PROGRAM

The second out-of-the box idea and program we offer is the Immediate Buyout Program for our sellers. This is exactly what it sounds like. We give the seller a cash offer in 24 hours. This is an investor offer that's less than the recommended list price. The closing date can be flexible, based on the seller's timeline. We've closed as quickly as seven days and as lengthy as 45 days. Many times if the homeowner is occupying the property they'll request at least a month. I've done several immediate buyouts, and I've acquired listings as an alternative to the immediate buyout as well. Many sellers will be suspicious of this offer and will sometimes call or inquire just to get the details or to find out if it's a legitimate program. Clients are pleasantly surprised to learn that the program is valid and not a scam.

After setting an appointment to see their home and doing an evaluation of the property, I can offer an immediate buyout price. At this time the seller has options. The seller can take the offer and avoid the hassles of listing and waiting to find a buyer, control the closing period and get the sale wrapped up easily, or opt for a full-service listing if the immediate buyout is less than what they want to sell for. This is also a great way to get a well-priced listing and an opportunity to net more money for myself and the seller. If the seller takes advantage of the immediate buyout, additional opportunities arise. This takes us to the next pillar of the unconventional real estate agent's arsenal.

APPROACH #3: INVESTOR INVOLVEMENT

Having one or more investors is an important component of a successful, unconventional real estate agent. If you don't have the ability to invest in real estate, find someone who does! In any market there's endless opportunity to make money in real estate. The investment side of the business is vital in order to reach the maximum potential in your business. When offering the immediate buyout, you must be able to put your money where your mouth is. The check must be written, and the funds must be available. If you offer a homeowner 70 percent of their home's value and they agree, finish the job. I have investors in line waiting for these opportunities, and so should you.

After completing the transaction, the investor should be ready to list the property with you again for another quick sale. Investor involvement should arise on many levels; the immediate buyout is just one. Other opportunities include, but are not limited to, short sale and bank-owned property purchases, county auctions, and bulk purchases.

In every situation I'm thinking about how I can net each individual the most amount of money, including me. I'm always looking for a chance to sell properties multiple times. My favorite transactions result in a 12 percent commission: 6 percent from the immediate buyout, then another 6 percent from finding a new buyer once the property has been listed and sold with the investor.

APPROACH #4: SHORT SALE IMMEDIATE OFFER PROGRAM

The fourth alternative approach targets distressed homeowners. How many real estate agents think that "short sale" is a negative phrase? I used to be one of those agents. I hated short sales, on the buyer or seller side. I discouraged buyers from entertaining a possibility of purchasing a home that was a short sale, and I ran the other direction from sellers who were inquiring about short selling their home. Not anymore! Now I seek out distressed homeowners and look forward to helping them. This has become one of the most rewarding aspects of my business for many reasons. I believe that as a trusted consultant, our responsibility as real estate agents is to advise homeowners and direct them through these difficult times. While I offer no legal advice, I can provide my experience and knowledge. I can give homeowners a legitimate, immediate offer on their home and instant interaction with their lender. This jump-starts the short sale process and also gives the homeowner relief from the traditional short sale process. This also means they can avoid an embarrassing short sale sign in the front yard and the endless requests for showing their home for months on end. Results typically come more quickly, and the process is usually shortened. The process is innovative and simple, and many times leads to homeowners selling their home and getting cash from the lender at closing. This is a win-win for all parties involved when an agreement is reached with a lender and the short sale is complete.

APPROACH #5: THE BUYER VIP TREATMENT

The fifth pillar of my unconventional method is the VIP treatment given to buyers. I offer concierge service with cutting-edge technology. Buyers are a vital component of my business and a joy to work with! It's so exciting to be trusted with the involvement of finding a home for someone. What a delight it is to get to know the motivation for buying a new home. I think it's so thrilling to hand the keys to a new homeowner and see their excitement. This is a great motivation to ensure that the best home is found. I offer our buyers a backstage pass to our MLS. This allows them to search homes, look at pictures, save listings, look up taxes, schools, and so much more information right at their fingertips. They have access to as much information as they can handle. I also offer home buyers a unique exposure to bank-owned listings before they even hit the market. I list bank-owned properties and always try to give my buyers first chance at these opportunities. I also educate buyers on the best way to structure and present an offer, as well as how to make an offer that is 100 percent risk free. These are all value-added tidbits that assure my clients that I am indeed an expert and merit their trust.

APPROACH #6: THE TEAM APPROACH

The sixth and final unconventional approach I offer is a team concept. For a potential buyer or seller this may be the most important advantage I have. Everyone has heard the tag line "_T_ogether _E_veryone _A_chieves _M_ore"—well, it's true. I can offer my clients service through a team that individually I could never deliver. My team consists of buyer's specialists, who are 100 percent devoted to assisting buyers; inside sales agents, responsible for follow-up phone calls and customer care; a short sale consultant, for our distressed homeowners; an excellent office manager; virtual assistants; and a courier who doubles as a handyman. All these individuals have their specific areas of expertise and roles they play, and all are available to assist clients. Together we can move faster and more efficiently. We're available and more consistent and, therefore, offer a better quality of service to our clients. The attitude in our office is fun and upbeat, but always professional. I think that so many real estate agents fail to treat their business like a business. The mindset that real estate is a profession for part-timers or retirees is unfortunately widespread and ill-fated. As real estate agents we've been charged with a heavy responsibility, and it shouldn't be taken lightly. Working with a team not only sets me apart from other agents, but it makes the office extremely enjoyable and more exciting because success is shared!

Now's the time to change the game. No more follow the leader. It's time to break out of the mold, and stop being a clone! Be the trendsetter, the rule-breaker, and the exception to the norm. Let's embark in a new game. Dare to think differently, and make waves in the stillness and mundane ocean of other agents. It's time for you to set the rules and boldly go where no real estate agent has attempted to go. Make yourself so attractive to prospective clients, that there's no other alternative. Be the expert and be unconventional!

About Erin

Erin began her professional career in the retail industry and worked her way through the ranks to CEO of a billion-dollar company. Knowing that her passion was real estate she made a career change in 2007, when most agents were fleeing, and became a multi-million-dollar producer almost overnight. Erin believes that her high expectations have allowed her to become a real estate success, and she understands that this success is achieved through helping others. She prides herself in thinking outside the box and pushing the limits of conventional wisdom.

Erin is from Central Oklahoma and studied at Oklahoma State University in Stillwater. She brings a down-to-earth and friendly attitude that's welcomed among her clients. Her positive look-on- the-bright-side attitude is refreshing in the midst of the doom-and-gloom attitude that's so often portrayed.

In these confusing economic times, when the name of the game changes daily, homeowners need a trusted expert. Erin is committed to helping and assisting homeowners and homebuyers through these uncharted waters. Keeping current is top priority, and continually educating and guiding clients is a driving factor in the success of everyone involved. New techniques and ideas are ever-flowing to achieve the maximum benefit for each individual.

To learn more about Erin and her style in real estate, visit www.ErinCatron.com.

CHAPTER 27

T.E.A.M—Together We Achieve More

By Clayton Gits

I purchased my first home in June 2006. I distinctly remember the excitement of driving around and looking at different neighborhoods and at houses on the internet, trying to envision what my life would be like as a homeowner. I didn't know it at the time, but that first experience buying a home would forever change my life. You see, I was selling pharmaceuticals (legally) and not enjoying my professional life. As a matter of fact, because I hated going to work so much Monday through Friday, I would say that I pretty much hated my life for 269 days of the year, minus vacations and sick days. Weekends were the only highlights for me. Actually, I started to get depressed again on Sundays because I knew I had to go back to work on Monday.

I knew I needed a change, and as fate would have it, I decided to buy a home to break up the monotony of life at the time. I ended up working with a friend of mine who was, and still is, a highly successful realtor. When all was said and done, I realized I could sell houses. My perception of real estate was that you would just show up at a house that either you or your client picked out, open the door, turn on some faucets and flush some toilets (to make it look like you know what you're doing), and eventually your client says, "This is the one." You would then cash a $4K to $8K commission check and move on to opening more doors, flushing more toilets and turning on more faucets. Repeat this scenario enough times, and you could be rich. I'm no math genius, but an average commission of $5K adds up to $125K a year if you sell just 25 houses! Piece of cake, right?

OK, so I was wrong. Turns out therre's just a little bit more that goes into being a successful realtor that has a steady stream of predictable income and clients that become raving fans.

I started with a local real estate company in March 2005 and quickly realized I was working more than I ever had. However, I was happy. There was no one telling me what to do or how to do it. It was all up to me. Turns out, this is a double-edged sword.

By the end of my first year in business I had sold 28 houses and netted right around $78K. Not bad for a first year in the business. Although, I wasn't quite sure at that point what I was doing, I just knew I was having fun doing it. I also got married that same year, so I knew I had to make some changes professionally because working seven days a week didn't seem to fit into my wife's perception of what marriage was all about. Who knew? I hired my first assistant in 2006, and early that same year I realized real estate could be a profession I could be very happy with, so I decided to completely commit. Part of that commitment was exploring all options in terms of brokerages. I determined in June 2006 that Keller Williams Realty was a great fit for both my values and my professional ambitions. Although Keller Williams Realty wasn't the only company that offered training and coaching, it was the first company that introduced me to the power of these concepts.

I quickly realized *success was no longer a secret; it was a science,* and I began to spend more and more time with realtors from around the country who were where I wanted to be professionally. The one thing that kept coming up over and over again in conversation was the concept of having a team. I don't know what the stats are in terms of the number of realtors who have a team vs. the number who don't, but I do know that most of us work alone. The fundamental flaw associated with any business where you're the only employee is that you just can't be everything to everybody. Your growth is extremely restricted if you don't have the leverage necessary to focus on the things that matter most in your business. As far as real estate is concerned, listings are the most important piece of any successful realtors practice. I kept hearing this over and over from the mega-agents I had been spending time with from around the country. I knew I needed help to grow. After reading Gary Keller's game-changing book *The Millionaire Real Estate Agent*, I began to follow the model that so many successful agents had laid out before me. Remember, success is no longer a secret; it's a science.

The first step was accepting that I wasn't just a realtor; I was a small-business owner. So my focus began to shift from answering phones, delivering fliers, developing marketing material, working with buyers, etc., to delegating everything as quickly and efficiently as possible. As I began to delegate, something magical happened…exactly what was supposed to happen! My business grew. I went from $4.2 million in total sales and 28 units sold in 2005, to $31 million in 2011 and 138 units sold. Moving into 2012 I hadn't worked with a buyer-client in more than three years with the exception of my mother, which was a nightmare—just kidding mom! As I write this chapter I currently have a team of seven, and I'm in the process of hiring two additional buyer's agents and an inside sales agent.

Now to be perfectly clear, I have and continue to work extremely hard, but most important I've simply followed the path that has been blazed before me by other realtors. The path is clearly defined; we just have to have the passion, will and commitment to stay on it. Oh, and by the way, having a huge, hairy, *big why* helps with the passion, the will and the commitment. What's your reason for getting out of bed every day? Remember, we all get sidetracked and stray off the beaten path from time to time, but our ability to get back on it determines our destiny.

So what now? What are the steps to building a big real estate team? Before we begin, I would like to mention two critical areas that can really derail progress. One, if you have debt, work toward paying it off as quickly as possible. I'm a huge fan of Dave Ramsey's book, *The Total Money Makeover*. Dave outlines a clear and proven path to paying off debt and building wealth. Not just credit cards and car payments—all debt! That includes your mortgage(s)! It's a lot easier to follow the path and not get off track if you have little to no debt impeding your decisions. Two, pay your taxes! Always stay ahead of paying your taxes. Find a good accountant, and don't get caught paying taxes at the end of the year or right before tax time because again this can have a dramatic impact on your ability to make decisions to hire employees or invest in a marketing program that could help your business grow.

According to Gary Keller's *The Millionaire Real Estate Agent*, you must go through seven levels of success to reach that magic millionaire status:

LEVEL 1

At this stage you're on your own. You're either working way too much or way too little. You're everything to everybody. You're a bookkeeper, marketing director, janitor, dishwasher, receptionist, telemarketer, salesperson, runner, etc. We've all been there at one time or another. The key is to get yourself in a place where you can hire someone to help with the 80 percent that doesn't produce immediate income for your business. Once you're in a place to comfortably hire an assistant, it's time to progress to Level 2. I've always been told that a good rule of thumb to know when you're ready to hire your first assistant is when you simply cannot successfully handle the amount of business you currently have.

LEVEL 2

You're ready to hire your first assistant. According to *The Millionaire Real Estate Agent* model, your first hire should be an administrative and marketing assistant. I have to admit things can get a little tricky if you don't pay attention at this stage. Please make sure to ask the advice of others who've successfully built businesses and hired more than one employee. One of the most important aspects of hiring—which I had to learn the hard way—is to always D.I.S.C. your potential hires. The D.I.S.C. personality test is a behavioral model developed by Dr. William Moulton Marston. The acronym stands for dominance, influence, steadiness and compliance, and is an important factor in understanding whether or not a potential hire is a good fit for your organization. For example, you may want to think twice about hiring an assistant who has a high degree of dominance because you may find yourself butting heads with someone who just doesn't understand why they can't do things the way *they* want them done. Remember, most CEOs have high D personalities, so if you end up hiring a high D, you may end up reporting to them and not the other way around.

The second point I would make when hiring is to make sure that you have a predefined set of core values and that the potential hire matches with your company's culture and values. *Think long term,* and remember that the cost of a bad hire vs. the cost of a great one could be a major setback.

LEVEL 3

Don't be tempted. This is the stage where many agents step off the beaten path. Most agents either hire a buyer's agent before Level 3, or their first hire was a buyer's agent. The goal is to get as many of the administrative duties off your plate as possible, not to hire a bunch of salespeople before you have the administrative capability to handle more transactions. If you're not careful, you'll end up being the transaction coordinator.

At this stage, you should be able to effectively delegate all your daily responsibilities except for lead generation and working directly with buyers and sellers. In a sense, your administrative team becomes your gatekeepers. Their responsibility is to keep you on task and held accountable to your daily priorities. They should also not allow any distractions through the gate unless it involves either lead generation or working directly with buyers and sellers. If you've hired properly, there's nothing that two exceptional employees can't handle for you while you focus on "making it rain" and converting business.

LEVEL 4

You should only move to this level when you can no longer successfully work with buyers and sellers without burning out or without sacrificing service. You need to be ready to stop working with buyers and start focusing entirely on your seller-clients at this level. Again, it's important to note that you should always think long term when hiring. If you take your time (slow to hire and quick to fire) hiring your first buyer's agent, you should have an exceptional team member that can eventually take over and manage your entire buyer's agent division. You should see tremendous growth at this stage because you can now focus on the number-one development secret of almost all big real estate businesses: listings! Nothing can grow your real estate business faster than focusing the majority of your time and energy on converting and selling more homes. Period!

LEVEL 5

As you can see from the model, your real estate business is truly beginning to look like a business at this level. You may have a team of three to four administrative people working to support a team of three to four salespeople. The big growth strategy in this stage is that you're now in position to hire a listing partner. This very well could be the hire that could take over the most profitable division of your entire company, so continue to look for exceptional talent. You're still working with sellers in Level 5, but you're moving in the direction of taking yourself out of the sales department altogether.

LEVEL 6

Now we're talking! You're officially the CEO of your real estate business. You're now managing, training, and top grading your staff in preparation for the next level. Your new mission is to help others succeed. You're no longer working with clients; your employees are your main focus. Profitability is obviously always important, but as you begin to consider replacing yourself, you must make sure your business is highly predictable and profitable. If you can help others achieve their goals, then you can and should experience incredible success as you work toward handing over the proverbial rains on your way to Level 7.

LEVEL 7

Real estate nirvana! As you've progressed through the various stages of the "Millionaire Real Estate Agent Organizational Model," you no doubt have learned a tremendous amount about how to run a business. You've likely failed your way to success to achieve what few business owners have or ever will achieve: owning a business that can successfully operate without you being involved in the day-to-day operations. The great thing about owning a Level 7 business is you can practically do whatever you want if you've followed the model, have little-to-no debt, and now have a significant source of passive income to finance your next business, your passion or your retirement.

My sincere wish is that you understand that building a team and succeeding in real estate is not a secret; it is a proven repeatable process that has been duplicated over and over again. I think Gary Keller says it best, "Anyone can do it but not everyone will." Why not you? Why not make today the day you start your journey down the beaten path of real estate success? Happy trails!

About Clayton

Clayton Gits has been selling real estate in Richmond, Virginia, since 2005. Clayton is a Richmond native and is married with two daughters. Clayton takes great pride in being a realtor and enjoys having an amazing team of realtors who work together to deliver an extraordinary customer experience. Clayton is not just a realtor with Keller Williams, he is also a franchise owner, and he routinely coaches and trains agents in Central Virginia and is excited to share everything he's learned with other realtors who are willing to listen. Clayton's professional passion is to surround himself with people who are super talented and to build a business where his customers can honestly say they can't wait to share their home buying or selling experience with others. In 2011, in what some would say was a very challenging real estate market, Clayton and his team had their best year ever selling over 130 homes. In Clayton's spare time, he enjoys spending time with his family, reading, working out and traveling. To learn more about Clayton and his team, please visit www.SoldInRichmond.com, or call (804) 545-6690.

CHAPTER 28

3 Keys to Running a Successful Real Estate Office

By Heath Higgins

For a consumer who's thinking of buying or selling real estate in this period known as the Information Age, it's easy to get overwhelmed with the sheer number of choices when it comes to choosing the right company and/or agent to represent their needs. Every buyer and seller is different and has different timing and motivational factors for selling or buying a home, but the end results are all the same! They want their wants and needs taken care of with great care and diligence, and the least amount of hassle.

So what should a person look for when choosing a real estate company or team? The answer is simple, but the choices are few for the consumer in any market.

Why? Because change is hard and real estate companies have been around for years and tend to get stuck in "old" ways of doing business. Traditional real estate companies are on the verge of extinction! When you study the recent past, you find that the traditional real estate company/agent is walking the same plank as the travel agent, mom and pop hardware stores, local movie stores and neighborhood coffee shops. But the really scary thing is agents are oblivious to the "industry pirates" that are allowing them to walk, unknowingly, to their death—things like the internet, the death of paper advertising, traditional open houses, etc.

There are so many things to do to successfully market a home, procure a buyer, and get it from market to the closing table that it's near impossible to do it on your own. That's why, according to the National Association of Realtors, 70 percent of FSBOs (for sale by owners) end up listing their home with a real estate agent. Not only that, but in today's unpredictable market, upwards of 50 to 60 percent of listed homes are hitting the "expired" list, meaning these homes didn't sell through a traditional real estate agent either. What's a person to do with these kinds of statistics?

Panic, give up, and let the bank take it back? Unfortunately, that's the path many people have gone down. I'm not here to say there's a magic bullet for getting a home sold or to help a buyer secure their dream home with zero snags or problems, but there are key things to look if you want to secure the best odds.

The way to beat the odds is to swing them in your favor, and for selling a home, those odds get a whole lot better when you hire a company with a track record of selling!

Seek out and surround yourself with success, and you'll become successful in whatever you want to accomplish! In other words, look for a successful real estate team, hire them to sell your home, get your home sold!

How do you run a successful company/team that people want to do business with? "When in Rome do as Romans do," or for our purposes, "To run a successful company, do what successful companies do." You have to look at the practices of outside industries rather than just the traditional ways real estate companies do business to get a different perspective.

Would you expect to go to a doctor's office and see your heart surgeon answering phones and setting appointments? Then calling all his vendors and suppliers to make sure his medical supplies were in inventory, and sending out reminder letters and thank you cards to past patients. This wouldn't be expected and would even be a little disturbing.

If that's the case, then why should real estate customers, who've decided to hire a professional to buy or sell their largest asset, expect to hire a single agent (who in most states are classified as independent contractors) to do the 100 things it takes to sell a home. Yes, I said 100 things—you can see the complete list at www.heathhiggins.com.

After 10 years, I've found there are three keys to running a successful real estate company.

KEY #1: SURROUND YOURSELF WITH A SUCCESSFUL TEAM

If you needed life-saving surgery, would you want a team of specialized surgeons and nurses, or only a single practitioner? It's an easy question to answer, isn't it?

The traditional real estate company has an office full of independent contractors, who are all competing to get the same client, lead, buyer and seller. Today's "new" real estate office has a "team mentality," in which everyone is working toward the same goals and objectives! Even inside traditional real estate offices, you're seeing more and more "subcompanies" taking shape in the form of teams. I refer to them as subcompanies because they're running their business like a business, not as an independent contractor operation. Successful agents realize there's too much to do as one person, and the only people that suffer are the customers.

When you're shopping for a real estate team to sell your home, what should you look for? There are many hats that have to be worn when it comes to selling real estate. On my team, in addition to the licensed agents who specialize in working with buyers and sellers, I also have a closing coordinator, listing coordinator, inside sales agent, director of first impressions (aka, the office assistant), follow-up coordinator, short sale specialist, photographer and a runner. Using a team approach for selling your home is critical, because there are just too many details to trust the process to just one person. Instead of hiring one agent to do an average job at best on everything, why not employ a team of *specialized experts* so each step of the process is outstanding!

One thing is for sure, if the company/agent you're hiring is doing it on their own, you better make sure you're their only client!

KEY #2: SURROUND YOURSELF WITH GOOD VENDORS AND SUPPLIERS

As real estate professionals our clients look to us for advice on many areas of the real estate transaction that go further than just the buying/ selling process. These areas include legal advice, home inspections, title companies, lenders etc.

Most successful real estate companies/teams, who are keeping up with the times and trying to provide a smooth real estate transaction for the consumer, are making the process as easy as possible by having strategic partnerships within an arm's reach to supply their clients with the best possible experience.

Inside my brick and mortar building, my company has an in-house lender for making the preapproval process easy, an in-house insurance agent who gives fast quotes on potential homes for clients, and an in-house home inspector that works for buyers when purchasing a home and also does prelisting inspections for home sellers to fix any potential problems that might come up during contract negotiations.

It has been my experience that some companies don't want their agents recommending vendors to their clients simply to eliminate liability. It's my belief that our clients look to us for these recommendations and as professionals we should know who to recommend so our clients don't blindly choose someone who might not do a good job.

KEY #3: MAKE IT FUN!

This might seem obvious or even silly, but I believe with all my heart that if you don't wake up everyday and love what you're about to do for the day, then you need to change something and change it fast!

I know there are some days that just stink and can't be fun no matter what you do, but the secret is to not have too many of these days in a row. How does this translate to a real estate office?

Simple. As the team leader I have to keep looking for ways to keep it fresh and spirits up. If you look at the history of real estate on a time line, it's a constant up and down (i.e., either a buyers' or sellers' market), which means emotions can run high in the good times and low in the slow times. It's been shown that a happy worker is more proficient and gets more accomplished in a shorter amount of time, so it's important to keep those spirits up, even in the down times. For evidence, look at Google and why it's always ranked as one of the top-five companies to work for in the world. They practice a few of simple philosophies I believe should be adopted by every company:

1. Appreciation is the best motivation!
2. Work and play are not mutually exclusive!
3. Life is beautiful!

(*Source:* http://www.google.com/intl/en/jobs/lifeatgoogle/toptenreasons/index.html)

We can't practice real estate with blinders on and not prepare for the slow times. A good team leader will take advantage of the slow times with team building/training activities, which help keep their team with the eye on the mark.

Negativity in any office is like a cancer and needs to be removed at all cost. How many of us know the "Negative Ned or Nancy" in the office. The person who just talks about people, how bad everything is, and how it's never going to get better, no matter what!! This kind of talk is like fingernails on a chalkboard, so to deal with it, my rule is simple: *Don't do it here!*

We start our weekly staff meetings with one question: "Tell me something positive that's happened to you or that you're going to make happen this week!" We also make a point of greeting people with "Tell me something good!" Rather than "How are you?"

Try it; it's so powerful to ask someone to "tell you something good!" Watch their reaction and facial expression when they think about your greeting and as they try to think of something positive to tell you.

By surrounding yourself with positivity it just makes everything else a little more bearable. As Henry Ford said, "Whether you think you can, or you think you can't—you're right."

The three keys to running a successful real estate office really are that simple! First you must surround yourself with successful people who share your vision and goals, and the only way to do this is to share *your* vision and goals with the people who you surround yourself with. These people must compliment your weaknesses and accentuate your good traits. Second, you must have a network of good vendors who can back up your recommendations and take care of your clients' needs. Finally, the only way this works is to run a positive office that's a place where everyone either wants to work or do business with.

I hope you find this information helpful and informative, and would appreciate any feedback. You can find me on Facebook at Realty Executives of Mid Missouri.

This chapter is dedicated to both my wife and kids who support me in everything I do and who I love more than anything in the world, and also to my work family who stick with my through all of my crazy ideas and ADHD moments!

About Heath

After graduating from Central Missouri State University in Warrensburg, Missouri, in 1998, I married my college sweetheart, Amy, in 1999 and started my family in 2000. My daughter Trinity followed, then my son Tagen in 2003, and my youngest daughter, Tayte, in 2008.

After college I went to work for a local computer company, selling network solutions to companies around mid-Missouri. I also started a home business selling "stuff" online, becoming one of the first eBay Power Sellers.

In 2001, I started in real estate kind of by accident. I had a little bit of money from selling so much stuff on eBay that I decided it was time to invest in some real estate. I started enjoying looking for and trying to buy investment properties, so I decided to get my license and went to work for a local franchise company. The internet was really beginning to boom for all industries, and I wanted to make sure I was there for real estate marketing as well. I soon realized that real estate was my thing, and that this was where I needed and wanted to be.

I was a quick learner and traveled around the country attending seminars and networking with some of the top realtors. I was an implementer! I quickly developed a team in 2002 and hired two buyer's agents and an office manager. The funny thing was, I had no buyers and only one listing. That didn't last long: With my determination, we quickly grew to the company's top producer and the top 10 in the state of Missouri for Coldwell Banker. We earned this title every quarter for 24 consecutive quarters before leaving to start my own company. In 2007, I purchased a Realty Executives franchise and have grown my team every year since.

Awards include: Four-Time Consecutive Gold Executive Club Member & Top 50 for Realty Executives Mid-America Every Year

Designations include: GRI, e-Pro, ABR, RDCPro

Heath Higgins
Broker/Owner
Realty Executives of Mid Missouri
(573) 761-3343
heath@heathhiggins.com
www.heathhiggins.com

CHAPTER 29

First-Time Home Buyers:
How to Get Real About Real Estate

By Alexandra Kennedy

I've been involved in real estate since 2005, and I love my job as a realtor. That's because I love to meet new people and help them reach their real estate goals. I find that process the most rewarding when I have the opportunity to help a first-time home buyer through their initial real estate transaction.

That's why I focus my real estate practice on those who have yet to own their own home. I've helped would-be homeowners as young as 19 make this huge decision, and it's incredibly gratifying. By putting my extensive knowledge to work for them, I'm able to take them by the hand and ensure they end up with a purchase they can feel good about.

I don't do this job primarily because of the money, nor do I look at my clients and see dollar signs on their foreheads. I do it because I really enjoy working with them; it's not about me, it's about *them*. Of course, I end up staying so close to the process, because I feel as though it's *me* personally buying around a hundred houses a year instead of my clients!

I think that's the reason I don't need to advertise my services all that much—most of my clients come to me by personal referral. I also think it's the reason my realty business has grown over the past few years, while many others have either shrunk or closed down altogether. When you have a passion for what you're doing, others can see it, and they want that passion working for *them*.

But I obviously can't personally work with everyone reading this book—unless y'all are planning to move to Mobile, Alabama, where I work. Instead, in this chapter, I'd like to share how I work with first-time home buyers so they can avoid the big mistakes that can come back to haunt them later. I understand those mistakes...because I've made them myself!

MY REAL ESTATE DISASTER

Before I relate to you the story of my traumatic home purchase, I want to explain how Alabama real estate law is different from many other states. In Alabama, "caveat emptor" basically holds sway—that's Latin for "let the buyer beware."

And the buyer *should* beware, because when someone sells you a home that's already been lived in, *they're not required by state law to disclose anything about the property.* What's more, after you sign the final closing papers, all the issues with the house become *yours*—and you have no recourse but to fix things yourself.

This is why, in addition to focusing on first-time buyers, I also concentrate on selling newly constructed homes. The "caveat emptor" principle doesn't apply to a new house—the builder must disclose any problems. Not only that, but generally, new construction comes with certain guarantees and warranties on things, such as the air conditioning system or the hot water heater. This can give some real peace of mind to a first-time buyer with a tight budget.

Peace of mind is exactly what I lost with my home disaster, along with a lot of sleep and money. I purchased a resale home, and none of its major problems were flagged during the home inspection. There was trouble with the roofing, the plumbing and even the foundation. I didn't know that until after I put in a new living room—and then a nearby toilet overflowed all over it. That meant my brand-new carpet wasn't going to get any older, and I quickly replaced it with tile. But it still wasn't over. During the next hard rain, the living room ceiling caved in, once again flooding it with water and also ruining all the new lighting fixtures I had just installed.

Fortunately, good things come out of bad—that experience motivated me to do everything I can to help my clients avoid that kind of nightmare when they buy a home.

STARTING THE HOME-BUYING PROCESS

I'd like to walk you through how I work with my clients to make sure buying their first home is as good an experience as it can possibly be.

One of the first things I do is get them preapproved for a mortgage; that way, they know what they qualify for and what they'll be able to afford. As a former loan officer, I know the ins and outs of the mortgage industry and can provide a lot of valuable advice in this all-important financial arena. There are a lot of different programs available for first-time home buyers, which I'm happy to explain to them.

Once I get them approved, we sit down and discuss what they're looking for. If it's a married couple, I make sure both people are there so everyone can agree on the goals. If they have kids, I don't mind if they're involved—it can be fun for them to be a part of the process, too. The main questions we have to answer are what kind of home do they want, what area, what school district and so forth.

We also figure out the highest price they should pay for a home. Even if the lender has approved them for a certain amount, the mortgage could still translate into monthly payments that might be hard for them to handle. I don't want my clients to end up "house-poor"—buying a house should improve your lifestyle, not make it worse. You want to be able to decorate as you wish and build equity, not blow off going to the movies because you have to pay the power bill, or abandon your yearly vacation because you can't afford one.

That means I go through their budget and ask if they have any other monthly expenses, such as tuition or child care, that didn't show up in their credit report. We balance that budget against what their mortgage payments might be, and we make sure they'll be comfortable. It's kind of simple to get an initial loan approved, but once you've defaulted on one mortgage, it's hard to go back and get another one.

I also strongly advise them to get a 30-year mortgage that they can pay off earlier if they're comfortable making the extra payments. For example, if you're able to set up automatic payments where half your mortgage payment gets paid out on the first of the month and the other half on the 15th, you're able to reduce the years on your mortgage by eight; and, if you're able to afford making an extra payment a year, you pay off the mortgage in 17 years instead of 30. Since interest rate is accrued daily, you're only paying for 15 days of interest instead of 30. I direct my clients to use the online mortgage calculator at www.bankrate.com so they can test out different options themselves.

MAKING SURE IT'S THE RIGHT HOME

Once my clients have zeroed in on a home they're interested in, it's time to make an offer. I like to negotiate; I think it's smart. But I also think it's crazy to ask for too much from a seller if it's an attractive property. The strategy really depends on the house, but if it's something the client really wants, they shouldn't ask the seller to lower the price by $15,000, then demand they pay the closing costs as well. You're going to miss out on opportunities that way.

For example, I worked with a couple who insisted on hardball tactics like that in their offers. That couple lost three houses in a row that they really wanted by pushing the seller as far as they could. Even though the real estate market has been hammered in recent years, you still can't overplay your hand when it comes to a beautiful home that may only be on the market a few days before it gets snapped up. There's no need to risk that.

To me, a good deal is: a) a property I love, b) a property that meets all my criteria, and c) a property that, to me, is *affordable*. I don't believe in going by price; I believe in going by affordability—if it's a house you love and you can comfortably make the payments, you should go for it! Getting the seller to lower the price by $15,000 may only save you $90 a month on your mortgage, so you have to ask yourself, "Is that $90 worth losing the home you've decided you want?

If the offer is accepted, then, especially if it's a resale, a home inspection is the next step to make as sure as possible that the property is in good shape. Any property that was either built or renovated in the 2005 to 2008 time period also needs to be checked to see if faulty sheetrock was installed. During those years, drywall from China was imported that contained harmful toxins, particularly to young children and the elderly.

If the property has a septic tank, it should also be thoroughly inspected. Sometimes these tanks collapse and sellers will put the drainage hose right into the ground instead of connecting it to a tank. Obviously, that creates big (smelly) problems down the line.

As I mentioned before, buying a newly built house helps you avoid getting stuck with those types of major hidden problems. My years in the business have enabled me to know who every single builder is in Mobile as well as what they have to offer. I like to recommend that my clients actually do a presale with one of these builders—by negotiating a price in advance, then having the house built to their specifications. With a presale, the client can pick out the lot, ask for certain amenities and design it from the get-go. That ensures they get exactly what they're looking for.

In addition, newly constructed homes are built with the most recent building codes, and they're very energy-efficient as well. You no longer have to think you can only afford an older home that might be 10 or $15,000 less in price. The truth is your mortgage payments will be higher with new construction, but you'll probably save *more* than that difference in monthly payments, thanks to lower utility bills.

APPROACHING THE CLOSING

As closing day on a property draws near, it's time to make necessary last-minute checks on the house. When it's new construction, most builders will usually have a preinspection, where we do a walk-through and make a list of things that need to be corrected or fixed. Closer to the day of the closing, we go through the property again to make sure everything on that list was addressed.

If it's a resale, there's also probably a list of things my client has requested be repaired by the seller before closing. The seller will either agree or negotiate what will actually be repaired. Whatever we settle on, I make sure the seller lets us know when the repairs are done so we can come in and review the work.

And I *always* do a final walk-through of the property within a day or two of closing and—in some cases—within a couple hours of the closing. Many agents don't, but I insist on it, and one incident will vividly illustrate why.

We were set to close on a Tuesday, and we went in on the Sunday before for the final walk-through. One of the attractions of the house was that it had all new appliances installed—dishwasher, refrigerator, washer/

dryer, etc. Well, when we visited on that Sunday, all those appliances were suddenly gone!

Not good. I called the seller and said, unless those appliances were put back in the house, the closing wasn't going to happen. The seller didn't have the funds to replace them, so we arranged to have the money to cover them (and their installation) taken out of the seller's end during the closing process.

Finding solutions to these kinds of unexpected problems is a big part of my job. I always want to make sure my buyers don't stress, so I do what I need to to put them at ease. It's not their responsibility to fix problems—it's *mine*.

EXPERIENCE MAKES THE DIFFERENCE

Since the vast majority of my clients are first-time buyers, they're desperately in need of someone with my kind of experience in real estate. I always give them advice that's in *their* best interests, not mine. Without the right kind of experienced guidance, they can really land in hot water.

For instance, I recently worked with a couple who had bought a foreclosure through another agent. They thought they were getting an amazing deal. The agent told them just to put in an offer for the full asking price and not request a home inspection. Because the price was so low, they thought it was no big deal.

Well, they ended up almost going bankrupt. They kept fixing and fixing and fixing things, but just couldn't see the end of their misery in sight. They came to see me. I found out that the wife had bought the house in her name, so I knew we would be able to get a mortgage on another house in his name. I found them another resale home, but we did inspections and negotiated the right price. They then disposed of the other home in a short sale.

None of their troubles would have happened if I was their agent in the first place. I don't say that because I'm so great; I say that because I believe they were pushed into a home they never should have bought in the first place.

Whether you're buying your first home or your tenth, you always should seek out an agent you're comfortable with, someone you feel you can trust and work with. And you should feel free to say anything you need to say to that person to protect your own interests.

I always tell my clients, "Don't worry about hurting my feelings; you're the one who's paying for the house. You have to be happy with the end result." Buying a home if you've never done it before can be a terrifying prospect. Real estate is usually the biggest purchase anyone will ever make in their life. That's why it's important for first-timers to find someone who will help them through the process in a caring and knowledgeable way.

And that's just what my professional and personal goal is with every client.

About Alexandra

Alexandra Kennedy, owner of Weichert Realtors Premiere Properties in Mobile, Alabama, is widely considered an expert on Gulf Coast real estate and is sought out for her expertise on the her local market and new construction in particular. Alex has appeared on FOX and NBC affiliates, as well as making regular appearances on the "Ask the Expert" segment on News Radio 710. Through the years, she has been sought out by numerous builders to represent them throughout her area. She has also been endorsed by Sean Hannity and Glenn Beck as having an effective system for attracting buyers and for being a "superstar agent" in the Mobile metro area.

Alexandra's passion is helping first-time home buyers and others, who never knew they could own a home, realize their own version of the American dream. Her clients love her for her infectious personality as well as her knowledge, experience and negotiating skills; so much so that nearly 77 percent of her business comes from personal referrals.

To learn more about Alexandra Kennedy, visit her at www.homes4mobile.com.

CHAPTER 30

7 Simple Steps to Starting a Real Estate Investment Portfolio

By Gary and Deb Atchley

It was in the late '90s when we first heard Gary Keller, founder of Keller Williams Realty, ask "What is your big *why* in life?" He gave us several exercises that caused us to think about what others call their "bucket list," basically asking what is it you really want to achieve in your life.

Our list included physical, spiritual, financial and enjoyment goals. When we started the process of dreaming and then mapping out the *how*, it was clear that building wealth was an incremental step in getting those "earthly" accomplishments acquired. *And the fun began*!

Both of us are competitive. We enjoy setting goals, picturing something, then breaking it down into simple one-by-one steps. Gary is the master at sales, negotiations and relationships. Deb is the master at strategy, analysis, and has exceptional business acumen. Two minds working toward a common goal inside a robust real estate career and a budding real estate investment portfolio that's out performing Wall Street.

We embrace the concept that goals are wants, desires, dreams and things we'd like to see in our daily lives. Yes, goals are truly personal. Without them you never know when you've arrived at your intended destination. We believe goals are the scorecard in the game of life. Who's winning?

This chapter is about seven steps to start or accelerate a real estate portfolio. *Steps we've personally taken* and shared with our team members and clients. We're passionate about real estate and how it can be a catalyst to change lives, bring about financial freedom, fund dreams, and feed the dreams of others through your own generosity.

TIP #1: KNOW YOUR BIG "WHY"

Actually knowing your *why* (dream or destination) is a step so many people miss out on enjoying. This is the true gift of why we're human beings—we have choices. We choose where we want to live, what we want to do with our lives, and, if we're purposeful, what it will look like when this life on earth is completed.

Take some time away from the noise and clutter of day-to-day activities and invest that time in dreaming. You know, that thing you did as a kid ....under a tree or on a swing thinking about what you could do when you grew up.

We actually do this whenever we're faced with a big decision. For example, we had been blessed to fulfill one of our bucket list dreams by purchasing 80 acres just minutes from Oklahoma City. Being realtors, proximity and location are huge priorities and necessities.

After the purchase, we continued to check off our dream list:
- nice barn with small riding arena ✔
- barn living quarters ✔
- outdoor riding arena with lights ✔
- ponds with nice landscape ✔
- and so on until we had our 80 acres almost complete ✔

After both our parents passed from lengthy illnesses, we knew we needed to regroup. Our mutual love for the western lifestyle and horses could now take a larger role in our personal lives. Living in our barn-apartment, we had a blast. Also, it gave us the opportunity to entertain and share our dreams with others. Then came the time when Gary felt we should build a home. He recognized that growing old in a barn wasn't his long-term vision.

With the decision made to start our dream home, we again went back to our "why" exercise. What's the mission of having a home on this property? How does it make financial sense? What purpose will it fulfill? How can we serve others? We even made the design of the home a "why" exercise.

- Why have a living room that's transparent from north to south? To see the beauty of the prairie and ponds.

- Why have multiple porches? Because the wind blows on average 20 plus miles an hour and selecting a location out of the wind is desirable.

Every room had a "why." The same questions made sure each decision in the design and function of the home had market appeal for resale. After all, our home ultimately is a major part of our financial portfolio.

The "why" for real estate investments is two-fold. First, purchase to make long-term gains in the appreciation of the property. Second, expect your initial investment to have a return of 8 to 10 percent annually. These numbers play a role in your overall financial-wealth goals both for now and possible retirement income. Consider doing the "reinvest profits" exercise to shorten mortgages and make additional investments. Our goal has been a portfolio of 12 single family residential properties with a return above 9 percent and debt free by the time we reached a certain age.

TIP #2: LIVE BELOW YOUR AFFORDABLE MEANS UNTIL YOU'VE REACHED YOUR GOAL

This is nothing new, but it speaks volumes about what's wrong with our country's credit crisis. To build real estate wealth, you need laser-focus on what you want to achieve. A rule of thumb is to live on no more than 70 percent of yearly earned annual income, save/invest 20 percent, and give back or tithe 10 percent.

Avoiding consumer debt, not financing personal lifestyle, is a great way to get your house in order. If you have credit issues, now's the time to speak to a reputable mortgage or credit counselor about the steps to take to improve your credit scores. Your goal should be to have the financial prowess to buy your first home and/or multiple real estate properties with the result of building a healthy financial future.

A great way to look at this is to sacrifice high-consumption today for financial independence tomorrow. Respect money as a resource that should be used wisely and frugally. Buy expensive things when you've achieved your goal, not before the anticipation of becoming wealthy.

For about 12 years, we've used an assets and liabilities balance sheet showing our net worth as a compass for how we're progressing on our goals. Sometimes the sheet says "good job"; other times it says "caution." Be careful not to get off the "good job" portion of your big-picture goal. Some experts recommend doing this exercise monthly along with a personal budget.

TIP #3: BUY AND PREPARE TO HOLD

Let's be very clear about this. Right now the mortgage rates and home prices have created the ideal real estate market for buyers wanting to take advantage of the environment.

According to MSNMoney.com, the Case-Shiller home price data shows (see chart, below) that from January 1, 2000, to November 2012, if you were to graph the Dow Stock Exchange average it would show a modest 11 percent gain. The S&P 500 (-10.3 percent) and NASDAQ (-30.3 percent) haven't performed positively at all. Yet overall real estate is still up over 43 percent if you go all the way back to 2000. Nationally the real estate market took a hit around 2006 continuing through 2011. But if you look back to 2000, the people with real estate investments have weathered the storm.

Return on Investment

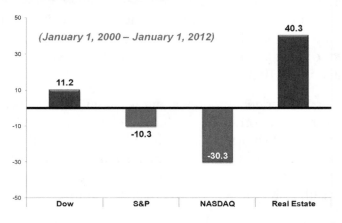

(January 1, 2000 – January 1, 2012)

MSN Money.com, Case Shiller

Financial journals and analysts are promoting "It's Time to Buy That House." In fact, that was a headline in the *Wall Street Journal* (10/15/2011). The article said, "It's an excellent time to buy a house, either to live in for the long term or for investment income."

One thing we know this *isn't* a time for buying and flipping, with the exception of overly distressed properties that require extensive rehab, and you have the time and muscle to invest—better known as sweat equity. The quick-flip environment of a few years ago has truly waned.

In 2011, owning a home vs. renting shifted dramatically. Mortgage rates decreased by 2.6 percent, and rents climbed 5.9 percent in the same time period. Whether you're buying your first home or investing in rental property, *now* is your opportunity!

TIP #4: BUY "IN OR BELOW THE MARKET," NOT ABOVE

Ideally, in purchasing investment property you would like to have a 10 percent cushion between your purchase price and market value. However, with lower mortgage rates, available homes that are clean, renter-ready and in stable neighborhoods, you don't want to miss the opportunity to purchase a home that will have long-term capital gain.

When making an offer on a home, be aggressive and cautious at the same time. Have your realtor show you comparatives—how area homes have been selling, price spreads within the neighborhood, the list-to-sell ratio—then balance these against days on market before getting a contract. This will set the tempo of how strong you can expect to negotiate to get your desired property. *Just remember, your pearl may be someone else's diamond.* If the home is new to the market and is a strong contender, expect competition.

We also recommend, whenever possible, making cash offers pending inspections with no repair costs. Meaning, you're going to buy regardless of the appraisal, and you may (or may not) finance, but that won't affect the sale. The home inspection is still done, and the seller knows he/she won't be expected to pay any additional repairs if the inspection is acceptable to the buyer. In certain states, items such as pests and roof insurability are taken into consideration for a successful sale to proceed. Most sellers respond favorably to this type of offer and are often willing to consider a deeper discount offer. We like that!

TIP #5: SELECT YOUR BEST FINANCE OPTION

Exciting news here! First, mortgage rates are at an all-time low. Second, Fannie Mae has lifted the mortgage limit from four to 10 for total loans. Investor loans typically require 20 to 25 percent down payment. Also, you must have a minimum of six months of mortgage payments in reserve (including tax/insurance).

If you have a 401(k), traditional IRA or Roth that has not been performing to your liking and there's enough cash, here's an opportunity to roll funds for the purchase of real estate investments. Ask a financial planner and/or an accountant about your options to make sure this change doesn't impact your taxable income—these rules can be tricky but are worth the investigation.

Recently, we've been working with clients who see the local real estate market as something they can understand much better than the stock market, which doesn't seem to be as safe. These clients have been guided to real estate investments that will generally net 8 to 10 percent annual income, and that doesn't consider any appreciation the property may gain over time.

TIP #6: STAY ALERT…WHEN OPPORTUNITY KNOCKS, BE READY TO OPEN THE DOOR

This strategy is about knowing what's a good deal and having the cash on hand to make it work. Cash (or access to credit) is ideal. A line of credit with a local lender is an excellent choice since you don't pay interest until you actually tap the funds. *Of course, a stellar credit score is a premier asset for getting a loan on a real estate investment.*

We encourage clients who are interested in real estate investments to identify neighborhoods where they'd like to own properties. We suggest they spend time driving the neighborhoods after 5 p.m. and/or on weekends. They should be looking for pride in ownership or overall curb appeal of the neighborhood. How many rent signs are out? How easy would the property be to market? What are the strengths and weaknesses of the area as it relates to crime rates, commute times, shopping, schools, etc.?

Knowledge of existing rental and occupancy rates is essential information to have when making quick decisions. You need to know which way the supply-and-demand swing is shifting. Nationally, rental demand is strong. Here in Oklahoma City and surrounding communities, single family homes in safe neighborhoods are in high demand. An investor can expect about 0.85 to 1 percent of the market value in monthly rent. For example, a $110,000-valued home in the Oklahoma City area, with 3 beds/2 baths around 1,600 square feet might rent for about $1,050.

Also, we tell clients to have all their leases expire May 31. This strategy will help you get the home re-rented quicker and typically for more money in June or July. It has been our experience that buying a home in the fourth quarter is also a good time to get tenants for January 1 occupancy.

If the property that you're purchasing needs some updating or repair, allow time to get the work done and be ready to hit the rental market at peak times if at all possible. This can increase your rental market price by as much as 4 percent.

TIP #7: FIND A RELIABLE REAL ESTATE EXPERT ADVISOR FOR PROFESSIONAL GUIDANCE

Working with a trusted real estate expert to find a sweet deal is a good practice. First, discuss your overall goals and investment targets. Give the expert as much insight into how you wish to "work on the property." Do you like doing the work yourself, or do you want the property to be "rent-ready"?

Second, discuss with your realtor the average sale price in the community where you wish to own a rental. Typically, you want to purchase a home below the average so you're seeking properties that are more affordable.

Ask your realtor if he/she is a real estate investor. You'll gain wisdom from those who have walked the path before you! Their experience can be a massive asset to your long-term goals. Build a relationship by keeping them in the loop of what you're looking for, and make sure they understand you're serious and ready to move on a great deal!

Your realtor can customize a multi-list search, using parameters such as:

- price per square foot less than a certain dollar or range (what makes the cost-to-rent ratio appealing; your realtor should be able to help you determine what that number should be for your market)

- school district boundaries
- minimum bedrooms (3+ desired)
- minimum square footage
- age of the property
- other amenities that might be unique to your area, such as attached garage or basement
- eliminate from your search mobile homes, well/septic systems, acreages, properties that require more maintenance
- square mile radius from major highway systems, shopping, health or commerce centers

Finally, develop a relationship you can "mine for diamonds" over time. Your realtor should know you well enough to be a "jewel prospector." As your realtor gets new listings (either into their inventory or when he/she hears about great homes coming on the market), *you get the first call!*

About Gary and Deb

Gary and Deb Atchley—*The Perfect Fit*

If ever there was a magic formula for the perfect fit in business, it's Gary and Deb Atchley. Each bringing to the table their own collective talents, these Oklahoma natives have carved out a successful niche in real estate. Ask Gary how he knew he'd wind up a realtor, and he'll tell you sitting in on his builder father's open houses. Even at an early age, he knew he had a desire to fulfill others' dreams of owning a home.

Successful forays in other entrepreneurial venues only strengthened his desire toward the real estate profession. His strong work ethic, integrity and a dogged pursuit caught the attention of the local real estate market. This led him to be offered an ownership opportunity with the then-new Keller Williams Realty Edmond Market Center.

Another perfect fit. Within a short time, the office took and maintained dominance as Oklahoma's "top brokerage." With this momentum, Gary's own real estate production receives "top dog" awards regionally and nationally with Keller Williams Realty. It has maintained a steady hold on that ranking. A leader in the real estate community, Gary has served as the local board president and continues to receive multiple awards from his peers for cooperation and leadership.

Gary says the smartest move he ever made was hiring his wife as his business partner. Deb's background in strategic planning and marketing was the perfect fit for further developing a business model that had a win-win strategy. Today, that model has evolved into a dream team with multiple agents, a top-notch support staff, and cooperative vendor relationships providing a superior client experience. Needless to say, The Gary Atchley Group has a strong referral base.

Together they have an enthusiasm for sharing their wealth of knowledge. They truly want folks to succeed in achieving their dreams. This bleeds over into sharing their knowledge of real estate investing and building wealth. Ask Gary and Deb how you can start expanding your investment portfolio by emailing them at expert@atchleygroup.com.

CHAPTER 31

Going for It All!
How to Become a Real Estate Investor Without Losing Your Shirt

By Donald G. Wilson

During the real estate boom of 2006, selling a house was so easy a monkey could've done it. Realtors were relegated to being order takers, and some investors threw caution and expertise to the wind. Recent negative reports about home values and the number of people "upside down" on their mortgages abounds. So, naturally, a person might be misled to think that real estate isn't a wise investment. The naysayers would have you believe that you'll lose your shirt in real estate, but I believe you should be *going for it all* in real estate right now! I'll show you how to do it correctly so you maximize your profits and don't get stuck with a bad investment.

Don't believe me? Here are some statistics you might not have heard; if you purchased a home on January 1, 2000, and held it until October 1, 2011, your property value would have *increased* 42 percent! Conversely if you had made other investments in the same time period, they didn't do as well (as shown in the stats below):

- Dow Jones   - 1%
- S & P   -19%
- NASDAQ   -39%

So if you've now decided that an investment in real estate is a good idea, where do you invest? Where's the property that will allow you to go for it all?

First, think about your exit strategy. Always keep your exit strategy in mind; are you renting, flipping or renting to own? Will you be paying cash or financing the acquisitions? The best investment will offer you a win on every exit strategy.

Here are five other things to keep in mind when researching your go-for-it-all property:

1. Where Should You Buy?

a. Choose a *location* without months of bad weather, such as snow. Harsh winters can mean big repairs.

b. What's the *demand*? Look at areas that are in high demand. You want an area that will attract more than one type of tenant or buyer.

Here are some questions to ask yourself:

- Is this an area where a renter would like to live?
- Is this an area where I can resell the property?
- Would a retiree move to this area?
- Would a second home buyer purchase here?
- Would a foreign buyer purchase here?
- Would a vacation home buyer purchase here?
- Would a vacationer rent here?
- Would someone want to relocate here?
- Is there a good economy here to support my purchase?

2. Which Type of Home Should You Purchase?

a. *Single family home:* These homes provide the best appreciation as well as the broadest appeal for all exit strategies. The other thing is to look at the costs of ownership. Taxes and insurance are among these, but the most important thing is the homeowners' association fee. This one thing can make or break the investment. I recommend homes with no homeowners' association fees.

b. *Condos/Townhouses:* These homes on the surface offer the best-looking numbers for investors; however, the costs on these properties can easily take a great-looking investment and ruin it. The homeowners' association fees on average run quite high. Appreciation on the value of these properties tends to run at a much slower rate than that of the single family home.

c. *Multifamily homes:* Multifamily homes can be a great investment. However, the purchase price will be higher because the value of these homes are generally based on the income of the property. Once again evaluate the costs and consider your exit strategy before taking on one of these properties.

d. *Mobile homes:* Mobile homes can be a highly profitable investment strategy. The purchase price of these homes are usually quite low, and the overhead costs are generally low as well. However, mobile homes aren't good for the investor looking for long-term appreciation. They're more for short-term gain and are ideal for rent to own.

e. *Commercial property:* Commercial property isn't for the amateur investor. These investments require lots of analysis and money. The returns can be extremely good but can also be an ongoing expense for the investor.

f. *Vacant land:* This type of investment isn't recommended because it doesn't generate income. The exception would be a property that can be leased.

3. What's Involved in the Purchase Process?

When you've determined the type(s) of properties that will best suit your exit strategy, your next step is to learn about the purchase process. I can't stress enough the importance of using professionals for this process. I recommend the following professionals make up your team: a licensed real estate expert, an attorney to look over your closing paperwork, a licensed home inspector, a licensed wood-destroying organism inspector, a reputable title company, and a licensed professional property management company. If you will be financing the property you also will need to enlist a licensed lender or mortgage broker, a licensed appraiser and a licensed surveyor.

Although some investors will take shortcuts and not use certain professionals, I highly recommend that no shortcuts be taken. In our office we use an entire team of professionals that work together to keep costs down. Even though the team works together, each member is a licensed professional and is bound by their state licenses to represent the buyer. Each member of the team charges a flat rate and isn't earning a commission based on the sale. They simply look out for the buyer and have no gain as to whether the purchase is finalized or forsaken for another property. The only person who is earning a commission is your real estate agent who is paid by the seller.

4. What Type of Property Management Team Should I Hire?

After purchasing your property, you should consider hiring a property management team who will look out for your investment. This is especially important if you'll reside far away from your investment property.

We highly recommend using a real estate expert to locate the right property. You don't want your buyer's agent to be your property manager because if they're good at what they do, they'll only have time for one facet of the business—either sales or property management. In our company, we have separate people who handle these responsibilities. With this team concept, you'll be assured that the home you're purchasing will be in an area that can be rented. Here are a few things to consider in a property management company:

a. *Size of management company:* How many properties do they manage? Does the property manager also sell property? I recommend you use a professional property manager that only manages property.

b. *Experience:* Does the company have experience? Do they take ongoing training? What is their occupancy percentage? Property management companies should run a vacancy rate of about 5 to 8 percent. If they're 100 percent rented, they're renting the homes too low. If their vacancy rate averages higher than that, either their advertising isn't working, or they're charging too much for the property. How long does it take them to rent a property?

c. *Assurances:* What if my tenant doesn't pay their rent? What if the tenant tears up my home? What about the eviction process? What about pets? Do they give any guarantees? Do they offer any assurances to help the investor if any of these situations occur, or do you, the owner, have to pay all the costs associated with this?

5. How Will You Handle Property Repairs?

Consider that you'll have to maintain your investment property, or run the risk of compromising the value of your investment. Ask yourself, do I have a mechanism in place to handle repairs? How can I get these repairs done and paid for efficiently? Do I get a warranty with my work? How do I know the price quoted is fair?

These are a lot of questions and this chapter scratches only the surface of items to be considered when becoming a real estate investor. What I've found through years of testing, as both an investor and as a licensed real estate professional, is you need to work with someone who has experience.

As an example, my company will take an investor and interview that person to find out their likes and dislikes, as well as determine their investing goals. We will then start to locate properties. We put the properties into a proprietary program we created to analyze the property using several different exit strategies. This program tells us if that property is the one for you. If you're unable to visit the prospective property, we'll visit it for you to photograph and make movies for you. At the same time, we'll evaluate the property for needed repairs and estimated income. We have a professional home inspector and wood-destroying organism inspector prepare reports on the property. Once we have all the information, the final decision is made whether or not to purchase the property. At this point in the process the investor has spent less than $500.

At my company we have a property management division, so every property is evaluated as to its value as a rental property before the purchase is made. We consider "if this property is one we want our managers handling?" So often I see investors who've been sold a piece a property by a real estate agent just so the agent can make a commission with no regard to the entire investment process. Once the investor closes on their property, we'll already have started marketing for them and any repairs are started immediately.

A repair company makes up another division of my company. This isn't a big profit center for us, it's simply a service we provide to help our investors in "going for it all." We constantly shop for quotes with outside companies to make sure our prices are the lowest. The vendors we use offer warranties on their work and are supervised by the property manager. With proper supervision, the owner can rest assured that the repair is done properly, on time and on budget.

One final thing my company offers, which you might want to look for when investing, is assurance plans. We realize that a major headache for investors is non-payment of rent and possible eviction of tenants. We asked ourselves, "What can we do to make this go more smoothly for both the client and for us?" We sought out and contracted with a company that offers an assurance plan to protect the investor if a tenant stops paying the rent. This plan pays the owner up to two months' rent while we go through the eviction process. The plan also will pay up to $1,600 toward the legal fees for an eviction, which is more than enough for an uncontested eviction. This unique plan is an added value to investors.

Maybe you'd like to offer your home with an option of no security deposit since some quality tenants may be inhibited by the need for large security deposits. We also have a plan where a security deposit assurance can be purchased for a fraction of the normal deposit. We also offer up to $500 for any pet damage when an owner gets our pet protection plan. All these plans can be structured in a way that the tenant will actually pay for them if the owner wishes.

As a real estate expert, I've created an environment where an investor can step in and make an investment in real estate with as little risk to them as possible. By following my simple plan, you can not only reap the rewards of the aforementioned 42 percent increase in the value of your property, but you might also be able to save money in the areas of management costs and repairs as well as be financially protected by an assurance plan in the process. Going for it all in your real estate investments isn't a pipe dream. It can be your reality. Go for it!

It's tangible, it's solid, it's beautiful. It's artistic, from my standpoint, and I just love real estate. ~ Donald Trump

About Donald

A native of Central Florida, Donald G. Wilson, has been involved in the real estate business since the 1970s. He's often sought after by investors from all over the world for his ability to see the market for what it really is and not what the media and government tells us it is. In fact, Don has been seen on ABC, CBS, NBC and FOX affiliates speaking about real estate. He has also been featured in several local newspapers. He uses facts and figures from many sources inside and outside the real estate industry, along with a source rarely used by his competitors, called common sense, to evaluate the market and come up with a custom plan for every client. Don has been involved in all aspects of the real estate industry, including construction, investing, buying, selling, and being a landlord of his own properties as well as other people's from all over the world.

Everything that Don has ever committed to, he has found himself rising to the top. In the early 1980s, he took a $1,000 investment and turned it into a company that grew to $1 million in sales and more than 18 employees. People have often asked Don why he never works with the status quo, and he quickly replies, "If it is worth doing, its worth doing better than anyone else."

Together with his partner, Olympic medalist Ivan Katz, they own several real estate businesses in Central Florida that reach worldwide. The core value of these businesses is helping people have a rewarding experience in real estate.

To learn more about Don and how he can help you reach your real estate investment objectives as well as receive a sample investors report titled Making Money With Real Estate in Any Market, simply go to www.NewRiseinRealEstate.com or call his office at (352) 241-7000.

CHAPTER 32

A Dream Come True:
Buying a Piece of New York City

By Elisabeth Mohlmann

New York City is one of the most exciting cites in the world, with its rich culture in the arts, theater and entertainment, as well as its world-class shopping, dining, sports and business opportunities.

You can find everything you ever wanted or ever wanted to do in this one city. New Yorkers know that the sure way of really enjoying all that New York has to offer is to own a residence here. Not surprisingly, many foreigners have been thinking along the same lines, whether to live full time or just to have a *pied-à-terre*. Last year more than 20 percent of all the real estate sales in New York were to non-Americans. Real estate in New York, depending on the area, ranges in price from reasonable to pricey, but on average it's less expensive than in other major capitals like London, Paris or Tokyo.

The process of buying real estate in New York is unique in a number of ways that I'll explain in this chapter, so it's important to be advised by someone who knows the ins and outs. I specialize in helping people find New York real estate, mostly at the upper end of the market. My clients range from those who want to buy simply to be part of the dream, who want to buy for their children who come here to study or work, who want to make an investment, or who want to buy a *pied-à-terre* for themselves and their friends.

My clients come from all over the world: France, India, Turkey, Persia,

Brazil, China, the United States, but also from many other countries. Each client has his or her unique story to tell. Each client makes his or her special mark on the city by coming to live here. Working with clients from all over the world and seeing the pleasure and pride my clients feel when they find the right residence makes my profession.

I was born in Germany but grew up in Rio de Janeiro, where my father was a diplomat. I've lived in many other places: New York, Africa, India, France, Germany, Italy, and England, and have traveled to many others. My professional activities prior to real estate allowed me to travel and experience different cultures, and once I moved to the United States, I naturally wanted to do something that was in-line with my cosmopolitan background, knowledge of languages, and desire to help people make their dreams come true.

After building an event company with a focus on cross-cultural weddings in the United States and Mumbai, I was asked by Apollo Real Estate Advisors to take care of many of their real estate-related events. I eventually became part of the team involved with a specific luxury high-rise development: 10 West End Avenue. This experience allowed me to find my true passion, as a real estate broker in New York City.

Dreams come true. As I've said earlier, each client has his or her own story, and I have many fascinating stories to tell. Following are just a few:

A couple from Thailand needed outdoor play space for their children. We started looking in Battery Park City. It seemed like the ideal location, with its excellent security, child-friendly environment, playrooms and waterfront properties. Very quickly the clients became interested in and made an offer on a beautiful two-bedroom apartment with water views. However, they began to reconsider their original choice when a friend of my clients told them about Roslyn, a lovely suburban community with a great school district, that's a short train ride from Manhattan. So we went to Roslyn to look at single family houses. Within a couple of weeks we found one that had everything my clients wanted: four bedrooms, a basement that could be built out, a back and front yard, and a private community with extensive outdoor and sports areas for the children to play. For them it was the perfect location and property at one-third less than the price of the apartment in Battery Park City. The clients enjoyed working with me, so they decided to continue our relationship and look for a house in the suburbs, even if the suburbs weren't an area I specialized in. However, they knew I was familiar with their preferences and trusted me to scout out all the available options and to educate myself quickly about areas I didn't know. I'm grateful for their loyalty.

A lady from Connecticut and I started working together slightly over a year ago. She wanted to sell her magnificent 5,000-square-foot waterfront house and buy a smaller apartment in Manhattan. She had never lived in New York City and was used to a lot of space. Her criteria were very specific: She wanted a 3,500-square-foot apartment on a high floor, with views, but didn't want to spend more than $5 million. We had only a few choices to work with but found her the perfect apartment within the first two weeks. Her grown children came to give their input, and we started negotiating. Because we knew the developer was under pressure to sell, we were able to get him to reduce the price to $4.2 million, with additional concessions.

For a gentleman from Mumbai, India, the most important criteria were that the apartment needed to face Central Park and be an investment. The layout also had to be Vastu compliant (Vastu is an ancient doctrine that consists of precepts born out of a traditional view on how the laws of nature affect human dwellings). We needed to look for the right floor plan to make it work. I showed him two apartments that were suitable, and we were very fortunate that the seller of the apartment the client liked best wanted to lease back the apartment for several years. This allowed the client to purchase the right apartment without losing time finding a tenant.

Here's one last story: Let's call this client Jean Claude. He's a worldly and brilliant French investor who knew exactly what he wanted but needed my help to narrow down the search and get the best price in what was to him unfamiliar territory. I found him an incredible deal on an apartment with magnificent full waterfront views. He loved it, but then we found out that the price we were able to negotiate was so favorable because there was a problem: a dispute between one of the partners of the developer and the other partners. I spent weeks of intense effort trying to get the seller to sign the contract, and I was able to get it signed by the developer just before the dispute escalated, and the sales office was closed down for several weeks. Working with the client's lawyer we were able to protect him from any negative fallout. Ultimately, the dispute was resolved, a new developer took over the property, and the sales office was reopened. The new developer increased all the prices, but because the client had a signed contract at a lower price, which the new developer had to honor, he was able to purchase a three-bedroom, 1,800-square-foot waterfront apartment for $2.3 million. One year later, this apartment is worth $3 million-plus!

This scenario isn't typical. Situations like this don't happen every day. But they do happen, and it tells you how important it is to have a seasoned broker, as well as a team of lawyers specializing in real estate, mortgage consultants, and architects and engineers that I can recommend to my clients.

These stories illustrate some of the key lessons you need to learn if you want to buy real estate in New York City or the surrounding areas, whether for yourself, your children, as an investment, or for any other reason. Most important, you need to find a broker whom you can trust. Trust is the most critical factor in any relationship, but particularly one as important as buying real estate. You need to work with someone who cares about what you want and isn't trying just to sell you any property, who won't be offended if she or he spends a lot of time with you even if you don't buy anything, who will be as happy as you are when you purchase the apartment you wanted.

Following are the nine key factors I've identified that make for a smooth real estate purchase in New York:

1. *Select a broker who knows your segment of the New York market.* This is a very specialized market. The high-end tier of real estate is different from all the rest, so you need to work with someone whose practice is focused on this one market. Some brokers specialize in neighborhoods while some, like me, are knowledgeable about the entire city.

2. *Choose a broker with knowledge about how to structure a purchase and to recommend the right advisors.* A broker representing foreign buyers needs to have a basic understanding of how to structure a purchase to maximize the tax advantages and must be able to recommend an international tax professional to put in place the appropriate structure (purchase in the client's name, in the name of a U.S. company, offshore company or trust).

3. *If you're planning to rent the property, select a broker who can advise you about renting it.*

4. *Work with one broker.* Unless you have a great deal of time, you'll find that you can do everything much faster and with fewer problems by working with one broker you trust. Since citywide listings of properties for sale are available to all brokers, unlike other cities, in New York City one broker can show you everything in every neighborhood. Working with several brokers ultimately becomes inefficient since you need to specify your criteria over and over to different people.

5. *Do your homework.* Before you contact a broker or do anything, browse some real estate websites to get an idea of what the New York City real estate market is about. Start to identify neighborhoods you like and the price you want to pay. Consider your likes and dislikes. Are you a theater or an opera lover? Do you like eating out? If so, the area around the Lincoln Center, on Manhattan's West Side, is a good option for you. Are you someone who likes loft apartments and a unique blend of shopping, restaurants and nightclubs but have no need for amenities such as doormen and a gym in the building? If so, Soho and Tribeca would be a good option for you. Your daughter goes to NYU, and you want her to be within walking distance? Greenwich Village and East Village are good neighborhoods to look at.

6. *Know your ownership options.* Keep in mind that in New York there are various ownership options: cooperative apartments, condominium apartments and townhouses. If you want to make an investment or buy a *pied-à-terre*, then a condominium apartment would make the most sense, particularly if it's in a new construction, sold by the sponsor, since no purchase application or board approval are required.

7. *Do you want an apartment with a tax abatement program?* Some new developments have the benefit of tax abatement programs (called "421a abatements"). The 421a Tax Abatement Program was set up to encourage development in certain areas. In a building with a 421a exemption, the real estate taxes are phased in over a certain period of time (10 years in most parts of Manhattan or up to 20 to 25 years in Brooklyn, the Financial

District and Harlem). with increases every two years up to the maximum market rate. This means that your annual expenses are much lower than other, comparable apartments.

8. *Consider less favored neighborhoods.* If you're interested in longer-term capital gains, you should consider neighborhoods like Harlem, Long Island City, parts of Brooklyn and Roosevelt Island. These neighborhoods are well located, but for one reason or another aren't currently as much in favor as other neighborhoods. There's a good chance they'll grow in value over the next few years.

9. *The United States is a stable country, and New York City is its financial and cultural capital.* Despite the current worldwide downturn, the United States remains the premier economic power with a stable political and social system that works. That isn't going to change in the near future. Within the United States, New York City has a special place as its financial and cultural capital. Our market is consistently stronger than the rest of the country. Over time, New York real estate has proved to be a good investment, whether you want a steady annual return or capital gains.

Hopefully, you've learned something from reading this short chapter and you'll visit my website at www.elegran.com/em. My hope is that someday we may meet and if I can help you to make your dream of buying a residence in New York come true, it will be my great pleasure and honor to do so.

About Elisabeth

With her intimate knowledge of Manhattan real-estate, international background, negotiating savvy and poise, Elisabeth Mohlmann, associate broker at Elegran Real Estate and Development, serves a global clientele seeking to sell, buy or rent a residence in New York.

She's also very likely to speak your language, literally. Fluent in English, German, Italian, French and Portuguese, Elisabeth has handled numerous high-end sales for clients in New York, Paris, Bonn, Istanbul, Zurich, Mumbai, Hong Kong and many others. Her global savvy and professionalism is why the prestigious boutique New York real estate firm Elegran sends her many of their international clients.

A successful actress and model in Europe and the United States, Elisabeth has exceptional people skills and a vibrancy and energy that have helped her successfully serve and anticipate the needs of her clients. Her background includes running a thriving event-planning company with a global clientele in New York for 13 years. Planning major festivities across Manhattan sparked her deep appreciation and knowledge of high-end Manhattan real estate.

Her roles in various facets of the local real estate scene include her involvement developing 10 West End Avenue, a 33-story condominium on Manhattan's Upper West Side.

In a frantic and fluid real estate market, clients often find that what they come most to appreciate about working with Elisabeth is her poise—a calm and ease cultivated living among different cultures of the world.

A Munich native, who spent her formative years in Rio de Janeiro, Brazil, Elisabeth studied at the elite Ludwig Maximilian University. She's lived and worked in Europe, Latin America, India and Africa, and has a gift for guiding foreign clients seeking to buy, sell or rent in New York. As a long-time resident of the Upper West Side of Manhattan, Elisabeth has a great affection for all things New York. For many years, she has also served as a spirited and tireless volunteer for various nonprofits serving the city.

Elisabeth Mohlmann
New York City
Elegran Real Estate & Development
Cell: 917 428 0932
Email: em@emglobalrealestate.com

CHAPTER 33

A Logical Alternative:
Rent Your House and Let Your Tenants Pay the Mortgage for You

By Randy Huntley

The rental option could work, but it all depends on the situation. Homeowners deciding whether or not to do a short sale might benefit. Others who are facing the prospect of foreclosure might also consider renting their house for a few years. How about the family who wants to move up but can't sell right now? Or, what happens to the soldier who recently purchased and then receives transfer orders? And speaking of transfers, in my marketplace there are thousands of State Department personnel who routinely move overseas but choose not to sell because they'll eventually want to move back. There are also estate and tax questions that might demand that a property not be sold just yet.

Renting may not be your first choice, that is, if you're not an investor; however, it might make sense to at least consider your options. After providing my clients with a rental market analysis, if I think there's a good chance to successfully rent, I encourage them to speak to their accountant, attorney or lender (regarding shorts sale or foreclosure situations). The other examples I included have a lot to do with timing, convenience or specific real estate financing goals. After all, in some markets the rent value might come close or even surpass the monthly mortgage (also adding in taxes, insurance, homeowners' association/condo fees). Each decision you make, however, comes with a set of consequences—some you can live with easily, while others might be adverse and difficult.

Assuming you have a reasonable chance of success—meaning that renting is your alternative of choice—I've listed several things in this chapter that will lead to a great landlord/tenant experience. With 23-plus years as a property manager, my goal is to encourage you as well as warn you that being a landlord is a contact sport.

QUALITIES OF GREAT LANDLORDS

I have identified five qualities of a good landlord:

1. Does not expect perfection
2. Knows the rules and is fair-minded
3. Sets reasonable lease terms and boundaries
4. Maintains a clean, updated property, and upgrades where necessary
5. Willing to accept advice, or at least learn

As a landlord, you have to be ready for anything! Anything means just that—fire, flood, storm damage, injury or death of tenant, nonpayment of rent, repairs, additional boarders, broken windows or locks, unkempt yard, abandoned cars, intentional damage, fallen trees. The list can go further, but the point is made. Alternatively, a good tenant will pay the rent on time, take care of the property and yard, report damages promptly, and allow showings for future marketing. Good tenants don't interrupt property appreciation; they enhance it.

You should occasionally praise tenants for their faithfulness in paying their rent. This almost never happens, but imagine the pleasant surprise a tenant feels when he/she opens a personal note of gratitude from the landlord! This encourages a tenant to cooperate even more.

You should never stoop to name calling, accusations, threats or verbal abuse. Nothing turns off a tenant more than landlord abuse. Landlords must always stay within the bounds of the governing laws. If not, you may end up defending yourself in court.

QUALITIES OF GREAT TENANTS

Clean Credit Report

Normally someone inquires about an available rental, sets an appoint to see the place, completes an application, and waits to be picked as the next tenant. However, there are quite a few things that go on behind the scenes before the final choice is made. For one, credit check should be ordered and reviewed thoroughly because this will reveal the credit-worthiness of an applicant. Credit reports confirm the following useful information:

- Social security number and current address (identifying the correct person)
- Current employer along with former ones
- Number and types of inquiries over the previous 18 months
- Existing credit accounts with balances
- Open accounts
- High credit amounts
- Late payment history (30, 60, 90, 120-days late, or charge-offs)
- Types of credit: installment, mortgage, school loan, car, credit card
- Adverse information, such as collections, bankruptcies and public records

Not every applicant is creditworthy. Great credit records don't guarantee future performance, but they're certainly a good indication.

References

On a typical application there's usually room for references. This is important because references vouch for the character or performance of the applicant. There are personal references like Mom, Dad, other living relatives, friends or associates. These become useful if tenants vacate "in the middle of the night." Personal references always know where and how to find the tenant, and they help describe the applicant personally, in addition to what they put down on paper. Professional references will answer questions regarding job or rental performance. It's good to get an idea of the applicant's work ethic and general personality in a professional setting.

Job and Income Verification

It's prudent for a prospective landlord to verify an applicant's job and income. This confirms the tenant's ability to afford the rent. It also confirms job stability. Good questions to ask include:

- How long has the applicant worked at this particular position?

- Is the applicant expecting any promotions?
- How likely is the applicant to be transferred?
- Will his/her company compensate for the landlord's loss of rent?
- Will the tenant's supervisor offer a personal reference?

Once again, satisfactory answers don't guarantee performance, but they definitely add to the applicant's credibility.

Reason(s) for Moving

It's useful to know the reason someone wants to move. Generally applicants put down reasons like job transfer, moving up, lower rent, bigger house, got married, got divorced, better commute, better schools, and sold house. Nobody ever lists reasons like burned my house down, pet problems, eviction, didn't pay, evading authorities or got fired. Verifying job and income will also lend credibility to their reason for moving. Additionally, speaking to the applicant helps landlords decide if their reason for moving is reasonable, logical and truthful.

Rent History

Verifying rent history is different than checking references. Whereas references describe opinionated and character issues about an applicant, rent history gets down to facts. How long did he/she rent, and was the rent paid on time? Did they pay on time and take care of the house? Any neighborhood complaints or excessive repair calls? It's wise to verify the two previous landlords because applicants tend to get very creative if they have some adverse rental issues to hide. Also, a future landlord has to be mindful of the answers previous landlords give because sometimes they really want to get rid of their tenants. In other words, they'll say anything they need to just to get rid of them!

REFUSING A TENANT

Bad credit can mean several things. It can demonstrate a lack of responsibility, or it can simply reflect a temporary setback. Just like good credit doesn't guarantee good performance, bad credit doesn't automatically guarantee bad performance. Find out the reasons why. There's always a story. There could be a divorce or a serious medical issue that led to the problem. Sometimes responsible people just fall into bad credit problems. Examine the credit report thoroughly, and more times than not, the real reason surfaces.

However, if applicants are overwhelmed with car payments, high credit balances, collections, excessive inquiries and late payments, then you should refuse this applicant. Tenants will pick and choose which are important payments to keep up with because things can easily be taken away or repossessed. Rent becomes less important because it takes so long (sometimes several months) for a tenant to be evicted. Here are some other reasons to refuse a tenant:

- Insufficient income is definitely a show stopper. Unless the tenant has someone else willing to pay the rent, this is automatic grounds for refusal.

- Lack of personal or professional references makes it difficult to gain perspective regarding the applicant. This, too, is grounds for refusal.

- Finally, refusal is easy if the applicant decides at the very beginning of the relationship that he/she sets the rules. Sometimes an applicant refuses to agree to terms of the lease, or might ask for too many changes—in other words, they set their own rules for the landlord to follow. Bye, bye to this one!

REASONS TO PULL IN A PROFESSIONAL!

Why might hiring a professional residential property manager be a good idea?

Lack of Expertise
Many people who happen to own rental property lack the expertise to find tenants and manage their property. Finding good tenants who will take care of your property and pay the rent on time is difficult. Abiding by federal, state and local fair housing, along with additional required laws also complicates matters. You might need to show several sets of prospects before settling on one; therefore, most landlords give up and simply take the first prospect who shows up. Day-to-day management, tenant demands and legal requirements are pitfalls that paralyze you into doing nothing, eventually costing you thousands.

Overwhelming Personal and Professional Demands
Managing property takes time, and good landlords see that tenants are comfortable and satisfied. They also communicate regularly with their tenants and perform periodic inspections. Please don't go more than six months without catching a look at your asset! Sometimes you'll have to

respond physically to plumbing, electrical, heating/air emergencies and neighbor complaints. It takes even more time to arrange repairs or replacements. After all, you have your own job and life to manage. Overwhelmed landlords eventually find themselves hoping against hope that they will not hear from their tenants—ever!

Absentee Owners

It's not practical for long-distance landlords to manage their own properties. Response time suffers and time-zone differences eventually take a toll on the landlord-tenant relationship. A tenant reports an emergency during daytime hours, but it could be middle of the night landlord time. How does a long-distance landlord know when his/her rent is paid, or that their property is properly cared for? Yet another challenge develops when responding to tenant requests are just not practical regardless of the time.

ALTERNATIVE TO SHORT SALE OR FORECLOSURE

Property owners who can't pay their mortgage(s) for various reasons must make serious and timely choices. One choice is to ask their lender for permission to sell short of what they owe (short sale); however, this option could take months to resolve itself. Another option is to allow foreclosure to occur, but this leads to eviction and huge personal trauma. Both choices are financially hazardous and will take their long-term toll on credit reports. On the other hand, picture someone who gets a cross-country job transfer after recently purchasing. Unless the employer picks up all expenses or losses, selling so soon will simply cost too much. Imagine this happening in a plunging real estate market—a transferred home owner could easily find himself upside down with little hope of recovery.

Renting the property might just be the answer. Finding a good tenant, charging fair rent, and having the property professionally managed buys the homeowner time. While the sales market value decreases, it's common that rents increase because people still need places to live. Tenants are conditioned to expect annual rent increases. Even if the rent is less than the mortgage, real estate taxes and insurance combined, oftentimes landlords can handle some negative monthly cash flow better than they can handle losing their home altogether, or coming up with several thousand dollars at the settlement table. One thing is for sure, despite typical highs and lows in the real estate market, generally real estate values appreciate over time.

DEALING WITH TENANTS

Honestly, some landlords, regardless of competency, locale, personal reasons, or financial situations just don't want to deal with tenants. They usually want to treat the rental and management from an arm's-length distance. Whether personal or professional, new landlords quickly find out if dealing with tenants is their forte. Tenants tend to take advantage of friendly landlords, while friendly, personable landlords sometimes consider tenants friends. This type of relationship is the recipe for failure because it's like doing business with family members. Whenever money is involved (rent and security deposits), it's never a good idea to breach the tenant-landlord line. It's very difficult to reset the tenant-landlord relationship after one or both parties abuse it. Landlords seem to fall into one of two extreme categories: Either they comply with every single tenant request, eventually exhausting their bank account and patience, or they ignore every request—even the reasonable ones—which also will eventually exhaust the account and patience. Two extremes; same outcome.

INVESTORS WITH MULTIPLE PROPERTIES

Calculate the time and effort it takes to manage one property correctly and multiply that figure by several properties. Managing property then becomes the "other" full-time job. Where there are existing mortgages, there might be very little profit after expenses, yet it still takes the same time to manage. It's a good idea for a multiple property investor to do what they do best and employ a professional company to do what they do best. Investors also know that nearly all expenses associated with rental property, including management fees, finder's fees, homeowners' association fees, general repairs, appliance and system replacements, interest and insurances are tax deductible. It makes financial sense for them to turn over their properties to a professional manager.

LANDLORDS WERE ONCE TENANTS TOO

You might as well give up now if you think all tenants were like you. Be honest: Did you have small, quiet dinner parties or invite the office over for a keg? Did you shovel snow after every storm or let it pile up and turn to ice? Did you write personal notes of encouragement thanking your landlord or add a few expletives to the check memo? Did you report all leaks or wait until your basement was ankle deep in whatever that was flowing from the basement toilet? Did you mow your yard at regular intervals or allow your yard to grow into grazing land? Did you park in the driveway or use the front yard as a supplementary lot? Did your gutters become mini tree farms and your refrigerators storage for furry little somethings? Were bathrooms a bacterial oasis? Blinds, what blinds? Oh you mean that flag covering the window? You get the picture...

A LOGICAL CONCLUSION

As I referred at the beginning of this chapter, renting might be your logical alternative, but it could be overwhelming unless you have help. You'll need to figure out what you want to accomplish with your particular situation, study the market, decide whether renting is beneficial or not, find professional help, and go for it! As a recipient of this book, feel free to contact me with any questions you may have about buying, selling, and especially renting and property management! Email me at residentialpmva@gmail.com, or visit my website: www.residential pmva.com.

About Randy

Randy Huntley has managed several hundred single-family homes and individually owned condo units since 1989. He's president of Residential Property Management Inc., which provides competent and accountable property management services to landlords worldwide. Randy began selling real estate in 1987. When the property management position became available, he took up the challenge, and so began his career in property management. Additionally, Randy is a real estate broker with Weichert Realtors and is a multimillion-dollar producer in annual real estate sales.

Originally from Iowa, Randy is a recently retired, 30-year veteran of the U.S. Marine Drum and Bugle Corps and U.S. Army National Guard Band (257th Army Band). Randy and his wife, Sue, have been married for 33 years, have four children, and five (soon to be six) grandchildren. His geographic concentration is the Northern Virginia area and also Washington, DC.

Managing property is his true passion, because as he says, "We're in the 'Peace of Mind' business. We receive a huge sense of satisfaction knowing that landlords can focus on their lives and professions wherever in the world they are, and they don't have to worry about their rented property back home. In other words, we have their backs!"

Just recently the local area experienced an earthquake, hurricane, and extreme storms and flooding all within a three-week time span. Randy's staff got busy and began alerting landlords, describing various situations; they contacted their tenants asking for feedback and updates on the property condition, coordinated repairs and necessary services, and kept the communication lines open. Where many service companies simply reverted to voice mail, Randy's staff did their best to answer the phones live and reassured both landlords and tenants that all was going to be OK.

Here's just some of the positive feedback Randy and his team received: *"As always .... Thanks. I'm sore from bailing water here in Connecticut to prevent flooding. It helps to not worry about the house down there."*—Landlord Elaine L., South Windsor, Connecticut. *"All good here! Thanks for the utility and emergency contact information. Glad you are there for us."* —Tenant Judy C., Arlington, Virginia.

Randy credits Buffini & Co. for teaching him how to grow his business by referral, develop deep and lasting relationships and being accountable. In addition, Jay Kinder and Mike Reese of Kinder Reese Real Estate Partners, and his broker, Steve Gaskins, have been true inspirations and have contributed greatly to his business success.

Also, Randy is constantly adding to his referral base through Business Network International. Finally, Residential Property Management is a member in good standing of the National Association of Residential Property Managers.

CHAPTER 34

The 2-Year Flip:
4 Steps to Investing In Your Own Home for Huge Tax-Free Profit

By Todd Tramonte

My wife and I started out in a 400-square-foot efficiency apartment that was basically a storage unit. Next we moved into a 630-foot apartment in an actual complex. She loved it compared to the tin-roof dump we had just moved from. Before long, I was investing in homes, and we decided we needed to own our home. I had no interest in following the normal formula of borrowing as much as we could, to buy as much house as we could, to look as well off as we could, to as many people as we could. We came up with a much better plan for owning a home, and we still use that original strategy to make huge amounts of tax-free profit each time we chose to move. You can do the same, if you follow the four simple steps I've laid out in this chapter.

STEP #1: PLANNING TO PURCHASE

Right off the bat, you'll need to adjust your mindset a little. You aren't ready to jump in the car and go look through everyone's medicine cabinets yet if you haven't decided exactly why you want to buy a house.

There are hundreds of reasons you might want a house, but for the purposes of this chapter, we're focusing solely on the idea of purchasing a home to live in as a two-year investment for cash profits.

At this point, you should visit with an experienced mortgage professional with a track record of educating clients through the process of buying a home. Remember, the fact that you can afford a house doesn't always justify its purchase.

Once you've determined what you're willing to spend, you need to find an experienced residential real estate expert. But not just anyone—you want a licensed realtor. This means this person has at least taken the steps to become a member of the National Association of Realtors. This, however, still isn't enough. You want to interview your prospective agent upfront to make sure he or she will operate as a knowledgeable consultant. You want someone who listens to your needs and desires, understands them, and then pursues them with you as a friend. You also want someone who will commit to specific results upfront. They should remove the confusion from the process. This person must display a high level of expertise in the market. Ideally, your realtor will be part of a team, and you'll have access to the resources of his or her team members as well.

STEP #2: PURCHASING THE RIGHT HOME IN THE RIGHT AREA

To approach the home buying process as an investor, you must eliminate as much emotion as possible. It's wild to think that one of the largest buying decisions in most people's lives is made based mostly on "warm and fuzzy feelings," but studies show overwhelmingly that this is typically the case. You must learn to look at a home as a source of value, as opposed to a showpiece for friends and family. Since you're going to live in the home during a two-year flip, you will not sacrifice happiness for profit. There will most definitely be sacrifices to be made, but regardless of how much profit a house generates upon a sale, a young couple with two babies and a Labrador probably shouldn't try to fit into a one-bedroom condo—even if it's selling at 25 percent below market value.

Once you understand how to approach the buying process, you need to decide what you're buying and where. Let me provide a few rules to live by when looking for your next two-year investment home:

- Buy an average size or smaller home based on bedrooms, bathrooms and square footage for your area.

- Don't buy a home in an area where developers plan to build for more than another year.

- Always buy a home that feeds into desirable schools.

- Don't buy a home that's been entirely updated or renovated. There won't be much opportunity for increased value left.

- Get a full home inspection by a licensed home inspector every single time you buy a house.

- Don't buy a house with a strange floor plan that can't be changed.

- Buy a house on a quiet, safe street.

- Don't buy a house in an area with little or no turnover.

- Buy a house with a backyard.

A perfect home for a two-year investment is a three-bedroom house in need of some repair, with two bathrooms and an attached two-car garage in a desirable area.

Have your realtor determine the turnover rate, which is the percentage of homes in the area that sell every year. An area with a turnover rate of 10 to 20 percent is ideal. Base your purchase price on the average price per square foot of similar homes in the area.

You'll hope to sell right at the average market value in two years, which will be determined by the price that home buyers are willing to pay for similar homes in the same market at that time. You can get a reasonable estimate by having your realtor use current data for homes that will be comparable to the one you're considering after you complete updates. Make no assumptions about the property value appreciating in addition to the value increase that comes from the updates you make.

STEP #3: IMPROVING THE HOME

Once you own the perfect house for a two-year investment, you'll need to build some additional equity into it by making the right improvements. Anyone who's watched television over the last few years has heard someone say that kitchens and bathrooms are the best places to make improvements to your home. For the most part, this is true. However, if you have a decent master bathroom and a bedroom with a sinkhole in the floor, you might want to start with the bedroom!

Home Is Where the Kitchen Is

When remodeling your kitchen, the best return on your investment will come from appliances, countertops, cabinets and lighting. Updating flooring and backsplashes are affordable and usually necessary as well. Here are a few tricks:

- Use complementing colors for your tile grout—never use dark tile with white grout.

- Try to refinish or antique older cabinets before throwing in the towel and buying new.

- Kitchen floors don't have to be exquisite, but they do have to be attractive. Some ceramic tiles have great slate, travertine and other natural stone looks, and sell for very affordable prices.

- Appliances should all match, and keep in mind that often you can switch the face plates on existing appliances from white to black, or even stainless steel, for big savings.

- Light fixtures are relatively low-cost items and can change a room immediately.

- Countertops need to be impressive. Granite is great but not your only option. Stone tile is an excellent option for average-priced homes and is regularly 20 percent of the price for the same stone in a slab. Ceramic tile also works for counters.

Update and Refresh Bathrooms

When the bathrooms become your focus, remember that the master bath is priority one. Here are some tips:

- The old tub doesn't always have to go. Try an aggressive cleaning and recaulking if it isn't too nasty.

- One-piece fiberglass shower/tub combos must go. These can be replaced with tiled walls and a new standard bathtub for a reasonable price.

- Old plumbing fixtures must go too. Just having the ability to say "new fixtures" in your marketing is worth the cost.

- If the toilet is old and dirty, it goes to the dumpster. No one wants to sit on someone else's 30-year-old john.

- Countertops are a great investment here, since they usually aren't that big.

- In the master, you should consider nicer surfaces like stone or stone tiles.

- In the second or third bath, ceramic tile or one-piece Formica tops can be done very affordably.

- Pedestal and cabinet sinks are very popular as well.

- Replacing huge mirrors with individual framed mirrors is incredibly affordable and very impressive aesthetically.

- Replace sinks and fixtures when updating counters for an added clean look.

- Cabinets in bathrooms can, in most circumstances, be cleaned up, painted or left alone.

Your Yard Says It All

When addressing landscaping, remember that buyers will either consider buying or disqualify your home within the first 8 to 10 seconds of seeing it. Here are some affordable, yet powerful ways to make your yard scream, "Buy me!" to passing prospects.

- Keep everything as neat and tidy as possible.

- Define the edges of your flower beds very clearly with stone, rock, sharp grass boundaries or plants.

- Color is great, but too much can hurt you. Focus the colorful plants and flowers near the front door so the buyer's eye is drawn toward entering the home.

- The grass is just as important as the flowers. Keep your grass green, thick and cut to maintain a healthy lush lawn that can be seen from down the block.

- Keep trees trimmed up to at least the roof line so the home can be seen from the street. Clean up small, new growth limbs each summer.

- Use landscape lighting on the ground to accent the home at night for a dramatic effect.

- Lights high in trees can make ordinary homes look like classic estates in the dark.

STEP #4: MARKETING THE HOME FOR SALE

You'll want to use a professional in order to effectively market your home for sale. Your realtor should present his or her marketing plan for your review. He or she should have an aggressive attitude toward getting information about your home in front of prospective buyers.

Here are a few tips for designing your home to sell itself:

- Allow as much natural light in as possible.
- Leave all lights on during showings.
- Keep the house as clean and fresh as possible.
- Keep the house smelling good, but don't have too strong of an artificial aroma.
- Thin out all cabinets, shelves and closets so they'll seem big.
- Make sure there aren't any visible family photos or photos of people anywhere.
- Remove as many rugs and rarely used furniture pieces as possible. This will make the rooms feel larger.
- Ensure you or your realtor take really great photos of the home during the day. A bright but cloudy day is best.

On day 730, you must remember that this home is an investment, so begin to detach yourself from the memories you've created with friends and family.

This is where the two-year time table becomes very important. You can turn your project into a three- or five-year flip, but it must be at least two years for the following reason.

AVOIDING CAPITAL GAINS TAX

There are a few basic requirements to avoiding the payment of taxes on your gains when you sell your two-year flip:

- You must occupy the home as your primary residence.
- You must own the home for a minimum of two years.
- You must keep track of what you spend on improvements.

A taxpayer can exclude up to $250,000 ($500,000 if married filing jointly) of realized gain from the sale of a principal residence [IRC Sec. 121; Reg. 1.121-2]. Gain (or loss) is computed based on the selling price, less expenses, of the sale and the taxpayer's adjusted basis in the residence.

Adjusted basis is original cost or—if the taxpayer postponed gain under former IRC Sec. 1034 when the residence was acquired—cost adjusted for deferred gain. The cost of improvements (but not repairs or fixing-up expenses) made to the residence increases the taxpayer's basis and any depreciation claimed on the property decreases basis (see IRS Pub. 523 for information on what constitutes improvements vs. repairs).

BEFORE AND AFTER

Now that you know what steps you need to take to make it work, here are some real-life financial and photographic examples of the two-year flip in action.

Oak Tree Townhome *2-Year Flip Summary*		*Bridle Lane Property* *2-Year Flip Summary*	
Hold Time: 26 months		Hold Time: 25 months	
Purchase Price:	$ 141,650	Purchase Price:	$ 125,000
Repair Costs:	$ 15,100	Repair Costs:	$ 30,000
Kitchen	$ 1,200	Kitchen	$ 9,800
Wood Floors	$ 4,000	Wood Floors	$ 5,300
Carpet	$ 1,800	Carpet	$ 1,800
Tile	$ 1,600	Tile	$ 1,300
Bathrooms	$ 3,600	Bathrooms	$ 4,000
Paint	$ 2,000	Paint	$ 2,000
Deck	$ 600	Landscaping	$ 700
Landscaping	$ 300	Walls/Ceilings	$ 2,900
Sales Price:	$ 230,000	Fence	$ 2,200
Marketing (Realtor) Fee:	$ 13,800	Sales Price:	$ 211,700
Closing Costs:	$ 2,866	Marketing (Realtor) Fee:	$ 12,702
Net Profit:	**$ 56,584**	Closing Costs:	$ 2,770
		Net Profit:	**$ 41,231**

Living Room Before 2-Year Flip

Living Room After 2-Year Flip
Painted, added trim around windows and
fireplace, added wood floors and blinds.

Kitchen Before 2-Year Flip

Kitchen After 2-Year Flip
Raised ceilings, new cabinets, new tile
floor, new slab granite counters, new
appliances and vent hood, new windows,
new lighting, removed walls, new back
splash and new bar top.

Hall Bathroom Before 2-Year Flip

Hall Bathroom After 2-Year Flip
Painted, added molding, tiled marble
counters, new sink, faucet, framed mirrors,
ceramic tile floors, painted cabinets,
and added new handles.

Kitchen Before 2-Year Flip

Kitchen After 2-Year Flip
Raised ceilings, new cabinets, new tile
floor, new slab granite counters, new
appliances and vent hood, new windows,
new lighting, removed walls, new back
splash and new bar top.

Breakfast Room/Bar Before 2-Year Flip

Breakfast Room/Bar After 2-Year Flip
New cabinets, tile floors, slab granite
counters, windows, paint, molding, trim,
lighting, and wine chiller

Master Bath Before 2-Year Flip

Master Bath After 2-Year Flip
New travertine tile, slab granite counters,
sinks, hardware, framed mirrors, painted
cabinets and walls, new handles, new
lighting, new shower heads, faucets and
towel racks.

Living Room Before 2-Year Flip

Living Room After 2-Year Flip
New wood floors, walls removed and
paint.

Dear Reader:

What you've just read is my personal plan, built with experience and hard lessons learned, written down in order to enrich your life in the same way it has enriched my family's and mine.

By now, I hope you've come to the conclusion that owning your home is a wise investment for your future and that approaching your personal home as an investment will only serve as an accelerant to the building of your personal wealth.

This strategy has been proven to work and requires minimal sacrifices. The central idea of this chapter can be written in a sentence or two, and here it is:

If you buy the right house, do the right repairs and plan well, you have the potential to sell your personal residence every two years and generate enough tax-free profit to cover the basic expenses you and your family will incur over the next two years while you do it again.

Best Wishes,

Todd Tramonte

About Todd

Todd Tramonte is well known as an innovator and leader in the areas of real estate marketing and sales. His passion for education and commitment to excellence are trademarks of his leadership of both his company and his clients. Todd is the author of *Live Free: The Art of the 2-Year House Flip*, which is currently in its second printing and available on Amazon for Kindle. Todd and his company have been seen on HGTV, Discovery and Travel Channel as well as in the *Chicago Tribune, Dallas Morning News, Examiner, People News* and *USA Today,* in addition to countless online news sources and blogs.

Todd began his real estate career while in college at Baylor University, as an investor specializing in wholesale transactions and quick remodel flips. After years of owning a major national real estate franchise office, in 2010, Todd built the business he had always dreamed of. Todd researched what consumers really wanted and needed and built his brand around meeting those wants and needs better than it had ever been done. His current team at Market Experts Realty is focused on the client experience and providing the most valuable service possible based on expertise, character-driven representation and a passion for relationships.

Todd regularly says, "There is no such thing as normal in real estate," and "Averages are liars." He continually stresses the importance of expertise-driven client advisory service that respects the individual nature of each client's needs. Todd also often says, "Real estate is not a one-size, one-price-fits-all business."

Todd is also an energetic and entertaining speaker on the topics of real estate, small-business development and his Christian faith.

To learn more about Todd Tramonte and how you can receive a free chapter of his book, *Live Free: The Art of the 2-Year House Flip,* visit www.ToddTramonte.com or call (214) 216-2161.

CHAPTER 35

Lifetime Value of a Customer

By Brian C. Reed

The general consensus by the public is that realtors are just out there to make a quick buck. They feel realtors are simply middlemen trying to get involved in a deal by any means necessary so they can get their piece of the pie. They're perceived to be dreamers in search of great riches and extravagant lifestyles without doing all the grunt work usually considered essential to achieve it. Let's face it, the perception of realtors by the general public is for the most part not always considered to be favorable.

I was completely unaware of this stereotype concerning real estate agents prior to entering the profession. Like most young professionals, when I set out to become a realtor I had all the intentions of becoming successful and providing a secure and a healthy lifestyle for my family. By no means, however, was I looking to make a quick buck, but rather I truly desired to be considered a knowledgeable and trusted advisor.

In my opinion, the reason our profession has been perceived to be filled with swindlers looking for quick riches is that for much of the last decade it truly was. At the boom of the real estate market in the early to mid-2000s deals were happening left and right, and even the least capable agents were able to sell homes just by waking up in the morning and managing to find their way to the office. In my first couple of years in the business, I saw many unscrupulous and unethical activities by some of my fellow agents. At times, I was ashamed to be associated with my chosen profession.

I had worked predominantly in commercial real estate prior to 2010, and my business partner of four years had worked mostly in raw land. In all honesty, though, we had never specialized, and it was uncommon in our area for anyone to do so. Most agents would just take what came their way and throw it against the wall and hope it stuck. We sold an occasional house here and there, but for the most part just worked with investors. The only bad thing was that investors soon became few and far between.

In 2009, we had four or five deals that fell apart at the tail end and some-times literally just short of the closing table. Instead of having solid six-figure incomes for the year, we were struggling just to make ends meet. Needless to say, our investors were struggling as well and with their financial difficulties or lack of confidence in the market, they soon bailed out. The lead calls that had once been in abundance had come to a blistering halt. A percentage of the agents we once knew were gone along with the quick buck, as they now had to work for a living. My partner and I were at our wits' end and were both considering getting out of the business altogether.

We sat down and discussed what it was we liked most and least about the business and thought about the times we were happiest in our jobs. After much consideration, it became clear to us that we both found our jobs most rewarding when we were helping those who really needed and appreciated our services. Some of our best experiences were work-ing with first-time home buyers. My partner and I were both young—I had just turned 30 and he was just under 30—so we had the opportunity to work with a lot of young professionals who were in the beginning stages of new careers, just recently married, starting new families, or some combination of these things. We were given the opportunity to help these people from day one through the whole home buying process and were able to provide them with an overall memorable home buying experience. This is where true value lies.

For the majority of these people, we were in most cases consulting them in the biggest investment of their lives. These individuals truly appreci-ated the tremendous efforts we had made on their behalf and through the course they had made us an extended part of their families. It felt great knowing we had put these individuals in homes we were confident would not only function well for their family but also would serve as solid investments for their family's future. Being a trusted advisor for these families is where we found hope for our profession and renewed confidence in our careers.

In early 2010, my partner and I made the commitment that we would specialize in selling homes with a strong focus on first-time home buyers. We would provide our customers with the ultimate home buying experience. We decided to write down our core values and make it a purpose in our lives to live by these core values. Our hope was that every time someone purchased a home through us, by the time of closing, they would have a good understanding of our core values merely through our actions. We were going to give this real estate business one more shot and, regardless of the outcome, we knew we would at least be doing the right thing and having a positive impact on the lives of those around us.

All revelations aside, one of the biggest difficulties we faced early on as a home selling team was that the banking standards kept getting more and more stringent. In many cases, individuals with strong incomes and more than enough money for a down payment weren't qualifying for loans due to credit issues. On the flip side, people with decent incomes and just enough money scraped together for a down payment were getting qualified for loans. A considerable number of times, these credit issues were no fault of their own or were due to mistakes they made in their distant past. These were responsible people who should be in homes but were not due to the nation's financial crisis and the over-correction taking place by the financial institutions.

How could we help individuals who were prime candidates for buying a home but falling short merely because of their credit score? We began looking for solutions and the only option we could find was to send them to credit repair specialists. Many clients had already spent money to see these so-called "specialists" and saw nothing in return. We realized our mistake was referring our clients to those who did not share our same core values and that we could no longer affiliate ourselves with them. We wouldn't kick these clients to the curb like every other agent and lender had done previously; instead, we would help find a solution to these individuals' credit repair needs.

Credit repair is a tricky process, and it's impossible to guarantee results (although many out there will). We figured we just needed to associate ourselves with individuals who demonstrated the same core values in the credit repair business that we did in our home selling business. No guarantees would be made such as those by unscrupulous companies that charged absurd and continuous monthly fees with no incentive to complete their task. In contrast to these practices, our associates always pull our clients' results within a specified timeframe so they can see their progress, and most important, they don't take on clients that can't be helped (i.e., recent foreclosures, bankruptcy, short sales, etc.), just to take their money.

We started by helping a handful of clients by paying their credit repair fees out of our own pocket because we wanted to make sure it worked before asking our clients to make the investment. After several months of testing, it became apparent that we had a solution for these selected individuals. We saw 60, 80, even 100 point increases. It wasn't a solution for everyone, particularly those who were irresponsible, hadn't made payments on time for months, and clearly shouldn't be approved for a loan. However, it was a solution for those who had credit issues due to mistakes or unfortunate events in their past. These individuals were ecstatic, and so were we!

These people had been deemed "unsellable" by every other real estate agent, builder, lender, etc., who they had met prior to coming to us and were not given more than five minutes of attention by anyone. Instead we took the time to show them their options and provide them with alternatives. Showing someone how to fix their credit is basically showing someone how to put more money into their bank account. Talk about creating raving, lifelong fans! Once you have gone through the effort of helping someone resolve their credit problems, they are almost definitely going to trust your advice as a real estate agent and show you their appreciation by purchasing their home through you.

In this market the only agents who are going to survive are those who care. The agents who were in it for the quick buck have, for the most part, quickly fled the industry. Deals don't close in a matter of weeks like they formerly did. An agent is going to have to nurture and oversee every deal. If you don't, clients aren't going to have a favorable home buying experience and, most important, you're not going to get valuable referrals. Qualified clients are fewer and farther between these days, and in order to make it in this market, you're going to need to assist home buyers by creating the ultimate home buying experience for them. In return, you'll create raving fans who will go out of their way to send their friends and family to you to share a similar experience.

How can you create lifelong customers and raving fans? Follow these seven simple steps:

- *Determine your core values.* What's most important to you, and what message do you want to relay to your customers? Take the time to write them down so you can see them every day and under no circumstances do you deviate from or jeopardize these values.

- *Assure that your core values are shared and used by your team.* Make sure everyone on your team, from your administration to your buyer agents share and practice these same core values. If they don't, cut them loose. I promise you, if you have someone on your team who doesn't believe in these values it will quickly become apparent, and the only one who will come out looking bad is you.

- *Only associate with those who share these same values.* Our job as realtors isn't always to do everything but to direct our clients in the right direction to the right people. Only associate yourself with affiliates who share the same core values as you. If your clients get bad service from an affiliate, they'll assume they learned their values from you.

- *Don't kick clients to the curb: Be the solution to their problems.* Whether you're directing them to credit repair, helping them find temporary housing, or showing them how to create a budget, help clients resolve their issues or direct them to someone who can. This client might not be capable of purchasing a home immediately, but eventually they will be, and you want to be their agent when that time comes. If you help them find that solution, you will be rewarded for your efforts.

- *Create the ultimate home buying experience.* Buying a home is an overwhelming process to many individuals, so from steps A-Z of the home buying process you should have the systems and processes in place to make it as smooth and enjoyable as possible. You can work as diligently as possible for your clients, but if the experience isn't pleasurable, you won't be getting repeat business or those precious referrals.

- *Create raving fans.* If you've created that ultimate home buying experience, you'll inevitably create raving fans who'll go out of their way to send you referrals just to say thank you. You can't stop there, though, as people will only send you referrals if they remember you exist. Stay in touch, show and express your appreciation for referrals, and continue to show your clients your gratitude and how much you care by simply taking a vested interest in their lives.

- *Become a raving fan of your clients.* Just as your clients show you their appreciation and celebrate your accomplishments, you should go out of your way to celebrate their achievements no matter how large or small. If they have a baby, send them flowers. If they complete their first marathon, send them a congratulatory letter. We should be in the bleachers rooting for our clients and being their No. 1 fan.

It's the opinion of many that if our industry doesn't take major steps to change these perceived flawed practices and the image this creates, we'll be as extinct as the once-prominent travel agent. I don't believe this has to become a reality, because trusted advice will always be sought after when buying a home. A home is one of people's biggest assets, and buying a home can be an unfamiliar and scary process to many. However, if you don't position yourself as the expert advisor and the one who truly cares, your time as a real estate agent will likely come to an unsuccessful, speedy end.

When I tell people I'm a real estate agent, I sometimes hear, "Oh, I'm so sorry, it must be so tough in this market." It makes me laugh because I truly love this market. It has helped "clean up our house," and now all the pretenders are long gone or on their way out. Last year was our team's best year ever, and it came down to simply reflecting on our core values and getting back to the basics of what the customer should be able to expect from us.

So what is the lifetime value of a customer? The lifetime value of a customer is for the most part immeasurable, but it is simply the biggest return on investment you can make in your business. When you stop to consider it, the only real investment you have to make is time for others. Create that ultimate home buying experience for customers, create raving fans and be a raving fan!!! I can promise you one thing: If you start by taking the focus off of yourself, at the very least your life will be much better. It is my hope that your business will soon follow suit.

About Brian

Brian Reed, along with his business partner Ryan Peterson, formed The Ryan & Brian Real Estate Team in 2006. Their unique team system is the secret to their success and allows Ryan & Brian to provide unparalleled service to their clients. The Ryan & Brian Real Estate Team take pride in their mission, culture and core values. Their focus is on their clients and keeping them informed in every step of the real estate transaction. They have separated themselves from the herd by showing their clients that they care and never kicking them to the curb by providing solutions to their obstacles. They're dedicated to providing their sellers and buyers with the ultimate home buying or selling experience.

Their mission is to create the most productive and influential real estate team in the Rio Grande Valley of South Texas by focusing on teamwork, leadership and personal growth to achieve their goals, and only working and associating with those who share this same focus. By providing world-class service, they'll create raving fans of their team. They've created an image that's known throughout their community for service, results and innovation.

To learn more about Brian Reed and The Ryan & Brian Real Estate Team, visit www.RyanAnd Brian.com or www.RnBTeam.com, or call toll-free (855) RnB-Team (855-762-8326).

CHAPTER 36

Important Ingredients in the Real Estate Recipe:
A Note to the Public and Practitioners Alike

By Derek R. Bauer

Passion is a formidable thing, and it's a blessing when someone identifies what they're truly passionate about in life. Ralph Waldo Emerson said, *"It* is a fact often observed, that men have written good verses under the inspiration of passion, who cannot write well under other circumstances." That says a lot about what someone can accomplish with passion at the helm. It seems fitting to also include a quote about passion from "The Donald":

> *"Without passion, you don't have energy; without energy,*
> *you have nothing. Nothing great in the world has been*
> *accomplished without passion."* ~ Donald Trump

I'm truly pumped to share my thoughts with you about something I'm very passionate about: how real estate agents and brokers should service their clients, and what our clients should expect from us.

It's an awesome privilege and responsibility to facilitate a home purchase transaction knowing that a couple will raise children within those walls; to market a home for top dollar so a family can relocate for a promotion and start the next chapter of their lives; or to responsibly guide a homeowner through financial distress on to brighter days. To enact positive change, facilitate life-changing experiences, and be welcomed into homes to do so is truly awesome and is a driving force for me each day.

The guiding principle of The Door to Dreams Home Selling Team is to help our clients make good decisions. This is core to our brand and is the reason we use a lighthouse in our logo, conveying that we are a bright vision and a beacon of trust for our clients. We feel that as long as this concept guides the advice we give, supports the contracts we structure, and illuminates the homes we sell, then our clients will win every time, and we'll be fulfilled in our exceeding their expectations.

When it was time to create our mission statement, it was extremely important to communicate the principles outlined in this chapter. For that reason, our mission statement begins:

Our purpose is to express our core values of expertise, integrity, professionalism, and resourcefulness to do what is ethically right and in the best interest of our clients, always, by helping them make good decisions.

These words are posted on the wall in our office, in our brand marketing, and are demonstrated daily in our representation of clients.

I've recently been transformed by the teachings of Dave Ramsey, and to say that it has impacted my life is an understatement. In fact, this transformation has certainly improved my life, probably prolonged my life, and possibly even saved my life. Dave has a very defined and deliberate formula for financial success and peace. If you don't know who Dave Ramsey is, make a note to look him up as soon as you finish this book. Thanks to Dave, in the handful of months leading up to this book, I downsized my house, eliminated a lot of debt, lost over 100 pounds, grew spiritually, and achieved peace as a result. When personal peace combines with professional passion, you can add value like never before!

As a daily podcast listener to Dave's show, and as someone who now shares Dave's passion for eliminating debt as quickly as possible, I often speak aloud about the advice I presume Dave will give before he invokes his wisdom. This passion spills over into my real estate business, as many times clients request things that may not be in their best interest. I'm not shy about sharing my opinion when a client suggests something that may not be in their best interest, although it may very well be in mine. We would rather turn someone down then let them down, always.

After a buyer-counseling interview two weeks ago, we determined what types of properties were and were not a good fit for a new client. This particular client contacted me last week and was in a hurry to view and likely pursue a property that was clearly distant from what we had defined. I could have rushed out, encouraged a transaction, and certainly realized a fast commission ... but instead reminded this first-time buyer about the decisions they'd made, why they were going to avoid these particular homes to begin with, and to really consider if this was a wise choice. They were thankful for the guidance, and we're still on the hunt for the right home. To see a first-time home buyer make a decision based on logic rather than emotion is very rewarding in and of itself.

The economic downturn in recent years has brought with it hardship for some and opportunity for others. While some try to find opportunity after hardship, which we certainly support, others have tried to position a hardship to create opportunity, and in that we will not participate.

An example of this is where a homeowner who's "underwater" yet financially able to pay their bills wants to "short sell" their house because they feel good money is being thrown after bad. We frequently receive calls to represent these clients and situations, and refuse to do so 100 percent of the time. If you have a bonafide hardship, we want to help you! We will, however, forgo any potential commission before participating in what's an ethical end-run. This is an example of how core values guide our business, why they should guide yours, and why these traits should be important to the consumers of our real estate services.

I'm reminded of one particular scenario in early 2011 when some folks contacted me to purchase a home, and they arrived at my office prepared with a letter from a loan originator stating they could purchase a home up to a specific amount. It was, however, very interesting to uncover that their current residence was up for sale as a short sale. I suspected after a short interview what was taking place, as it appeared they could have easily afforded the house they owned and that which they wanted to purchase. No thanks—relationship over before it started.

Real estate agents who are members of the National Association of Realtors are obligated to abide by a code of ethics and standards of practice set forth by the association. This code is comprised of 17 articles and further defined by standards of practice. I just completed my third year on our local committee whose purpose is to review individual cases in which realtors are accused of violating one or more of these articles in their dealings with the public and/or their colleagues. This is important because of my passion for the quality of service the public should expect and receive. It has long been my position that the overseeing departments and agencies should make it more difficult to become and remain a real estate professional, but I must qualify this by pointing out that some states are stricter than others. Look at it this way, if you were getting lasik surgery, how important is the education and experience of the doctor? By the same token, if someone is going to guide and lead you through one of the most monumental financial transactions of your life, what standards should they be held to?

Let's break this down further to the consumers of real estate services and then to real estate practitioners.

To those of you who will soon or someday need representation in the purchase or sale of property, I encourage you to do the following six things:

1. Make a list of the professional characteristics you require from your agent *(do this before going any further or peeking ahead)*

2. Add "passion," and "selflessness" to the list if they're missing.

3. Identify three local real estate experts to interview.

4. Focus the first part of the interview on determining if this agent is aligned with your required professional characteristics. If for instance, "organized" is on your list, you may choose to ask, "What's an example of how you or your staff/team track all the necessary duties in the listing of our house?" If you ultimately deem this agent to not be a good fit based on their responses and lack of your required professional characteristics, then you need not continue and it's on to the next candidate.

5. Focus the second part of the interview on the marketing savvy of the agent *(for sellers)* and on process and negotiation strategies *(for buyers)*.

6. Make the right hire, keep them accountable, keep an open line of communication, and be loyal to them.

If your agent isn't serving your best interests, then it's time for an honest conversation and possibly a change in direction if things don't improve. Good and great agents invest a lot of time and resources into their clients and deserve your honesty and loyalty. In addition, you also deserve the best they have to offer.

You may be drawn to a particular agent by their big billboards, their direct mail pieces, how many homes they advertise that they sell each year, or even by a clever program that guarantees your home will sell, or they'll purchase it from you. At the end of the day, though, make sure the agent you hire is passionate about you and focused on *your* best interests and accomplishing your real estate goals.

To those of you working in real estate who may be contacted for this job interview, I encourage you to do the following six things before going further in your career:

1. Make a list of what you're truly passionate about *(do this before going any further or peeking ahead)*.

2. Is your real estate career on the list? If so, is it near the bottom? Ask yourself if you're truly passionate about the real estate business and about the net outcomes of your daily efforts … paychecks aside. If you're not, then the exercise was good and you've determined another career may be best for you.

3. If your real estate business was on the list, make another list of the reasons why you're in the real estate business *(do this before going any further or peeking ahead)*.

4. If "I'm a people person" and/or "I really like houses/architecture/design" is part of your very short list, you may want to reassess if real estate is the best fit for you. I strongly recommend utilizing the DISC as a starting point, as it has been a valuable tool for me and those I have chosen to learn from and model my career after. The DISC is an exercise to identify an individual's predominant "behavioral style." DISC is an acronym for a behavior model which is comprised of the following four primary traits: Dominance, Influence, Steadiness, and Compliance. While each of us have some degree of all four traits, the DISC helps uncover the levels at which they exist in you. I strongly endorse this is as it is a proven way to gain career direction, a useful tool in the development & growth of an organization, or

even used solely for the benefit of you and those close to you, allowing communication to occur on a more powerful and effective level.

5. If you're truly passionate and are in the business for the right reasons, yet you may be struggling at this minute, seek out an expert in your market whom you admire and ask for some advice and guidance. The rainmaker agents who are true professionals should have no problem helping you down the road to success. I completely enjoy giving a struggling agent advice on how to grow their business or tweak something they're doing. Les Brown said, "Help others achieve their dreams and you will achieve yours." Les also says, "*You don't get in life what you want; you get in life what you are.*" What *are* you?

6. Do the right things, for the right reasons, and follow your passions. The rest will fall into place.

The most recent Gallup data available at the time of this publication reflected that 23 percent of the public had a positive perception about the real estate industry, while 23 percent were neutral, and a majority 52 percent had a negative perception of the real estate industry. Although that was more favorable than what the same report for the federal government reflected (which showed 17 percent positive and 63 percent negative), it indeed leaves much room for improvement. In fairness, Gallup.com went on to report "the bad image of the real estate industry most likely reflects the housing crisis that has beset the country in recent years." Regardless, as is the case in many companies, industries, markets, etc., there are both good and bad practitioners. When you're passionate about your business and represent your clients in a selfless manner, with complete focus on their needs and outcomes, only then will you separate yourself from the stereotypes, from the public perception reflected in these statistics, and from your competition. I strongly encourage my colleagues to operate their businesses this way, and that future home buyers and sellers make an agent's passion and selflessness a requirement in your interview process to determine who deserves to be awarded your trust and business.

To my fellow real estate professionals or to those considering the career, you may be or were drawn to the real estate business by the flashy cars you see some agents drive, by the big houses they live in (both of which I have done away with…thank you Dave Ramsey!), or by some other material measuring stick. Dig deeper, though. It's very true that if you find something you love and are passionate about, the money will follow. So find that passion for yourself and add value to the lives of those you serve, regardless if that's in the real estate industry or if it leads you elsewhere.

A career in real estate is very rewarding, fulfilling, and honorable when done the right way, for the right reasons. According to the Bureau of Labor Statistics at the U.S. Department of Labor, the number of licensed real estate sales agents and brokers is projected to increase 14 percent by 2018. As we grow in numbers, let's also work hard to deservedly improve those Gallup figures so that sooner rather than later the majority of the public recognizes the value and worth of good and great real estate experts.

As the descendant of farming families, I learned about hard work and selflessness from my mother, father and grandparents at a very young age, and that still embodies who I am today. Let passion and selflessness guide you in everything you do, from raising your family to growing your business; from volunteering at the animal shelter to mentoring someone in need of your care and support … and anything else you can think of.

So get out there, focus on others, be passionate, inspire, add value, and make a difference! You'll be amazed at the results, and others will appreciate you for it.

It was my pleasure and privilege to spend some time with you.

About Derek

Derek Bauer is the creator and leader of the Door to Dreams Home Selling Team in Michigan and is a real estate broker with more than a decade of experience. Derek has been recognized by RIS Media as one of America's "Top 50 Realtors on the Rise," has been a guest lecturer on real estate and technology at a Michigan University, and wins customer service and sales volume awards year after year. Prior to Derek starting his real estate business, he was a technology and process consultant for then the world's largest consulting firm, which provided Derek with a foundation of tracking metrics, implementing technology, and using systems and processes for efficiency and results. Today, Derek's expertise is helping property sellers get the absolute most money possible for their properties, using a variety of proven techniques. If you or someone you know has a property in Southeast Michigan to sell, be sure to include Derek on your list of experts to interview. To learn more about Derek Bauer and the Door to Dreams Home Selling Team, visit www.DoorToDreams. com, and be sure to check out their channel at www.YouTube.com/DoorToDreams. You may also speak with Derek or a team member by calling (248) 820-7222.

CHAPTER 37

Clients Before Profits:
Raising the Bar on Real Estate Customer Service

By Emmett R. Carr and Jason Peck

There's no question that technology has altered the face of almost any business you can think of—in particular, the internet. From shopping to travel reservations to reading a newspaper, online interfaces allow you to do virtually anything—and to do everything virtually. Even the local restaurant posts a menu on it's website, so you can see whether it's serving what you're hungry for.

The fact is that the two of us are in a real estate partnership, even though Emmett is located in Atlanta and Jason works out of Denver. We can't be sure that would even be feasible without today's technology.

But, as is almost always the case, when something is gained, something is lost, and the real estate industry is no exception. Before the rise of the internet, our business was mostly one-on-one personal interactions between clients and agents. Now, it's transformed into a blizzard of emails and voice mails. While it's certainly easier and more efficient to communicate this way in most cases, the human element pays the price. And the need for more information at a faster pace is just accelerating the process.

We've made a concerted effort to reverse this trend, at least in terms of providing a *premium customer service experience* to all our clients. In this chapter, we'd like to discuss how we're putting that concept into action and offer some more thoughts on what you should expect from your real estate agent when you're pondering either the sale or purchase of a home.

THE TURNING POINT

First, we'd like to admit that we embraced the new technology and all its advantages with complete enthusiasm. From our perspective, we saw only good things coming from it for our clients: They received more property information at an ever-increasing speed and were able to make more informed decisions. That brought good things for us: We sold a lot of homes and received many awards for our sales performance.

But, interestingly enough, we soon saw a dark undertow to this profitable surge. While our transaction count was increasing, while the awards and the accolades were piling up....our referral business was declining and our repeat business lagged. Our real estate "family" of clients wasn't experiencing the growth it should have been. It didn't really seem to make much sense, because the customer satisfaction ratings that we received from the initial transactions we handled were high, and, again, our sales were strong. It was impossible to reconcile our ongoing success on the balance sheet with the growing problem of keeping clients in our orbit.

We didn't understand the root of the problem until one day, a very wise business coach made a comment that resonated with our situation: "Being on the transaction treadmill left a lot of business on the table." That statement hit us like a Mack truck; we had become the epitome of the "transaction treadmill." Yes, our clients loved the fact that we quickly found them the property of their dreams. Yes, they were happy about the fact that we aggressively negotiated them a favorable price, as well as the terms and conditions they needed to have in place. And yes, they certainly were fans of how we looked after the home inspections and made sure needed repairs were completed and the closing went smoothly.

But what they *weren't* doing was sharing all these aspects of their great experience with us with their friends and family. This meant we weren't generating the necessary referrals that are crucial to a real estate agent.

After months of introspection, evaluating how we approached our business, and documenting every process to see where we were falling short, we realized why being a "transaction treadmill" was a short-term boon and a long-term problem. We had become a machine, and people don't bond with machines. We handled real estate sales and purchases efficiently, aggressively—and coldly. With the new technology, we had everything in place to handle property transactions at the highest level but nothing in place to build *relationships* with our clients.

This was a huge problem. As every real estate professional can attest, most property transactions are *emotional* in nature. Supposedly, 20 percent of real estate purchases fall apart even after contracts are signed. Statistics show that some fall through for appraisal and financing problems, but the rest don't get completed because either the client lost—or never had—an emotional connection to the home.

Experience bears this out: All agents have been in a situation where they had a client who was convinced they'd found the perfect home on paper...only to walk into another house and immediately and deeply connect on a personal level with it. That second home may have been the complete opposite of the one they *thought* they wanted, but that just didn't matter.

Beyond anecdotal evidence, scientific research further confirmed how important an emotional bond was to a business. A Gallup survey found that, over a one-month period, a customer emotionally connected to a business spent 46 percent more money than one who was happy with the service but *not* emotionally bonded.

The fact is, the heart usually wins out over the head. Feelings will matter more than carefully thought-out plans; it's what makes us human. Now, we had to figure out how to make our *business* human.

PUTTING ON THE RITZ

As we were brainstorming different ideas to put into action, we began to see certain similarities between the real estate and hotel industry. We began to see that we resembled the Marriott hotel chain. We delivered customer value in an efficient manner, just as a Marriott would, but most people wouldn't say they felt very *attached* to a Marriott—or us.

In contrast, there's the Ritz-Carlton group of hotels. Noted for their five-star business, the Ritz-Carlton management likes to say they're in the business of "wowing" their customers. They've won countless national and international awards for their exemplary customer service model. Anyone who has stayed at a Ritz knows and appreciates the personal touch you receive at one of their hotels. They approach each customer interaction as if they're asking themselves, what can I do to improve this customer's experience. And then...they do it!

How could we become the Ritz-Carlton of the real estate industry? How could we balance this kind of customer service and maintain our technical advantage that we painstakingly built over the past 15 years?

The foundation had to come from putting into action the principle of "Customers Before Profit." That meant slowing down the machine and sacrificing a higher transaction count for higher customer retention and satisfaction. This meant not just attending to the machine's health, but also attending to what our clients really wanted from us, which was personal attention and empathy.

Like everything else in life, it's a juggling act—and juggling isn't easy. It causes you to sometimes drop a ball or two. Our transition to making customer service a priority has meant a few missteps on our path to improvement; processes have had to be adjusted and so have some of our personnel decisions, as top-level customer service demands an additional skill set that not everyone has. But it's also brought us to a more positive destination—one where we enjoy a more fulfilling personal relationship with the clients we serve.

PUTTING THE PERSONAL TOUCH INTO ACTION

What have we learned from this retooling of our business? We'd like to share three of the more prominent points we've put into action.

1. Human beats high-tech. If realtors want to remain relevant and build customers for life, they need to not use technology as a crutch—or a hiding place. Our clients may feel the internet gives them more than enough information to make their own real estate decisions, but they don't realize that our day-to-day dealings in the marketplace put us ahead of the online game. We understand where prices really should be rather than what might be posted on a real estate website.

That's why it's important to employ the personal touch—to cement the bond with our clients and let them know how well we'll care for them. For example, many agents don't even bother to write a personal note to a past, current, or even potential client. Instead, they think a generic email will do the trick. They think a quick text is better than actually picking up the phone and having a conversation with a client. Or that a website filled with pages of information takes the place of a one-on-one meeting at the realtor's office.

It's a little passive-aggressive, to tell you the truth, and the question has to be asked: Is this approach in the best interests of the consumer?

As we've noted, we don't think it is. That's why it's important to ask if your current marketing and communication processes help or hinder your client relationships.

2. Emotion is essential. Every realtor, including ourselves obviously, has to remember that a home purchase or sale is an incredibly important and emotional transaction for a client. It's a transaction that affects their ongoing lives in a big way. That's why a realtor has to make sure they're meeting their clients' emotional goals as well as their fact-based goals.

As we discussed earlier, many clients will describe the nuts-and-bolts specifics they want from their next home: what price they want to pay, what kind of layout they want it to have, what size they want it to be, what area of the community they want it to be in, etc. What they may not talk about, if you don't ask, is what this next home represents to them in terms of where they are in their lives.

For example, if your clients are a married couple, are they going to have more kids? Or are they about to be empty-nesters in a few years? Are potential home buyers looking at the property more as an investment or a place where they intend to stay for many years? It's crucial to see how they're looking at their new home, beyond the black-and-white facts, so you can serve their big-picture goals better.

3. Information is not connection. Let's face it: Thanks to the internet, consumers now more than ever have greater access to real estate information. This has caused some in our industry to become lazy when it comes to personal customer service. Most realtors send their current and potential clients to their website to search for homes. They'll also place clients on automated email lists that send prepackaged generic updates and marketing messages. Too often, we wait for them to call or email us about a specific home, instead of being proactive and getting in touch with them to discuss what's available from our perspective.

Can realtors use technology to their advantage to improve the customer experience? There's no question the answer is a resounding yes. Obviously, it's in the client's best interest to be able to view properties online first without having to drive to every potential property on their list.

The problem arises when realtors rely almost exclusively on technology to serve their customers and put them on that transactional treadmill we found ourselves caught up in. According to a survey taken by the National Association of Realtors, 70 percent of people who buy a home say they would work with their agent again. But the truth is that only 10 percent actually do. That means, on some level, our industry is failing our customers.

That failure, however, is an opportunity. If the competition isn't doing something well, *you* can improve your performance in that area and find success. We just have to stop increasing sales by any means necessary and work on the overall customer experience to create lasting relationships that result in repeat business and reliable referral streams.

When a realtor closes a real estate transaction with a client, the relationship shouldn't stop there, not if you want to build a sustainable business that grows exponentially. The personal touch needs to be put back into our industry so we all enjoy better relationships and our clients know they're more than a dollar sign to us. The sooner we all get off the transactional treadmill, the more our clients can realize their true goals, and we can feel good about our jobs, as well as realize a deeper and more fulfilling level of success.

> *"Professional Service and Exceptional Results" isn't just a motto for Carr & Peck Real Estate Experts at Coldwell Banker Residential Brokerage; it's a commitment to giving the very best to each and every client.*

About Emmett and Jason

Emmett Carr

Jason Peck

Thanks to the power of the internet, Emmett Carr and Jason Peck were able to join forces to serve two very different real estate markets—Atlanta and Denver—with a "Ritz Carlton" level of service tailored to a very demanding and discerning luxury home clientele. The pair is known for combining innovative marketing techniques, cutting-edge technology and the emotional connection created when the right buyer sees the right home at the right time. Perhaps that's why, even in the challenging 2011 real estate market, Carr & Peck have been awarded the highest performance awards from Coldwell Banker and Prudential Georgia Real Estate in the representation of their clientele. The team sold a home every two days in 2011, netting their sellers a staggering 3.7 percent more than other agents in the same markets.

Atlanta-based Emmett Carr spent 13 years as a marketing and sales executive in the technology sector, servicing companies including Microsoft, Dell and Apple Computer. This experience working with a discerning Fortune 50 clientele prepared him well for the demands of the luxury real estate field. Today, he's a member of Fine Homes International at Prudential Georgia and Previews International in Denver. Since 2005, he has been certified as a Certified Luxury Home Marketing Specialist, Certified Residential Specialist and a Million Dollar Guild Member. Emmett is a member of the National Association of Expert Advisors and has been certified by both Prudential Fine Homes and Coldwell Banker Previews for exemplary performance in both the Denver and Atlanta markets. He has received numerous accolades and awards, including Regional Rookie of the Year honors, Triple and Double Gold Circle Performance Awards as well as International Diamond Society Performance Award for the last three years, a designation for outstanding performance in the representation of his clientele.

In his spare time, he volunteers with various charitable organizations and religious groups and serves as board member for the Chauncey Davis Foundation, focusing on early education to combat diabetes.

Denver-based Jason Peck is a customer service specialist—a skill he honed working in the restaurant industry. Today, he and his team are committed to providing a unique real estate experience that places the customer's best interest and goals first and foremost. Jason has served on the board of directors for the Denver Metro Association of Realtors since 2010 and is also a member of CAR, NAR, NAHREP and the NAEA.

He has been certified as a Previews Marketing Specialist and certified Real Estate Expert Advisor with the National Association of Real Estate Experts; he and his team are certified by Coldwell Banker Previews and Prudential Fine Homes. He has also been nationally recognized and won numerous local and national awards as a managing broker for Coldwell Banker.

Beyond real estate, Jason is a philanthropist and dedicates his time to volunteering with various charitable organizations to give back to the community he calls home.

CHAPTER 38

The Value of Using a Realtor:
Helping Clients When They Need It Most

By Kendall Haney

Looking for a realtor can be challenging in some cases, especially if you haven't bought or sold a home in several years. Referrals are always a great source when looking to find someone to help you with your real estate needs, but one thing you should always look for is a realtor who brings value to the task. With more than 25 years in the business, I've recognized that buyers and sellers are really looking for a realtor to take the lead and take care of their needs. Of course, everyone has different needs at different times in their life, but as a realtor we must listen to what our clients' needs are at that moment, and then act.

Over the years, I've been able to become in-tune with my clients' needs. I not only give them advice based on research and their current situation, but I also share the research with them so they can see what I'm talking about. By learning about each of my clients and knowing what they need, I'm able to earn their complete trust. By knowing and understanding the needs of two of my recent clients, I was able to give them the best advice possible and help them when they needed it most, which is the real value of having a realtor.

SELLING AND BUYING A HOME

Getting Ready to Sell
I recently worked with a single mother of 2-year-old twins. I listed her home for sale, and since her home needed a little TLC, I walked through

315

each room and shared with her things she could do to help her show its best assets. Within a few days, she had a friend come over and stage her home. Wow! She was amazed at the difference.

In most cases when I list a home I recommend that the seller have the home inspected by a qualified inspector prior to putting it on the market. At first she didn't understand why she should have the inspection when it's usually the buyer's responsibility. She also stressed to me that she had very little free time working full time, and when she's at home, she's even busier with her twins. I explained to her that if we waited until we had a contract, the buyer would be responsible for the home inspection, but we would have to negotiate repairs. Having the inspection done early would put a lot less stress on her already busy life, because she would be able to have a few items repaired at a time and not feel so pressured to have it all done at once. Plus, having the repairs done on the front-end helps put her in a better position to negotiate a contract with a buyer. The buyer will look at having the inspection already done as a huge plus because the seller has been proactive in getting repairs done. By giving the buyer a copy of the report and a list of all of the completed repairs, the buyer may decide not to have the home re-inspected. I also reassured her that she didn't need to worry because I had a list of reliable contractors that I've used on a regular basis for the past 10 to 20 years, which I could arrange to have all the work done for her at a reasonable price.

We received a contract on the house, and in this case, the buyer chose to have another inspection done. The report only turned up three minor repairs. This is when the seller really saw the value of having the inspection prior to putting her home on the market. She didn't have to stress out with getting tons of repairs done at the last minute and was able to focus on buying her new home.

Staging her home properly and making the repairs early put her home at the top of the list with potential buyers. She listened to everything I recommended and trusted that I was correct. Because of this, we were able to sell her home in less time than the average for the neighborhood and for more money.

Finding the Perfect Home

As we started searching for her new home, we not only found that none of them had been preinspected but that most didn't show well. Eventually, we were able to narrow down the search and found one in the right neighborhood, in the school district she wanted to live in. Before we put the offer in I researched all the sales in that neighborhood to compare prices, location, condition, days on market, square footage, etc. We discovered that the home was overpriced. It was so overpriced that I called the listing agent to express the buyer's interest, but I told the agent I was having a problem finding any homes that recently sold that would support the listing price, not to mention that the roof needed to be replaced. The listing agent was unable to send me any sales to help support the listing price but encouraged us to make an offer anyway.

Before we made an offer, I contacted a roofer I had used before to give us a bid on how much a new roof would cost. This would help put us in a better position to negotiate. Since this home hadn't been preinspected, we weren't sure what else we were going to find during the home inspection. At least we could make an offer based on our findings about the inadequacy of the price and having a new roof installed.

After a few counters, we were able to come to an agreement. Our next step was the appraisal and inspection. The appraisal came back at the current sales price we agreed to, but we found additional repairs that needed to be completed. Fortunately, we were able to come to an agreement quickly. After the repairs were completed and the new roof was installed, we were able to close, and my buyer could move into her new home. She even liked the color of the roof I picked out for her!

Throughout the process she learned to trust me. At closing she hugged me and told me that she couldn't have done it without me. She was able to see the value of having a professional realtor. By being on top of my game in order to make everything work in her best interest, I was able to guide her in the right direction and stood by her until the end.

It's a great feeling being able to help someone reach their goals and to see the next chapter in their life. So many of my clients are grateful because I helped them in ways they couldn't imagine, and I couldn't ask for anything better.

FIRST-TIME HOME BUYER

Earlier this year, I helped a young couple, who was currently leasing, find the perfect home. They came to me to see if it would be possible for them to purchase their first home. They wanted to buy but were unsure if they were quite ready. I asked them if they would be able to set up a time to meet with me so I could explore some options with them.

During our meeting I asked them many questions and shared with them that they would be able to qualify for a home loan. So I set them up with a mortgage lender to get them preapproved for their mortgage. We were able to get a preapproval letter within a few days, and then we began our search for the perfect home.

It only took a couple weeks to find the perfect home and make an offer. We were able to negotiate with the seller to pay all their closing costs, which meant that they would be able to buy their home with only a small down payment. The home was perfect and in great condition. We had the inspection done and negotiated the repairs with the seller. Within a few weeks we closed, and they were ready to move in.

After we closed they sent me a testimonial that I would like to share:

> *"The whole process from start to finish was amazing. Kendall was always 10 steps ahead of the process and was able to inform us as first-time home buyers on what to look for and what to expect from the whole experience. He certainly knows how to take care of his clients. His staff is amazing, extremely knowledgeable, friendly, and just wonderful to work with as a whole. He was also able to give me numerous contacts, from cleaning services to pest control to insurance agents. Each referral was just as professional and knowledgeable as Kendall himself. Needless to say, I will be using Kendall whenever we decide to sell our new home in the future."*

I truly enjoyed working with this couple, and as I write this chapter, they just called to tell me they're expecting their first child! A new home and a new baby—what a happy life experience. This is what it's all about!

TOP 10 VALUES TO LOOK FOR IN A REALTOR

1. Team: If possible, find a realtor who has a team, or at least a full-time administrator and a buyers' agent. There are, on average, 164 items that need to be done to close on your home. If the realtor has a team of administrators, buyer's agent, closing attorney, home inspector, contractors, insurance agents, etc., you tend to get better quality service.

2. Real estate expert: Find a full-time realtor who knows the real estate market inside and out.

3. Testimonials: Ask for testimonials—most great realtors will provide you with them

4. Contractors: When buying or selling a home, you most likely need to make repairs or improvements. Finding a realtor who has reliable contractors he can recommend is a great added value.

5. Lead generation website: If you're a seller, make sure they have a website in place to generate buyers for your home.

6. Staging: This is such an important step when selling your home, especially if it's vacant. According to the National Association of Realtors survey of 2,000 realtors, staging a home typically provides a 586 percent return on investment.

7. Showing appointment center: Make sure the realtor you choose to sell your home has an online appointment center. This allows you, the seller, to keep track of all showings and feedback on your home.

8. Photos: Make sure your agent takes a lot of photos to place on all the real estate websites. Your agent should list your home on at least 25 real estate websites. Some of these websites will allow more photos than others, and the homes with more photos tend to get more hits.

9. Technology: Make sure your agent is equipped with the latest real estate technology. This helps give your home the most exposure and expedites the real estate transaction immensely.

10. Home warranty: Your agent should be able to provide you with information about a home warranty. As a buyer, this will cover major systems in your home for one year. For a seller, it makes your home more sellable and can possibly save you money if you have to make small repairs.

About Kendall

Kendall Haney has been serving his clients for more than 25 years. He has spent his entire real estate career training to become better at helping his clients in the ever-changing market. To this day, Kendall continues training with his real estate coach. He has earned many real estate designations, including the designation as a Certified Home Selling Advisor—less than 0.5 percent of all realtors have this designation.

Kendall gives back by serving on his local board of realtors. He has served on the board of directors and other various committees throughout his career. He's also involved in various community activities.

Kendall owns his own real estate company and has a team of experts who work with him on a daily basis so he can provide the best possible service. He's always looking for better opportunities to serve his clients to ensure that all of them have a great real estate experience. Because of his continuous endeavor to be the best possible agent, Kendall has created a raving clientele, who support him in many ways. So many of this clients send him referrals, and many are repeat clients.

To learn more about Kendall Haney, go to www.kendallhaney.com or email him at kendall@kendallhaney.com.

CHAPTER 39

Get Real in Real Estate

By Kristy Moore

An elderly woman was meeting with me to sell her home because she wanted to move closer to other family members. She had worked with another real estate agent and received poor advice and her house didn't sell. As we began our conversation, she looked at me with tears welling up in her eyes, lips quivering, and then looked away as if she was ashamed for being so emotional in front of me. I put my hand on her shoulder and moved my head to look into her eyes and said, "It's OK. Whatever it is, you're not alone and I can help. I just have to know if there's anything keeping me from helping you." Her tears intensified, and she became more emotional. This sweet elderly lady who reminded me of my grandmother began to explain to me what had her so upset. Her oldest son was forcing her to pay a large portion of her home equity to him by not allowing her to see her grandson. He said she deserved it since she took his father away from him when she left him, when all she was trying to do was get out of an abusive relationship. She told me all the horrible stories about what his father did to her. She said she never told their father that he couldn't see his kids—he chose to do that on his own. Now, her son was making her pay for her decision.

At this point, all she wanted to do was move to another state to be closer to her sister and her other son who has always treated her well. Now, she felt all alone because her oldest was her only family here. She was having a hard time selling the house and still getting what she needed to buy in the other state with the amount her son wanted from the proceeds from the home sale. Even though he wasn't a party to the title or had any legal claim on the proceeds, she said she wanted to honor the amount he requested to avoid any further problems with him and maybe even see her grandson again.

I've heard stories like this throughout my career. Strong, independent and educated women have told me about their abusive husbands, and decent men have told me about their cheating wives. I've heard everything from both sides of nasty divorces to charming stories about how newlyweds met. Parents have told me about their kids' struggles with cancer, mental illnesses and other diseases as well as their own. Other stories are about the passing of their loved ones and the births of their precious children. When it comes to finances, people have told me all of the smart and stupid decisions they've made as well as the hardships outside their control.

In real estate, I deal with people's hopes as well as their hopelessness, their successes and their failures, the beginning of their lives, as well as the end. Through all this, I've come to realize what people want is someone who really cares and can help them through all the chaos of their lives while maintaining some normalcy.

However, finding someone in this business who's genuine and authentic can sometimes seem like an impossible task. Most people I've met in this business have their business persona, which is separate from their real lives. In a world full of reality shows and social media, where people are always on a public platform, sometimes it's difficult to tell if the person is who they say they are. When someone is posting an update on a social media site, is that really who they are? It's difficult to really get to know people when we are on stage all the time.

People want to know who they're really dealing with. When I ask my clients why they chose to work with me, they almost always say its' because I'm real. Anyone who grew up with me will attest to the fact that I've never been one to hold back what I think. I never had a filter between my brain and my mouth, often causing me to stick my foot in my mouth. However, it has also caused me to have greater success in my business by connecting with people. They know I'm telling them what I think, not saying what I think they want me to say. This builds trust and allows me to have deeper conversations with the people with whom I work, which ultimately allows me to help them more.

I live outside the nation's capital but grew up in a small town. Since I never learned how to be politically correct or diplomatic, it was quite the shock when I started selling real estate outside of Washington, DC. People working in a fast-paced, competitive, political field operate a little differently than I did. I certainly didn't grow up privileged, as my parents were on welfare when I was a child. They were just doing what they had to do in order to survive. My parents weren't trying to climb a corporate ladder, attend dinner parties with owners of companies, or network their way into politics. They were just two folks from an even smaller town who worked as hard as they could to provide for their kids and do what's right. From what I could tell, what's right isn't always what's done in any kind of political atmosphere. Saying what you're actually thinking is almost detrimental for people who have to operate in that environment. When you grow up in a large Irish Catholic family like I did, you learn how to speak your mind very quickly if you ever want to be heard.

When I first moved to Washington, DC, I tried to be politically correct and diplomatic. I would hold my tongue and not say what I wanted to, since it seemed to be proper etiquette. In time, what I noticed is that you can only pretend to be someone else for so long. Eventually, I would say something spontaneous and look at my clients with my eyes wide open as if I was the cat that ate the canary. They would start laughing, realizing I thought I had said something wrong, but they appreciated the candidness. At other times, I would share something personal, even embarrassing, about me, and people would feel more comfortable sharing more intimate details of their lives with me.

Even though I'm serious about my business, deep down, I'm still really goofy and appreciate a good laugh. Being myself has helped people loosen up around me and realize I'm just a human being, not some robo-businessperson. Realizing I could be myself and didn't have to live up to the idea of what a successful person is allowed me to double my business in one year. Marketers spend millions of dollars a year showing consumers how their products are different from the competitors. If you're the face of your business, all you have to do is be who you are—and you're automatically differentiating yourself. You're not like everyone else running around, trying to be the big shot. People pick up on authenticity and lack thereof. You're unique, so be you, be authentic, and your business will thank you.

Following are five steps to authenticating your business:

STEP #1: KNOW WHO YOU ARE

It's really easy for us to get caught up in what other people want us to be and have a persona for other people. When I first got into sales, I thought it was all about being the high-rolling, fast-talking and slick salesperson. I thought this was who I was supposed to be. However, the more I was true to my core values, the more people trusted me. They knew I was being true to who I am and thus being honest with them. Get to know what your core values are. What do you stand for? Once you know your core values and operate from those principals, the more purposeful your life and your relationships will be with those whom you do business.

Once you know your core values and who you are, you can open up to people because you're comfortable in your own skin. When I was at ease with sharing my personal stories and the hard times I've endured, people were more open with me, sharing their goals and difficulties they were experiencing. We've all experienced challenges in our lives. The more we share our experiences, the more we connect with other people. Sharing these experiences is something people will never forget, and you'll change each other's lives in the process.

STEP #2: REALIZE YOUR PAST
DOESN'T EQUAL YOUR FUTURE

When I looked back on my childhood, I realized how difficult it was for my parents to provide the basic necessities in life. I felt like I was supposed live the same lifestyle as well. Sometimes, I felt guilty for being successful because I'd say to myself, "I don't deserve it" or "Why is this happening to me?" I once had a mentor of mine tell me, "You're not a poor girl anymore. You work hard. It's OK to want and have more." I never forget this. He knew my mindset of thinking I was poor was keeping me from being successful inside and outside myself. Just because I grew up in a household that had a hard time making ends meet didn't mean I had to have a difficult financial life as well. Plenty of stories exist of people coming from unbelievable poverty, only to make their wildest dreams come true. Instead of thinking, "Why them?" I started thinking, "Why not me?"

Realizing I had the choice to have control over certain aspects of my life and be who I wanted to be made an enormous impact on my future. If you know who you are and you know where you want to go, you start to live your own truth. Don't focus on the past; you've lived it and it's gone. However, make decisions today that will affect your future. Knowing this can empower you and your clientele to make good choices. If they're experiencing hardship, and you've been there and back, you know there's a better road for them ahead if they make good decisions.

STEP #3: GET HELP IF NEEDED

We all have issues—some of us have more than others—because we're all human beings. We can't expect our family and friends to solve all our problems for us. I would argue most of us need help processing our feelings. We all have baggage from our past. A skilled, trained professional can help to resolve the problems holding you back and can be a very effective path to moving forward. One of the most life-changing decisions I made was going to therapy. I know people think it means you're weak, sick or even a loser if you go to therapy, because I was one of those people. However, I hit a breaking point where my anxiety was controlling my life. I would literally hide in my closet when I was having anxiety attacks so my husband wouldn't see me being "weak."

I determined at this point it was time to get over some traumatic events in my life I pretended never happened. I was the type of person who buried my emotions instead of dealing with them. I also disconnected from other people because it was a defense mechanism to not get hurt. It took me over a decade to get to this point, and it took only months of therapy to help me cope with my past and let people into my life. I feel like this was the single biggest breakthrough in accepting me and connecting with others on a different level. Just changing my perspective on the events in my life that hurt me the most, I was able to become a better person. Finally, not being afraid of who I was or anything that happened in my life helped me be more open and authentic with people and more empathetic toward what they were going through. As humans, we all have issues, so I shouldn't judge people on how they deal with their own.

STEP #4: COME FROM A PLACE OF UNDERSTANDING AND ACCEPTANCE, NOT JUDGMENT

Knowing who you are, processing and dealing with difficulties from your past, and working on yourself constantly isn't easy. Going through those steps will help you better understand yourself, which will help you understand others. You'll realize not everyone processes emotions the same. Some people act irrationally or even callously when they're stressed out while others would rather hide in a bathroom. Understanding what people are going through and why they're acting a certain way can help you better help them.

Understanding who you are in all your glory and darkness and accepting yourself will help you accept other people for who they are. Let other people be who they are whether you agree with them or not. We all have differences in opinions, life experiences, challenges and privileges, which makes life exciting. Accepting people for who they are and not trying to change them is to love them. If you're accepting of them, they'll be more accepting of you.

I had a lot of difficulty dealing with people not doing or saying things the way I thought they should. This caused me a lot of stress because I couldn't understand *why* they would do such a thing! No one likes to be told how to live or they're wrong, so why even go there? Once I realized people are who they are and accepted them as such, my business grew.

STEP #5: BE ACCOUNTABLE TO YOUR ACTIONS

People don't want to hear excuses. If you make a mistake, own up to it. Fix the mistake and apologize for the error, and don't be embarrassed by it. Even if one of the other people involved in the transaction has made a mistake, let the client know it will be taken care of, even if by you. Taking responsibility for your actions will earn you the respect of your clients and staff as well as win you referral business for being a person of your word. You're only as good as your reputation. Do you want to be known as the person who owns up to their mistakes and makes it right, or the one who only makes excuses?

About Kristy

Kristy Lynam Moore started her real estate career after transferring to Michigan for a job in the lending business. Soon after moving, the company declared bankruptcy during a major recession. Despite this adversity and knowing few people in one of the worst markets in the country, she excelled in the new area. She was awarded the Rookie of the Year Award and went on to be a President's Club Member and one of the top agents in the country within one year. Since then, she was relocated with her husband to the suburbs in Northern Virgina, outside Washington, DC. While not knowing anyone at first, she was able to build her business again from the ground up and has been a Multi-Million Dollar Sales Club member as a top producer every year since. As of 2011, she is in the top 1 percent of all agents for Keller Williams in her region. In addition to her sales production, she has written how-to booklets for agents on marketing effectively on the internet. These books have been used by hundreds of other agents nationwide as a premier guide on generating leads for free online.

CHAPTER 40

Relocation or Dislocation?
An Exciting Adventure or a Painful Memory!

By Lucretia Pinnock

A few years ago, while on a ladder painting a room, I stepped wrong and dislocated my kneecap. I was in a mess, and I needed the services of a physician. In many ways, moving or relocating your home to a new home can also be very painful and traumatic. However, with the help of the right professional with the right skill set, the details of the move can be made more manageable and positive.

As an Army wife, I had moved more than a dozen times when we were assigned to Ft. Bragg, North Carolina. As it appeared that we were calling North Carolina home, I began thinking of a career, and real estate held an interest for me. I felt that moving across the country as well as internationally had somewhat prepared me to help people in similar situations. Thus in 1984, I set out to build a career in real estate

Since obtaining my realtor license in 1984, relocation and referrals have been at the center of my business. In fact, when I opened my own company, it was named Pinnock Real Estate & Relocation Services Inc. to emphasize that aspect of my services and expertise. Though that's a long name for a little company, it helped to establish the vision and scope of my business.

In October 2011, Fannie Mae's national housing survey found that the top four reasons people buy a home are:

1. To find a good place to raise and provide quality education for their children.

2. To have a physical structure where they and their family feel safe.

3. To provide more space for their family.

4. To gain control over what they can do with their living space, like renovations and updates.

People look for a new home for many reasons, and the search for the new home is made more stressful when it involves a job transfer, military move, or even the decision to retire to a new area. Who, what, when, where, why, and how are the words that come to mind as I begin to work with people "on the move."

My real estate career has been a labor of love and hard work combined. My childhood roots were in Oklahoma, where many generations of my family relied on their strong wills and determination to survive and thrive in very difficult situations. My mother would often say, "When you bite off more than you can chew, you just keep on chewing." As I've helped buyers and sellers achieve their goals with their real estate investments and built my real estate company, those words have often been an encouragement to persevere, work hard and never give up.

With relocation being a major focus of my career, relocation companies, such as the Employees Relocation Council, have been a source of business. Referrals from past and present clients as well as realtors in other areas have been important to my business. Knowing why people want to move to my area specifically is also important, of course. People relocate to our area for a variety of reasons, from climate and hobbies to jobs in the military and other industries. Pinehurst and Southern Pines, North Carolina, have long been an area that appeals to people wanting to retire to the "Sunny South." Many yearn for the climate where they can play golf or ride horses every day! We're also located next to Ft. Bragg, so our market attracts many military personnel, active duty and retired, as well as government contractors. Other people move to the area due to corporate moves in industry, medicine or business.

Nothing makes my day any brighter than to receive a note or phone call from a past client or friend who has a friend moving to our area. Their trust is so important, and I always promise to take great care of them. So I make keeping in touch with people a priority. At first my database was contained entirely on the pages of a yellow legal pad. Now I use Top Producer software to maintain contact information for my past and present clients as well as the people in my sphere of influence. Using the data, I mail newsletters, handwritten notes, calendars and other items to key contacts throughout the year.

I give credit to Brian Buffini who stresses the awesome power in personal notes. Whether it's a thank you note, congratulatory note or note of sympathy, handwritten notes carry with them a personal connection and concern to the recipient. Personal notes have not only helped my business grow, but they've kept me personally connected to people who've touched my life.

I also have great success with special events, client parties and movie nights, for example. These events are fun for everyone, especially when they have unexpected "touches" that are meaningful to my clients. At one client barbecue, for example, I arranged for Air Force Combat Controller Joel Juett, an expert skydiver, to surprise everyone by parachuting into the middle of the festivities. Though my heart began to pound for fear something awful would happen to him, his perfect landing earned him—and me—the claps, cheers and memories of my guests. And now Joel is a part of my real estate team!

I've also rented the local movie theatre and invited clients, friends, colleagues and prospects to join me to see special movies. We provide popcorn, soft drinks, candy and door prizes. Of course, these events are free to our guests. It's so much fun to chat with people as they arrive. It's a relaxing evening. The hardest part of the movie night is choosing an appropriate and fun movie. That in itself has been a fun exercise in team building.

Another critically important area I feel is important to success is expertise and knowledge. Professional knowledge and ongoing education are critical parts of being successful and effective in the real estate business. In fact, it's essential. For example, in January 2011, North Carolina made a significant and important change to our offer-to-purchase contract. Anticipating lots of issues with this new "due diligence" portion of the contract and wanting to ensure I could give my clients top advice and service, I attended three continuing education classes, each with a different instructor. It was important to me to make sure that my understanding was solid. With that preparation, I was ready to use the new contract. As Carla Cross, another real estate expert that I admire says, "Competency builds confidence!"

The importance of personal skill-building can't be underestimated. Self-education is an important key to success. There are great coaches, educators and trainers in the real estate business. Brian Buffini, Rick DeLuca, Barbara Corcoran, Danielle Kennedy, Carla Cross, Howard Britton, and, most recently, Michael Reese and Jay Kinder have been powerful influences in my business. It's important to attend professional seminars and conferences. The speakers and trainers provide up-to-date information, and networking with other attendees is a valuable connection as well.

Reading and studying businesses outside of the real estate industry has also helped me grow my business. The internet has become such a powerful part of real estate, and as I searched the internet for a new car, I saw firsthand how automotive manufacturers used the internet. They were quick, consistent, and answered my questions in detail. The car dealers followed up quickly and consistently when I visited their websites. I observed the customer service policies of the dealership, and this inspired me to seek ways to increase the quality of our company service and communications. I've applied these same principles with our lead-generation websites by stressing quick calls and continuous communication. Technology is a very real and important part of our business.

Many industries use surveys to evaluate their service or performance. As a company we send surveys to buyers and sellers at the conclusion of a transaction. When we started, our return rate was nothing spectacular, but while I was at a National Association of Realtors meeting, I noticed a survey at a restaurant. We adapted that survey, and it has made a significant difference in our rate of return. We send a thank you note, the survey, a postage-paid envelope and a gift to our clients at the conclusion of the transaction. This mailing is the first of our continual efforts to stay in touch with each client.

HERE IS OUR SURVEY:

HOW DID WE DO?

Please relate to us your overall real estate experience by completing the little face below. It can be as simple as a smile, or as detailed as you like. We hope that it won't be a frown! If you would like to tell us more, we've given you space for that below.

The Good Stuff

The Bad Stuff

Do we have your permission to use your name and/or comments in our advertising? Yes ❏ No ❏

Recently, a special survey was returned. The client added a big smile, bright eyes, a nose and curly hair to the little round "blank" face. Their comments made my day and are a treasure to me: "Twenty years ago, Lucretia was recommended to us by a family friend who was a realtor in the town we were from. Lucretia showed us many homes in the Pinehurst, Southern Pines and Whispering Pines areas. After deciding on a home in Whispering Pines, Lucretia continued to help us with the negotiations and purchase of our new home. Twenty years later, we again chose Lucretia to help us sell our home. Lucretia is still the same professional, honest and hard working person that we met 20 years ago. Our home sold in 8 weeks." —*Ron and Judy McLaurin*

Inspiration for ways to improve our business and services comes many sources. Mark Sanborn's book *The Fred Factor: How Passion in Your Work and Life Can Turn the Ordinary Into the Extraordinary* is about a postman who made everyone on his mail route not only feel special but be special. Making others feel and be important makes real estate more fun and rewarding. Fred paid attention to the details of the lives of people on his route and made a positive impact on them. That has been a goal and challenge for me as I interact with my buyers and sellers. I would recommend this book to everyone, by the way, regardless of their career path.

Going that extra mile with cooperating agents as well as buyers and sellers adds an extra measure of joy into the transaction for all concerned as well. Along those lines, I recently learned a short, succinct variation on the golden rule: "Do what you can, when you can, because you can!" That expression, attributed to Caroline Harsant Whitley as she was fighting for her life with terminal brain cancer, is a great illustration of when and how we can all make life a little better for others, including our clients.

A few months ago, after the excitement of closing on their new home, my buyer client headed to their new property. Upon arrival on a Friday night at about 5:15, they discovered they had no electrical power, and it was the first cold fall night. A phone call to the electric company revealed that workers had mistakenly disconnected the electrical power rather than connecting it. The power company said it wouldn't be able to connect the power until Monday. It was going to be a cold weekend in a home filled with boxes! Learning from Caroline's message, I wanted to do something to help. Help came in the form of a generator that I was able to buy along with an extension cord and gasoline. This was literally a "housewarming" gift for this family. With some strategy from the homeowner, the generator powered a lamp, a small heater, microwave and computer. While waiting for the "real electrical power," the generator helped turn the situation into a bit of an adventure instead of a truly miserable weekend.

Not only is this a great business, but I also believe that real estate is a one of the best investments available. My real estate business has paid bills, provided a living, and helped educate my daughters. However, my personal investment in real estate has helped build my estate and provide a retirement plan. In one of the seminar's I attended with Brian Buffini, I came away with the decision to buy rental property. I now own my office building, two rental houses, and, of course, my personal home. I've sold three houses, and with the profits, now own my office building free and clear. The knowledge of the market is a perk of working in the real estate business. We work hard to find good deals for others, and we can find good deals for ourselves as well.

Participation in community events and taking on leadership roles in organizations that are important to us provide many widespread benefits. The experience and exposure build confidence and cement your alignment with service. Further, as we're successful in our real estate businesses, we have the ability to share our financial gain with people who need our support. Opportunities for serving our communities are vast. Through service to such organizations as the local chapter of the American Red Cross, I've made lifelong friends and given support to people in need locally and nationally. Our area's "Backpack Pals," which provides needy schoolchildren with a weekend's worth of meals packed in a nondescript backpack, has been another group that touched my heart. Working together as a team to make comfort kits or deliver food has helped to build closeness in our work family.

From the time I began my career, I decided that if I did the right things, the bottom line would take care of itself. That philosophy remains my mantra. Living the golden rule as stated in the Realtor Code of Ethics has always been important. Treating cooperating agents respectfully, fairly and honestly while working through the difficulties of our transactions pays great dividends.

I'm passionate and patriotic about the opportunity of home ownership that we enjoy in the United States. The ownership of private property is a fundamental guarantee of the Constitution and is at the heart of our system of democracy. I've lived in other countries where only the very wealthy owned real estate. In America, ordinary people can own their own home! I'm proud to work in this industry and to be a realtor.

It has been an honor for me to share some of my history and philosophy regarding my career. I love real estate and the business of real estate. Even though the market has been bruised and battered for the last few years, I still believe it's a great investment. Though there are other investment vehicles, such as gold, silver, stocks and bonds, but none will provide safety, shelter and much, much more!

About Lucretia

Lucretia Pinnock believes in the value of real estate and is passionate about helping her clients. Lucretia was born in western Oklahoma, and her work ethic was taught by the example of the generations of a hard-working family whose family history includes the pioneers who settled Oklahoma in the days of the land rush and then survived the Dust Bowl of the 1930s. Her family history also included records showing that her ancestors in Wake County, North Carolina, were some of the official witnesses for land sales. It seems that real estate was in her blood!

After moving to the beautiful Pinehurst and Southern Pines areas of North Carolina as an Army wife, Lucretia began her real estate career in 1984. Having moved her family dozens of times across the country as well as internationally, Lucretia had lived the relocation process and wanted to make the way smoother for others. Thus began her almost 30 years of serving, providing resources, and being a housing "matchmaker" for hundreds of people.

Real estate education and professionalism are top priorities for Lucretia. She was president of her local realtor association as well as Realtor of the Year in 2003. She is currently listed on Barbara Corcoran's International Real Estate Network, Inner Circle; is an Endorsed Local Provider for Dave Ramsey; and has earned several real estate designations, such as ABR, CDPE and CIAS.

Lucretia is a member of the Pinehurst Southern Pines Association of Realtors, the Fayetteville Association of Realtors and the National Association Realtors. She's the owner/president of Pinnock Real Estate & Relocation Services Inc., as well as the mother of three daughters, Marci Houseman, Melodi Knudson and Morgen Reynolds; and grandmother to Carina, Lindsey, Ben and Luke Houseman; Caroline Knudson; and Isaac, Lucretia (Lucy) and Emma Reynolds.

CHAPTER 41

The Core:
At the Heart of Success Is a Personal and Professional Value System

By Matthew Sipera

"Your beliefs become your thoughts. Your thoughts become your words. Your words become your actions. Your actions become your habits. Your habits become your values. Your values become your destiny."~Mahatma Gandhi

Mahatma Gandhi is arguably one of the greatest political and spiritual strategists of his generation. Gandhi seems to have understood the principle that living out your values builds a foundation for a successful destiny. This principle is not found only in philanthropic areas. Many top producers in real estate also seem to have discovered it. As they've applied their *core values* in their businesses, in turn those values help pave for them a successful *professional* destiny.

Many people believe that the common thread in successful organizations or individuals is their relentless pursuit of money or financial success. Obviously, financial success is a great motivator. However, if you observe top producers, such as real estate mogul Donald Trump, visionary Steve Jobs, or an industry leader such as Bill Gates, you'll see that one of their common keys to success is having a well-defined personal and professional *core value system.*

Knowing your *core values* is not just helpful in business; it's an important (seemingly invisible) part of our lives. In talking with people about what's important to them when choosing a political candidate, certain issues inevitably surface. There's a checklist of things they hope to find. However, when it comes time to actually cast that vote, people seem to choose the person who holds similar values. We hope the candidate will truly represent us in what we think and believe is important.

Similarly, people may go through a filtering process when choosing a husband or a wife. Many people have a checklist or wish list of expectations for a future spouse. A friend of mine once shared how important values were for her when it came to "decision time." She'd been dating a great guy for almost a year but had witnessed so many unsuccessful marriages. She wrestled with the fear of becoming another divorce statistic. So during that unexpected moment, when the ring was out of the box and "the question" floated in the air, there was a long pause. She was able to overcome her fear and take the risk after remembering they both held the same moral and ethical values. She believed that their shared values would help them work out any future kinks they would encounter.

Sixteen years later, they're leaning on those values and trying to pass them on to their son.

During my high school and university years, soccer was a key component in how I developed my own personal core values. As a high school soccer player, my team was ranked in the top five in the nation. Soccer provided me with the great opportunity to travel abroad and to ultimately pave the way to a college degree. Soccer taught me many values such as the power of mentorship, never giving up and accountability. Soccer also taught me that a diverse team of players from different cultural backgrounds can all come to the field with a single goal—and come home winners! These values, among others, have become the foundation of my real estate business.

The real estate profession plays an important part in providing one of people's most basic needs: shelter and a place to call home. People invest so much of their labor and income into their homes and businesses, both for themselves and their families. This being true, it is vitally important to take all the necessary steps to insure the best real estate outcome. One way to best serve your clients is to provide all the information needed so they can make the best choices for their families or businesses. However, it takes time and dedication to become a real estate expert. Many things must be considered, such as lead generation, knowing your market, and understanding the local and state laws and rules governing your area. Nonetheless, there's nothing more important for the real estate expert than creating core values.

Core values are built on your beliefs. You think about and reflect on what you believe. Those thoughts are released as words and ultimately actions—that will either lead to your successful or unsuccessful habits. Your habits (frequent behavior) then shape your future. Those who practice regular exercise will probably shape a healthier future than someone who doesn't. This is why core values are the heart or "core" of your real estate business. They're the pulse from which everything originates. The "core" is the foundation of your business culture, philosophy and the compass that directs all your decision-making and guides your interactions with your staff, vendors and clients. By identifying, living out, and sharing your core values with your clients and colleagues, you can achieve success and still avoid becoming the next Bernie Madoff... or one of his financial casualties.

As I shared in my soccer experience, people can come from different perspectives, yet still agree on the same goal. The following are the core values I hold and find useful in guiding me as a real estate expert.

CHARITY

"We make a living by what we get, but we make
a life by what we give." ~Winston Churchill

Charity is an important value because it creates a positive climate that can be reciprocated. Giving back to your local community is a way to say thank you to all those who support your business. Charity is essential because it lets your clients and local communities know that you're aware that you need them and you're creating yet another environment to meet their needs. There are many great philosophies and creeds that reinforce the practical need for charity in a successful business. The old saying "You reap what you sow" is a long-held traditional value for many people because it illustrates the thought that if you do good to others, then it's more likely good will be returned to you. "Paying it forward" is another phrase made popular by Hollywood, which underlines the need to do good deeds and pass financial reward to others less fortunate. When you give to the community, the community will give back to you.

MENTORSHIP

"Before you are a leader, success is all about growing yourself. When you become a leader, success is all about growing others." ~Jack Welch

Mentorship is an ancient tradition; it can be traced to early Greek mythology. Mentorship provides expertise to less experienced individuals to help them advance their careers, enhance their education, and build their networks and/or net worth. It's important in any thriving real estate business that all team members be committed to continual education and self-improvement. It should be the goal of every real estate expert to educate, advise, and *mentor their clients*. Whether the client is a first-time home buyer or a seasoned real estate investor, the real estate expert's role is to mentor their clients to improve the client's knowledge base and protect their financial interests.

PERSEVERANCE

"Success seems to be largely a matter of hanging on after others have let go." ~William Feather

In a well-established and successful real estate business, failure is not an option. The difference between the real estate expert and an agent is the agent *tries* and the real estate expert *delivers*. The real estate expert must be committed to discipline and excellence in providing outstanding service that *exceeds* the expectations of their clients. When dealing with clients, the real estate expert must be able to perform at an optimum level at all times. Clients aren't interested in your efforts, only in your *results*. In order to be identified as a real estate expert, you must possess a good sense of human nature, humor, and the best knowledge of real estate products and services in your market area.

The real estate expert is expected to find a way (legal and ethical) to make the deal work for his or her clients. This means that every angle must be examined and the ability to think outside the box is a necessity. Surrounding yourself with experienced men and women who are also committed to being the best is also a must for the real estate expert. As one of my mentors stated, you don't have to be the smartest person in the room… if you're sitting next to them.

ACCOUNTABILITY

"Accountability is the foundation of trust."
~Author Unknown

Accountability for the real estate expert has many levels. The first level of accountability is to *oneself*—to be committed to being among the best in your field. The second level of accountability is to be *ethical* in your real estate business practices and show the upmost respect to your clients. The third level of accountability is to be absolutely committed to your core values.

One of the fastest ways to destroy your credibility with your clients is have a lack of personal accountability. Accountability presumes that you first *have an ability* for which to give an account. A person must have a specific set of skills to be accountable or *responsible* for them in a specific industry. For the real estate expert, accountability means possessing the skills necessary to help their clients develop strategies to sell high, buy low, and increase their overall net worth through investing in real estate. Real estate experts also realize they're accountable to have the most current market statistics and analysis in order to provide their clients with the best informed options available. Finally, real estate experts must apply all knowledge ethically to protect their clients' and their own reputations.

Benjamin Franklin was one of America's Founding Fathers who stated: "He that is good for making *excuses* is seldom good for anything else." Accountability must be a *core value,* which means at the end of the day there are two types of realtors: the realtor with excuses and the real estate expert with results. In dealing with your real estate needs, which one would you prefer?

EFFECTIVE COMMUNICATION

"Take advantage of every opportunity to practice your communication skills so that when important occasions arise, you will have the gift, the style, the sharpness, the clarity, and the emotions to affect other people." ~Jim Rohn

Effective communication in real estate may be defined as the ability to use words, media, and directed-behaviors to inspire *trust, rapport and confidence* with your client as the real estate expert. John Marshall, the longest-serving chief justice of the United States, emphasized the flip side to communication: *"To listen well* is as powerful a means of communication and influence *as to talk well."* In order to meet the client's needs, we must listen intently and seek out what's truly wanted and needed. At times we'll need to correctly read between the lines.

Successful communication also encompasses the *effective use of time, follow-through and keeping your word.* It has been my experience that one of the primary reasons that clients continue to do business with me is that when I give my word—I keep it. Clients want to know that the real estate expert has their best interest as the centerpiece of every interaction. This requires the real estate expert to promptly return calls and emails, proactively keeping the clients informed, and respecting the client's time by keeping your appointments as scheduled.

Aaron Goldman, the chief marketing officer at Kenshoo, shares a new twist on the golden rule. He advises to "Communicate unto the other person that which you would want him to communicate unto you, *if your positions were reversed."* What a great place to start for the agent seeking to become a real estate expert.

LOYAL FANS

"Do what you do so well that they will want to see it again and bring their friends." ~Walt Disney

My real estate business is located in a city were there are lots of choices for food, entertainment and other services. One day I found myself in need of a chiropractor. I tried a few and was very dissatisfied with the service and the skill of the chiropractors. A friend, who's a loyal fan of her chiropractor, recommended hers to me. During our conversation, she spoke very highly of the chiropractor's ability and professionalism. What interested me most was when she stated that she would never go to anyone else. My friend is a person who could financially go anywhere she wanted, but it was her *loyalty* that convinced me to see her chiropractor. Today, he is the only chiropractor that I would use or recommend. Now I'm one of his loyal fans.

My chiropractic experience taught me that by being the expert in your profession you can create loyal fans who will be clients who will refer you to other potential clients. Loyal fans are those individuals whom you have proven yourself as the preferred real estate expert. Your loyal fans become your walking and talking referral source. Anyone with a successful real estate business will tell you that referrals from loyal fans are the most cost-effective advertisement with the best conversion rate. It is my commitment to this *core value*—to provide a *quality of service* that will instill this kind of confidence and loyalty in all those I do business with. It is my commitment that my clients' experience in working with me as their real estate expert will persuade them to become loyal fans of my real estate business.

The "core" is essential for any real estate expert who wants to be in a position to give his or her client the ultimate service experience. It's the real estate expert who expects the very best of himself or herself at all times to provide their clients with innovation, technology and individualized personal attention. When the real estate expert sets a foundation of charity, mentorship, perseverance, accountability and effective communication the result is...loyal fans.

About Matthew

Matthew Sipera is a licensed realtor in Georgia and Florida, who has multiple years experience working with sellers, buyers and investors in and around the Atlanta Metro area. Matthew is a Certified Distress Property Expert (CDPE) who has successfully sold and bought more than 100 short sale homes. His core values are respect for his client's needs, good communication and excellent customer service, all of which has made him a successful realtor. Matthew's business and life philosophy is one and the same—to treat people with integrity and respect, and value their time.

Matthew has a master's degree from the University of Central Florida, where he graduated among the top 5 percent of his class. He began to invest in real estate and became a licensed realtor in 2005. Matthew is also an entrepreneur who built a large international distribution company in the mid 1990s. He's a member of the 400 North Board of Realtors and a member of the National Association of Realtors.

For more information about Matthew's services, visit www.ShortSaleGA.com or www Buy-A-Home-In-Georgia.com, or call (770) 778-3026.

CHAPTER 42

The Real Estate Revolution:
Work With a Winning Team

By Mike Grbic

THE TEAM MANIFESTO

Imagine a modern car assembly line. You're putting together a car, piece by piece. Installing the electronics and wiring, doing the paint work, and installing the engine.

Now imagine there's only one worker on that assembly line. He's struggling, out of breath, running from one position to the next in sequence, desperately trying to keep up. He's doing everything himself and being forced to do things he's not even good at.

Ridiculous? Of course, it is. It's ridiculous, inefficient and impractical. Would you want to be the person who buys one of his cars? The welder and painter are typically not the same person—and they shouldn't be.

In virtually every industry you can think of, there's a solid team in place working together—a team that contains various specialists who make sure every step of a process is completed as well as possible. Whether it's a bank, dentist office, factory, or any other kind of business, no one expects one person to be able to handle every single task that has to be accomplished. Even in a restaurant, you wouldn't want to see the dishwasher suddenly cooking your meal or the waiter cleaning the bathrooms.

In the real estate business, however, that kind of "one-man band" has always been the norm. A single real estate agent, with virtually no support staff, is expected to be the expert at photography, staging, marketing, web development, graphic design, contracts, home inspections, mortgages, pest control and on and on. It's just not possible anymore. Some of the most likeable Realtors in the United States are terrible at paperwork and at managing the dozens of details during the contract period.

It's an idea that, more than ever, is almost as ridiculous as that one worker manning an entire assembly line. Buying and selling homes has never been a bigger challenge than right now. When people who want to buy or sell a home rely on a lone agent to cover all the bases, they're putting one of the biggest transactions they'll ever make in their lives at risk.

And why should they?

That's why I say the traditional real estate business model is essentially dead—or at least should be. The same team concept that's applied to every other major industry in this country should be the norm with our business. We've done it with our Wichita real estate operation, and, as a result, our clients enjoy more service, more marketing, more value, and more security in their real estate transactions.

It's the ultimate win-win for them—and for us.

WHY A REAL ESTATE TEAM?

It's 6 p.m. on a Friday evening. A homeowner who's ready to sell decides to call our offices. Since it's after 5 and the start of the weekend, they expect to just leave a voicemail. Instead, a real live human being answers our phones and schedules an appointment. Myself or one of our highly experienced listing agents meets with them right away. Monday morning at 10 a.m. our staff photographer is at the home to do the photography and virtual tours. He uses high-end photography equipment, no less. By Monday night the listing is already on our website, complete with photos and virtual tours, fliers printed, and our full 87-point marketing plan is in full effect.

The client is ecstatic and blown away by the speed and efficiency of our team. If she'd contacted a real estate agent that worked as a solo act, she probably would have gotten a voicemail…and waited and waited. She certainly wouldn't have gotten her listing up and marketing done for many days.

But we do it every day, because we work as a team.

Our real estate office of 25 professionals expertly serve our clients each and every day—all specialists at what they do. Like many other top teams in the country, our team includes listing coordinators, buyer agents, listing agents, transaction managers, marketing coordinators, graphic designers, photographers, web designers and so forth. Matched to their job by personality profile, skills, interests and experience, they each know their individual jobs and they each do them extremely well.

Putting this kind of team in place just makes sense. Instead of one person taking pictures of properties, managing marketing, taking care of necessary paperwork and, oh yeah, actually providing friendly, personal service to clients in their spare time, a group of highly skilled and experienced pros are able to do things faster and better. Each are handling hundreds of transactions a year, instead of the average agent's seven to eight homes a year.

Why has real estate traditionally been a one-person job? I believe it all springs from the fact that it's a 100 percent commission-based occupation. Creating and employing a real estate team incurs a considerable amount of overhead, which is a high-risk situation for a 100 percent commission industry. No real estate brokerages and few agents are willing to risk that level of expense.

The little-known fact is that the traditional real estate company does zilch for agents. They don't provide leads or clients, they don't provide any marketing for the agents or for their listings, they usually don't even provide office space unless the agent pays rent. Photocopies? That's extra. All marketing expenses are the responsibility of the real estate agent, and because the real estate company isn't paying for it, they can't require a minimum level of marketing or service of their agents. Because of this, clients even using the same company, often have a very different experience.

It's relatively easy to become a real estate agent. In Kansas, you can become a real estate agent in just under two weeks and for less than $1,000. Once licensed, most real estate companies will immediately take you on because they have nothing to lose. If you sell something, great; if you don't, that's fine too. There's no investment in the agent or their client, and, therefore, not much benefit to the consumer. It's a low-risk, high-recruitment business model and runs completely contrary to the team concept. The traditional real estate model offers little team-work and no continuity.

ADVANTAGES OF THE TEAM APPROACH

The services delivered by a real estate team far surpass what a solo agent can deliver in a number of important ways. We see it every day for ourselves, and we're grateful we can perform at such a high level for our clients.

Here are just a few of the advantages a seasoned real estate team can provide:

- *More time for the agent to focus on you:* Instead of a single agent multitasking his or her way toward exhaustion, a real estate team has specialized support staff devoted to doing paperwork, sched-uling appointments, marketing listings, and every other step of the process. Consider the amount of time the average agent has to spend just finding clients to work with, much less attempting to give some level of service to them. Agents on our team are incredibly grateful for that kind of team support, because they have more time to personally devote to their clients and their real estate business, and our clients appreciate that.

- *An awesome marketing machine:* If you want to understand why real estate has radically changed in the past 15 or so years, look no further than your web browser. In 1995, less than 2 percent of people searched for real estate on the internet—today, that figure is at 93 percent and climbing.

  Internet exposure now isn't just important, it's critical, and the more places your listing is featured, the better off you are. Be-cause we handle more than 365 real estate transactions a year, we have a solid marketing machine in place with a generous advertising budget. The more homes a team sells, the more they can promote their clients' properties. Because large teams are ne-gotiating advertising for hundreds of properties, we have greater leverage and can get better pricing. This allows us to provide even greater levels of marketing.

Our marketing machine first kicks into gear with our professional photographer, taking the best possible photos of a home. There are a few real estate agents still taking photos of their clients' homes on their smartphones, and occasionally from sitting in their car, believe it or not! But we employ a pro who knows how to properly capture the most attractive pictures, as well as another who knows how to stage a home to the best effect for those photos. We know that, if the average internet user doesn't see pictures that capture his or her attention, that person isn't going to bother to come look at the home. Presentation is everything.

Next, the homes have to be placed on websites where the maximum number of people can see them. Those sites have to be researched to see which gets the most traffic and, therefore, are the most powerful for potential sales. Teams have the budgets to upgrade to more "enhanced" listings (listings that get more space on the site and feature more photos, for example) on the most popular sites you want to be featured on. If someone is relocating from Seattle to Wichita, they're going to be looking on a national real estate site like Zillow.com, Realtor.com, Trulia. com, Homegain.com and a host of others; not necessarily just a local site. You want them to be able to see *your* listing. If no one knows your home is for sale, they can't buy it.

Sadly, most agents know absolutely nothing about online marketing. How can they? They're too busy trying to sell houses. Even seasoned agents, know very little. Successful teams can provide the best of both worlds: experienced, customer service-minded agents, as well as computer-savvy pros who know the online marketing game. Teams can do much more for their clients than a solo agent, who might be thinking twice about how much he or she wants to spend to sell your house. Remember, the average agent only sells seven to eight homes a year!

You see, a team isn't a group of agents getting together to share office space, each responsible for generating and servicing their own clients. The team model we speak of is a real business, not a job. The marketing done by the team provides clients to be expertly served by its members.

- *Faster and more efficient service:* Even when an agent is unavailable at a meeting or out on an appointment, there's always someone in our office who can answer a quick question or help with an urgent situation. You don't have to risk not hearing back from someone for hours or days at a time as you might with a solo agent. Solo agents are often too busy trying to "do it all." Like many top teams, we guarantee that if you call our offices between 8 a.m. and 9 p.m., seven days a week, you'll talk to a real person and not to a voicemail system.

Most important, if you're selling a home, a real estate team like ours is going to be much more responsive to potential buyers. Teams often have agents available at all times to answer incoming calls during their "phone duty." Buyers can get frustrated and move on to another property and another agent. Our society is now geared for fast responses and, when they don't happen, we move on. You don't want an interested buyer to move on from *your* property, and we make sure that doesn't happen. Teams have the people in place to schedule appointments and show homes at all times, no voicemail.

- *A specialist for every job:* Imagine how well a football team would play if every player regularly rotated into every single position at random. I don't believe you'd see that squad in the Super Bowl, or anywhere else for that matter, because a team just can't work that way. Well, a solo real estate agent has to try to be a team of one, playing every position, and, more and more, that approach just doesn't work.

A properly run real estate team, however, puts the best possible person in place for each stage of your real estate transaction. Every one is a specialist who knows their specific job, just as a running back, a safety, a quarterback and a guard knows theirs. That brings a client a higher level of service and more effective results.

- *More buyers for your home:* Fact: Most buyers don't purchase the home they call on. Because we're a team with a large number of homes for sale and handle a lot of transactions, we're able to cross-sell our listings. We share information on our other properties and steer "hot leads" to team listings. This kind of "internal marketing" means more showings for your home and more prospects, who are ready to buy.

- *The ultimate combination of experience and expertise:* The solo real estate agent may have been in business for six years or six months. He or she may be selling one home a year, or 20. (Even the newer agents on our team sell more than 25 homes a year.) Because teams handle many hundreds of transactions a year, there aren't many real estate problems we haven't faced and solved before. The collective knowledge and experience is a tremendous asset. We know where the price points are in the market, how to get you top dollar if you're selling, and how to negotiate the best deals if you're buying. If one of us doesn't know something, it's a lock that another one of us does and is happy to share the information. Because teams do more transactions than agents and share their experiences, our skill levels are extremely high—and our clients benefit from those skills every day.

When you put a real estate team to work for you, you've got a collection of dedicated professionals determined to give their very best at every single stage of your buying or selling experience. One person just can't do the job anymore, especially in a real estate market where you need to stack the deck in your favor. How about a full house?

When you're ready to take on your next real estate transaction, I urge you to work with a realtor who has embraced the team concept. I guarantee you'll see the difference where it counts—in your bank account.

Now more than ever, real estate truly is a team sport! Game on!

About Mike

Mike Grbic, a realtor, associate broker, team leader, and coach of Mike Grbic Real Estate Experts, Select Homes, has sold well over 2,000 homes in his career. Mike Grbic Real Estate Experts has been recognized as the No. 1 Agent Team in Kansas (2005-Present), and ranked as a Top 50 Team in the United States, ranked by the Wall Street Journal (2006-Present) by units sold.

Mike has been a licensed agent since 1994, but it wasn't until 2002, when Mike studied and implemented the team concept, that the real estate business really took off. Today, Mike spends most of his time selling real estate, coaching agents, and helping the team implement new marketing strategies, systems and technologies. He thrives on staying on the cutting edge and thinking outside the box. "The customer is our only focus. If you ask yourself, what does the customer want and start there .... you can't go wrong."

Mike Grbic Real Estate Experts, Select Homes, is a team of 25 specialists, consisting of both real estate agents and support staff serving the Wichita, Kansas, and surrounding areas. To learn more about how hiring a team can benefit you, contact them. They can be reached at (316) 684-0000 or at www.mikegrbic.com.

CHAPTER 43

Calling the Right Plays In Today's Real Estate Market

By Mark Stock

As a well-traveled NFL football player who played for four professional teams and two of the best football coaches in history—Joe Gibbs and Chuck Knoll—I'm confident in saying that picking the right plays at the right time of the game was easily the difference between winning and losing on most Sundays.

Not surprisingly, I've experienced the same situation as a real estate agent in Northern Virginia over the last 11 years. As the market has changed dramatically, going from fever pitch in the early 2000s to virtually down and out at the end of the decade, we, as real estate agents, have had to dig into our sales "playbooks" to find the right solutions for homes sellers and buyers to accomplish their goals.

At the end of the day, if you can't adapt, think quickly on your feet, and come up with strategies that help you come out on top, you'll get stopped in your tracks in both the NFL and real estate business. And you never want to stand still in the NFL or in the real estate business because that's when you get run over.

Unfortunately, many agents in today's marketplace play it a little too safe and use the same plays over and over again…even when some of those plays don't work. As a result, they, too, have been stopped dead in their tracks.

If you're going to succeed in this real estate market, you really need to have the right play for just about every situation that comes up.

WHAT'S RUNNING YOU OVER?

Much like NFL coaches, we need to minimize the impact of our clients' weaknesses on their and our situations and at the same time look for opportunities to exploit the weaknesses in our opponent—the current real estate and mortgage markets—to get our clients the results they want and need.

Today's home sellers and buyers need agents to be creative, dig deep and find solutions that get them the best possible results no matter what the market environment is at the time. Getting run over really isn't an option if you want to thrive, even survive, in today's market and beyond.

Here are some of the things that run agents over every day in today's real estate market:

- You lose a buyer to a one-year rental because the family's credit got crunched in a recent short sale.
- You have seller who moved to your area for a better job and bigger income, only to find out that they're upside-down on their house and are having a tough time getting it sold.
- You're talking with sellers who are motivated to sell their home because they really want to downsize, but the contraction in the market makes it such that they feel they're "giving away the farm," and they choose not to sell.
- You have buyers who qualified for a mortgage a month ago, but due to an income change or a change in underwriting guidelines, they no longer qualify for a mortgage.

These are all real situations, and they run us and our clients over on a daily basis. The good news is that there's a play you can run to avoid getting knocked down, and it's way better and safer than a Hail Mary.

YOUR PLAY FOR TOUGH SITUATIONS

What I'm about to share is not a new idea, but it's proven, successful and most important, it's beneficial for the seller, buyer and real estate agent...in every market environment.

The play I'm calling a lot lately is the *contract for deed*. Before you turn the page, please keep reading. This solution is as good a one you'll find for the situations I mentioned earlier and others as well. In many cases, it can help the "stuck" seller and the buyer who can't get financing for a year or two. Using it properly could mean the difference between putting a deal together and it crumbling before your eyes.

A contract for deed, also called an *installment land sales contract* or a *land contract*, represents a security agreement between a buyer and a seller where the seller agrees to finance the purchase. In essence, the seller serves as the lender while continuing to maintain any existing loan(s). The seller becomes the bank of choice for a buyer whose mortgage options may be limited.

Here's how it works:

The contract for deed sale is basically structured as an installment sale, where a buyer may acquire possession of a property by taking advantage of the seller's existing low interest rate financing. To achieve this, the parties sign a contract for deed, which sets out all the specifics of the financing. Then a deed from the seller to the buyer is executed and held in escrow.

Once the paperwork is completed, the buyer makes monthly payments to the seller, who then forwards the payments to the lender. Contracts for deed constitute a sale for IRS purposes, thus allowing the buyer to obtain the tax benefits of a homeowner. A form 1099 is issued by the settlement company, and timeframes for capital gain rollover or exemption are triggered.

At a time in the future (usually a preagreed-upon time), when the buyer is financially able to obtain a new loan or assume the existing loan with lender permission, the deed is recorded and the seller's liability is extinguished. Should the buyer default on the payments, the contract for deed includes remedies for the seller, including but not limited to forfeiture of any funds paid to date, execution of a quitclaim deed that eliminates the buyer's interest in the property, and/or a judicial foreclosure.

In short, rather than take a lump-sum sale, the seller agrees to hold the note and take payments over time—at a price, of course. Through this transaction, the buyer becomes the new owner, paying the taxes and maintaining the property, while taking advantage of the mortgage tax deduction.

The seller continues to pay down the existing mortgage and banks the difference between the original interest rate and the higher rate settled on in the terms of the contract for deed.

A contract for deed is really a win-win for every party:

- The seller gets to move from his/her home to the next place he/she wants to be, with a buyer who will cover the mortgage.

- The buyer gets to move into a home he/she wants to at a price he/she can afford and enjoying the home as an owner would.

- The real estate agent involved gets a commission for helping bring the parties together.

There are lots of i's to dot and t's to cross, but done properly, the contract for deed can be a great play to pull from your playbook when the time is right.

EXCELLENCE IS IN THE DETAILS

What makes this substantially different from a rent-to-own agreement is that the buyer becomes the *de facto* owner at the time of the agreement. No late night calls to the seller that there's water in the basement; no unexpected visits by the seller to check up on the property; no landlord-tenant disputes.

Everything is spelled out in the contract, and both parties walk away winners.

- The seller finances the purchase for the buyer.

- The seller continues to hold the title until full payment is made.

- The buyer receives what's known as an equitable title.

Once the property is paid off, the seller provides the buyer with a deed to the property.

It's important to note that negotiating a contract for deed requires a real estate agent—one who's able to think 10 steps ahead of the deal to determine what could go wrong, who could renege and what the penalty should be if they do, and what would happen if.., plus a whole lot more.

Here are some questions an agent would consider when putting together a contract for deed for a seller and buyer:

"What happens if the buyer stops making their payments?"

The contract needs to stipulate that the seller can foreclose under the power of sale. It should also delineate the time frames in which this could happen as well as the particular laws regarding default in the state where the purchase takes place.

"What happens if the original lender disallows such a 'sublet' on the sale of their mortgage?"

The contract should include language that the buyer has verified permission to give title. Some lenders restrict this reselling of a loan. While it's the buyer's responsibility to check on this, any realtor overseeing a land contract should make sure this is done.

"What if the buyer decides to resell the property before it has been paid off?"

Language should be included in the contract on whether the seller is willing to accept a new buyer under the same arrangements. In most cases, the seller should stipulate that any new arrangements would assume new terms.

There are many other questions that can and will arise. It's important to arm yourself properly before putting a contract for deed deal together.

TIME TO BREAK THE HUDDLE

Once you've gotten your head around what it takes to put one of these deals together, the contract for deed can be a great go-to play for your business.

You'll find that the most likely candidates for an owner-financed transaction are motivated sellers having a hard time finding conventional purchasers and/or purchasers who have a solid income but challenged credit. The buyers in this category may be able to secure a loan, but it would be one with a less-than-desirable interest rate.

Why not help these folks find each other and put a deal together that benefits them and you.

Another demographic to consider are renters who cannot imagine owning home, in part, because they can't scrape together enough for a decent down payment. For a motivated seller who would rather make a sale than receive a lump sum, renters are a much-overlooked pool of potential buyers.

Also, for investors looking for a fixed rate of return on their investment—at a higher interest rate than CDs or mutual funds, but sharing an upside of limited risk—a contract for deed may be the way to go. They can have someone cover the monthly payments on the home and pick up the spread between their payment and the payment the buyer makes. It makes for good cash flow, too.

In fact, for anyone inclined toward leveraging OPM (other people's money), contract for deed sales are an untapped sector. Think how many houses have been languishing on the market since 2007. Consider how many renters would love to own a home, if it weren't for the loan and limited down payment. You could be just the person to turn won't-work into a huge win-win.

Not long ago, I sold a home through contract for deed. The seller and his family were moving to Africa to serve as missionaries. They were not only motivated to sell, but the clock was ticking on their deadline to leave the country. They really needed a sale—and fast.

The buyers had their own set of challenges. They had undergone a medical bankruptcy, and their credit was shot. With a contract for deed, we were able to get top dollar for the seller and the buyers became homeowners—a dream that had almost died under a mountain of medical bills.

Certainly, a contract for deed isn't for everyone. It won't work in every situation, but if you see the right opportunity to use this play, make the right call, break the huddle and go for it.

It could very well be just the winning strategy needed for you and your clients for years to come.

If you would like more information on the contract for deed and winning strategies for owners and investors, please contact Mark at www. soldbystock.com.

CHAPTER 44

Selling the American Dream:
Using Today's Low Rates to Invest In Real Estate and Earn Long-Term Income

By T. Scott Ashbaugh

My only claim to fame is being followed into a restroom at the St. Louis airport by three gentlemen who were more than convinced that I was Kurt Warner. Understand Kurt used to play in St. Louis and had a legendary season and career in professional football. It would make sense that Kurt had come back to town for a visit. The more I tried to assure them I wasn't who they thought I was, the more they assumed that I was, in fact, Kurt, traveling, busy, and didn't want to be bothered. How cool is it to be mistaken for a Super Bowl MVP?

Well, if I'm not famous, why am I writing in this book, you ask? The answer is that I have a very unique way of dealing with real estate, setting up an investing business, and making transactions happen.

I'm a dairy-farm kid who grew up in the middle of small-town America, where milking cows and scraping manure were my daily rituals. My dad will attest that I avoided these duties with great passion, dedication and creativity. Looking back now, I realize just how fortunate our family was as I was taught a do-it yourself attitude. I eventually got into the tool-and-die trade. Over the years, I worked my way up through engineering positions, always looking for something better. I dabbled in real estate investing and thought I saw great promise. I was right! I hope to give you a glimpse of real estate investing that you may have never considered.

THE PROBLEMS/OPPORTUNITIES

Times have certainly changed in the world of real estate. There are many economic factors, layoffs, job cutbacks, adjustable rate mortgages failing at ever-growing rates, all causing skyrocketing foreclosures. Qualifying for new loans is drastically more difficult than before, cutting many deserving buyers out of the market. Buyers and sellers are greatly disrupted.

In addition, consider those who have stocks, bonds and mutual funds in the current market, relying on their investments to grow and flourish. Many have expressed to us that they were tired of seeing their monthly statements decrease every month. Self-preservation alone has forced investors to pull their capital out of the stock market at historic numbers, parking their capital in cash, until they feel that a worthy, viable option exists to once again start growing their capital.

Many lose out in this economy:

- Those who can afford to buy their own home but can't meet the new higher requirements to qualify for a bank loan
- Sellers who really need to sell but have lost the vast supply of buyers
- Investors who feel there's no safe or viable opportunities in which to place their capital

These situations spell "incredible opportunity." Through some research, asking lots of questions, and studying those who've been successful, I've found some incredible answers and insights. Let me explain what it is we're doing and what you can do as well.

For me, this is where it gets exciting and is truly my passion. Please, you really need to understand this! *Fact:* The commodity of real estate, the single greatest source of wealth this country has ever known, is selling at deep discounts. Five major crash zones are hardest hit: the I-5 Interstate corridor in California, much of Florida, Phoenix, Las Vegas, and many areas of Michigan. *Fact:* You have to go back about 75 years to find home valuations this discounted. *Fact:* Mortgage rates are at historic lows. *Fact:* Demand is still high to own, rent or lease a home. *Fact:* At no time in our nation's history has there been such a large amount of capital sitting in cash, basically uninvested. Some experts have labeled this "The Perfect Storm"—many factors have all come together at once to make this an incredible time to invest.

THE SOLUTION

We've positioned ourselves to maximize this opportunity, both for ourselves and for our investors, to buy houses at deeply discounted prices from the current market and sell to deserving buyers at above-market prices, and best of all to use the do-it-yourself attitude that I've learned and eliminate the need for bank loans. We get great monthly cash flow, huge equity, and some of the best tax benefits the IRS has to offer, together producing incredible rates of return.

I set up a business whose intent is to buy and hold real estate for long-term income and asset accumulation. By using self-directed IRAs, the business was able to invest retirement money into single-family houses. Few people realize you can place your retirement money with a management company, allowing you to invest in the house at 123 Main St., instead of stocks or mutual funds. The use of retirement money for investing in this manner still allows the maintenance of your tax-deferred or tax-free status. I'm not here to give financial advice, but your stock broker or financial planner won't tell you about this. It's high risk *to them*, because they'll lose their commissions on your money and you'll be in control, no longer needing their services.

Our business used the self-directed IRA money to buy properties (all cash) so the deepest discounts were received on each purchase. We then advertised these houses on a "lease to own" basis or a land contract (*contract for deed* in some areas of the country), with no bank qualifying, owner financing. This advertising draws many phone calls, especially in today's economy. Those who are interested are screened. A high credit score isn't our main criteria; we confirm applicants' income and debts, ensure they can afford the monthly payments, and that they have a decent pay history. We're looking for deserving people, and each applicant is evaluated looking at the individual situation and the risk that would be taken by selling to them. A down payment is established, possibly as low as 2 to 5 percent of the purchase price, higher if there's more risk. We "sell them" the house for 30 years or more, if that's the length of time it takes to complete the sale. We get great cash flow each month and tax write-offs, as we own the property. Typically, they cash us out before the end of the contract and pay off the equity that we call the huge back end.

I've taken the properties that were purchased and used them as case studies to potential investors, showing actual cash flow, rates of return and expenses. Investors "joint venture," or partner with us. We set up a jointly owned LLC business, and using their cash and the business's systems, buy properties in the joint venture's name. My business manages everything: buying, any required prep work, marketing, filling the property, then splits the earnings after costs. This is what we call the "Win-Win-Win-Win Business Model."

Win #1: The sellers we buy from win, because the market is so stagnated. We can buy their property so they can move on, or if it's a bank-owned house, it comes off their books and returns as a performing property to the local tax base.

Win #2: Those we sell to, the buyers, win. They get their fair chance at the American dream, owning their own home.

Win #3: The investors we partner with win. They get monthly cash flow, a great cash-on-cash return and huge built-in equity.

Win #4: I have a thriving business and make not only a wage, but profits, thereby building long-term assets for myself and my family, not to mention for my investors as well.

However, investors at this level don't make a move until their investment criteria are met. They tell me the following six criteria are some of the most important characteristics an investment must entail before they enter in and why they've chosen to partner in real estate as a successful option.

1. Sophisticated investors tell me first and foremost that they look for an investment to be *safe*. Our rules include only buy in neighborhoods we know and buy at significant discounts from current market value, not what it was two years ago. We also stay in the price range that the average homeowner can afford. Stay away from "slum lord," or "war-zone" areas. Although investors in these areas can make substantial cash flow, it's not worth the effort. The low end has much higher maintenance on the properties and the buyers that lead to more complications than the average person can handle. This is a special niche best left to the extra hearty!

Stay away from the higher-priced houses. The number of people who can afford these houses and neighborhoods are far fewer, a smaller market and more risk. White-collar neighborhoods foreclose at a much higher rate than blue-collar ones. Also, white-collar buyers expect the house to be far closer to perfection when they move in, whereas a blue-collar buyer looks for and desires a fixer-upper so he can gain that sweat equity. Less initial cash outlay for repairs and upgrades equals a higher rate of return.

Ideal properties are 20 percent above and below median home sales prices. In this price range, you have the largest selection of properties to buy and the largest volume of buyers who can afford to own their own home. Let's face it, the opportunity to own your own home is what we're selling.

2. Also on top of the list is *security*. To ensure a secure investment, have systems that ensure all your bases are covered, documented safely and correctly, and the proper documents filed at the courthouse. In the real world, things do go wrong. Learn from someone who's very experienced and knows the best ways to do things step-by-step and correctly.

3. The next most important thing is to look for *long-term opportunities*. No quick flips, no buy low and try to sell high (appreciation plays), not in this market. Buy rock-solid houses in solid family neighborhoods. Invest in a property and expect long-term income from it. Once you go through the work of finding one, buying one, and marketing to put a family in one, keep it "working for you" month after month, for years and decades to come. Can you see the benefit of an investment of this type?

4. *Cash flow* is next. Only invest in properties that create substantial cash flow *from day one*. No speculation, No hopes of making your return on appreciation. Investors who used that business model have found themselves out of business and bankrupt. Remember, *long-term return, safe and secure*.

5. Let's not forget *favorable tax treatment*. Although it's not the primary investment purpose, fully take advantage of some of the best tax benefits the IRS has ever provided to real estate owners.

6. Finally, there's *above-average rates of return.* By buying properties below market value and in an already deeply discounted market, you lock in an above-average rate of return. When offering owner financing on a home, additional value is added, enabling you to sell at above-market pricing.

I often hear, "Are you *nuts?* Don't you hear the news? Why would you be thinking about real estate at a time like this?" I simply respond by asking this question, "When would you want to go to Macy's shopping—when everything is full price, or when everything is 75 percent off?" *You need to clearly understand this! Now* is the time to invest. This will be a once-in-a-generation opportunity, and the deep discounts that are available today won't last forever. Regardless of the media, and even the government comments, owning your own home is still the American dream!

Recently, I attended training with many of the top realtors in our country. Apparently, I was one of the very few investors there, and as we discussed this economy, the realtors became very excited by my partnering with investors to buy real estate. They could see by embracing the idea of eliminating the need for bank loans, working with investors, and incorporating this into their advertising campaigns, they could offer such a greater service that it would grab the attention of potential sellers. This idea would make them more valuable as a realtor and set them apart from the herd. If they use headlines like "I can have an all-cash offer in your hands and close on your house quickly," wouldn't that get your attention? Of course, the house and the situation would need to meet certain criteria, but the realtors I spoke with were more than a little excited by this concept. They understood how many people would find this appealing—and what a great addition it is to their services.

I can tell you from my personal experiences doing exactly what I'm describing, that everyone involved wins. I've had people whose house I bought break down crying and hug me because they had their house listed with two different realty agencies and couldn't sell. They were going to lose their home if they didn't get out from under it. I've also had had buyers break down all choked up. They badly needed a new place for their family to live, and for one reason or another couldn't qualify for a bank loan. Their children stayed in the same school with all their friends, and I got a big hug for making this happen. I've also invested money for people who had pulled their capital out of the stock market and quadrupled their income from the interest they were earning at the bank, and in an investment that was safe, secure, long term and offered monthly cash flow.

One thing I haven't really touched on is the fact that your investment capital goes right back into our local communities. You become the facilitator of deserving families attaining the American dream of owning their own home. When we buy, people are relieved, the people we sell to are ecstatic, and our investors think we're geniuses. By providing this opportunity and a great service to them and their families, they're all thrilled about what we do. It's not investing in Wall Street; it's investing in Main Street, with a much higher and safer rate of return. An added plus—and this is bigger than I expected—when your head hits your pillow at night, it's a pretty darn good feeling knowing what a great investment doing the right thing is. My dad told me that being raised on a farm always gave me a trade I could fall back on. We sure did learn a lot, worked hard, and we really did have a ball, but… I don't ever remember the cows hugging me for milking them nor did they hug me when I scraped manure. I'm kind of liking this business a little better. Dad, I hope you understand, I think I'll stick with this.

I'd be happy to answer any questions you may have; my contact information is listed in my bio information.

About Scott

Scott Ashbaugh is the founder and manager of Ashcraft Properties Inc. and a realtor with Evenboer-Walton Realtors located in Kalamazoo, Michigan. Previously, Scott was an engineer and manager in the automotive industry, managing large groups of skilled trade, staff and engineers in businesses that each brought in $20 million per year in sales, as well as managing automotive car launches worth more than $40 million per year in sales. Scott has experience managing technical and diverse teams with widespread responsibilities.

Today, Scott has created a new career, taking a hobby—investing in real estate for the past 12 years—and built it into a full-time career. Ashcraft Properties works with investors by partnering with them to acquire and manage real estate holdings. By following his passion, he has helped both sellers and buyers do what they couldn't do the old fashioned way. Scott is affiliated with many other investors as well as a handpicked team of professionals, building a stronger and broader network of those who can help.

He's committed to ethical and creative ways of providing a "problem-solving" real estate mind-set to the marketplace, as well as an ongoing commitment to building long-term relationships with his clients, and private lenders/investors, to benefit and support their involvement with his organization and further improve their investments and holdings.

For any questions or for more information, we would be happy to help. Contact Scott at Scott@WMHomeSales.com as well as our company's main website at www.AshcraftProperties.com. We can be reached directly by calling (269) 978-1985.

Ashcraft Properties Inc. is located in the Kentwood area of Grand Rapids, Michigan, at 6026 Kalamazoo Ave. SE, #184, Kentwood MI 49508.

CHAPTER 45

5 Fatal Mistakes Homeowners Make When Selling Their Homes
(and How You Can Avoid Them)

By Brett Jennings, Broker, NAEA Certified Expert Advisor

Getting the highest price for your home is a priority for almost every home seller. How much you sell your home for and what you net from the sale will have the biggest impact on what options you and your family have when buying your next home.

According to the MLS, the sad reality is that more than 26 percent of the homeowners who list their homes for sale will fail, and their homes won't sell. For those who are successful in finding a buyer, many will leave as much as 18 percent of their sales price on the table, simply because they didn't have the right agent or weren't aware of the pitfalls to avoid in the home selling process.

So what is it that's shooting down 26 percent of the home sellers out there and causing them to lose money? It can be narrowed down to five mistakes. The good news is that all are easily avoidable, and this chapter will provide you with a step-by-step system for preventing them and help put the sale of your home on a track to success.

The ideas I'm about to share come from the cumulative experience of thousands of the best real estate professionals in the country and remain consistent from market to market, city to city. As charter members of the National Association of Expert Advisors (NAEA), we have the privilege of bringing together ideas like these from the top 1 percent of real estate agents across the country to help homeowners like you make and keep more of your hard-earned wealth.

Here are the top-five mistakes that are causing homeowners to fail in the process of selling their homes.

MISTAKE #1: OVERPRICING YOUR HOME AND THINKING "I'LL LOWER THE PRICE IF IT DOESN'T SELL"

This a mindset many homeowners adopt during the home selling process. They price their home too high in the beginning and think they can lower the price later if it doesn't sell. Unfortunately, it's also the biggest mistake homeowners make, and it can backfire horribly. If you make this mistake, statistics tell us it will likely cost you at least 2 percent of the sales price of your home.

Why? You see, the single biggest factor in the marketing of your home is price. It's not that the condition of the home and what your agent does to market your home aren't important, because they are. It's just that if everything else is done right and the home is overpriced, it likely won't sell. Showings don't happen, offers don't come or, if they do come in, they come in low and slowly.

Timing is Everything

When selling your home, sooner is always better than later. Not selling your home right away, in and of itself, might not sound like a problem. But when you understand the life cycle of your home's listing, you'll see why overpricing your home in the beginning puts you at a huge risk of leaving lots of money on the table.

This graph, at the top of next page, illustrates the level of excitement and interest in a new listing over time. When a property is first listed, it generates a very high level of interest from prospective buyers, which reduces dramatically over time. This is why it's so important to be priced correctly and be as attractive as possible from the start, during the peak of this curve, to have the best chance of landing a good offer.

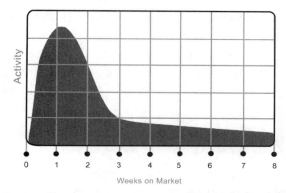

Weeks on Market

Experience shows that your property will get maximum exposure and showing activity in the first 10 to 20 days.

Your List Price Determines the Exposure You Get

When you overprice, the number of buyers who come look at your home also drops significantly. You simply don't get nearly as many showings for your home as if your home were priced correctly.

Many sellers mistakenly think that if their home looks great and is just a little overpriced, buyers will still come to see it. In fact, the opposite is true. Overpricing your home paints a picture to buyers that you're unreasonable. To buyers, the idea of getting in their car to drive across town to see a great-looking, overpriced property is waste of time when they could be looking at quality homes that also appear to be a good value.

The chart below illustrates the importance of pricing correctly. The center line represents market value. As you move above this market value, you attract a much smaller percentage of prospective buyers, greatly reducing your chances of a sale. Conversely, as you move below market value, you attract a much larger percentage of potential buyers.

In the end, if your property is priced in-line with the market, approximately 60 percent of the available buyers in the market will come see your home. If you're priced just 10 percent above the market, only 30 percent of the available buyers will come see your home. And if you overprice by 15 percent, only 10 percent of the buyers in the market will come see the property.

When you overprice your home at the outset, fewer buyers will come to see the home, ultimately requiring you to reduce your price. By the time you reduce the price to become more attractive to the market, you'll have already missed out on a big surge of interest and the opportunity for a reasonable offer. Overpricing your home is detrimental to getting the equity you deserve from the sale, making pricing it right the first time one of the most critical components in your overall plan.

MISTAKE #2: NOT GETTING INSPECTIONS UP FRONT AND FIXING WHAT'S BROKEN

In negotiations, the party with the most information usually comes out on top. In fact, once you've accepted an offer on your home, the tables turn in favor of the buyer, and you lose 80 percent of your negotiating power. Eighty percent!

After you accept an offer on your home there's very little you can do to improve your position, but there are a lot of conditions remaining for buyers that they can use to potentially renegotiate a better price from you.

In general, inspections are one of the things a buyer can use against you after you've accepted their offer. According to market research, you'll give up $4 to fix something after a home inspection that would normally cost $1 to fix before the buyer finds it. It's almost always cheaper to fix all those little things yourself than to let the buyer use it against you.

So to protect yourself, spend a little time and money up front, before you accept an offer to have a home inspection completed. Find out what's wrong with your property and work with your agent to determine which of the things in your inspections is a priority to get repaired.

It's also important to know that insisting on an "as-is" offer doesn't remove this risk. As-is simply means you don't need to do any work on the property. It doesn't waive the buyer's rights to perform an inspection or their ability to ask you for a credit or concession for any issues found.

Finally, before you accept any offer, make sure your agent requires prospective buyers to review and acknowledge any and all inspections and disclosure reports you have. This way, the buyer can't act surprised and blindside you about issues with the property they would have known about prior to entering a contract with you.

MISTAKE #3: NOT TAKING THE FIRST OFFER SERIOUSLY

Here's one that's often missed by homeowners and even many agents. Studies show that unless you're in a rapidly appreciating real estate market, the first offer you get on your home is usually the highest. As stated earlier, the best exposure you get for your home is right when it first comes on the market. This is when buyer activity and demand for your home is generally the highest. This is naturally when you're most likely to get the highest price.

So if you aren't thrilled about the first offer, talk it over with your agent, and think twice about the advice he or she comes back with. More often than not, taking time to hold out for a higher offer usually works against you, and you end up with a stale or stigmatized listing.

MISTAKE #4: SELECTING AN AGENT
BASED ON THEIR NUMBERS

Every home seller has the same goal: net the most amount of money. So it seems natural that you would want to list with the agent who quotes you the highest estimated value and the lowest commission. Right? Wrong!

Selecting an Agent by the Highest Suggested List Price

Using the "highest suggested list price" as your selection criteria can cost you dearly. If you select an agent based primarily on the fact that his or her estimate of the value of your home was the highest of any of the realtors you interviewed, chances are his or her estimate is above the market.

It's a strategy commonly used in the industry by unscrupulous agents and is called "Buying a Listing." The agent "buys" the listing by overestimating the value of the home, preying on the seller's desire to walk away with the most amount of money on the sale. The agent then gets the homeowner to sign a long listing agreement at the inflated price, knowing it won't sell. After the home is listed on the market for several weeks with no activity, the agent pressures the seller to reduce the price until they get the necessary price reductions, hoping all along that it sells.

As stated earlier, being overpriced at the start causes you to miss out on optimal exposure and showing activity. By the time you lower the price, most of the serious buyers are gone, and you have to make drastic price reductions just to get the buyer's attention. Additionally, you end up chasing the market down and lowering the price until it sells. It's a costly and frustrating position no seller should be in.

Choosing an Agent Based on the Lowest Commission

On the surface, it seems that paying a lower commission will net you more money. However, one of the most crucial roles your realtor plays in the sale of your home is as your negotiator. In every state, real estate commissions are negotiable, and most professional realtors charge a flat percentage for selling a home.

Now think about this: The professional you're hiring is negotiating the sale of the largest asset you'll most likely own in your lifetime. Do you really want to hire the negotiator that discounts their service and gives up their own money quickly and with no resistance? If they're so fast to give up their own money when negotiating for themselves, just imagine how quickly they'll part with your money when they're negotiating for you? I'm not recommending overpaying for an inexperienced, ineffective real estate agent. I'm simply stating that you should hire and pay for the best in order to get greatest results.

MISTAKE #5: PRICING YOUR HOME BASED ON YESTERDAY'S REAL ESTATE MARKET

This mistake is pretty common as the majority of realtors out there are still using the outmoded method of pricing a property, called a Comparative Market Analysis, or CMA. The problem with using only a CMA for setting a list price for your home is that it relies solely on what happened in the real estate market in the past and reflects only where the market has been, not where it's headed.

There's still no crystal ball for the market, but if you're going to be successful in selling your home, you need to have some sense about where the market is going with some kind of forward-looking indicator. Home buyers today have access to tons of market information at the click of a mouse. Many of them may know what's happening to market values at the time they're looking, which makes it imperative that sellers keep pace with the market on the sales price of their home.

Pending and closed sales are the main data points used by agents to determine CMA values. Most agents will price a property based on this data, *and this data alone*. But is a price or estimate of value based solely on yesterday's market activity the best way to position your home on the market today? If 26 percent of the home sellers and agents are failing to sell the homes they list, probably not.

The good news is there's a new model for positioning or pricing your home for the market that's much more effective than the old CMA, and it yields success rates of more than 90 percent. This new pricing model relies on CMA values in addition to a few key indicators that give you a view where the market is headed. One such indictor is called *absorption rate*, or *pace of sales*. It lets us know the relative strength or weakness of the market, and from this we can easily determine your strategy on price going forward.

The other key indicator that has been driving pricing in the real estate market more recently is foreclosure activity. In most states, the way foreclosure works is that banks are required to file notices before the foreclosure. With years of stats behind us we can accurately estimate the number of foreclosures that will be coming to market based on the number of foreclosure notices filed. The more foreclosures coming to market, the more downward pressure there is on prices. The fewer fore-closures, the better the chance that prices will be level or go up. It's a pretty simple formula.

Using a combination of these two indicators along with CMA values, we can get a good read on where the market is heading and how you need to price your home in the market to ensure a successful sale and net you the highest possible price.

So there you have it. Those are the top-five mistakes homeowners are making when selling their homes. Making these mistakes when you don't know what you're doing is expected. Making mistakes when you access to an Expert Advisor in your area to help you avoid them is insanity. If you're getting ready to sell your home, contact your local Expert Advisor and let them guide you through the home selling process. You'll be glad you did.

About Brett

As an award-winning realtor, Brett Jennings understands real estate and is a respected leader in the real estate industry. Brett has been assisting homeowners and real estate investors minimize taxes and grow net worth for more than nine years. Prior to his career in real estate, Brett was the founder and vice president of a boutique financial planning firm specializing in asset protection. His diverse background in consulting and financial planning enables him to bring a fresh and creative perspective to your real estate needs.

As a Silicon Valley resident and homeowner, as well as an income property owner and manager, Brett understands the challenges his clients face when making important real estate decisions. Brett uniquely blends his marketing savvy and financial planning expertise and real estate knowledge to help you maximize the investment potential of your home or other real estate. With this strategic approach, he can help you reach your financial goals on, or even ahead of schedule.

A recognized expert in his field, Brett Jennings is often called on to teach conferences and workshops for agents and investors. He has been a member of the leadership council of various brokerages and continues to volunteer his time to train and teach other agents on what it takes to be successful in a shifting market.

To learn more about Brett and how you can receive a free digital copy of the special report *5 Fatal Mistakes Homeowners Make When Selling Their Home*, visit www.TheBrettJenningsTeam.com, or call (408) 427-9220.

CHAPTER 46

How to Maximize Your Price In Any Market

By Josh Hisaw and Michael Mosteller

When it comes time to sell their house, it's been our experience that sellers have many misconceptions about what's important in determining the price of their homes. As listing agents it's our job to educate sellers on what factors will affect the price of a house. Oftentimes, we find sellers believe their house is superior to other homes, and somehow the market hasn't affected the value of their property. We also find many sellers have heard so much information from friends, family and the internet, that it's difficult to see through all of the information and focus on what's really important. Our goal in this chapter is to help you understand the most important factors of getting the most for your property.

There are several factors that will affect the price a house will sell for. We'll discuss what we've learned about getting more money for the sellers who've hired us to sell their homes. This chapter is intended to help guide you through the process so you can sell for more money in less time, with fewer hassles. That's what you want, right? We'll walk you through determining what your home is worth today in its current condition and what we can do to effectively maximize the price. There are some factors we can control and others we cannot. We want to help you focus on what you can do and what needs to be done to achieve the highest sales price. This chapter will help you sell your home in a timely manner with minimal setbacks.

DETERMINING PRICE

Any time I enter a clients' home, one of the first things they want to know is how much can I sell my house for? Price is a sensitive subject: Considering this house is your "home" you have a higher perceived value of your property. From this point on we'll refer to your "home" as your "property." Calling the property your "home" keeps you tied to the property emotionally. In order to look at pricing objectively, you must disassociate yourself from your house. One must step away from the emotional aspect of selling your property, and open the door to a business transaction. With that said, let's look at some of the key factors in pricing your property. There are four criteria we'll consider when pricing your property. We'll look at supply and demand in the market, what has sold, what's for sale, and what was the condition of the homes sold.

A factor in pricing your property in which we have no control over is "the market." When people talk about the market, you may hear things like "it's a buyer's market" or "it's a seller's market." You may also hear, "the market is at an all time low" or "or a great market to sell." What do all the previous statements really mean? It's as simple as any freshman-year marketing class: supply and demand. How do you get the best price in *any market*? You must analyze the market trends in your local market and price your house accordingly.

First, we'll look for how many homes like yours have sold in the last six months. Properties sold is the key word. The sold houses are the current statistics of what has actually been selling. Looking at the big picture—analyzing the last six months of homes sold—will help us predict how many homes should sell in the next six months. This is the "demand" of homes in your market. Looking at comparable homes that have sold illustrates what buyers are willing to pay for a comparable property.

Second, we'll look at how many homes similar to yours are currently for sale in your area. This is your competition and "supply" of the market. The houses on the market are what the buyers are going to be comparing your house to. Based on this number, we're looking for how many months of inventory is on the market. If there's about a four-month supply of inventory, we can conclude the market is balanced and prices are stable. It there's less than four months of inventory, prices are pushing upward due to the demand for properties. If there's more than four months of inventory, prices are pressing downward due to a saturated market. Consider this scenario: There are 10 buyers all looking for a 3-bedroom, 2-bath property in a certain area. There are only three houses for sale that meet the buyers' guidelines. These buyers are willing to pay more for these three properties because they're the only ones on the market. Market trends helps us determine whether we price your home higher, lower or comparable to what has sold in the past six months.

Condition will be the last factor in pricing your home. We'll discuss this point in-depth later. The condition of your home is the only true factor you have control over. To sell your property for the highest price in any given market, your property must be in the best condition possible.

Now that we know how many homes have sold, what they sold for, and how many homes are currently on the market, we can predict how long it will take to sell. For example, if there are six homes like yours that sold in the last six months, we can conclude six homes is a six-month supply of inventory. This means statistically one home per month is selling. Basically if no other homes are placed on the market, it will take six months for all of them to sell. This means we need to position the price of your home competitively. Considering the scenario above, there's a slight downward pressure on price therefore we must price just below the comparable sales in order to maximize your sale's price.

THAT CRITICAL FIRST IMPRESSION

The condition of your home will maximize the price in any market, and it's the only variable you have control over. It's a first impression. This is where you need to step out of your home and become the buyer. Think of why you bought your home? Was it the curb-side appeal? Was the kitchen recently updated? Was the house move-in ready? Think about what you would be looking for when purchasing a new home. The truth of the matter is buyers want to invest in something that looks like it was taken care of. Purchasing a home is one the biggest investments a person will make in their life. Not only is this a costly purchase, but they're also purchasing a home, a place to live, raise their children or retire. Condition can make or break a deal for a buyer, both emotionally and investment wise.

As a seller you want to create a "wow" experience for all perspective buyers. Imagine being the prospective buyer and stepping out of your car for the first time at your property. The lawn in is good condition with nice landscaping, the sidewalk is clear, the house appears newly painted. At first glance the property looks perfect. You don't see anything that needs to be fixed. This is all about curb-side appeal. This will set your client at ease the moment they step out of their car. "Ah, this house has been taken care of."

A buyer wants to step into a property that looks and feels like a well-kept home. The seller must declutter, organize, rearrange and depersonalize the property. Decluttering is one of the most important steps in making your home appealing to buyers. Get rid of everything you don't use daily. Pack up these unused belongings and donate or store them. After removing the clutter, begin organizing. A buyer will assume you've taken good care of the house if you seem very organized. Organize closets, cabinets and your DVD collection. Organize everything down to the last detail. Have cups neatly placed with handles going in the same direction, dishes neatly stacked, pantry food in order, shirts all hung in the same direction. This may all sound silly, but in reality the buyer won't be distracted by your personal belongings. Your main goal in preparing the inside of your home is to impress upon the buyer that this house is move-in ready, creating the illusion of what it's like to live in this house.

Finally, is your house is working order? Having your home preinspected is key to ensuring the buyer isn't going to find something wrong with your property during their inspection. Some sellers have even left the home inspection on the kitchen counter for potential buyers to review in order to demonstrate that the home is in working order and has been maintained. The less work a buyer has to do before moving into your home, the more they'll be willing to pay for it. There's great value to a buyer in the convenience of not having to repair, replace or remodel before moving in. Removing the concerns a buyer may have about the home is imperative to getting the highest price for the current local market.

PRICE ATTRACTS; CONDITION SELLS

With today's technology and flow of information on the internet, we find buyers are educated on the market and its current offerings. Buyers looking for homes like yours will be knowledgeable about the current inventory of homes available. With this said, we're able to reach thousands of potential buyers through online marketing. There are hundreds of real estate websites that buyers will be surfing daily. We have the ability to create virtual tours where buyers can view every room in your home from their computer screen. The question then arises, How are we going to entice buyers to leave their current home to view yours? The truth is, if your price is attractive, buyers will take the time to physically tour your home. If your price isn't attractive, they'll move on and view other properties with a more attractive price. Showings are simply the market responding to your price. If there are multiple showings and no offers, then there's a conditional issue with your home. The conditional issue will ultimately be overcome with a price reduction, until the buyer is satisfied that they're paying a price that best represents the home's condition. Until the buyers are attracted to your price, your property will stay on the market. Too many days will eliminate any opportunity you may have with creating demand for your property.

The final key in getting the highest price in your marketing is having a plan. You want your house to hit the market with the right price and the best condition possible. This will create a momentum of urgency among buyers. If all conditions are right, a buyer will be ready and willing to purchase your home. If you decided to list your house for higher than your market price, even though your house in the best condition possible, you're missing your golden opportunity to hit the ground running. Once a buyer has viewed your house online and decided it was too expensive, you've already missed out on potential buyers. Price and condition need to match or exceed the market value in order for you to receive the most for your property. With these two conditions correct, you create an urgency that you'll be able use as leverage to maximize your price in your market every time and anywhere.

Josh Hisaw

Michael Mosteller

About Josh and Michael

Josh Hisaw and Michael Mosteller, well-known for their business acumen in the Memphis area, have joined forces to change the status quo of real estate practices today. They were recently cited in the Memphis Business Journal and Memphis Commercial Appeal as the "New Breed" in real estate. Known in their market as "The Hisaw Team," they help their clients achieve their goals by structuring opportunities through marketing and pricing strategy specific for each client. Josh and Michael bring about a no-nonsense accountable approach to sale or acquisition of your property. Josh and Michael's recent articles demonstrate a seller's ability and opportunity to maximize the return on the sale of their home no matter the current market conditions. To learn how and more, please visit www.JoshHisaw.com.

CHAPTER 47

The 20 Biggest Fallacies in Real Estate Today

(And Why You Shouldn't Believe Them!)

By Jason Cianflone

Anyone thinking about buying or selling a home can easily get lost in the avalanche of real estate "truisms" that are routinely quoted by people who don't necessarily know what they're talking about. This chapter is a great place to discover the actual "reality of real estate."

As an expert realtor who's part of a top-level team of specialists, I've experienced enough real estate deals through the years to know what makes sense—and what seems senseless. So, without further ado, here are what I consider the 20 biggest fallacies in real estate today.

- *Fallacy #1: We're going to wait for the exact house that has everything we want—including an incredible price!* When people are looking for a house to buy, they sometimes go on and on with the list of things it "needs" to have: stainless steel appliances, granite counters, hardwood floors, etc. Well, that kind of home might cost $800,000—and their budget might be only $250,000. When you set your sights on the perfect home at the perfect price, without sitting down with a real estate professional to see what's actually realistic for the money you can afford, you'll inevitably be disappointed. Start by seeing what the local market actually is like at the moment and what your best options are from there.

- *Fallacy #2: We're going to wait to sell, because interest rates are going to go up and houses will get cheaper!* Well, that may be true about the interest rates. And it may be true about home values going down as a result. The problem is, if that's the reason you're waiting to sell your existing home and buy a new one, you may get a better price on a property you want to buy, but, at the same time, you'll get a lower price on the property you're selling.

- *Fallacy #3: We'll just make an offer on a house based on the list price.* You should never make an offer on a home based on the list price. That offer should be based on the actual *value* of the home, which is something only an experienced real estate pro can help you accurately determine. Of course, value can be subjective: The home may be two doors down from your mother's house, so, in theory, it's worth more to you. A savvy realtor will help you nail down the numbers and write an offer than makes sense for all parties.

- *Fallacy #4: I'm going to make sure I get an amazing deal on a property.* Are there any truer words than, "Everybody wants a deal?" Yes, nobody wants to give a great deal to someone else." If you were selling your house, you certainly wouldn't want to cut the price by $40,000 just to be wonderful and give a buyer a break. When you approach real estate with this "amazing deal" mindset, you're thinking like an investor, not a homeowner, and you'll find yourself making no progress in your house hunting.

- *Fallacy #5: There are so many things wrong with this house, the price has to be drastically reduced.* If you're selling a home with a great many problems, you probably think you have to sell the home for a fire sale price just to get rid of it—maybe $100,000 for what should be a $500,000 home. What if it only cost you an additional $100,000 to restore it to a level worthy of that full sale price? It would be worth making those repairs to make that extra $300,000, right? Right.

- *Fallacy #6: Fixed-rate mortgages are better than variable ones.* The facts say otherwise: A survey done from 1960 through 2010 demonstrated that if you had a variable rate instead of a fixed rate on your mortgage, you would be much further ahead. I understand that some people want the security of a fixed mortgage payment, so here's my solution for them: Because a variable mortgage payment will be around $100 to $200 cheaper per month, simply put aside the money you're saving on a fixed-rate mortgage and bank it. You'll have the extra money in place if interest rates rise.

- *Fallacy #7: Purchasing a used home is a much better deal than buying a new one.* While I can't say this is always a fallacy, it definitely shouldn't automatically be regarded as a truth. The used home and new home markets fluctuate, depending on the area and the cost of building a home—all the numbers need to be analyzed. With a new home, the advantage is you can work with the builder and get exactly the home you want. Not only that, since you're committing to the home in advance of it being built, you'll typically build up some equity in the six to eight months it takes for it to be finished. Your property values will also stay high, since you'll typically be in a development that will have a higher proportion of amenities, such as parks and new schools, that will attract other homeowners. This ultimately means you may be able to comfortably live in a new home longer.

- *Fallacy #8: One of our family members has bought numerous homes, so they're advising us on our house purchase.* Suppose I met someone who wanted to be a doctor and put band-aids on their children when they had small cuts. Should I consider this person to be an experienced medical professional? That's obviously not how it works. A real estate team has the professional background, the necessary certifications and, most important, the experience to understand what your best choices are. Your relative isn't buying the home for you, and they're not going to live in it either. A real estate pro does this every day and can provide real, actionable advice that will get you the best deal.

- *Fallacy #9: The best way to get a great mortgage rate is to shop around.* Let's say you're about to buy a home, and you want to get the lowest mortgage rate possible. You drive to one bank—maybe they quote you a 2.6 percent rate. You go to another bank—they go down to 2.5 percent. The third bank? They'll do the loan at 2.3 percent. Great! Except for the fact that they can't approve you. You see, every time they run a credit check on you, as each of these banks did, your credit score goes down, and you basically end up kicking yourself out of the mortgage market. The other fact here is that, by yourself, you don't have the purchasing power to get the best rate. You want to hook up with a real estate team that does a lot of deals, since they already have prenegotiated the best mortgage rates for their clients. That's a lot easier than driving from bank to bank.

- *Fallacy #10: Buying a home using a single realtor is no different than using a real estate team.* When you hire a lone realtor, you have to believe that agent is working for you 24/7 and you're their only client in order to get the best out of them. Obviously, that can't be the case. I used to be my own one-man operation, and let me tell you, it's impossible to do the job as well as you should. You can't be the listing agent, the website developer, the secretary, the marketing manager, etc. all at once, but you have to be. A real estate team, however, has the best possible people doing the best possible job in their individual duties, which means you get the benefits of a group of specialists all working in your best interests. Ninety-five percent of agents are, in fact, single realtors, but they never have the time or ability to focus on 100 percent of your business, because they simply can't.

- *Fallacy #11: Listing a home is the same as selling.* A lot of homeowners believe that, as soon as they list their house, they're going to sell it. Well, the truth is, listing doesn't really cost them anything. and it has nothing to do with *selling* their home. That's where a real estate team is essential. They'll go beyond a simple listing to actually marketing your home and creating demand for it.

- *Fallacy #12: Needing money urgently justifies a high selling price.* Let's say a couple needs to move, but they have little equity left in the house. They need as much money as possible for a move, so they want to list their property at $330,000 instead of its market value of $270,000. Well, it's one of those cases where just because you *say* something, doesn't mean it's true. Just because you need more money from a sale, doesn't mean you're going to be able to buck the entire market and get that price. Your personal situation doesn't drive price or the quickness of a sale...unless, of course, you're willing to take a lot less money.

- *Fallacy #13: Take your time before you sign an offer to buy a home.* When it comes to contracts, people tell you to beware. But in real estate, that doesn't work. You should sign the offer to purchase right away—just to be sure to put conditions into that offer that have to be met. You sign quickly, and do away with conditions slowly. Those conditions are your exit hatch; if you do need to get out of the deal. Otherwise, you could risk not getting the home you really want.

- *Fallacy #14: All builders are basically the same.* When you want to buy a new home, you may interview up to four or five different builders to do the job. And you'll soon discover that they're not all the same. They're all unique, with very different products. Keep in mind that a builder who constructs hundreds of homes a year is going to be able to build at a lower cost because they can get better deals on the large volume of materials they buy. Also research which builder will give you the best terms and guarantees, as well as a five-year warranty period.

- *Fallacy #15: The perfect lot for a building will come up eventually.* Waiting for the perfect lot can be like waiting for the perfect home: a quest that seems endless and ends with you paying too much money. Land prices always go up, so you should move as soon as you can on something you like. Lots are released in stages, usually in blocks of 10 or 20. The only way to get the "perfect lot" is to reserve the spot with a refundable deposit long before the lot is officially released on the market. You must be first to show up to make that reservation, and you must make an official agreement. If you buy one that isn't perfect, well that will work out, too. You can always build up equity and sell down the line for something you like better. That's what real estate is all about.

- *Fallacy #16: Investing in real estate is easy. You just have to buy a book.* If you think you can learn all you need to about how to make millions from real estate from some book...well, let's just say that we in the industry don't see this happening on a regular basis. We actually don't see it happening at all. What you really have to do to understand real estate investment is connect to people that have invested themselves for 20 years or so and experience enjoying the highs and riding out the lows of the marketplace. Here's my golden rule for working with other investors: Make sure they're investing themselves and taking the same amount of risk as you are. If somebody is a billionaire and investing just a few thousand like you are, that's not really a risk for that guy.

- *Fallacy #17: You can sell a home by yourself as well as you can with a professional realtor.* If you want to represent your own home on the marketplace, you have to ask yourself, what's your availability? People are house-shopping on their own schedule, and someone has to be there to respond 24/7— or they move on to another one. Also, a homeowner doesn't have the same reach as a professional real estate team. They don't know how to market and properly price properties. Finally, realtors have processes in place to protect the seller legally—legalities that the homeowner is unaware of. They say a man who acts as his own lawyer has a fool for a client. I'd have to say this goes for real estate, too.

- *Fallacy #18: Springtime is the best time to sell a home.* This is not at all true. It's true that you'll find the highest activity in our market at that time and the lowest in December and January. Does that mean the winter months are a bad time? No, you have to look at all the factors involved. A professional can help you determine when the best time to put your home on the market is.

- *Fallacy #19: Upgrading your home with the latest and greatest features makes you the most money.* Let's say you want to put $70,000 into your home to make it more "saleable." Before you do that, you should really sit down with a pro and see if you can actually make that money back. Some areas simply won't yield a price above a certain level, and you could be wasting your money. Your taste also may clash with potential home buyers—they may not like the colors or materials you've chosen. That's why a consultation with a realtor is important.

- *Fallacy #20: Statistics tell us all we need to know about the market.* In my opinion, statistics are the worst thing in the real estate industry today. Let's say in one market the numbers say that market prices have increased by 9 percent, so a homeowner in that area automatically assumes his property has enjoyed that gain. That could be totally wrong, depending on what street and specific neighborhood you're in. Maybe you're in a beautiful new development, which has actually enjoyed a 15 percent gain in value. You can't know without the specifics of your home and location!!!

I hope these fallacies have been of help to anyone interested in buying or selling a home now or in the near future. Remember that a professional and experienced real estate team should be an essential part of your process. They'll have the information and the marketing firepower to make your home dreams a reality!

About Jason

Jason L.F. Cianflone, better known as "The Real Estate Game Changer," is a leader and innovator in real estate marketing, advertising, project consulting and investments. Founded on the principle of genuine, caring, personal service, he consistently exceeds all customer expectations, providing a memorable experience and exceptional value. Jason has been seen on NBC, CBS, ABC and Fox affiliates, as well as in the *Wall Street Journal, USA Today* and *Newsweek.*

Jason has grown his real estate companies at a remarkable pace in the past five years. Already known as one of the top advisors and professionals in North America Jason's following continues to grow nationwide like wildfire. With Jason, there's no stopping at just helping people buy or sell homes. Jason's growing team of rising experts and professionals commands a reputation for excellence coupled with the mandatory rule of treating everyone as family! Jason continues to strive to provide the best service and advice from marketing to project consulting and more!

To get to know Jason on a more personal basis and to extend your knowledge in the real estate world, visit www.JASONCIANFLONE.com, or call (204) 772-7777.

CHAPTER 48

The Baby Boomers' Dilemma:
What to Do With Mom and Dad's Estate

By Jon J. Maniscalco

"Harry got up, dressed all in black, went down to the station, and he never came back." ~Don Henley, *"New York Minute"*

Mary Stevens awoke that morning in a great mood. The day before she had confirmed her reservation for her sixth cruise of the year and was excitedly awaiting the departure date. Painting was her passion, and she had just completed a portrait of her granddaughter, Mimi, and was quite proud of the results. Last week her doctor had given Mary a clean bill of health, both physically and mentally. Her home was paid for, she had a new car, plenty of money in the bank, and she had a close circle of good friends. More important, she had Ken and Audrey, her wonderful, attentive children, and, of course, Mimi, her granddaughter and precious "gift from heaven." Not bad for an 89-year-old former schoolteacher. The missing element was her husband of 60 years, Chester, whom Mary had lost several years ago. She wished her lifelong companion was still around to share her good times.

No matter, it was a beautiful day to go grocery shopping and run a few errands. After her morning ritual of green tea, toast and vitamins, Mary got in her car and began her journey. As Mary moved through the upscale neighborhood she had occupied for most of her married life, she thought of the items she needed: cottage cheese, rye bread, orange juice, eggs…when, suddenly, everything went black. The next faded, blurry image Mary encountered was that of a masked surgeon, who was forefront among a backdrop of nurses, assistants, and the glaring bright lights of an operating room. During the next few hours, the surgical team desperately tried to repair Mary's badly damaged body. A broken leg, punctured lung, internal bleeding, and head trauma were the major obstacles to Mary's survival.

What caused Mary's leisurely trip to the grocery store to turn into this catastrophe? She had been blindsided by a 20-foot delivery van, speeding on the main road Mary had attempted to merge onto after stopping at her intersection. The Jaws of Life had been used to extract Mary from her mangled, new car. She had been rushed to the nearest hospital. Tragically, her injuries were too severe for Mary to overcome. She died that beautiful day. Her children were summoned to the hospital to receive the devastating news.

Losing a loved one is never easy. Sometimes, as in Mary's case, the loss is shockingly sudden. Other times, the process breaks down into a long, arduous succession of doctor appointments, debilitating treatments, procedures, surgeries, perhaps a stay at a rehabilitation facility, or full-time home care, all of which usually results in some sort of constrained, limited, painful, frustrating existence. The end may come in a hospital room, where the patient is surrounded by their loving family, all with the intent of being supportive to one another while also having to deal with their own emotional tribulations. And despite those long, tortuous journeys, the final exit is still as heart-wrenching, traumatic, and tragic as Mary's unexpected demise.

Regarding Mary, some may say she led a full, productive and fruitful life—that it was her time. Those words are of little comfort to those closest to Mary, who are deeply and profoundly affected by her death. Time heals all. However, before that time passes, Mary's children will be confronted with a seemingly endless barrage of questions, thrust upon them when they're emotionally ill-equipped and unprepared to handle the onslaught. Funeral arrangements will have to be made. If buried, which outfit will Mary wear for eternity? Which type of casket best suits her? Who will write the obituary? What will it say? Who will be notified, when and how? Who will be allowed to speak at Mary's service? Should there be a family gathering afterward? What food shall be served? And so on.

Once those decisions are made and Mary is laid to rest, the next matter of attention presents itself: settlement of the estate. Did Mary have a will? A living trust? A list of bequeathed items? Who should be enlisted as advisors? Will there be estate taxes due? How will they be paid? What about Mary's house? Should it be sold? Should it be rented? How much rent should be charged? Should family members be allowed to live there? Surviving beneficiaries are confronted with these issues and many more, all at a time of heightened emotional sensitivity. The time after a loved one's death can seem like a whirlwind, and the most important personal issue, grieving, can be suppressed or delayed by all this activity, decision-making, and deviation from a normal routine. Emotional outbursts and deteriorating health, experienced many weeks after the loss, are not uncommon. To call this period of time "stressful" can be a gross understatement.

Fortunately, for Ken and Audrey, Mary had planned well for the inevitable. She had created a will and living trust. Included in these documents was a list of personal items and the individuals designated to receive those items. Mary had a trusted estate attorney and an accountant who helped her children with many of the issues they faced in settling the estate. As a value-added service, Mary's accountant recommended a real estate company that specializes in the disposition of estate real property; in this case, Mary's home.

Ken and Audrey had quickly decided they didn't want the responsibility of becoming "accidental landlords." Becoming a landlord is a business. In fact, many municipalities require the procurement of a business license (and the subsequent payment of taxes and fees) in order for individuals to rent property. Not wanting to deal with the headaches associated with property management (e.g., tenant screening, rent collection, property maintenance, knowledge of tenant/landlord laws, emergency calls in the middle of the night, and having to be intimately familiar with the rules and procedures of tenant eviction, among many others), Mary's children chose to sell the house. The real estate company, recommended by Mary's accountant, offered a unique collection of services designed to ease some of the stress and relieve the majority of the work required to prepare the house for sale.

After Ken and Audrey had ensured Mary's bequeathments were complete, they turned their attention to Mary's house—a house full of memories and a lot of stuff! Not that Mary was a hoarder; let's just say nearly every square inch of the house was occupied by something. They were items Mary valued, but to others, these items amounted to just more stuff. Furniture, appliances, dishware, cleaning supplies, food (refrigerated, frozen, dry and liquid), toiletries, bedding, artwork, files, office supplies, clothes, Mary's art studio supplies, and a rather large collection of old magazines were found. In the garage, they discovered tools, gardening equipment, fertilizer, pest sprays, paint cans, car cleaning products, oil, etc.

Ken and Audrey asked themselves, "How do we dispose of the things we don't need or want in the best possible way? And how are we going to be able to take even more time away from work and family to accomplish this overwhelming task?" The real estate company had the answers. Their services included providing the family with a detailed inventory of the items in the home. At Ken and Audrey's discretion, specific items were earmarked for sale, donation or appropriate disposal. Spoiled food was obviously placed with refuse, while food with continued shelf life (canned and dry goods) was donated to the local food bank. Some large-ticket items (furniture and artwork) were purchased by a wholesaler, and other items were donated to various charitable organizations. Hazardous waste products were taken to the appropriate facility. Ken and Audrey had no idea the old thermostat they found in the garage is considered hazardous waste because it contains mercury in the switch. Likewise, the fluorescent tubes their Mom had neatly stacked in the laundry room closet are hazardous waste. The house was quickly relieved of these items, cleaned and staged for sale.

Because of the real estate company's efforts, the house sold for top dollar, maximizing that portion of Mary's total assets. Ken and Audrey, while saddened by their mother's tragic and sudden death, were grateful she had entrusted her estate to a group of expert advisors who helped get them through this most difficult period of their lives. They were especially grateful for the accountant's recommendation of the real estate company that treated them with respect, kindness and consideration for their plight, while performing their duties with utmost professionalism—all completed for a fee other agents charge just to list the house. A value-added proposition, indeed.

This story illustrates a situation most baby boomers will confront at some point in their lives: how to handle their parents' real property.

Baby boomers are generally defined as the generation born between 1946 and 1964. They're informally referred to as "a pig moving through a python," because of their immense numbers. The socioeconomic impact of this generation has been well documented and is unprecedented. An interesting and inevitable consequence for the national real estate market has to do, not with the boomers, but with their aging parents. As their parents reach the age where they can no longer live at home, boomers are faced with the dilemma of providing home care or moving their parents to an assisted living facility, both expensive options.

When the home is left vacant due to failing health or, in Mary's case, a sudden tragedy, what happens to it and its contents? Usually, due to the fact the majority of this "Greatest Generation" were frugal savers, the house is owned free and clear and can ultimately be used as a source of funds to pay for the elders' care. Renting the house and becoming a landlord has its pitfalls as mentioned earlier. The worst-case scenario is the failure to properly screen tenants, which can result in your family home's condition suffering disrepair and abuse while you're trying to collect three months of past due rent—not an appealing alternative. Hiring a property management company is costly and diminishes the potential income from the property. There's still no guarantee of the tenant's integrity.

Regarding the contents of the house, once the valuable family items are removed, who would want to subject themselves to the emotional turmoil of having to physically empty the entire contents of their parents' house when memories abound in every room and with many objects? Without specialized knowledge, how does one determine where the items should be routed to provide the most benefit to the estate and, possibly, to those in need via a charitable contribution? Improper disposal of hazardous waste is not only harmful to the environment, but it can be illegal and punishable by fines if reported. A better alternative is to allow a third party to handle the entire process.

If you find yourself executor of an estate containing real property located in the San Diego County area, there's help immediately available. Horizon View Properties has created the solution to this dilemma. The company provides the services necessary to help relieve some of the stress, work and direct involvement associated with preparing the property for sale, while maximizing the proceeds of the sale of real property.

This is a significant benefit to the surviving beneficiaries and executors. These value-added services produce an orderly, systematic process of converting real property to liquid assets; assets a family can use for elder care, beneficiary distributions or charitable contributions. Other candidates for this invaluable program include estate attorneys, accountants, and anyone named as executor of an estate.

Ken and Audrey came out of their experience with a great appreciation for the collective group of expert advisors their mother had assembled to help them through this incredibly demanding, emotionally challenging ordeal. Mary had left them in good hands. What a great final gift she left to her loved ones—helping them through their own personal version of the baby boomers' dilemma.

About Jon

Jon Maniscalco has been an entrepreneur since age 12, delivering newspapers on his bike in his hometown of San Diego. At age 20, while still attending college, he and his brother, Michael, started a wholesale produce company. San Diego Produce was the first local produce wholesaler to incorporate its own in-house processing facility. This value-added proposition allowed customers to choose between whole fruits and vegetables or table-ready products. New concepts and exceptional customer service propelled the company from seven to more than 250 clients, 30 employees, and annual sales approaching $8 million.

Always interested in real estate since purchasing their first home in 1984, Jon and his wife, Marlene, decided to apply the value-added approach to their niche in the real estate industry. Today, Horizon View Properties specializes in the conversion of real property to liquid assets for estate equity or distribution. The company provides a group of services designed to ease the stress and relieve tedious tasks facing family members trying to sell "Mom and Dad's home." These services are also invaluable to estate attorneys, accountants, or anyone else who finds themselves in the role as executor of an estate. Horizon View Properties currently focuses its efforts in San Diego County. If you need assistance in selling estate real property, contact Jon or Marlene. They're compassionate, caring, empathetic to their clients' circumstances, and responsive to their needs. Visit their website, HorizonViewProperties.com, for more information. Remember, "At Horizon View, It's All About You!"

Jon is a graduate of San Diego State University with a bachelor's degree in business administration/marketing. He and Marlene live in Del Mar, California, with their two dogs, Toto and Skipper.

CHAPTER 49

What You Need to Know to Get a Home Sold the Right Way

By Kim Williams

In the world of real estate, what you don't know may not hurt you, but it certainly *will* cost you. And sometimes, it will cost you dearly.

Look at these scenarios and check off the ones that have happened to either you or someone you know in the past. Have you ever:

☑ Signed a contract without fully understanding what it says?

☑ Sold a home by yourself or with an agent and let a potential buyer move in before closing without a rental agreement signed and an agreement stating the procedures for the buyer to move out due to nonpayment?

☑ Gone to a closing at 5 p.m. or later only to find out that the buyer's driver's license is expired and not an acceptable form of identification for him/her to use to sign closing documents?

☑ Sold or purchased a new construction home and not gotten an occupancy permit to let you legally move in and live there?

☑ Blown up a transaction (or had it blow up on you) because of a measly $500 disagreement?

☑ Been stuck paying two mortgages because you just "knew" your first home would sell when you moved into your new home before both payments were due (only to not have enough money to cover both of them).

☑ Found out the day of closing that you'll be supplying more funds or receiving less than anticipated at closing?

☑ Made your decision to move forward with a sale or purchase based solely on what was "said" by the other parties, rather than getting it in writing where everyone has a copy?

☑ Assumed that because you have a contract on a home that the home is *sold*.

☑ Been told by an agent that any problems on the home inspection will be covered completely by the seller, only to find out they're not?

☑ Listed a home with an agent because they had the "perfect buyer" waiting to buy it, only to find out there was no buyer?

☑ Not taken the first reasonable offer and negotiated it only to have the next offer(s) be less or cost you more money in concessions?

How many did you check off? Chances are you checked at least one, if not more than one. And unfortunately, every single one of these problems doesn't have to happen if the right person is in charge of the transaction—a real estate expert. The challenge is, it's tough to find an expert if you don't know what you're looking for.

WHEN AN EXPERT IS NOT AN EXPERT

Everyone thinks they have what it takes to expertly handle every detail of a real estate transaction properly, when honestly, less than 20 percent of the real estate agents on the face of the planet (and a few industry experts) actually know what it takes to make things happen correctly from start to finish. That includes attorneys.

It's not surprising that this is the case. Take a look around you, and you'll see that most everyone you know at some point in your life is: a) active in real estate sales, b) attempting or has attempted to gain a real estate license, c) interested in real estate at some level, or d) related to an active real estate agent in one way or another.

In fact, it's not shocking at all when you realize there are still more than

1.02 million real estate agents in the United States, according to the National Association of Realtors (down from 2.4 million in 2008).

You see, the bar for becoming a real estate agent is still pretty low across the country. It takes almost 1,000 hours to become a hair stylist, but only about 75 to 90 hours to get your real estate license. That's bad news because a bad haircut will always grow out, but you may never recapture the thousands of dollars you lose when you pick the wrong agent.

As a result, many people become real estate agents and don't do it for the reasons you or I, as a buyer, would want them to do it for, because it's their passion and they love helping people buy and sell homes.

In fact, they become agents because:

- It's a default choice for them because they retired or another job/career didn't pan out.

- They wanted to make a boatload of money and were hoping that real estate would be their ticket to riches.

- Someone told them they would make a great agent (without knowing what makes a great agent).

- The agent who helped them buy or sell their last home did a terrible job, and they thought they could do it better.

- Their mother, father, brother, sister, uncle or cousin was an agent, and they thought it was in their genes.

- They thought it would exciting to give real estate a "try" for a change of pace to do something different.

Please know that I'm not a dream stealer and that I believe in the United States; it's our constitutional right to have any job we want at any time if we meet the minimum requirements for the position.

That said, please also know that I stand for excellence and want everyone from hamburger fryers to neurosurgeons, from construction workers to accountants, from car salespeople to landscapers, and everyone in between to be the best they can be, love what they do, do it with passion, and be an expert in every sense of the word in their field.

Anything less than that means you're doing a disservice to your prospects and clients, especially in the real estate industry where people are buying and selling their most valuable asset in almost every instance.

Said another way, those looking to meet minimum standards as part of their daily job need not apply.

KEEP YOUR EYES PEELED FOR EXPERT STRATEGIES

True real estate experts spend time honing their craft, work full time at their career, and have created a system you can count on to get a home sold fast and for top dollar. More important, they know exactly what they're going to do for home sellers and buyers long before they sit down and meet with them face to face. It's systematic, proven, and most of all, it's centered on creating a world-class experience for the client.

Here are five highly effective and recognizable tips the experts use to get homes sold fast and for top dollar in any market environment.

1. *Use professional pictures for listings.* A picture, as they say, is worth a thousand words. In the real estate industry, pictures can be the difference between a house being shown and sold, and not being seen at all. The better the picture quality and the more of them you have, the more likely it is that a home will be seen and subsequently sold. Professional pictures make a statement of the quality of the home, and more important, they lend themselves to helping prospective buyers stoke the fire of their excitement about potentially buying your home. Surprisingly, some listings on the MLS (and even on certain websites) don't have any pictures at all. This is the kiss of death because not having pictures virtually guarantees the home won't sell because most buyers and agents, including me, won't go to look at a home where we haven't seen the pictures first. Put your best foot forward and use professional pictures in all your marketing materials online and in print. It is a game changer.

2. *Stage the home before it's listed.* It's a simple strategy but one that's not often used by real estate agents and For Sale by Owners (FSBOs) alike. According to the American Society of Home Stagers and Redesigners, a staged home sells for 5.1 percent more than one that isn't staged, and it sells about 21 days faster. Giving the home a personal touch that makes it feel warm and "homey" as well as cleaning up the landscaping draws buy-

ers into the home and makes them take a longer look when shopping. While I recommend hiring a stager, you can do some staging yourself by simply allowing your five senses to guide you as to what needs to be done to make a great impact. For instance, having a few decorative pieces around the home make it look like a model home instead of lived-in. Also, small-cost fix-ups, such as caulking, insulation, painting your front door, removing small appliances, professional house cleaning, replacing cabinet hardware, repairing some boards on your deck, cleaning the carpet, replacing windows and/or doors, removal of bugs and decluttering have a huge effect on getting top dollar for the home.

3. *Hold a proper open house.* Make sure the people in the marketplace know the home is for sale. Take the time to extend personal invitations to each potential buyer to walk through and "feel" like they're owner(s). Be sure to invite neighbors as they may have a friend or may come into contact with someone wanting to move into the area. While at the open house, have something tangible with pictures for prospects they can take with them so they'll remember the home. People usually visit multiple homes in a day, and it's hard for them to distinguish between all the homes. A good take-away piece is always valuable. Lastly, be sure to follow up with everyone who came to the home. Not only is this feedback vital, but the time spent at the open house should lead to a legitimate buyer opportunity for the subject home or another home in the marketplace.

4. *Know the property inside and out.* The more information that's available on a home, the easier it is for the buyer to make an educated purchasing decision. Good things to know are demographics, schools, how to get creative financing on the home (as well as the conventional, FHA, VA and USDA regulations). It's also important to know about taxes, upcoming construction in the area, whether the area is mostly rentals or owner occupied, what the trends of prices are in the area, how the neighboring homes have stood up over time, and what sort of demand there will be for the homes in the future. Knowledge is power, and proper use of that knowledge is even more powerful.

5. *Get the home closed.* There are a spate of variables to manage in a real estate transaction, and many of them happen between the time the property goes under contract and the closing itself. Be sure to use a checklist so that *all* steps are covered and nothing slips through the cracks. Dealing with each of these professionals in the transaction to get the home *sold,* including lenders, appraisers, attorneys, inspectors, repairmen, carpet cleaners, locksmiths, etc. is a huge job. They all need to be communicated with and kept in the loop for each of their services to occur in a timely manner and have all their paperwork in hand for each closing. One missed step could cost you the sale...period.

There are several other strategies experts employ to get the home sold for maximum value in reasonable time periods, but these are some of the big ones. If you're selling your home yourself, you'll want to at least consult with an expert before you get started.

However, if you're going to interview and hire a real estate expert (which I strongly suggest), make sure you interview them thoroughly and put them to the test to ensure that they're truly experts.

Remember, experts have a system to get your home sold that they can show to you. More important, they're more interested in you reaching your goals than they are in getting paid.

Every expert advisor is a real estate agent, but not every real estate agent is an expert.

About Kim

Kim Williams, also known as "The Staging Broker™," is a real estate marketing expert. She's known for constantly asking the questions: "How is the market doing now? When is it going to turn? and How can I sell my listings quick and for more profit?"

She founded the Real Estate Insider (REI) in 2009, a company that provides marketing services for clients statewide, focusing on sellers, and offering a menu of options to fit their specific situation and pocketbook, as well as providing tips and suggestions to help them with the marketing process and professional advice to get the property sold. REI also provides a unique teleseminar for FSBOs (For Sale by Owners) where they can dial in to listen and make comments regarding what the market is currently doing, what's predicted, and how the mortgage rate change affects sellers, followed by a question and answer session. The Staging Broker™, a branch of REI established in 2011, is a staging, decluttering and organizing solutions service that helps clients create the "model home" look and feel in their own homes. Kim started REI because all homes are different and should have a customized marketing plan to cover what that unique property offers.

To learn more about Kim Williams, The Staging Broker™, and how you can receive the free special report FSBO: Understanding Your Home, as well as search thousands of properties instantly, go to www.theInsideBroker.com, or call toll-free (800) 735-1398, ext. 1500.

CHAPTER 50

Leah Santos' Guide for How to Attract the Right Buyer and Get Your Price

By Leah Santos

I'm grateful and delighted to live in South Florida. The place where rehabbing and marketing homes for sale became my passion and where I have achieved personal and professional success. South Florida is my home. The pulsating nightlife of downtown Miami, the cool elegance of Coconut Grove, the sophisticated dining in Coral Gables, Brickell's fast-paced trendsetting vibe, the spectacular Miami beaches—who wouldn't want to live here.

What I love to do is find new buyers and develop marketing plans for beautiful homes. Every time I close a sale, it's a celebration for both the homeowner and the buyer. And, of course, I wouldn't be honest if I didn't say that the money is not important. When you put your home on the market, you deserve the highest possible price. It's only fair, isn't it?

Selling your home is as much an art as it is a science. I've been very fortunate to have achieved success at selling hundreds of homes, and I'd like to pass along some of the lessons I've learned. Whether you work with a realtor or sell your home yourself, here are seven key concepts to

407

help you sell your home more quickly and at the highest possible price.

1. HOME STAGING

When a potential buyer visits your house, you want them to fall in love with it and see it as their dream home. First impressions are critical. If the house isn't appealing, a prospect won't even go inside. Your home may be beautiful to you, but every home needs to be presented to its best advantage. This is what we call staging.

You can spruce up your house without a big budget. On the exterior, trim the lawn and shrubs, paint the front door a nice bright color, take all the toys off the lawn, and fix any broken lights. Park your car either in the garage or away from the house. On the interior, you should repaint the walls and trim if necessary. Put away personal family photos and pet stuff. Make sure the drapes are open and the lights work. The kitchen and bathrooms need to be clean and fresh. If you have an old shag carpet, get rid of it. Put out fresh flowers on the dining room table.

The goal is to make your house look and feel like a model home that you would see in a magazine. You may choose to hire a professional staging service, and they'll come in and make your house look its very best.

You may want to consider investing in major repairs. New countertops in the kitchen or a new toilet in the bathroom will give your home that just-remodeled look. Your return on investment will far outweigh the costs and will bring bigger returns when you sell your house; research shows that spending a reasonable amount to upgrade your property can boost the price to more than cover expenses.

I once handled a lovely home that was located on a very busy corner. It had sat on the market for months and eventually expired. The owner contacted me for a consultation, and we determined that potential buyers disliked the location on the noisy street. So the owner agreed to plant a barrier wall of shrubs that shielded the house from the traffic and created a sense of a cozy, enclosed courtyard space. In just 23 days, the house was sold to a very happy buyer. Clearly, the modest investment in shrubs had made a huge difference.

2. DETERMINE YOUR HOME'S VALUE

What makes your home interesting, unique or different can raise its value. Perhaps you have an open kitchen and great entertainment area. Wine cellar? Great location? History? This may sound counterintuitive, but don't be afraid to highlight the negative in order to separate the lookers from the real buyers. For example, if you have no view, target prospects who don't care about the view but want a trendy downtown address at a lower price tag. Or how about making a spice garden on the wall that semi-encloses the balcony? Think about lifestyle, ask yourself what lifestyle your home represents, and then advertise to that.

3. REAL ESTATE ABSORPTION RATE

When you price your house, you need to understand the local real estate market and know the real estate absorption rate. It's a very reliable indicator of the relationship between the asking price and how quickly you can expect to sell your home.

The absorption rate is the current housing supply divided by the current rate of sales. The resulting figure is the number of months that a market-priced home will stay on the market until it's sold.

In a neutral market, the average home will sell in five or six months. When the market is slow, a typical home may remain on the market for nine months. In a fast market, a home might sell in three months. If you want to beat that average, you might consider pricing your property more aggressively to attract buyers more quickly. I'll discuss that in the next section.

4. DETERMINE THE ASKING PRICE

Pricing real estate is a function of supply and demand. It's important to set the price according to objective standards, and not by the seller's ego or presumed need.

When pricing your home, you'll want to look at comparable homes that have sold in the past six months, and if possible, within a half mile of your home. Also, if you live in a building or condo community, keep comparables within the same building or community. Here are the four steps to accurate pricing:

1. Research the sales in your particular ZIP code and divide into price bands.

2. Determine the number of sales in each price band.

3. Study the market absorption rate, which is the level of inventory within these price bands. The Average Days on the Market Before Sold (ADOM) in your community can vary from 0 months to more than 12 months. Use this guide to find the optimum price for your home:

- *0-2 months ADOM:* Price with the market and up to 10 percent above market.

- *3-4 months ADOM:* Price aggressively with the market.

- *5-6 months ADOM:* Price with the market and as much as 5 percent below market.

- *7-12 months ADOM:* Price 10 percent below market.

- *Over 12 months ADOM:* Price 10 percent or more below market.

Pricing your property on the lower end of the scale can actually lead to a higher selling price. How? By creating a buyer frenzy that drives up the price to, and even beyond, the market value. The combination of this strategy, along with an immaculately staged home, can be very effective.

A pre-listing appraisal is recommended for high-end luxury homes, homes with large acreage, or large tracts of land that may be difficult to find comparable sales. Be sure to attach this to your property's website or on the property listing MLS database if using a realtor.

5. MARKET YOUR PROPERTY ONLINE

In our new internet-connected world, everyone shops for property online. Syndication of your listing and international exposure are must-haves.

Visuals are important. Visit my website's "sell page" for in-depth information on how to photograph your home. On your property website, have a minimum of 20 full-color wide-angle photographs that capture entire rooms. Exterior shots should be taken without vehicles in the driveway or toys in the yard. Interior scenes must be well lit, with the drapes open and lights on. Remove pets, toys and personal family items from the scene.

For even more impact than still photos, provide a virtual tour with a short video clip. We often make a short video that guides the visitor step-by-step through the house.

In your video, describe the best features of the interior. Beautiful hardwood floors? A stone fireplace? Granite countertops in the kitchen? Solar heat? These are things buyers love, and they'll make them want to see your house—and pay more for it.

Remember the old saying "location, location, location"? Be sure to mention if you're close to shopping, museums, parks or the beach. Many buyers with families want to know about the school district, or whether you're on the school bus route. Don't be shy! Everything and anything that makes your property appealing is something a buyer needs to know about.

6. BE CAREFUL WITH OPEN HOUSES

In a buyers' market, it's not enough to tie a bunch of balloons to the mailbox and open the doors to anyone who walks in. When it comes to prospective buyers, quantity doesn't equal quality.

I always work with my clients to carefully prepare and stage an open house. A list of prospects is made, paying special attention to target specific groups or buyers that your home or location would appeal to and have invitations sent to them. The signage in the yard or at the curb is professional and inviting. Serve light snacks, and always have a guestbook for prospects to sign and leave their contact information. I do not recommend a homeowner be present. You want them to envision this as their home. If the homeowner is present, he or she should stick to talking about the features of the property. If selling with an agent, let the realtor handle the sales process that's what they're trained for.

You might try a real estate soirée, which is an invitation-only targeted event used to create "buzz." They're especially effective with homes that showcase a unique lifestyle choice, are celebrity-owned, newsworthy or historic. For instance, a home with an eight-car garage should appeal to car enthusiasts or collectors. How can you best reach this target group? A home with a large wine cellar might appeal to serious wine aficionados. These are examples of what we call in real estate "the hook." Determine your home's hook. Creativity is key in developing your target invitation-only group and establishing a proper marketing plan for today's luxury home sale and real estate soirée.

7. USE QR CODES AND OTHER DIGITAL RESOURCES

What's a QR code? The letters stand for "quick response." It's that checkerboard pattern that you photograph with your smartphone. The barcode-like design links you to the property website, where you can get information. We can place a QR code on a lawn sign, on a paper flier, in the office window¾just about anywhere a prospect will see it. In seconds, prospects can get full-color photos, listing information, and anything else they need to become interested in the property.

We also use a real estate hotline. It's a toll-free 800 number that prospects can call and get immediate information about a listing, or even get connected directly to me or my office. It's there for them 24 hours a day, seven days a week.

These tools are powerful. Let's say a couple is out driving on a weekend, and they pass your house. The prospects can use their smartphone and capture an image of the QR code on the lawn sign. The code will connect them to the website where we've posted a video tour of the home. They can call the real estate hotline and talk directly to me or one of my professional staff. After making sure they're qualified, we set up an appointment with them to visit your house. Within 15 minutes of the prospect seeing your house and the "for sale" sign, you're halfway to making a sale.

By the way, in print ads for homes, I never provide the list price. If you give potential buyers too much information, they have no incentive to contact you to learn more. Instead use the opportunity to drive prospects to your property's website, or very interested prospects will call to ask for the price. We get to know them and introduce them to your house as effectively as possible.

In today's real estate marketplace, you have many choices. I'm so pleased to have assisted many valued clients with selling their properties, and I'm also happy that we can offer our FSBO (for sale by owner) package to people who want to do it themselves. Either way, with the right planning and professional assistance, selling your home can be a profitable and pleasurable experience.

About Leah

Leah Santos, principal of South Florida Group of Companies, has a history of building successful organizations and relationships within the Miami community and giving back to the community through sponsorship and association with the Environmental Coalition of Miami and the Beaches, chamber of commerce and other community associations.

Leah's father, now retired, was a builder and self-made entrepreneur for all his adult life. He built numerous companies throughout the time she was growing up: Elro Enterprises, builder and developer of new homes and apartment complexes; Puerto Rico Floor Service, a direct supplier of commercial janitorial products and services; and the family even owned a coffee farm in their native Puerto Rico called Café Borinquen. In short, they were never bored and never lacked anything. This grew in Leah a love for entrepreneurism. Being surrounded by real estate while she was growing up really stayed with her.

Leah began her career with the Limited Companies, Victoria's Secret. She quickly moved up the ranks to general manager, where she won several achievements in sales volume and was quickly recognized and sent store to store to clean up and get the location performing at its top sales volume. Leah then transitioned to account executive for a major eyewear distributor, Linea Roma, going to trade shows and selling their products to business owners and suppliers all over the world. While it was a fun job and she had many good experiences, she had a burning desire to get into real estate, purchase and rehab properties and enjoy a higher quality of life while adding value and bringing quality solutions to people's lives.

Leah began her professional real estate career with one of the top real estate companies at the time, Coldwell Banker, well-known for their advanced training program. This was the best decision she ever made, as much of what she learned she still uses, even today. Simultaneously Leah started buying and selling residential property for profit and selling homes to her friends and family and sphere. When the market went down, she decided to go into her first real estate venture, despite the market downturn, and opened as co-founder and partner Imobilia Real Estate and Renter's Café on Miami Beach (www.renterscafe.com and www.imobilia.com, respectively). Short sales quickly became mainstream, and Leah closed more than 50 transactions that year (2007-2008) when many agents didn't even know what a short sale really was. Then in 2009, she decided to cut ties with the partnership and branch out on her own and created what she has today—founder and principal of South Florida Property Group & Management.

Leah's new venture is all about creating value and building long-term customer relationships with customers in order to create customers for life. Leah's biggest pleasure is when she helps customers who share in her commitment or have been referred by other happy clients from her raving fan club. She also enjoys meeting new, committed customers, solving problems and helping these customers reach their goal of homeownership or investments. More often than not, Leah can usually lead them to their own conclusion about what they want in life when she asks them the right series of questions. Leah is hooked on constantly gaining more knowledge about the industry so she can provide added value and best help her clients. Leah is always interested in new, innovative ways of doing things differently, attending conferences, and looking for ways to gain more knowledge about the industry so she can best help her clients and provide this value to consumers, which is what sets Leah apart.

When she's not working on her business and representing home buyers and sellers, she's on vacation, skiing, traveling and spending quality time with her family.

For more information about Leah and South Florida Property Group and to subscribe to Leah's blog or to download other great articles and resources for preparing your home for sale, please visit www.southfloridapropertygroup.com. To schedule a private marketing consultation and receive an in-depth market analysis tailor fit for you, call Leah at (305) 639-8374.

CHAPTER 51

6 Simple Strategies to Sell a Home In Any Market

By Sandy Steen

Clearly defining your motivation is the first step to successful selling. Before deciding to put your home on the market, always give careful consideration to your reasons for selling. Having a frank discussion with those involved and affected by your move about your motivating desires will ensure everyone is on the same team while your home is on the market.

Your level of motivation will directly determine the amount of success you'll have selling your home. Are you relocating for a job or because your financial position has changed? Are you downsizing or wishing to be closer to family? A consultation and candid conversation with an agent about all of the many reasons you've decided to or need to sell is critical.

An agent who helps you determine whether your level of motivation is consistent with what it takes to sell under your current local market conditions, will do you, other agents and buyers a great service. Always choose an expert advisor and be willing to heed their advice. There's nothing worse than having no showings on your home, while behind the scenes, you're miserable and exhausted from keeping your home show-ready. So where do you start?

VALUATION/EVALUATION (STRATEGIES 1-3)

Appraisal

An educated seller always starts with a presale appraisal. Have you ever wondered why top agents won't even take a listing without a current appraisal? They understand the process and have seen repeatedly that the traditional way a transaction is carried out is fundamentally flawed. With more foreclosures on the market than ever before, many sellers have lost more equity than they ever imagined. Many deals are lost because homes fail to appraise at the price needed for the buyer to obtain financing and the seller to satisfy their mortgage payoff. Obtaining an appraisal reflecting current market value helps you determine whether you still want to sell, can afford to sell, or whether you should just hold. Your appraiser is a good judge of where the market in your area is headed as well. They see trends developing in the local real estate markets, and while your home may not be worth as much as you hoped, it may still be a great time to sell if your market is projected to lose yet another 7 percent in the coming year or if you're simply in a must-move situation. Once you determine you're willing and able to sell the home at or below the price the appraiser has indicated, your next step is to obtain a presale inspection.

Presale Inspection

The most glaring example of a fundamental flaw in the traditional real estate transaction is the failure to obtain a presale inspection and uncover any hidden secrets before a buyer does. Why would you market your home for sale, find a buyer and then let them inspect all of your home's warts only to return to you demanding repairs, purchase-price reductions, or worse, threatening to abandon the sale?

This leaves the seller desperate to hang on to the sale. You can be certain buyers will always overestimate the cost to cure imperfections, and they often make unreasonable demands, which sellers will concede in order to protect their sale. Failing to obtain a presale inspection clearly places you in a weakened negotiating position and should never happen. It can cost you thousands or result in lost sales. Often repairs that could have been done by the homeowner can't be accomplished once the real estate transaction clock starts ticking, therefore, the seller is forced to hire out corrections and repairs that would have normally only cost them an investment of their time in order to meet deadlines. Another consideration is how quickly buyers may spread the word about the house they were going to buy until it failed inspection. Don't risk this kind of negative press about your home.

Title

This is another step not to be missed. In fact, if you're considering listing your home, a top agent will always have your title work available for review at the first consultation. Confirm that you have clear title without discrepancies, mistakes or unexpected liens. Tax problems and mechanic's liens filed by contractors can lead to nasty surprises if you postpone this step until you've already accepted an offer. If you have an outstanding mortgage, a home equity line of credit or any other seconds on the home they should appear on the title. Take this opportunity to confirm your payoff with the mortgage company and check the balance on your home equity line of credit or second mortgage. Know the total of your financial commitments that must be satisfied *before* you offer the home for sale.

IMAGES (STRATEGY 4)

More than 85 percent of home buyers start their home search online. You must compel them to take the time to visit your home in person over all of the other homes they're seeing on dozens of internet websites. For this reason, professional images are critical to this process. Amateur photos will ensure your home is ignored by online traffic, which will reduce your showings and cost you a sale. In most cases, you don't want your real estate agent taking marketing images of your home. I say in most cases, because there are a select few agents who've studied photography and have the necessary equipment. This isn't the time to hire a hobbyist or an agent with a pocket camera. A professional photographer will use a tripod, a wide angle lens, and adjust lighting, flash and shutter speeds for the best results. To give your home the advantage, be sure your photographer has a minimum of 50 great shots of your home to use in your online marketing. Many large homes require upward of 100 photos, and all homes should have video footage posted online, or at a minimum a video tour of still images. Many high-end cameras that photographers use are capable of capturing the quality of video required. Your photographer should be professionally skilled in the use of the latest image- and video-enhancement software.

STAGING (STRATEGY 5)

Make no mistake, home selling takes work these days. Gone are the days that a sign in the yard was all it took to prompt a bidding war that yielded a seller more than asking price. Real estate economists agree that those market conditions won't return to many markets for a decade. I describe our current situation as a "beauty contest and a pricing war." You must be willing to bring the home to top condition and keep it there until closing. If you're selling, roll up your sleeves and get ready to clean, scrub, paint, polish and weed.

The appearance of your home when a buyer visits can make or break the deal. Every time your home is shown, one of two things can happen: 1) The buyer likes what they see for the money, and you get an offer, or 2) you cause another property to look more attractive in comparison, and they get the offer, and you get crossed off the list.

Failing to have your home professionally staged can be a costly mistake. Studies show that great staging translates into your home selling faster and for more money. There's a misconception that staging is only necessary for vacant homes and bachelor pads. Understand that the buying process for most people is an emotional process. Appropriate staging softens your home, makes it feel inviting, and allows buyers to feel at ease. It creates a desire in the buyer to be in that pleasing environment and make it their own. There are very few homes that can't be improved upon by a staging.

Keeping your home and yard clean and clutter-free with made beds each morning is just the beginning. In tough markets, it takes a magazine-ready home to make a sale. Your property should look move-in ready. Requesting a two-hour showing notice so you can tidy up is always a better strategy than letting a prospective buyer and their agent see you at your worst. Agents are quick to tell their associates not to bother showing a property that they felt was messy. If you have animals in the home and have a difficult time keeping up with pet hair, consider boarding your pet with a friend or family member for the first 30 days your home is on the market. Unless you're overpriced, you should have the most showings during this time.

HOME WARRANTY (STRATEGY 6)

Offering a seller-paid warranty at closing indicates a level of seller confidence in the home. For a fee at closing, the buyer is covered for up to 13 months. This provides the buyer assurance that they won't have any large, unbudgeted expenses in their first year of ownership should expensive systems malfunction. You should enroll in a home warranty that offers both seller and buyer coverage. Many warranty companies that offer seller coverage will cover you during the listing period, even though you haven't yet technically paid for the warranty. This can help you avoid an unanticipated costly repair if you have a major system failure within your listing period. You would simply pay your deductible of $50 to $100, and the warranty company covers the cost of the repair.

FINAL ADVICE ON MARKETING AND POSITIONING

Once you've invested the time and effort to accomplish your presale strategies, be sure to take full advantage of your upfront preparation. Review your current competition by scouring every active for-sale property you can find on the market and calculate how many homes sell in any given month in your price range to determine how many months of inventory are available in your price range. Determine what seller-paid concessions you would consider making. Would you be willing to help the buyer by paying some of their closing costs? Should you be offering a landscaping, painting or carpeting allowance when you compare your property to others available?

Use your appraisal and market-absorption rate to set your asking price. In some areas, homes will sell at appraised market value, but be prepared to position your home to sell by pricing it below appraised market value. Some markets require as little as $500 below appraised value to attract offers, while in other markets the inventory is so high and the competition so stiff that you'll have to price 2 to 10 percent below appraisal to get offers in a reasonable amount of time, sometimes to get offers at all.

Bravo! You've done your due diligence in determining what your home is worth, while insuring the buyer won't find any costly problems on inspection. You don't need a lot of "wiggle room." You know the amount it will take to clear all debts against the home and your cost of sale. I caution you not to fall prey to the old strategy of pricing "a little higher" so you have room to negotiate. You're asking for failure by using this tired strategy. Buyers are value shoppers today and pricing your home even a little higher than the price you would accept often results in the very person that would have bought your home never even seeing it in the first place.

With a proven marketing plan, you're testing the purchase price of your home in the market and the reaction of the buyers to that price. Keep in mind, you don't set the price—the market does. The market doesn't care that you took out a second to pay off your boat or that you're moving to a more expensive area and need a higher down payment, or that your spouse will be unemployed as a result of your move. The market is indifferent to your personal situation, and you can't expect to compensate for your personal situation through the sale of your home.

I encourage you to come out swinging with your *very best price*. When you receive an offer below what your very best price is, simply counter back with your original price. The buyer will understand and respect that you've offered your home at your bottom dollar. If the buyer requests help with closing costs or other concessions, simply add them on top of your very best price. When you're priced below current market value, there should be room in the appraised price to cover small concessions that you might consider making.

Many sellers in today's market have their homes for sale and don't realize they're on the market but not in the market of homes that will actually sell. They've priced their home unrealistically using an outdated refinance appraisal, an old-school Comparative Market Analysis, or by choosing the agent who said they could get them the most for their home. The vast majority of these uninformed homeowners get zero.

Capitalize on the homework you did upfront by using marketing remarks that indicate you're priced below appraised market value, and offer the appraisal for inspection. Draw attention to the fact that you've already done a home inspection, and offer a copy of the inspection report and follow-up that shows corrections were made. Let buyers know that your title work has been reviewed and is clear. These commitments made by you indicate you're a serious seller, and you will most certainly attract a serious home buyer. Now it's time to celebrate! Your offer will be coming in any day.

About Sandy

Sandy Steen is the CEO and broker of Signature Realty Partners and Signature Property Management in Springfield, Missouri. Sandy has drawn on more than 15 years of her own private real estate investment and development experience to deliver world-class service to her many clients throughout Southwest Missouri.

Sandy uses the business talents she honed as an Air Force officer and the listening skills and compassion she developed while practicing medicine for almost two decades to create strategies that provide effective solutions for her real estate clientele. Her goal is to fundamentally change the way properties are marketed and sold industrywide.

Sandy believes that professional development is the cornerstone of any successful career. Setting herself apart from her peers, Sandy has invested thousands of hours pursuing advanced educational and professional designations in real estate to better serve her clients.

Sandy is a Graduate of the Realtor Institute and holds both the Master of Real Estate and the Senior Real Estate Specialist. She was also declared a Certified Residential Specialist by the Council of Residential Specialists, reserved for elite agents.

Holding the two most coveted designations in the entire real estate industry, the Certified Property Manager through the Institute of Real Estate Management and the Certified Commercial Investment Member, Sandy has proved that not all agents are created equal. These accomplishments place her in the top 1 percent of all agents worldwide.

Demonstrating her giving nature, Sandy is the exclusive broker in Southwest Missouri to participate in Homes for Heroes, a national organization that funds local charities every time a home is bought or sold by a firefighter, police officer, veteran, healthcare worker or teacher. This program puts thousands of dollars back into her local community.

Sellers, buyers and investors alike are thrilled to have the opportunity to work with Sandy because of her professionalism and profound real estate knowledge and experience. She's one of the most sought-after agents in her market. Her clients describe working with Sandy as a first-class experience.

CHAPTER 52

Penny-Wise, House Foolish:
Purchase a Home Wisely and Avoid Ending Up Underwater

By Tait Zimmerman

The old adage that homes always increase in value may be true, at least over the last 60-plus years, but as millions of homeowners are discovering, dips in the housing market can and do occur. These can put those homeowners who bought at the top of the market in a lot of trouble, especially if they're compelled to sell their home within several years of purchasing. The historical assumption has been that if someone buys a home, it will appreciate over the next few years so that the homeowner can then turn around and sell it, recouping closing costs and commissions, and hopefully getting a check back at closing. Unfortunately, while this may be the case in a rapidly appreciating market or over longer periods of time, it's not the case in a declining, flat or slightly increasing market, especially if one has to turn around and sell quickly. I'm not advocating that you not buy. In fact, I'm a huge proponent of homeownership and its benefits; I just want to enable you to make wise home-buying decisions that will help when it comes time for resale, as well as help you avoid a future short sale situation.

First, an all-too-common story. Then we'll look at some practical tips on how, as a buyer, you can make wise purchasing decisions and avoid ending up underwater like nearly half the sellers I'm currently meeting with.

John and Mary were first-time homebuyers, chasing after the American dream of homeownership. It was the era of sublending, zero down, and stated income prequalification. Getting a loan was easy, and everyone was doing it. The universal test among many lenders seemed to be, hold a mirror under a buyer's nose, see if it fogged, and if so, get them into as big a loan as possible. It was the bubble before the crash, and things were exciting!

John and Mary had been told their whole lives to use other people's money as much as possible. Their lender prequalified them at $350,000, based off both their incomes. Who would have thought that John, a manager at a local grocery store, and Mary, a waitress, could qualify for a $350,000 home with zero down? Elated, they carried out their home search over the next few months and finally fell in love with the perfect home, listed at $375,000. After going back to their lender, they got their preapproval amount bumped up and purchased their dream home! Even more exciting, they found out they were expecting. Soon, their beautiful baby girl arrived! Life was good.

Time passed, and John's anticipated pay increases didn't materialize in the now downward moving economy. In fact, he had to take a pay cut. Mary had always wanted to become a stay-at-home mom, but this hope now seemed impossible. Truth be told, they had barely been able to make their payments before, let alone now. They were slowly dipping further and further into the red. Meanwhile the housing market in their local area declined, not drastically, but significantly enough.

After several years of scraping by, they decided to sell their home and downsize. Their agent brought comparable sales and showed them what the potential bottom line would be at closing. In order to price their home within the market, they would have to list it at $345,000 ($30,000 below their purchase price of $375,000) and pay commissions and closing costs on top of that. When they bought, they had put no money down and had accumulated little if any equity in the property. Their bottom line at closing after commissions and closing costs: $317,000. John and Mary had no savings to speak of. Their agent suggested a short sale, as long as they could convince the bank that they had a hardship, since they weren't actually behind on their payments, had not lost a job, weren't being transferred, etc. There was the very real possibility that the bank wouldn't accept their appeal. Their only other option was renting the home out, which, of course, posed its own problems and complications.

John and Mary weren't in an easy situation by any means. Yet today, many Americans find themselves in this same predicament.

This story isn't specific to one individual but is rather a compilation of the stories of dozens of sellers I've met with recently. Within this pool of sellers, there exist varying levels of distress. Some are upset they'll come away from closing with only a few thousand dollars for moving expenses. Others are just breaking even. Many are required to bring thousands, if not tens of thousands of dollars, to the closing table. Then there are the sad cases in which the owners are behind on their payments and owe too much on their home to sell it, which results in a short sale. Some are heartbreaking situations. Fortunately, in many areas at least, the housing market isn't showing the decline that it did directly after the housing bubble. But even in a flat or slightly increasing market, the following tips and tricks could save your bacon should you end up needing or wanting to sell in the next several years. We'll explore when to buy, how to qualify for a loan, and how much home to buy to help you avoid the pitfalls John and Mary fell into.

- *Pay cash.* I know that this may sound fuddy-duddy, old fashioned, and not in line with our instant gratification, "put it all on the credit card" mindset, but I'll repeat my point. Pay cash, if at all possible. Or at the very least, put as much cash down upfront as you can. Why? Security, mainly. Many buyers live from paycheck to paycheck. One little hiccup (e.g., a pay cut, loss of one income stream, extra hospital bills, etc.) is usually enough to cripple a borrower and send him into a tailspin, which often leads to a short sale or foreclosure. In a downward economy, debt is like an anchor and chain around a person's neck. Even with historic low interest rates of around 4 percent, in order to justify investing that cash in the stock market, for instance, instead of putting it into your home upfront and saving on interest, the return on your stock market investment would have to exceed the percent interest on your home. I understand there can be tax benefits associated with a mortgage, but just make sure to make an accurate comparison, rather than just assuming the benefits are there. I understand that paying cash, while certainly beneficial, isn't a workable option for the majority of us. So let's look at some pointers on what you can do to minimize your risk factors if you do need to get a loan.

- *Don't plan on making money, at least in the short run.* Some markets may have hit rock bottom; others may still be falling. By most projections, the housing market could get a little bit worse before it gets any better. Those economists predicting a turnaround are usually setting it out several years. If you're viewing your home as an investment, you should plan on staying there for the long haul. If you're looking at your home as a home, as a place to live, a place where you can modify features to your specifications without worrying about a landlord, then now is a good time to purchase, as we're seeing some excellent interest rates. To at least break-even on a future home sale, your home would have to increase in value enough to cover commissions and closing costs, something that's not likely to occur in the next several years in the majority of markets. The obvious exception to this rule would be fixer-uppers. Just make sure your potential sale price after renovation takes into account a flat or slightly declining market.

- *Qualify on one income.* This just makes sense. If you buy a home as a couple, try to qualify on one income. That way, if one of your incomes changes significantly, your ship isn't completely sunk.

- *Put money down.* One challenge with the zero-down loans of yesteryear was that since 100 percent financing was so readily available, a buyer had no equity and hence no cushion for falling prices if he ended up needing to move within several years. Toward the beginning of a loan, most of the payment goes toward interest, so when no money is put down, payments contribute little toward equity. Putting money down on a property creates a boost in equity, which can be a needed buffer if plans change and you need or want to sell in the short term.

- *Go with a 15-year mortgage.* Essentially what you're doing here is paying more on your home, paying it off more quickly, and paying less in interest. Obviously, if this causes you to make a higher payment than you're comfortable with, this could backfire, so it might entail looking for a home in a slightly lower price range. The good news is that your interest rate will probably be lower for a 15-year note vs. a 30-year one, and you'll be putting a lot more money toward principal, which helps build that buffer against a quick move or downward-moving market.

- *Make extra payments.* It's amazing the difference making an extra payment, or adding a little bit more to your regular payment, can make! The additional money pays toward principal, quickly building equity. For example, if you pay $100 more a month, plus $1,000 once a year, your $200,000 30-year loan would be paid off in just 23 years. Not only will your home be paid off more quickly—for those of you who aren't planning on staying in the property for that length of time—but your equity will grow astronomically! Discipline required? Yes. But the rewards are great!

- *Buy less home.* While upgrades, extra square footage, a larger garage, a big back deck, jetted tub, granite countertops, etc., are all nice, I'm constantly meeting with people who bought too much home and purchased at the top of what they could qualify for. As a result, they're now more or less financially stretched. This group of homeowners encompasses all economic levels, from engineers to plumbers, cashiers to doctors. Buying less home is a wise move in today's market. Let's take this a step further. Imagine you could qualify for a $1,500/month base payment. Now imagine that you purchase a home with a base payment of $1,250 a month. Instead of spending the additional $250 on other things, you apply it to your mortgage, in addition to your required payment, decreasing the length of payoff and building equity.

- *Take advantage of low interest rates.* A lower purchase price isn't the only way you can save money. Interest rates drastically affect how much home you can afford and how much your payment will be. Let's take a home that has a purchase price of $200,000, on a 30-year mortgage:

At a 4 percent interest rate, your payment would be around $950 a month.

At a 5 percent interest rate, you'd be paying around $1,075 a month.

This may not seem like a lot, but it certainly adds up! Plus, lower interest rates mean you can qualify for a higher price point and make the same payment. For every 1 percent increase in interest rates, you lose about $10,000 of purchasing power for every $100,000 the home is worth. That means that if you could qualify for $200,000 at 4 percent, you could only qualify for $180,000 at 5 percent. As long as you keep each of the other points we've discussed here in mind, recent historic low interest rates provide an excellent opportunity to purchase a home!

In closing, let's look at a slightly different story than our opening. John and Mary were first-time home buyers, chasing after the American dream of homeownership. Instead of following other buyers, like lemmings off a cliff, John and Mary decided to be as prudent with their home purchase as possible. While the lender told them they could afford a $350,000 home, John and Mary realized this would be stretching themselves far past their comfort level. One slip, and they'd be underwater.

Instead, John and Mary decided to buy a nice home in a nice area for $250,000 with a 15-year mortgage. It didn't have vaulted ceilings, fancy flooring, or granite countertops, but it was neat, well cared for, and moderately updated. It was home. Soon a baby was on the way, and Mary was able to fulfill her dream of staying home with their beautiful little girl. Not only were John and Mary able to set aside a good chunk of money for a rainy-day fund, but they were also able to discipline themselves to make extra payments from time to time, drastically escalating the payoff of their property. They were able to rest securely in the knowledge that if they ever had to sell, they would actually get money back at closing, instead of having to bring money to the closing table.

About Tait

Tait Zimmerman is a lifelong Alaskan, raised in a real estate family. He has been involved in the development and marketing of the family-based business since 2000 and has helped his team grow from 25 sales a year to well over 100. Since 2004, he has been mentored on a weekly basis by various top real estate experts. Together, Tait and his father Don, the broker of The Zimmerman team, won the Rock Star and Commitment to Excellence award given to Kinder/Reese coaching members for outstanding achievement. Tait's goal in working with clients is to give them such a high level of service that they feel compelled to refer friends and family to The Zimmerman Team. Tait and his wife, Lauren, have three boys. In addition to real estate, Tait enjoys working on nonprofit projects, hunting, fishing, hiking, and enjoying the beautiful outdoors of Alaska.

CHAPTER 53

The Secrets of Selling a Luxury Home in Today's Market

By Daniel P. Hamilton

With all the recent changes in the real estate market, selling a luxury home today is more challenging than it ever has been. Gone are the days of simply sticking a sign on your front lawn and sitting back while multiple offers come rolling in. Today, it's a lot trickier. In my area of Greenville, South Carolina, for example, there is a two- to three-year inventory of luxury homes, all competing for the same pool of buyers. That means if you're in any hurry to sell, the process is going to be a little stressful.

My team and I try to alleviate that stress by making selling luxury homes as easy as possible. I like to look at it as providing a "Ritz Carlton" level of service, which matches the type of service for the kind of houses I sell.

I grew up here in Greenville, and I've been selling real estate in the area for more than a decade—through the boom times as well as more recent, not-so-booming times. I started in my 20s, working with a lot of young people like myself, helping first-time buyers enter the market and purchase their first homes. As they've moved up into bigger, more luxurious properties, I've moved along with them, expanding our focus to the high-end home market.

Along the way, I've learned a lot about what it takes to sell a home that may be significantly above the average price in the market. That's where that "Ritz Carlton" level of service comes in. It goes far beyond researching comparable sales, making sure a home is priced right, and hosting showings and open houses; instead, I go the extra mile to make sure my clients' luxury homes stand out from the other homes on the market. My team and I do everything in our power to showcase what's special about our clients' homes and help them move to the front of the line.

What steps do we take—and what can you do, wherever you might be—to give your luxury home that extra sales boost it needs in today's market? I'd like to suggest the following three steps that have worked wonders for my team as well as my clients.

STEP 1: SET THE STAGE

When you hear the word "staging," you might wonder what it has to do with real estate—it sounds like a term straight out of a Broadway theater, not selling a home. If you're a regular viewer of HGTV, however, you're probably very aware of the word as it pertains to my business. The popular TV channel is basically a 24-hour showcase for real estate, interior design and home improvement shows; in fact, the channel even airs a program called "Designed to Sell" that's all about staging.

What is it about staging that makes it important enough to warrant its own TV show? To be honest, HGTV, with its endless parade of perfectly staged homes, is partially responsible for the popularity of the practice. Today's savvy real estate buyers, especially those in the luxury home market, are looking for homes that are in what I refer to as "HGTV condition." This means homes that look a lot like model homes—in good, clean condition, free of clutter, with neutral paint, floor coverings and décor.

For a lot of people, the idea of decorating their house in tones of beige or taupe sounds boring, especially if they have a particularly quirky or colorful style. But when you're selling your home, it can be difficult to win over potential buyers by putting a lot of emphasis on *your* style. There may only be a few buyers out there who are going to appreciate your purple feature wall, or your prized NFL spoon collection. On the other hand, by providing as neutral a canvas as possible, you allow as many potential buyers as possible to picture your home fitting *their* style. Whether their taste is traditional, rustic or even modern, a neutral home provides a blank canvas that allows them to see themselves—and their furnishings—fitting in.

This is why staging is so essential. And by "staging," I mean anything and everything from repainting non-neutral walls to replacing those collections of family photos or souvenirs with simple accents and accessories. Staging also can mean clearing your kids' playhouse and Legos out of that room by the kitchen and renting a table and chairs to define it as the dining room most buyers will be looking for. Your overall objective is to make your home feel more spacious and maximizing "flow" by removing extra or oversized furnishings and even changing the way some rooms are set up, allowing potential buyers to move through your home more easily.

The reason so many people are passionate about staging is that *it really does work.* According to the Association of Staging Professionals, 94 percent of staged homes sell in 29 days or less, while nonstaged homes spend an average of 145 days on the market (DOM). Of course, since this data comes from a professional staging organization, it makes sense that it supports the importance of the work they do.

However, a recent nationwide survey of home sellers conducted by HomeGain backs up the idea that staging matters, concluding that simply by spending an average of $300 to $400 on staging a home, a seller can expect an increase in sales price of between $1,500 and $2,000. That's a 586 percent return on investment! My personal experience backs those figures up; we've taken listings that have gone unsold for months and even years with other agents, and, with a little staging, sold the home within days of putting it back on the market.

Of course, not every seller can look at their home and immediately see how to stage it. This is where a professional stager can be a valuable investment—getting homes ready for buyers is all they do. Many staging professionals are trained in interior design, so they can look at your home layout and design, your furniture and your accent pieces, and quickly and easily determine how to best use what you already have to make your home look beautiful. And if you happen to need some additional pieces—like that dining room furniture I mentioned—they have access to warehouses filled with a wide range of pieces that will work with any style of home.

STEP 2: SHOOT THE SCENE

We've all heard the expression "a picture is worth a thousand words. Well, in the luxury real estate world, a picture can be worth hundreds of thousands of dollars—provided it's the right picture.

Blame it on the internet. Back in the Dark Ages before "Google" was a verb, the first time a potential buyer would see anything beyond the façade of your house was the moment he or she walked through your front door. But today, the majority of potential buyers start browsing the online listings as soon as, and sometimes even before, they decide they're ready to look for a new home.

In fact, our studies show that a whopping 96 percent of home buyers begin their search online. So your first showing can happen anytime, day or night, on the internet, or on any number of thousands of websites that feature real estate listings. This means the photos of your house that you post online will most likely provide that crucial first impression that will either motivate a buyer to see it in person…or quickly move on to another listing without a second thought.

How crucial are photos? In the area I serve, one particular luxury home was on the market (with another listing agent) for more than a year. When the sellers switched to our agency, the first thing we did was stage the home and bring in a professional photographer, who specializes in real estate, to take all new pictures of the home's interiors.

Within a week of posting those new photos online, the house sold. The buyers told us they had seen the same house countless times online, but passed it by without a second look because it just didn't stand out from the massive sea of listings in their desired area and price range. It was only when our new, improved photos provided the right kind of show-case that they felt compelled to come look at the house—and ultimately make an offer.

In other words, professional staging only gets you part of the way there. The best staging in the world won't matter if the interior of a home isn't properly photographed. That means, once your home has been staged, you need to resist that overwhelming urge to pull out your digital camera and start taking pictures yourself. If you really want your home to stand out from the rest, and for the staging to really "shine," I highly recommend hiring a professional photographer who specializes in real estate marketing.

Why? Real estate photographers know and understand the tricks and techniques that will make your home look its very best. They know how to use angles to make rooms look bigger and more spacious. They have the lighting equipment to make your house look lighter and brighter. They know how to choose a focal point, and how to crop and edit a photo to make a great design feature like a fireplace or kitchen island pop.

How do you find the right photographer to showcase your home? Here are a few tips that I find helpful:

- *Review their portfolio.* The first step to choosing the right photographer is to look at some of the work they've done. Most photographers have a website where you can review some of their best and most recent shots. Of course, since the photographer will be shooting *your* house, it's best to meet him or her in person at your home. You can get an idea of how your home will be presented and ask questions to get the other information you need.

- *Ask about their equipment.* A professional photographer shouldn't be using a point-and-shoot camera. You may not know anything about photography, so ask if he or she is using a DSLR coupled with a wide-angle lens that has an effective focal length between 14 and 24 mm. In my experience, this is what I've determined is optimal for real estate photography.

- *Make sure they have the right photo-processing software.* No matter how good the photographer is, software will be necessary to edit the photos of your home in order to present it in the best possible light. Make sure any photographer you hire has professional, up-to-date software such as Adobe Photoshop to adjust white balance, exposure and saturation.

STEP 3: TELL THE STORY

Now that you have set the stage and photographed the scene, you may be wondering what's left to do besides stick that sign on the lawn. Well, there's one very important third step that, especially in the luxury home market, really makes a difference between getting lost in the crowd and standing out. That's video.

The recent rise of video marketing in real estate has been nothing short of dramatic. YouTube is the second most-used search engine on the internet, second only to Google. So it makes sense that more and more sellers are posting "house tour" videos on the site, which offer virtual walk-throughs and show off the best features of their homes. Video marketing is now so commonplace in the real estate world that it's no longer optional in the luxury space—it's essential.

If everyone has a video, how do you stand out from the crowd? What's important isn't just the presence of a video but the type of video you use. The best videos don't just tell potential buyers about your home and its features. They give them a sense of what it might be like to experience the lifestyle that your home will provide. And for that, you need to get a little bit creative and channel your inner Hollywood producer to tell the "story" of your home.

A good lifestyle video provides more than a narrated house tour and a list of features. It shows what living in your house is actually like. It might feature the man of the house leaving work, hopping in his luxury car and driving home through the neighborhood, past the shops, restaurants or parks that make the area special. It might show the lady of the house taking a bubble bath in the jetted tub, or cooking something delicious in the gourmet kitchen.

Our team hires professionals to create these videos, including professional models and actors to portray the homeowners. That means there's no worrying about how well you can operate a camera, or script a scene, or if the camera really does add 10 pounds to your body.

Just like a well-produced television infomercial, real estate marketing videos showcase your home and lifestyle in the best possible light, inviting potential buyers to "put themselves in the picture." In many cases, it's those images that motivate them to come see your house so they can experience the things they see in the video for themselves.

The three steps I've outlined in this chapter guarantee you're employing the best state-of-the-art methods to sell a luxury home in the fastest and most profitable way possible. To facilitate your luxury home purchase, you need to attract a high-end buyer. The way to attract that high-end buyer is through the proper investment of time, money and effort in proven upscale marketing methods.

Making your luxury home look as awesome as possible gives you the best chance of getting the fastest and highest offer possible in today's marketplace. Don't skimp—and you'll succeed.

About Dan

Dan Hamilton is the operating principal of Keller Williams Realty Greenville-Upstate, one of the largest and fastest-growing residential real estate firms in the Upstate with more than 100 licensed agents. To provide maximum service to his clients, Dan founded Hamilton & Co. of Keller Williams Realty, a real estate team that consistently ranks in the top 1 percent of Greenville-area realtors for sold transactions. Hamilton & Co. was recognized by the *Wall Street Journal* and *Real Trends* as one of the top 250 real estate teams in the country in 2010 for closed transactions.

Passionate about serving and improving his community, Dan currently serves or has served in the following capacities:

Board member, Carolina Hope Christian Adoption Agency

Board member and vice chairman, Greenville County Redevelopment Authority

Director and secretary/treasurer, Greater Greenville Association of Realtors

Advisory council member, Blue Ridge Council of Boy Scouts of America

Co-chair, Greenville Workforce Housing Trust Fund Task Force

Director and former chairman, Greenville Housing Fund

Director, Pinnacle Bank of South Carolina

In 2008, Dan was elected to serve his community in the South Carolina House of Representatives from district 20 in Greenville County. At the State House, Dan was selected by the Speaker of the House to be a Majority Whip, was elected vice chairman of the Freshman Caucus, and helped form and was elected chairman of the Upstate Caucus.

Dan married his college sweetheart, Kelly, in 1999. They have four children and reside in Taylors, South Carolina.

CHAPTER 54

Luxury Home Marketing Strategies That Produce Results

By Matt O'Neill

Selling luxury real estate presents marketing challenges beyond the traditional methods for real estate sales. Because luxury homes typically take longer to sell, luxury home sellers must maximize their marketing efforts and capitalize on every opportunity. The Institute for Luxury Home Marketing defines a luxury property to be one that's valued in the top 10 percent of home prices for a given market area. In this chapter, I'll explain five essential luxury home marketing strategies that must be implemented to have a successful home sale. Each principle is supported with an example of a successful luxury home sale completed by my real estate team in Charleston, South Carolina, within the past 12 months. If these five luxury marketing strategies are applied correctly, any luxury property has an excellent chance of selling.

STRATEGY #1: THE PRINCIPLE OF SACRIFICE

The principle of sacrifice is one of the least understood and least used marketing strategies in the field of luxury real estate. This principle states that it's better to advertise your property's shortcomings upfront rather than hiding them from your potential buyers by omitting them from your marketing materials. The majority of real estate agents focus purely on marketing to the masses. They feel that the more showings they're able to generate, the better job they're doing for their clients.

This thinking, while it may seem logical, is incorrect in the marketing of luxury homes. Rather than trying to market a luxury property to the masses, agents should focus on marketing their luxury home to the exact right-fit luxury home buyers for their property.

About eight months ago, I spoke with a home seller who was having a hard time selling a luxury property in one of the premier neighborhoods in Charleston. Their property had been listed by another agent who had ignored the principle of sacrifice and had advertised this home as a very traditional Southern home in order to attract the maximum number of showings. The problem was that this particular property was not a traditional Southern home but rather an extremely modern and contemporary property. The agent failed to mention the contemporary finishes in their marketing because they were afraid this would reduce their number of showings. While the agent did generate many showings for the property, he was not able to produce a single offer. His suggestion to the sellers was to drastically reduce the price in order to compensate for the contemporary finishes that the traditional home buyers disliked.

After his listing agreement was over, my team was hired to market this property. We obeyed the principle of sacrifice. Our marketing and advertising highlighted the contemporary and modern style of this home. Our flagship photo for the marketing campaign featured the modern kitchen with bamboo cabinetry and contemporary appointments reminiscent of the classic television show "The Jetsons." The first few lines of our marketing read as follows:

> *"Elegant, metropolitan living in stylish Hibben. Come see this meticulously finished designer home designed for a young, hip family who enjoys modern living and loves to entertain. This Charleston-style property has been blended with contemporary touches to create a fresh, crisp upscale home."*

The result of our marketing was a home sale within 33 days at 100 percent of market value. Through the principle of sacrifice, we sacrificed all the showings to buyers looking for a traditional home, and found our perfect buyer who was willing to pay a premium for something most people would only purchase at a discount.

STRATEGY #2: YOUR PHOTOGRAPHS MUST BE EXTRAORDINARY

Real estate agents are *not* professional photographers. There's a strange phenomenon with most real estate agents. For some reason, as soon as an agent passes the real estate exam, they feel they have somehow earned a professional photography certification simultaneously. It always amazes me to see multimillion-dollar estates advertised with horrendous photography. The fact is, photography is an art, and it takes years of experience, combined with actual artistic talent, to become a great photographer. When I began my real estate career, I admit, I too made the mistake of thinking I was the best option for the photography for my listings. Once I relinquished this control and hired a professional to handle the photography, the difference was night and day.

About a year ago, I began talking with a homeowner who was frustrated that her luxury home had failed to sell after two different stints on the market. The home was a custom-built masterpiece with an exceptional floor plan that used all of its 4,200 square feet exceptionally well. The estate was complete with an in-home movie theater, imported hardwood floors, a three-car garage, and a separate 2,000-square-foot guest house. The problem wasn't the property; the problem was the marketing. During the two stints on the market, the home had virtually no showings to speak of.

When the homeowners contacted me to get the home sold I instantly saw room for improvement in the photographs. I scheduled a photo shoot with the best luxury home photographer in Charleston County, and he spent three hours on the photo shoot itself. The two of us then worked together to narrow the shots down to the top 24 photographs that accented the best features of the property. The photographer digitally enhanced each of the photographs we chose to make every shot really pop. We hit the market with these premium quality photographs, and the results were immediate. We received an excellent offer on the property within 14 days and closed shortly thereafter.

STRATEGY #3: PRICE CORRECTLY, NOT LOWEST

Most agents have the same advice for their sellers when a property isn't selling: "Lower your asking price." This arbitrary answer is the "go-to" problem solver, but most agents don't actually know if a price reduction will make any difference in the home sale or not.

Just over a year ago, a real estate agent in our area contacted me to sell a luxury home that she personally owned. She'd been trying to sell this property for exactly 365 days without success. After a year of efforts, the agent called me to get some fresh ideas on how to get it sold. We conducted an extensive market study for her property. We compiled market graphs and meaningful statistics to analyze her pricing strategy. Among others, we examined the following:

- *The number of competing homes for sale in her greater market area by price bracket*

- *The number of competing homes for sale in her neighborhood by price bracket*

- *The number of homes sold in the last 90 days by price bracket*

- *The number of homes sold on average each month by price bracket*

- *The odds of selling her property within the next 90 days*

- *The number of months of inventory on the market by price bracket*

- *The average list-price-to-sales-price ratio in her area by price bracket*

- *The number of months some sellers may wait to sell by price bracket*

- *The number of homes under contract to close*

- *The average price per square foot for active, contingent and sold homes by price bracket*

- *The projected trend for home prices over the next six to 12 months in her area*

Our research identified a clear pricing strategy for her luxury property. The owner asked us to market her home at a price below our recommendations because she "wanted it sold." I explained that our research revealed that there were actually more home buyers shopping at the price level we had suggested. The seller agreed to go with our recommended price, and the result was a home sale in less than three months at 98.5 percent of asking price. By conducting the proper research, we were able to sell her home in a short amount of time and net her more money. It pays to do a little bit of research when it comes to pricing, and arbitrarily pricing a home lowest isn't always the best solution.

STRATEGY #4: HIRE A HOME STAGING PROFESSIONAL

Every luxury home seller should have a professional home staging consultation before they hit the market. Homes that have been staged professionally sell faster, and for more money, than homes that skip the staging consultation. While many of the suggestions a staging professional will recommend may seem like common sense, it's very difficult to see the obvious home staging blunders when it comes to your own home.

The staging of a home has almost as much to do with the sale as the house itself. A beautifully furnished home with lavish draperies, a sexy master suite, fresh flowers on the table, and a board game set up for children in the game room will push all of the buyers' emotional hot buttons. Conversely, a home with cluttered rooms will appear small. A home with cluttered closets will appear to lack storage space. A home with a small crack near a drywall seam will appear to have foundation issues. And, a home with too much of the seller's personal tastes will leave little room for the buyers to imagine their own belongings in the home.

Less than a year ago, I sold two luxury homes on the same street in one of the nicest golf course communities in the Charleston area. Both homes were listed within six months of one another and were of similar age, construction style, and offered similar finishes. We met with the first homeowners and suggested professional home staging to bring the home up to the condition needed to demand top market price. However, the sellers opted to decline home staging and decided to sell their house in "As Is" condition. After seven months, three price reductions, and 43 showings, their home finally sold. The final sales price was below the market average for their neighborhood and, considering the cosmetic improvements needed, we were lucky to get the price we did.

Conversely, the second set of homeowners chose to have the professional home staging consultation. They took detailed notes and diligently worked on the recommendations suggested by the staging professional. It took the sellers roughly one month to prepare their property for the market, and when we listed it, we hit the ground running. The first weekend on the market we had four showings and accepted an offer at 98.5 percent of asking price. The price accepted for this home was 22 percent higher than the price per square foot accepted by their neighbors just down the street. Both homes had the same professional photos, the same expert marketing techniques applied, and the same efforts used to get top dollar. The major difference was the choice to have professional home staging by seller number two. If netting 22 percent more money for your next home sale is important to you, I highly recommend you consider a professional home staging consultation before you list.

STRATEGY #5: DIFFERENTIATE YOUR PROPERTY WITH CREATIVE MARKETING

It's difficult to sell a property for maximum value if home buyers feel it's exactly the same as every other option available to them on the market. This was certainly the case for a set of sellers I was working with in an upscale resort community just outside of Charleston. I was contacted by the sellers because they had been unsuccessful at selling their luxury condo after 736 days on the market. To make matters worse, their condo was one of over 100 other condos for sale within this community, and the market for condos was literally at a standstill. All the condos were basically the same, and we were looking at more than three years of inventory on the market. So how do you differentiate a property that is basically the same as all the others and attract a buyer when there really aren't many buyers to speak of? These are exactly the questions I asked these sellers when we first met.

The sellers were honest with themselves about their unit. They admitted it was pretty much the same as all the other condos for sale. It offered a plane-Jane floor plan, below-average views, an average location within the community, and below-average finishes inside and out. With 100-plus similar units on the market, most agents would turn to a drastic price reduction in this scenario. While I did advise the sellers to price aggressively, we weren't the cheapest option on the market by any means. Rather, we did some creative things with our unit and our marketing to give us some separation from the competition. Our staging professional recommended the use of the color red to accent the unit. The sellers put fire-engine red chairs on the sun porch, painted their table lamps bright red, used red throw pillows to accent the couch, and used bright red flowers on the kitchen table. After these small and inexpensive changes, we had our professional photographer take interior and exterior shots of the unit, and the red accents did help our cause for differentiation.

Next, I hired a photographer with a high-resolution camera, which he affixed to a zeppelin balloon for aerial photography. The aerial photos he took looked 100 percent different from the marketing efforts used by our competition. While the photos didn't focus on our condo specifically, they did wonders for selling the lifestyle our unit had to offer. Based on the aerial pictures, buyers could see the beautiful golf courses and beaches nearby this condo. Of course, all the condos offered by our competition also had access to the golf courses and the beaches, but our unit was the only one to display this in an attractive and unique way. The results were fantastic. I sold the unit in just under two months and got our clients an excellent price. Not bad for an average unit, which had been on the market for over two years.

LUXURY MARKETING STRATEGIES SUMMARY

While selling luxury property does take more time, effort, money and thought, it can be done effectively if you apply the five principles outlined in this chapter. Use the principle of sacrifice to attract only your "best-fit" buyers. Be sure the quality of your photography matches the quality of your luxury home. Study the market statistics and trends thoroughly to price your luxury property correctly. Hire the best home staging professional in your market area, and be sure your luxury sellers take their advice before you hit the market. Lastly, use creative thinking to differentiate your property with your marketing. If you follow these five simple strategies correctly, your luxury property should sell faster and for more money than your competition.

About Matt

Matt O'Neill is a real estate expert and business owner of one of the most successful real estate teams in Charleston, South Carolina. His true passion is helping people realize their dreams, and he's able to live out this passion on a daily basis through his work in real estate. Matt is a Certified Luxury Home Marketing Specialist and a member of the Institute for Luxury Home Marketing's exclusive Million Dollar Guild. These accolades are only awarded to the top performing luxury real estate agents in the world.

Matt attributes his success in real estate to his thirst for knowledge and his desire to continually learn and grow. Driven by a need to be his very best for his clients, his determination to provide world-class service has transformed Matt into a true student in every since of the word. Matt can often be found reading a book or listening to audio from leaders across all industries in order to stay on the cutting edge and to continually hone his craft. Additionally, Matt travels the country on a regular basis to meet with other top luxury agents in order to share ideas about the best practices for marketing and selling luxury real estate.

Matt lives just outside of Charleston, South Carolina, with his wife, Katie, and their dog Copper. His love for Charleston runs just as deep as his love for luxury real estate sales. To learn more about Matt O'Neill, or to inquire about moving to Heaven on Earth (otherwise known as Charleston, South Carolina), visit www.MattONeillTeam.com, or call (843) 972-2411.

CHAPTER 55

Vacation Homes:
Making Dreams Come True

By David Connart

Buying or selling a vacation home isn't exactly like buying traditional real estate—there are different considerations, and as a realtor who specializes in the vacation home market, I know them well.

If you're a buyer looking for that "perfect" vacation home, your decision will end up being primarily an emotional one. That's because you're looking for the right place that will inspire you to relax, kick back and escape all your day-to-day stresses and problems—at least for a short period of time. Your dream might be to be close to the beach— adjacent to a golf course—or in a luxury condo in a building offering a wide range of amenities. Whatever your desires are, the property that you feel will most fulfill that idyllic agenda is almost certain to connect with your heart before your head. And therein lies the problem...can you trust those emotions?

On the other hand, you may be looking at a vacation home primarily as an investment. In that case, your head will take the lead, steering you toward a vacation property that will not only generate consistent income through rentals but also build equity over time. However, even without your emotions complicating things, vacation properties differ from primary residences, so much so that you will need to understand a different set of criteria to find the right property to meet your needs.

Finally, you may be ready to sell your existing vacation home. People's lives and circumstances change, and your property may not be relevant to your life anymore. If that's the case, you no doubt need to know the best selling strategy for your property so you can profit the most from it.

Whether you're buying or selling, whether you're a looking for a second home or for a solid investment, whether your goal is to make your dreams come true or to get (or pay) your dream price, the key to success is to understand the different "rules of the game" that vacation properties operate by when it comes to real estate.

VACATION DESTINATIONS

I run my own real estate company, White Sands Resort Realty, in Destin, Florida. For those of you who don't know Destin, it's primarily a vacation destination located on Florida's Emerald Coast, on a peninsula that separates the Gulf of Mexico and Choctawhatchee Bay. It features beaches filled with beautiful white sand and the emerald green waters that give the coastline its name, and it's near the western edge of Florida's panhandle.

This is where I've worked in real estate for more than 20 years. After graduating with a degree in real estate from the University of Mississippi, I started in Destin in 1990 with the local Coldwell Banker office—in the middle of a very bad real estate market, which they hadn't bothered to mention in any of my classes. I had to learn fast, and I guess I did—I was named Rookie of the Year at the office. But the honor that was a lot more gratifying for me was being recently named Realtor of the Decade, for 2000-2010, for generating the most sales volume in the area.

I think the reason for my success over the years, through all the ups and downs of the real estate market, is the fact that I don't regard myself as a salesman. We're in the business of helping people with their real estate purchases, we're not in the business of "selling" real estate. I've always found that if I try to sell someone a property, even if it might be in their best interest, they back out. Clients want to make the ultimate decision—and they should.

For my side, that means it's all-important to listen closely to clients say they want, to do everything possible to help them find what they're looking for and help negotiate the best price possible (without being overly aggressive and possibly jeopardizing getting a home they really want, which we'll talk about a little later).

If you're interested in buying a vacation property, this is exactly the kind of attitude you'll want your real estate agent to have. That's because, as I said at the beginning of this chapter, this kind of purchase is usually more emotional than logical. The agent shouldn't presume to get in the way of what the client wants or push that client toward a home the agent believes is better for him. There are intangibles involved that we real estate professionals can't understand. All we can provide is the best possible knowledgeable advice to guide the home buyer along the way.

You should also make sure you use an agent that understands the local real estate market thoroughly. And not just the overall market but also the various submarkets contained in it. Some may be appreciating, some may be declining—the news won't tell you what's really going on, but an experienced realtor will be able to.

UNDERSTANDING THE VACATION HOME MARKET

Another crucially important fact to know is about the vacation home market is that it tends to work on a "first in, first out" basis. What I mean by that is, when the economy is on the upswing, vacation home sales immediately go up, as consumers have extra money to spend on these kinds of nonessential purchases—"first in." On the other hand, when the economy stumbles, vacation homes are seen as a luxury and, therefore, something easily disposed of to cut expenses and generate cash—"first out."

Other factors can affect vacation home prices as well. Our market, of course, took a big hit when the economy began declining in 2007. We were just starting to come back when, on April 20, 2010, the history-making BP oil spill began pouring into the Gulf of Mexico. Prices here immediately fell back down. When they finally capped the well a few months later on July 15, prices began coming back. Of course, it helped that no oil ever did actually reach our white sand beaches, which remained pristine and beautiful.

The silver lining of that oil spill threat is that it made it a great time to buy a vacation home in our area. Prices are still off about 50 percent in most cases from the peak of real estate prices a few years ago because the oil spill caused prices to drop further than they should have. That means there's a great investment opportunity here; many buyers have already realized a 20 percent increase in equity.

The danger, however, can come in trying to aggressively make a great deal even better. For instance, we sell a lot of luxury properties that are REO foreclosures. One was for sale that was right on the Gulf; the seller was asking for $1.25 million. My client wanted the property but made an offer at a lower price. We were in negotiations with the seller when someone came in with a higher bid—and that person got the house instead of my client, who was upset he had lost the property. That sometimes happens when you try to squeeze a lower price out of what is already a good value.

BUYING A VACATION HOME

If you're interested in purchasing a vacation home, you should decide on your "must-haves" before you begin looking. Do you want to be a near a golf course? Are you looking for a condo with amenities, such as a pool and a gym? Do you want to sit on a balcony overlooking the ocean and watch the sunset? What does your budget allow?

Talking to an experienced real estate agent in the area you want to buy in can definitely give you a sense of what you can expect for what you can afford and help you make the necessary adjustments in your vacation home goals.

There are also long-term considerations to look at. For example, maybe you're planning on retiring to this home? In that case, you won't want to deal with a lot of stairs, unless there's elevator access. Also, you want to make sure you don't buy into a community where the maintenance fees are too high, as that will add considerably to your ongoing expenses.

If you're looking at the home as an investment, or as a part-time rental, the property that's able to sleep the most people will make you the most money; the higher the occupancy, the more you can charge for rent. Depending on the property and the rental rates, you can cover the entire expense of the home with rental income. This wasn't the case a few years ago, when the market was red hot and everyone was buying mostly to see the price appreciate. Today, the rental market is a lot stronger and very reliable.

When you've found the vacation property of your dreams, you'll want to know all the ins and outs of how to generate an offer that will be accepted. Again, this is where an experienced realtor can really make a difference. If the home's already priced where it should be (and your agent should know if it is), you probably don't want to go lower or you may lose it. When you offer less on a desirable property, you frequently lose out.

If it's an REO foreclosure property, this is particularly the case. We have that happen with everything from $40,000 properties to million-dollar properties; people offer less, they get into a multiple offer situation, they lose the house, and they're frustrated. If you offer full price, however, the bank may accept the offer; then even if bigger offers come in afterward, the bank will still honor your offer 80 to 90 percent of the time.

You do have to remember, if you're buying a short sale or REO property, that you must take that home "as is." If there end up being hidden defects, you can go back to the home's asset manager to see if they'll share in the cost of remedying the problem (such as a termite infestation). If it's a visible problem, however, like a crack in the wall or stained carpet, you won't be able to get the seller to do anything about it. The unwritten rule is, "If you can see it, don't ask for it after contract."

The upside to REO properties in some disrepair, as well as some older condos and homes, is you can go in, repaint and remodel, and create the exact home you want—and, at the same time, instantly build up your equity. You'll make your money when you buy.

There's one thing you'll want to look out for, however, when you're buying a condo. In order for you to qualify for certain financing, such as a 30-year fixed-rate mortgage, the building has to be approved by Fannie Mae or Freddie Mac. This might not be possible if the building has a lot of delinquencies (usually more than 20 percent) or doesn't have enough owner-occupied units. Even if you don't need this kind of financing, you should check on this in case you need to sell down the line, since your buyer more than likely will need to finance the sale for it to go through.

SELLING A VACATION HOME

If you're selling your vacation home, the first thing you should keep in mind is that there's a different psychology in place when it comes to a vacation home buyer. As I already mentioned, it's more likely to be an emotional decision than anything else. Not only that, but it's also a less *urgent* decision. For example, someone whose work causes them to come to a new area may be more interested in just finding something that works, because they have to start their new job quickly. Someone buying a vacation home, in contrast, can easily say, "Well, that home isn't quite right. I'll wait." That means you want to make your home look as good as possible and price it as competitively as possible to make it as attractive a deal as you can.

Let's start with the looks. A lot of work should be put into the staging of a vacation home to make it seem as though it's in perfect condition. Worn-out furnishings should be replaced, and rooms should be decorated to make a great first impression. And don't forget the exterior; if it's a home and not a condo, you want to make sure the landscaping is immaculate. Remember that you're selling not just a property but a vacation fantasy. And most fantasies don't include overgrown shrubs and patchy grass! You want to have the "wow" factor firmly in place so buyers are excited to buy your property.

You also want to take care of any needed repairs or other little problems that would undoubtedly pop up during a buyer's home inspection. Otherwise, you could hit a hiccup that could come back to haunt you. Do everything you can to make sure the property sails through the vetting process once you accept an offer.

As far as your selling price goes, you can determine the best number by looking at comparable sales and trends in the market, as well as the inventory and the number of sales being made. This is another area where your real estate agent's expertise is essential.

By the way, there's something to be said for the strategy of pricing your home *below* market price. This may seem risky, but it can also pay off. For instance, I was handling an REO sale and the seller wanted to list it at $145,000. I was a little stunned—I thought it was worth $199,000 according to how I read the market—so I asked if he was sure he wanted to list it at that price. He replied that he did, and he also wanted to accept the highest and best offer after 10 days.

Well, we received 35 offers on that property in those 10 days, ranging from $110,000 to $250, 500. The buyer offering the most was anxious to get the property, so anxious that he didn't want to lose it to a higher bid. Again, this strategy doesn't always work, but in this case, it gained the seller at least $50,000 more than what his property was really worth.

A vacation home can be either a dream purchase or a lucrative investment; as a matter of fact, it can even be both. When you work with an experienced vacation home realtor, you'll be guided to the best possible property—and the best possible result. Whatever your particular goals may be, I wish you the best of luck in your vacation home transaction.

CHAPTER 56

The Most Profitable Niche in Real Estate

By Hugo Balarezo

Let me introduce myself: My name is Hugo Balarezo, and I've been selling real estate since 1985. I've been involved in more than 4,200 transactions in my career, and I've been through two massive market shifts—one in 1993 and one in 2007. What's my secret—you'll soon find out.

While you're reading this chapter, I want *you* to start thinking about your business and what it's going to take to make it incredibly successful as well. Here's what you'll learn in this chapter:

- What's the most profitable niche in real estate.

- Four reasons why you should work this niche immediately. In fact, any single one of these reasons will be compelling enough for you to start working in this niche right away.

- The three ways to make more money in real estate. These three systems need to absolutely be part of your business for you to be a success.

- The reason why most realtors fail—which will absolutely blow you away.

The main components of the sales engine my team uses to sell more than 200 homes a year in this niche, and how to be productive vs. being super-productive. This concept alone will increase your productivity tenfold. So let's get started!

We can all agree that we're in a tough market right now. In fact, we're selling less homes and getting paid much less than ever before, because home prices have come down, and right now it's taking a lot longer to sell REO and short sales. So the selling cycle for these homes is much, much longer.

The two scariest times in my career were 1994 and 2007, but looking back, these were also the two times that really brought the best opportunities. So instead of complaining and being reactive, we need to be proactive and look at where can we make the most money in real estate today.

I started looking into this niche a while back, when I saw an interview with Barbara Simmons. Barbara is an agent who was crushing it in Los Angeles by tapping into this market, and she built a massively profitable virtual office, with virtual agents.

Bottom line is she was selling more than 400 homes a year and making a huge profit, so I immediately asked myself why I hadn't tapped this market before? The answer was simple: I was lazy and too comfortable. Maybe some of you can relate.

Fast forward to today: We all know REO assignments are down, and banks are just not releasing inventory. Short sales are really still taking way too long and are too much of a headache. So where are the biggest opportunities today? On the *selling side*. Let me say it again, the most profitable niche in real estate today is *buyers*, not listings.

Now, I'm wondering what's going through your mind right now. Are there any doubts about this? If there are, great, because that's exactly where I was five years ago. But if you gave me a choice today to make money fast, I sure wouldn't try to start doing short sales or chasing down new bank business. I would absolutely build a buyer business immediately. In fact, buyer sides are two to three times more profitable than listing sales. In fact, I know REO agents right now who make 70 percent of their profits from their buyer teams.

The truth is I would never have been able to sell more than 4,200 homes, if I didn't leverage this market. So when I saw what Barbara was doing, it became very clear to me that I needed to do the same.

Let's talk about four big reasons why this niche is so profitable.

1. *You can generate qualified buyers at a much lower cost.* There's an agent by the name of Brent Grove in Northern California who has a program called "Open Houses on Steroids." Simply put, what he does is handpick homes in great price ranges and locations, in which to hold open houses. He contacts the listing agents who aren't in his office, and invariably one of them will say, "Sure, go ahead and hold an open house."

What he'll do is put up 30 to 40 signs, which will attract an average of 30, 40, 50 people coming through these open houses. He'll do two of these a weekend, consistently. So when you really look at it, he's generating 400 leads a month just from open houses.

2. *Commissions on buyer sides right now are about twice as much as they are on the listing side.* Now listen to this: The average current listing commission on REOs is 1.5 to 2 percent. Most REO agents are actually netting half as much after all their costs are taken out, so think about that. Right now the trend is that listings are going to get tougher.

3. *The buyer side also allows you to close your transactions and get paid faster.* You don't have to wait four to six months to get paid; you can get paid in 30 days or less in most cases. Again, we're shrinking that selling cycle dramatically.

4. *The biggest reason why you should consider this niche is because the buyer side is underserved, so it's so much easier to build a buyer business today than ever before.* You can leverage your systems, referrals, showing agents, and lead coordinators. Later, I'll share with you a little bit about the buyer sales engine system I use.

First, though, let's talk a little about the three ways you can make more money in real estate:

1. *You can sell more homes.* If you can have a system where you're selling 60 homes a year instead of 30, you're obviously going to make more money.

2. *You can make more money per sale.* If you have a system where you're making two to three times more profit per sale, you're going to be making money two to three times faster, right?

3. You can sell and close homes faster. If you have a system where your average sale time is one-third, you'll be making money three times faster, right?

Imagine what happens when you combine all of these three moneymaking strategies, and that's what happens when you work buyers properly

With that said, why do realtors fail? Recently, I was on a plane flying back home and reading a report about why internet marketers fail. As I'm reading the report, I'm thinking, you know what, this applies 100 percent to real estate agents.

What's the symptom of an agent who fails? That agent buys anything that looks like it's going to make money and gets absolutely no results. And what's the cost? Opportunistic thinking; that agent is simply chasing the opportunity.

What's the business problem in this? A lack of strategy. The truth is we're describing two opposite ways of thinking: The first one is an opportunity seeker and the second one is an entrepreneur.

An opportunity seeker is always looking for the big opportunity to make lots of money—from the hot opportunity of the moment. This person's only criteria is, can I make money from this? Today it might be social media, tomorrow it might be blogging, and yesterday may have been video tours. Opportunity seekers buy lots of products but only use a few of them. The ones they do use get abandoned when the next so-called easy way to make money comes by.

The other way of thinking is that of a true entrepreneur. True entrepreneurs approach their businesses with a clear vision of what they want those businesses to become. Because they have a vision, they can analyze their own strengths and look at the pros and cons of each strategy, before they pick one that will help them achieve their successful vision.

The cool thing is that once you know exactly where you're headed and have the confidence that you can sell more homes, make more per sale, and sell homes faster, there's absolutely nothing that's going to get in your way.

Now, let me tell you a little bit about my team. I consider my team to be one of the very best in the country. I've coached this productive team for years now, and pound for pound, they're some of the most productive agents anywhere. In fact, my two top agents last year sold a combined 186 homes. The key to their success are the systems they use, and the systems we've implemented that make them focused.

We built our system around four conversion points:

1. The lead to showing appointment

2. Showing appointment to offers written

3. Offer written to escrows opened

4. Escrows opened to getting you paid

These are the conversions points that make our world go around. Every day our agents submit their daily schedules and update them every hour on the hour, so that way they know they're on task. We have a daily huddle—a 20-minute call—where every agent tells me what they're going to do in terms of sales, relative to their weekly goals, and what they're going to work on in their business.

What gets in their way? Mostly personal stuff. Things like email, people interrupting, their spouse calling; most of it is nondollar productive stuff that gets in the way of the dollar productive stuff.

Here are some of the key components to our sales system.

- *First you need leads, but you'll agree leads don't really matter unless you can convert them.* Again, it doesn't really matter how you generate buyer leads, or how many you generate, if you're not going to be effective in converting them.

- *Next, you need the right database.* The most important step in your business is to choose the right database. If you're going to be grabbing thousands of buyers every year, you better have the right tools.

- *Define your perfect buyer.* This is critical if you want to only work with motivated qualified buyers who are ready to do what you ask them to do. You need to be able to describe what they look like, and again, this is the best way to work with the best possible buyers.

- *Define the price range or your showing specialty.* This is where you can really start leveraging your time. If you focus most of your time on homes—let's say in the $200,000 to $350,000 range—guess what's going to happen? You're going to be generating buyers in the $200,000 to $350,000 range.

- *Develop your dialogues.* Having impactful dialogues will increase your call-to-appointment conversion rates; again, it's all conversion, remember. This one area will make a huge impact in your business. You need to know exactly what to say and when.

- *Define how you prioritize your clients.* When you say you have a high client, or a hot, medium or cold client, what do those look like? How will you deal with each of these priorities differently so you can sell more homes? This is critical because 80 percent of your commissions will come from 20 percent of your buyers.

- *Know your numbers.* How fun would it be if you knew that for every 20 high contacts, or clients you spoke with, you were sure to open one escrow within three weeks? Once you know your numbers and what they mean, you'll be able to leverage and grow your business exponentially.

- *Know how you're going to follow up your clients based on their priorities.* We talked about priorities before, but it bears repeating: Follow-up is everything. Remember, 80 percent of your business is going to come from 20 percent of your leads. You need to know how to prioritize them and then how to follow them up accordingly.

So again, in closing, everything we do is a system. This is why we can leverage, duplicate and scale what we do. Everyone on my team is following the same steps, and this is why I've been able to sell more than 4,200 homes throughout my career. You can learn more about our systems by going to AgentAcceleration.com/SellingSystem. I hope the information presented in this chapter will make a positive impact in your business.

About Hugo

My name is Hugo Balarezo, and I've sold more than three quarters of a billion dollars (yes, with a "B") of residential real estate in my career. You'd never guess that would be possible if you saw how I started in the real estate business. It was 1985, I was a college graduate with a degree in business, marketing and chemistry. I got into real estate because I wanted to make lots of money, and I thought I was hot stuff.

Fast forward 12 months later, I had racked up $22,500 in credit card bills and managed to close 2 transactions the entire year. Needless to say, my ego took a big hit! Reality finally slapped me in the face when I took my total earnings and divided it by the numbers of hours I had worked that year and realized my time was worth $2.17 per hour. I could have made three times more at McDonalds. I was frustrated, no one at my office seemed to care and I needed answers. . sound familiar??

So I went out to search for the answers I needed on my own. I didn't know exactly what I was looking for, but deep down I knew I could work harder than anyone and I just needed some direction. Then I ran across a sales bootcamp put on by a sales trainer. So I drove to Arizona, with pen and paper, and absorbed everything he talked about. When I came back I wrote everything out on cue cards, laid them out in sequence and memorized them. I then set up a daily schedule and blocked my time into three blocks: 1) prospecting 2) practicing 3) improving my business. The more I practiced, the more, confident I got, and I started getting results and scheduling appointments. The more I did, the more disciplined I became and the more homes I sold and my business started to grow

Fast forward to today … I've sold more than 4,250 properties since 1985, I currently have a team of 15, and I'm looking for the next chapter in my life. I received a ton of sales awards while at Re/Max, Keller Williams, and currently own two real estate companies in Riverside California. So I decided to share some of the things I learned along the way with you and hope you get one great idea you can implement. That's all it took for me to get my career moving in the right direction.

Check out more info at http://www.reacceleration.com/bestmarketniche. You can reach me at (951) 643-7410, or email me at info.reacceleration@yahoo.com. Here is to your success!

CHAPTER 57

Now's the Time to Buy Resort and Oceanfront Property

By Jerry Pinkas

The lure of the beach and ocean hasn't gone away; it has only grown stronger. In times like these people need to take a break and go on vacation—now more than ever. Because of this, I ask these questions: Is it getting harder to leave when your vacation is over? Have you ever wondered who owns the beach property you've enjoyed during your vacation? Do you want an investment with dividends like family fun, rest and relaxation? There's no better time than now! Whether you're setting your sights on a vacation or retirement home, or a property that can even meet your investment needs with positive cash flow, now's the time to buy. Successful investors have been waiting for more than a decade for this opportunity, and it's all about achieving a lifelong dream!

Many families are using rental income from resort property to help pay for their place on the beach. And the priceless part is, when it's time for their vacations, they have their own place at the beach!

With low interest rates and low prices, more buyers have been purchasing. Condominium sales have actually increased in 2011. These figures indicate that a strong condo sales trend will continue. While low interest rates have fueled demand among traditional condo buyers, first-time homeowners and empty-nesters have also increased the sales for second homes, vacation homes and investments.

DIVERSITY AND DESIRABILITY OF THE OCEANFRONT

There are many types of resort properties to choose from. Hotel-style condos, beachfront homes, golf resorts, intercostal waterway condos and homes, vacation properties, second homes, rental properties, and investment properties. Talk about diversity! Some vacationers will find a vacation condo easier to maintain than a vacation home. Families with young children realize that condominiums offer strong rental income and a great place for fun-filled family vacation getaways. There's an ample selection of designs and layouts, which range from ocean-view efficiencies with a small kitchen to five-bedroom, four-bath penthouses overlooking the beach.

The strip of area where land meets ocean is very limited. You can build a golf course just about anywhere, but you just can't go out and build a beach, making beachfront property very desirable and very limited.

It's no secret that properties on or near the water appreciate quicker than non-waterfront properties. Why is this? Our bodies are made up of 98 percent water, and our ancestors developed their villages and towns close to this scarce natural resource. Perhaps the natural instinct to build close to water still lies within us. Whatever the answer, there's something in all of us that draws us closer to water. But, of course, there's only a limited amount of waterfront property.

THE EASE OF OCEANFRONT LIVING

One of the main reasons beachfront condo sales have remained strong is because owners can take advantage of a care-free lifestyle. We're all busy and stressed out most of our life, but we all reach that point when we ask ourselves, "What's more important?" Would you rather spend your free time mowing the grass and maintaining the garden, or dining at a restaurant, relaxing by the pool, and staying fit and healthy going to the gym? When you're an oceanfront property owner, all these are only a few steps from your front door!

A hassle-free lifestyle remains at the top of the list of the main reasons that people love owning a condo. For condo owners, the "everything's included," relaxing lifestyle, is what they're looking for! They don't have to worry about lawn maintenance or exterior building mainte-nance. In most cases, water, sewer, trash service, pest control, and exterior property insurance are included in their affordable monthly fees. If you were to buy a beach house, you'd have to worry about (and pay for) all the extra maintenance. But being a condominium homeowner, you and other homeowners pay homeowners' fees. Individually, these inexpensive homeowner fees are very low but together cover the expenses and costs for upkeep of the entire complex.

Additionally, condominiums differ from traditional homes because everyone shares ownership of common land and has access to facilities. Associations oversee building maintenance, enforce rules and guidelines, and other policy-setting bodies on issues, such as taxes, insurance, bankruptcy, reform and fair housing. Whether you're a full- or part-time owner, a condominium association can be an extremely valuable asset. By upholding these standards, condominium associations ensure that the community is well-maintained and property values remain profitable. The quality of life at the beach is amazing. Many condo communities include amenities that are found in upscale single-family neighborhoods. Some offer designer-decorated clubhouses that host scheduled events. Amenities such as on-site pools, water parks, restaurants, bars, tennis courts and fitness centers cater to active lifestyles. Some communities even feature carwash bays and on-site guest suites that can be reserved for visiting family and friends! Condos, houses and complexes on the intercostal waterway may include boat ramps, fishing piers, crabbing docks and, in some cases, even full-service marinas. Homeowners in upscale complexes enjoy 24-hour concierge and even business support services.

Condominium owners also enjoy meticulously maintained and enhanced landscaping; water features, such as fountains and man-made ponds; and decorative and exotic exteriors, which add to the overall appeal of the community. As the demographics of the average American homeowner continue to change and condominium developments improve in quality and design, condominium popularity will continue to increase because of the comfort, lifestyle and convenience.

NOW'S THE TIME

The 77 million baby boomers born between the years 1946 and 1964 will soon be coming of age—retirement age, that is. While many of these boomers are still in their peak earning years, they also have disposable income available to enjoy a second home or vacation property. Many are working hard and looking forward to the day when they'll make the transition to leave the workplace and relax. When this happens, they'll take into account their favorite activities and their happiest moments with family and friends. Some may choose golf, restaurants, shopping, festivals, or days spent enjoying the beach. Lucky for them, Myrtle Beach offers all of this. Developers in Myrtle Beach have built in many community amenities that are geared for this lifestyle.

Here's a question for you: What's on the cover of just about every retirement brochure? It's the beach or the ocean, right? It's what the retirement agencies have been selling us on for years. This intersects with the number of baby boomers who will retire in the next few years. People have been saving their entire life so they can retire, be comfortable and have fun. These people are going to retire whether the economy is good or bad. A majority of our population will be looking to move to warmer climate to enjoy the beach lifestyle. This "great migration" of the population could shift property values in the next few years.

It's amazing how many people have always had a dream of owning an oceanfront property or second home. Many are snapping up deals right now. It's more affordable than it has been in years, and the deal of the decade happens about once a week!

THE GROWTH OF THE GRAND STRAND

Why invest in Myrtle Beach? Myrtle Beach continues to grow! It's the up-and-coming vacation city. When it comes to vacation destinations, Myrtle Beach ranks higher on the scale than locations in Hawaii and the Virgin Islands! Myrtle Beach is one of the most popular beach vacation spots in the nation today, with more than 14.6 million visitors annually. Myrtle Beach, South Carolina, is located in the center of a 60-mile oceanfront area known as the Grand Strand. Second-home owners are welcomed by year-round residents with gracious southern hospitality, fantastic year-round mild weather, and something for everyone to do. Myrtle Beach's philosophy, "First in Service," makes it's clear that the city of Myrtle Beach puts its residents and vacationers first. This above all else encourages more people to buy their vacation homes or relocate here.

The Grand Strand area is known as "the next best thing" because it continues to grow even when the rest of the United States is in a recession. Recent construction continues with the city expanding the downtown area. A new investment of $14 million in the mile-long oceanfront boardwalk features many new shops, amusements and cafés. The construction of the new oceanfront SkyWheel, which is the largest Ferris wheel east of the Mississippi, as well as Jimmy Buffet's very own Land-Shark Oceanfront Bar & Grill keeps the Myrtle Beach fun going. With more than a hundred golf courses (Myrtle Beach is the golf capital of the East Coast), fun amusement parks and a hot nightlife, there's something for everyone in Myrtle Beach. Owners can enjoy the ocean and beach, fishing off the multiple public piers, playing the many fun miniature golf courses or the beautiful award-winning golf courses, dining at more than 1,700 restaurants, or taking a relaxing walk on the beach. Myrtle Beach has become the land of pleasant living and is one of the nation's top choices for second-home living.

MAKING AN INVESTMENT IN OCEANFRONT PROPERTY

What do the gurus say about investments? Buy when selling, and sell when buying. Otherwise known as the investment phrase, "buy low, sell high." It's no secret you can buy oceanfront properties or golf course properties for the lowest prices in decades. I don't know how long this window of opportunity will last, but there are some incredible deals in the market right now!

Many people come to me seeking advice, and it all boils down to the same question, "Is now a good time to buy?" I discuss little-known information with them about leverage, opportunity and return on investment. Interest rates are the lowest they've been in since the 1950s. At current market prices, the high amount of rental income and cash flow allures buyers to purchase oceanfront property, not only for their personal enjoyment but to make a return on investment.

Many will look back at these times and say, "Wow! I should have bought oceanfront property back then." Don't miss the opportunity! If the media says the market is bad, then it's your time to take action and move quickly to find your dream property.

Remember a few years ago when the media told us to buy property during the stock market bubble? Think about it: You would have been better off if you did the opposite of what the media told us. The television and newspapers only report what has already happened. Once the media reports it, it's old news. Take advantage of the real estate market now before everyone else is informed.

WHY CHOOSE MYRTLE BEACH?

Why did I choose live in Myrtle Beach? I started investing in real estate, buying my first rental property at the age of 21. As the owner of a furniture store in Baltimore, I later moved to Virginia to expand the wholesale side of my furniture business. With my love of the beach and ocean, I continued my real estate investments in Myrtle Beach. I slowly purchased another property here or there until my part-time real estate investments became my full-time career.

Some of my fondest childhood memories are of the vacations spent with my family at the beach. After many years, I decided to move to Myrtle Beach full time. Moving to the beach was the absolute best choice.

Real estate is my passion! I'm truly honored to be considered the local expert advisor. I take great pride in knowing the real estate market inside and out. I feel it's my obligation to inform and educate my clients on being a pro in the local real estate market by avoiding costly common pitfalls. I work hard to always uncover the newest tips and secrets in the real estate industry. When I'm not helping other people achieve a lifelong dream, you'll find me spending time with my wife and three beautiful daughters, enjoying all that the Grand Strand has to offer.

THE ALLURE OF THE BEACH AND OCEAN

Take a moment and think of the game of Monopoly. What if you could to purchase the premier properties like Boardwalk and Park Place for 50 or 75 percent off what they sold for at the height of the market? Do you think you could make money? The formula for great wealth is found in real life, just as it is in the game. Every month, whether the stock market is up or down, many people who invested in oceanfront properties in Myrtle Beach continue to receive rent checks in the mail month after month. The advantages of resort real estate make it a phenomenally powerful investment. Now go back to your childhood, and try to think of where everyone wanted to go for summer vacations—9 out of 10 people will say they wanted to vacation at the beach. Life becomes a vacation when it's by the beach. Life is definitely more alive near the ocean than other places that are inland. Recreational actives are everywhere by the sea. The allure of the ocean is deep-seated and in all of us. Now it's your time to take advantage of this window of opportunity in Myrtle Beach.

About Jerry

Myrtle Beach Real Estate Expert—Jerry Pinkas

Jerry Pinkas is an award-winning real estate professional at Jerry Pinkas Real Estate Experts, a successful investor, business owner and author. He has taken years of experience and positioned himself as one of the top real estate professionals in the country. Always eager to help others, Jerry was determined to find a way to share his simple and effective business practices to more people through his Real Estate Experts team of agents.

In 2010, Jerry Pinkas' team was named No. 1 in the Carolinas and No. 7 in the world with Exit Realty International. Jerry was propelled into real estate stardom in 2011 when the Wall Street Journal named him company one of the "Top 250 Real Estate Teams in the Nation."

Owner of Oceanfront Condo Rentals and Jerry Pinkas Real Estate Experts, this award-winning team of realtors is always ready to help. They take great pride in sharing the information they've learned.

For years, Jerry has worked to develop the most effective real estate system in the industry and is intent on continually gaining knowledge to pass on that success to his clients. He has appeared numerous times and been quoted in some of the top local and national newspapers and magazines.

The Jerry Pinkas Real Estate Experts team raises the bar on the level of knowledge and advice, and has many proven systems. If put to work for you, you'll get guarantee results!

Average just doesn't cut it any longer. With the many changes over the last several years in the real estate industry, you want the expert advisor who brings you a wealth of information, a strong work ethic, and is committed to your success.

If you ask Jerry's friends to describe him, they'll say he's driven and hard working. He just loves what he does and throws all of his energy into helping his clients. It's what makes working with Jerry so enjoyable.

His philosophy is very simple: Why waste your time building something average. Life can be a real adventure when you apply what you have learned, and then help others to do the same.